C000140634

THE PAST, PRESENT AND FUTURE OF THE EUROPEAN UNION
Edited by Alan V. Deardorff

LATIN AMERICAN ECONOMIC CRISES
Trade and Labour
Edited by Enrique Bour, Daniel Heymann and Fernando Navajas

ADVANCES IN MACROECONOMIC THEORY
Edited by Jacques H, Drèze

EXPLAINING GROWTH
A Global Research Project
Edited by Gary McMahon and Lyn Squire

TRADE, INVESTMENT, MIGRATION AND LABOUR MARKET ADJUSTMENT
Edited by David Greenaway, Richard Upward and Katherine Wakelin

INEQUALITY AROUND THE WORLD
Edited by Richard B. Freeman

MONETARY THEORY AND POLICY EXPERIENCE
Edited by Axel Leijonhufvud

MONETARY THEORY AS A BASIS FOR MONETARY POLICY
Edited by Axel Leijonhufvud

ECONOMIC DEVELOPMENT IN SUBSAHARAN AFRICA
Proceedings of the Eleventh World Congress of the International Economic Association, Tunis
Edited by Ibrahim Elbadawi and Beno Ndula

IEA Series
Series Standing Order ISBN 978–0–333–71242–9

You can receive future titles in this series as they are published by placing a standing order. Please contact your bookseller or, in case of difficulty, write to us at the address below with your name and address, the title of the series and one of the ISBNs quoted above.

Customer Services Department, Macmillan Distribution Ltd, Houndmills, Basingstoke, Hampshire RG21 6XS, England

The Industrial Policy Revolution I

The Role of Government Beyond Ideology

Edited by

Joseph E. Stiglitz
University Professor, Columbia University, United States of America

Justin Yifu Lin
Honorary Dean, National School of Development, Peking University, China

First published 2013 by
PALGRAVE MACMILLAN

Palgrave Macmillan in the UK is an imprint of Macmillan Publishers Limited, registered in England, company number 785998, of Houndmills, Basingstoke, Hampshire RG21 6XS.

Palgrave Macmillan in the US is a division of St Martin's Press LLC, 175 Fifth Avenue, New York, NY 10010.

Palgrave Macmillan is the global academic imprint of the above companies and has companies and representatives throughout the world.

Palgrave® and Macmillan® are registered trademarks in the United States, the United Kingdom, Europe and other countries.

ISBN 978–1–137–33516–6 hardback

ISBN 978–1–137–37452–3 paperback

This book is printed on paper suitable for recycling and made from fully managed and sustained forest sources. Logging, pulping and manufacturing processes are expected to conform to the environmental regulations of the country of origin.

A catalogue record for this book is available from the British Library.

A catalog record for this book is available from the Library of Congress.

Typeset by MPS Limited, Chennai, India.

Contents

List of Tables

List of Figures

Foreword

In 2012, the International Economic Association (IEA), the association of national economic associations/societies, convened a two-part series of roundtables on the theme of industrial policy. The first, "New Thinking on Industrial Policy," was hosted by the World Bank in Washington, D.C. on May 22–3, and the second, "New Thinking on Industrial Policy: Implications for Africa," was held in Pretoria, South Africa, on July 3–4, in partnership with the Economic Development Department of the South African government, and with the further financial support of UNIDO and the Department of Economic and Social Affairs of the United Nations. The two roundtables assembled an outstanding group of scholars to discuss the breadth of the topic of industrial policy, focusing in the second meeting on the African context. These scholars have all grappled with issues of development and growth over many years. The insights generated at the roundtable are critical in our policy debates, and are captured in this two-part IEA publication, which is the 151st volume of the International Economic Associations Proceedings of Roundtables and World Congresses. (The second part of the volume is titled "The Industrial Policy Revolution II: Africa in the Twenty-first Century.") Taken together, the two-part volume includes more than 30 papers selected from those presented at the Washington, D.C. and Pretoria roundtables, in addition to more than 20 commentaries on those papers, written by other roundtable participants. In many cases, the papers were revised after the conclusion of the roundtable to take into consideration discussions that took place at the event.

The roundtables were convened in recognition of the fact that industrial policy is a sort of lynchpin for the economics of development, that the countries which have been most successful in development have undertaken a wide variety of industrial policies, and that different countries can and should learn from these experiences.

Africa provides an especially clear example of why this refreshed emphasis on industrial policy is so important, and worthy of convening international experts on the scale achieved by the IEA in 2012. The continent has one billion people: potentially a great producer and consumer base for the development of strong, dynamic manufacturing industries. It has a large and growing workforce, with a youthful population. It has significant energy resources, from traditional feedstocks such as coal and oil to renewables in the form of rivers, sun and wind. It has enormous natural resources, with a host of minerals and swathes of rich agricultural land.

African growth rates have climbed in the past decade or more. Between 2000 and 2010, six of the world's ten fastest-growing economies were to be found on that continent. Yet that growth was largely fuelled by the export of raw materials to the production centers of Asia, Latin America, and Europe. The commodity price boom supported Africa's rapid growth. Oil made a significant contribution, as did higher prices for metals and agricultural products. But domestic manufacturing, which has been central to those countries which earlier achieved sustainable growth, lagged as a contributor of growth.

Yet the reality is that while Africa has many of the inputs and markets that would support the rise of a large manufacturing sector, the continent has a small industrial footprint and arguably saw a degree of deindustrialization in the commodity boom of the mid-2000s – a continuation of deindustrialization trends that have been in places since the structural adjustment programs.

According to UNCTAD data, for Africa as a whole, between 2000 and 2010 manufacturing fell from 13 percent of total value added to 10 percent. The decline was steepest in sub-Saharan Africa, where manufacturing dropped from 13 percent of value added in 2000 to 9 percent in 2010. In 2010, the share of manufacturing in value added in sub-Saharan Africa (excluding South Africa) was only just over half the global norm.

Meanwhile, between 2000 and 2010 raw materials climbed from 72 percent of all African exports to 78 percent, and manufactures dropped from 21 percent to 17 percent. In contrast, for the rest of the world in 2010, raw materials made up just 27 percent of exports and manufacturing some 67 percent.

Manufacturing matters, and especially so because Africa has to create millions of new jobs to meet the needs of its young people and the growing pressures of urbanization. And it has to create higher-quality jobs that can raise incomes on a large scale. Manufacturing is central to any sustainable job creation effort. It creates jobs directly, generally quality employment. It generates more jobs in supplier industries, from mineral processing to services. And its labor force supports still more jobs in agriculture, retail, production of consumer goods and infrastructure.

Manufacturing generally has a positive impact on foreign exchange earnings and the balance of payments, both increasing export earnings and reducing the import bill.

Recent economic history has shown that it is still possible for countries to achieve substantial growth in manufacturing, becoming successful in both manufacturing goods and product innovation. Many of these successes are found in Asia, from Japan's early lead, to Korea's development as an industrial economy and the present-day rise of China as the factory of the world. But successes can be found on a smaller scale for specific industries on the African continent, in countries as diverse as South Africa and Tunisia.

What these examples point to is the return of industrial policy as a valid focus of public policy. However, this resurgent industrial policy has learnt the lessons of both failure and successes elsewhere. It is smart industrial policy.

But modern industrial policy is not just concerned with expanding the industrial sector. It is predicated on the belief that government can play a constructive role in shaping the economy – indeed, there is no choice but for it to do so. That may entail encouraging the economy to move in more environmentally sustainable ways than it otherwise would; or to create more jobs. It might seek to create an economy with less inequality, or with a stronger research and development sector, or a more productive agriculture sector.

So how do societies industrialize and modernize successfully in a globalized world? And how do they maintain dynamic competitiveness?

This two-part volume seeks to lay the basis for a discussion that will look at lessons to take industrial policy beyond the provision of subsidies alone. Every successful industrializing economy used a wider toolbox of measures, one that drew on core state functions. These include:

- Shaping infrastructure and supply chain logistics to ensure that the output of emerging manufacturing industries can move cheaply and quickly between countries and from production centers to markets.
- Innovation and R&D as well as technology policies that deepen the local technological base especially by diffusing production and product innovations on a large scale. Critically, we must encourage the development and use of innovations that meet Africa's specific needs, including in rural areas, with technologies geared to the climate, biology, and logistics challenges facing the continent.
- Education, skills, and productivity policies that identify the best ways to empower millions of African workers and entrepreneurs.
- Competition policies that simultaneously improve market access and act against abuse of market power, not as aims in themselves but as tools to promote employment and industrial capacity.
- Trade policies that integrate markets, creating the critical mass and economies of scale, while maintaining space for new industries to emerge especially on a regional basis.
- Macro-policies that ensure stability and a competitive exchange rate.
- Financial policies that ensure access to finance at affordable terms, even by small and medium-sized enterprises.

Participants noted the long-standing challenge of the resource curse – that the very abundance of natural resources may inhibit the development of competitive downstream industries because entrepreneurs and governments can survive off the extraction of natural resources.

But the roundtables went further to reflect on the channels of competitiveness: what countries can do in developing skills and technology policies that spur industrialization. Crucially for policymakers, the participants looked at the role of institutions, drawing on the insights gained from the experience of fast-growing industrializing economies.

Washington, D.C. proved an ideal jumping-off point for the two-roundtable series. Pretoria, South Africa was a fertile and appropriate location for the Africa-focused companion roundtable. In total, the two roundtables drew 39 attendees, who participated in dozens of presentations and plenary discussions spread over different sessions, each focusing on a different aspect of industrial policy. This afforded a truly diverse and international range of perspectives, not always in agreement on the particulars, but with broadly shared common goals.

Part I of this volume, edited by Justin Yifu Lin and Joseph E. Stiglitz, encompasses the Washington, D.C. roundtable. Its chapters move from the broadly theoretical to the case-study specific, reflecting the organization of the meeting, which was divided into six sessions: (1) Conceptual Issues and Principles of Industrial Policy; (2) Special Issues for Developing Countries; (3) Instruments of Industrial Policy; (4) Regional Case Studies of Successful and Unsuccessful Industrial Policies; (5) Country Case Studies of Successful and Unsuccessful Industrial Policies; and (6) Industrial Policy Redux.

Part II of this volume, edited by Justin Yifu Lin, Ebrahim Patel, and Joseph E. Stiglitz, encompasses the Pretoria roundtable. The arc of the conference was similar to that in Washington, moving from the general to the particular, but focusing on how industrial policies could help transform Africa. After reviewing the results of the Washington meeting, and seeing how these and other broad perspectives that formed the foundations of the Revolution in Industrial Policy could provide general insights for policies in Africa, the discussion centered on certain key issues facing the region: Can the "Development State" work for Africa? How does the New Global Order affect prospects for African Reindustrialization? What are the most important things for African governments to do to create a good environment for industrialization? How can financial policies be used as an instrument of industrial policy? The conference then proceeded with papers analyzing the role of industrial policies in particular sectors, and by participants sharing experiences of industrial policies (with examples from Brazil, Mauritius, Singapore, South Africa, and Africa more generally). After an Open Discussion of the Role and Opportunities for Industrial Policy in Africa and Directions for Future Research, the Roundtable concluded with a panel for (and partly by practicing) policymakers.

The two volumes in this IEA Industrial Policy Roundtable series do not provide comprehensive records of all the papers that were presented at the roundtable, but hopefully they give a picture of the richness of the discussions and the potential for (and cautions in) the use of industrial policy. The editors have taken the liberty of rearranging the chapters. The whole program of the roundtables may be accessed by visiting the website of the IEA: http://www.iea-world.com/roundtables.php.

The convening of the conferences benefitted from the guidance of leading economists from across the world. In particular, the members of the Scientific Committee, Laura Alfaro, Mario Cimoli, Josh Lerner, Kaushik Basu, and K.Y. Amoako, deserve special mention for their work in formulating the agenda. Their wisdom, academic expertise and leadership, organizing competence and generous sharing of time made the roundtables enormously successful academic events. The IEA also owes a debt of gratitude to those who helped organize the roundtables on site in both Washington and Pretoria: Claudia Sepulveda, Julia Cunico, Nthato Minyuku and Pilar Palacios.

In addition, the hard work of the administrative staff and student assistants at the two roundtables ensured that the roundtables' operations ran smoothly, for which the IEA is also grateful. The IEA is grateful to Laurence Wilse-Samson for the invaluable assistance he provided as a rapporteur in Pretoria. We especially want to acknowledge the work of Eamon Kircher-Allen in both pulling the book together and in general editorial assistance.

The roundtable in Washington was financially supported by the World Bank, while the Pretoria roundtable was financially supported by the World Bank, the South African Economic Development Department (EDD), the United Nations Department of Economic and Social Affairs (UNDESA), and the United Nations Industrial Development Organization (UNIDO) The IEA would like to express deep gratitude to these donors for their generous support.

And finally, we are indebted to all the staff at the IEA Secretariat and Palgrave Macmillan for their great help in shepherding the volumes from conception to completion.

Joseph Stiglitz
IEA President

Notes on the Contributors

Editors

Joseph E. Stiglitz is University Professor at Columbia University. In 2001, he was awarded the Nobel Prize in economics for his analyses of markets with asymmetric information. He is currently the President of the International Economic Association (2011–14).

Justin Yifu Lin is honorary dean and professor of National School of Development at Peking University. From 2008 to 2012, he served as Chief Economist and Senior Vice President of the World Bank. His many books include *Demystifying the Chinese Economy, the Quest for Prosperity*, and *the New Structural Economics*. He is a corresponding fellow of British Academy and a fellow of the World Academy of Sciences for the Developing World.

Contributors

Laura Alfaro is the Warren Alpert Professor of Business Administration. She served as Minister of National Planning and Economic Policy in Costa Rica from 2010 to 2012. Professor Alfaro is the author of multiple articles published in leading academic journals, and of Harvard Business School cases related to the field of international economics and, in particular, international capital flows, foreign direct investment and sovereign debt. She is also Faculty Research Fellow in the National Bureau of Economic Research's International Macroeconomics and Finance Program and Faculty Associate at Harvard's Weatherhead Center for International Affairs. In 2008, she was honored as a Young Global Leader by the World Economic Forum.

Carlos Alvarez is the Deputy Director of the OECD Development Centre. He has developed his professional career in the field of the competitiveness and innovation policies, holding positions of the highest responsibility for the Government of Chile, among them, Vice Minister of Economy (2004–2006) and Executive Vice-President of the National Economic Development Corporation – CORFO (2006–2010).

Mr. Alvarez is Industrial Engineer of the University of Chile holds an MSc in Economic Engineering from the same University (1990). He also obtained his Master in Public Administration at the John F. Kennedy School of Government (1995-Harvard University).

From 1990 Mr. Alvarez served in different positions in the Chilean public sector, having played an important role in the design, implementation and management of the set of programs to support economic competitiveness that exist today in Chile. Specifically he has made significant contributions in the fields of the technological innovation, promotion, attraction of investment, and promotion to the SME.

Yaw Ansu is the Chief Economist at the Africa Center for Economic Transformation (ACET) based in Accra, Ghana. Prior to joining ACET in 2010, he spent over 26 years working at the World Bank in various capacities including: Research Economist, Country Director, Director for Economic Policy and Head of the Economists Sector Board, and Regional Sector Director for Human Development for Africa. Yaw Ansu holds a B. A. in Economics from Cornell University, and an M.S. and a PhD in Engineering-Economic Systems from Stanford University in the U.S.A.

Pranab Bardhan is Professor of Graduate School at the Department of Economics, University of California, Berkeley.

Ha-Joon Chang teaches economics at the University of Cambridge. In addition to numerous journal articles and book chapters, he has published 14 authored books (four co-authored) and ten edited books. His main books include *The Political Economy of Industrial Policy, Kicking Away the Ladder, Bad Samaritans,* and the best-selling *23 Things They Don't Tell You About Capitalism.* By the end of 2014, his writings will have been translated and published in 34 languages and 38 countries. He is the winner of the 2003 Gunnar Myrdal Prize and the 2005 Wassily Leontief Prize.

Robert Cull is a lead economist in the Finance and Private Sector Development Team of the Development Research Group of the World Bank. His most recent research is on the performance of microfinance institutions, African financial development, the effects of the global financial crisis on developing economies, and the design and use of household surveys to measure access to financial services. He has published more than thirty articles in peer-reviewed academic journals and is the author or editor of multiple books. His most recent co-edited book, *Banking the World: Empirical Foundations of Financial Inclusion,* was published by MIT Press in January 2013. He is also co-editor of the *Interest Bearing Notes,* a bi-monthly newsletter reporting on financial and private sector research.

Robert Devlin is a Professorial Lecturer at Johns Hopkins SAIS and Associate Director of Communiqué International. He previously worked at the UN Economic Commission for Latin America and the Caribbean, Inter-American Development Bank and the Organization of American States. He has a Ph.D. in Economics from American University. His most recent book is *Breeding Latin American Tigers: Operational Principles for Rehabilitating Industrial Policies* coauthored with Graciela Moguillansky and published by World Bank Publishers in 2011.

João Carlos Ferraz is Vice President at the Brazilian Development Bank (BNDES). He is responsible for Corporate Planning, Economic Research, Credit and Rating Assessment and Risk Management.

Claudio Figueiredo Coelho Leal has a Masters degree in Economics from the Universidade Federal do Rio Grande do Sul (UFRGS), Brazil (1995). He has been working within the Brazilian Development Bank (BNDES) for 19 years, where in 2010 he was appointed as deputy managing director of the Planning Division.

Ariel Fiszbein is Chief Economist for the Human Development Network at the World Bank. He holds a Ph.D. in economics from the University of California, Berkeley. He joined the World Bank in 1991 were he started his career as Country Economist for Colombia. He has held several positions including that of coordinator of the poverty reduction team at the World Bank Institute, coordinator of the Bank's program in human development for the Southern Cone countries in Latin America, Lead Economist in the Human Development Department for Latin America and the Caribbean and Adviser to the Bank's Chief Economist and senior vice-President for Development Economics. In the latter position, he coordinated for several years the Bank's Development Impact Evaluation (DIME) initiative. He has published extensively on a range of issues of social policy. Most recently he co-authored *Conditional Cash Transfers: Reducing Present and Future Poverty*. He has taught at the Universidad de San Andres in Buenos Aires and was the secretary of the Latin American and Caribbean Economic Association (LACEA) between 1998 and 2005.

Indermit Gill is the chief economist for Europe and Central Asia at the World Bank. Before his current position, he worked in East Asia and Latin America, including an assignment in Brazil. He was the director of the 2009 World Development Report, Reshaping Economic Geography, and the principal author of reports such as *Golden Growth: Restoring the Lustre of the European Economic Model* and *An East Asian Renaissance*. He has a Ph.D. in Economics from the University of Chicago, and an M.A. from the Delhi School of Economics.

Bruce Greenwald is a Professor at the Graduate School of Business, Columbia University.

Ann Harrison is a Professor of Management at the Wharton School, University of Pennsylvania. She has also taught at the MBA, PhD, and undergraduate levels at various other universities, including Columbia Business School, the University of California, Berkeley, the Kennedy School of Government at Harvard University, and the University of Paris.

Before joining the Wharton School, Professor Harrison spent two years in Washington D.C. as the Director of Development Policy at the World Bank. Prior to that, she served as the head of the research team at the World

Bank on international trade and investment. Between 2001 and 2011, she was Professor of Agricultural and Resource Economics at the University of California, Berkeley. Professor Harrison received her PhD in Economics from Princeton University and graduated with highest distinction in Economics and History from the University of California, Berkeley.

Professor Harrison is a Research Associate at the National Bureau of Economic Research and an affiliate of the International Growth Centre in London. She is on the editorial boards of the *Journal of Economic Literature*, the *Journal of Asian Economics* and the *World Bank Research Observer*, and on various other advisory committees at the World Bank, the United Nations, and elsewhere. Her research is in the areas of emerging markets, multinational firms, international trade, productivity, and labor markets. She has lectured widely, including at most major US universities and in India, China, Latin America, Europe, the Philippines, and North Africa. Her latest research analyzes the anti-sweatshop movement, the impact of offshoring on wages and employment, the role of industrial policy in economic development, and the determinants of productivity growth in India, China, and Africa.

Mushtaq H. Khan is Professor of Economics at SOAS, University of London. He was educated at Oxford and Cambridge and previously taught at Cambridge University. He has also been visiting professor at the universities of Chulalongkorn in Thailand and Dhaka in Bangladesh. He is currently a member of the Committee of Experts on Public Administration at the United Nations. His research interests are in the areas of institutional economics, industrial policy, governance and political economy.

David Kupfer is Associate Professor of Instituto de Economia da Universidade Federal do Rio de Janeiro, Brazil, where he coordinates the Research Group on Industry and Competitiveness (GIC). Among other activities, he is editor of the *REC – Journal of Contemporary Economic* published by IE/UFRJ, a member of the Economic Council of FIESP and columnist for the newspaper *Valor Econômico*. He is an Advisor to the President's Office at the Brazilian Development Bank (BNDES).

Keun Lee is a Professor of Economics at the Seoul National University. As the founding director of the Center for Economic Catch-up, he is a globally recognized expert on economics of catch-up. Owing to his achievement in this field, he is appointed as a member of the Committee for Development Policy of UN, a co-editor of *Research Policy*, and a member of the governing board of Globelics. He obtained a Ph.D. degree from the University of California, Berkeley. He has had working experience at the World Bank, University of Aberdeen, and the East West Center, Hawaii. He has taught or been a visiting scholar at the University of California at Davis, Tsinghua University in Beijing, Hitotsubashi University in Japan, Hannover University in Germany, and Punjabi University in India. He has authored and edited several books, and written about 80 articles in international journals. One of his most widely-cited articles – with approximately 530 citations (Google Scholar) – is a paper on Korea's Technological Catch-up published in *Research Policy* (2001).

Josh Lerner is the Jacob H. Schiff Professor of Investment Banking at Harvard Business School, with a joint appointment in the Entrepreneurial Management and Finance Areas. His research focuses on innovation, venture capital, and private equity. He directs the National Bureau of Economic Research's Productivity, Entrepreneurship, and Innovation Program and edits their publication, *Innovation Policy and the Economy*. He founded and runs the Private Capital Research Institute, a non-profit devoted to encouraging data and research about venture capital and private equity. In the 1993–94 academic year, he introduced an elective course for second-year MBAs on private equity finance, which remains consistently one of the largest elective courses at Harvard Business School. He is the winner of the Swedish government's 2010 Global Entrepreneurship Research Award and has recently been named one of the 100 most influential people in private equity over the past decade by *Private Equity International* magazine.

Wonhyuk Lim is Director of Global Economy Research at the Korea Development Institute (KDI). Since he joined KDI in 1996, his research has focused on state-owned enterprises and family-based business groups (*chaebol*). He has also written extensively on development issues, in conjunction with policy consultation projects under Korea's Knowledge Sharing Program (KSP). He received a Presidential order from the Dominican Republic for his work. After the 2002 Presidential Election in Korea, he worked for the Presidential Transition Committee and the Presidential Committee on Northeast Asia and helped to set policy directions for the restructuring of the electricity and gas sector and for Northeast Asian energy cooperation. Dr Lim was also at Brookings as a CNAPS Fellow for 2005–06, and worked as a consultant for the World Bank and the Asian Development Bank Institute (ADBI). In 2010, he helped to formulate the G20 Seoul Development Consensus for Shared Growth. His recent publications include "Chaebol and Industrial Policy in Korea" (*Asian Economic Policy Review*, 2012), "Joint Discovery and Upgrading of Comparative Advantage: Lessons from Korea's Development Experience" (World Bank, 2011) and "Global Leadership in Transition: Making the G20 More Effective and Responsive" (Brookings and KDI, 2011, co-edited with Colin Bradford). He received a B.A.S. in Physics and History and a Ph.D. in Economics from Stanford University.

Graciela Moguillansky is an economist from the Universidad de Chile. She is an international consultant in product development and innovation with experience in Latin American countries. She previously worked at the UN Economic Commission for Latin America and the Caribbean.

Célestin Monga is Senior Advisor at the World Bank where he has previously held various positions, including as Lead Economist in Europe and Central Asia, and Manager of the Policy Review team in the Development Economics vice presidency. He also served on the Board of Directors of the Sloan School of Management's Fellows Program at the Massachusetts Institute of Technology (MIT) and taught at Boston University and the University of Bordeaux (France). Prior to joining the World Bank, he was Department Head and Manager in the Banque Nationale de Paris group. His books have been translated into several languages and used as teaching tools by academic institutions around the world. He holds degrees from MIT, Harvard, and the universities of Paris 1 Panthéon-Sorbonne, Bordeaux and Pau.

Felipe Silveira Marques has a Ph.D. in Industrial and Technological Economics from the Economics Institute of the Federal University of Rio de Janeiro, Brazil (2009). He has been working within the Brazilian Development Bank (BNDES) for six years, where he is currently Advisor to the President's Office, working with industrial policy, the Planning and the Economic Research Divisions.

Volker Treichel is the World Bank's Sector Leader for Cote d'Ivoire, Benin, Burkina Faso and Togo and is responsible for the economic policy dialogue and the budget support operations with the four countries. He was a Lead Economist in the Office of the Chief Economist and Senior Vice President from 2010–2012. During this time, he co-authored several Working Papers with Justin Lin, including on the global financial crisis, the crisis of the Euro-zone, and growth strategies for Latin America and Nigeria. From 2007, he was the World Bank's Lead Economist for Nigeria. During this time, he edited the bestselling book *Putting Nigeria to Work* and led the first subnational Development Policy Operation in sub-Saharan Africa in Lagos State. From 1993–2007, he was at the IMF, including as mission chief for Togo and resident representative in Albania. He holds a Ph.D. in Economics from Kiel University and an Advanced Studies Certificate in International Economic Policy Research from the Kiel Institute of World Economics.

Marcelo Trindade Miterhof has a Master degree in Economics from the Universidade Estadual de Campinas (Unicamp), Brazil (2000). He has been working within the Brazilian Development Bank (BNDES) for eleven years, where nowadays is Advisor to the President's Office.

Shahid Yusuf is currently Chief Economist of The Growth Dialogue at the George Washington University School of Business in Washington DC. He holds a Ph.D. in Economics from Harvard University, and a BA in Economics from Cambridge University. Prior to joining the Growth Dialogue, Dr. Yusuf was on the staff of the World Bank. During his 35 year tenure at the World Bank, Dr. Yusuf was the team leader for the World Bank–Japan project on East Asia's Future Economy from 2000–2009. He was the Director of the *World Development Report 1999/2000, Entering the 21st Century*. Prior to that, he was Economic Adviser to the Senior Vice President and Chief Economist (1997–98), Lead Economist for the East Africa Department (1995–97) and Lead Economist for the China and Mongolia Department (1989–1993).

Dr. Yusuf has written extensively on development issues, with a special focus on East Asia and has also published widely in various academic journals. He has authored or edited 27 books on industrial and urban development, innovation systems and tertiary education which have been translated into a number of different languages.

Xiaobo Zhang is a "National 1000-Talent Program" chair professor of economics at the National School of Development, Peking University, and senior research fellow at the International Food Policy Research Institute (IFPRI). His research fields are Chinese economy and development economics. He has published widely in top economics journals, such as the *Journal of Political Economy*, the *Journal of Development Economics*, the *Journal of International Economics*, and the *Journal of Public Economics*. His recent books include *Governing Rapid Growth in China: Equity and Institutions* (2009), *Regional Inequality in China: Trends, Explanations and Policy Responses* (2009), *Narratives of Chinese Economic Reforms: How Does China Cross the River?*, and *Oxford Companion to the Economics of China* (forthcoming). He is a Co-editor of *China Economic Review*. He was selected as the president of the Chinese Economists Society from 2005 to 2006.

Introduction: The Rejuvenation of Industrial Policy

Joseph E. Stiglitz, Justin Yifu Lin and Célestin Monga

Knowledge validation has never been a painless process. It often takes a major, disastrous historical event for even the most self-evident ideas to gain wide recognition. It is therefore not surprising that the Great Recession of 2008–09 – whose global economic and social cost is still yet to be quantified – has led to a rethinking of many aspects of what might be thought of as the conventional wisdom in economics.

This book is about one important area in which there has been a major rethinking – industrial policy, by which we mean government policies directed at affecting the economic structure of the economy. The standard argument was that markets were efficient, so there was no need for government to intervene either in the sectoral allocation of resources or in the choices of technique. And even if markets were not efficient, governments were not likely to improve matters. But the crisis showed that markets were not necessarily efficient, and indeed, there was a broad consensus that without strong government intervention – which included providing life-lines to certain firms and certain industries – the market economies in the USA and Europe may have collapsed.

Today, the relevance and pertinence of industrial policies are acknowledged by mainstream economists and political leaders from all sides of the ideological spectrum.

In the United States, President Barack Obama was not shy in saying, in his 2013 State of the Union address, that his "first priority is making America a magnet for new jobs and manufacturing." After funding the creation of a manufacturing innovation institute in Youngstown, Ohio, he announced the launch of "manufacturing hubs," where businesses will partner with the Departments of Defense and Energy to turn regions left behind by globalization into global centers of high-tech jobs, and he asked Congress to "help create a network of fifteen of these hubs and guarantee that the next revolution in manufacturing is Made in America."[1]

In the United Kingdom, Conservative Prime Minister David Cameron promised "to have a proper industrial strategy to get behind the growth

1

engines of the future."[2] Observing that "market forces are insufficient for creating the long term industrial capacities we need," his government vowed "to identify British success stories as identified through success in trade and explicitly get behind them at the highest political level" (Cable, 2012). These would be "areas where we need a more strategic and proactive approach using all of the government's policy levers – rather than simply responding to crises after they have developed, or waiting to see what the market dictates." In Japan, the conservative Prime Minister Shinzo Abe recently created a new governance body for microeconomic policy, the Economic Revitalization Headquarters, which includes an industrial competitiveness council whose purpose is to formulate growth strategies.

In the European Union (EU), where the global crisis may have done the most profound long-term economic and social damage, almost all governments are reassessing their industrial strategies, trying to learn from successful experiences of Finland or Germany. Within the EU, where the idea of industrial policy has long been rooted, the thinking has evolved significantly. Departing from its stated commitment "to the horizontal nature of industrial policy and to avoid a return to selective interventionist policies" (EC 2005), the EU Commission has now adopted "a fresh approach to industrial policy" aiming at "bringing together a horizontal basis and sectoral application [*that*] will consider appropriate measures to inform consumers and promote industrial excellence in given sector." Specific sectors are identified for support (motor vehicles and transport equipment industries, energy supply industries, chemicals, agro-food, and so on) and sector-specific initiatives recommended to promote them (EC 2010, pp. 4 and 23). An entire department at the EU Commission is currently devoting much financial and human resources to design and help implement industrial policies across the Eurozone.

In emerging economies such as China, Russia, Brazil, India, Indonesia, or Nigeria, where the largest fraction of the world's poor reside, policymakers are also eager to encourage new thinking on the various ways in which smart industrial policy can help sustain growth and open up new possibilities for employment creation. Dani Rodrik has aptly summed up the sea change of attitude in relation to industrial policy by pointing out the apparent irony of the firm McKinsey, the global symbol of managerial capitalism, advising governments all over the world on how to do it right (Rodrik, 2012 and Rodrik and McMillan, 2011).

Clearly, there is a new impetus for industrial policy, and the general recognition – even among mainstream economists – that it often involves good common-sense economic policy.

But what exactly is industrial policy? Why has it raised so much controversy and confusion? What is the compelling new rationale for it, which seems to bring mainstream economists to acknowledge its crucial importance and revisit some of the fundamental assumptions of economic theory and economic development? How can it be designed to avoid the pitfalls of some of the seeming past failures and to emulate some of the past successes? What are the contours of the emerging consensus and remaining issues and open questions? The collection of papers presented in this volume and initially discussed at a roundtable[3] try to provide answers to these burning questions. This book is a contribution in the large body of ongoing analytical work that focuses on the rejuvenation of industrial policy in the post-crisis global economy,[4] discusses the evolving conceptions of industrial policy, takes stock of intellectual progress, documents the challenges of implementation, and outlines the remaining intellectual and policy agenda.

A short biography of an idea

The famous, late Nigerian writer Chinua Achebe often complained that many of the great literary critics who like his work do so "for the wrong reasons," which made him feel uncomfortable even among his strongest supporters. Industrial policy[5] can be said to be in the same situation: it has too often been celebrated and advocated for the wrong reasons.

The 1960s and 1970s were marked by interventionist government policies to promote economic nationalism and development in many of the developing countries. It was evident that the market economy – so far as it existed under colonialism – had not resulted in development. There were many motivations for the establishment of state-owned firms: a shortage of private entrepreneurs, the lack of depth of local (private) capital and financial markets able and willing to finance new enterprises or the expansion of old ones, the inability of local enterprises to bear the risks of large-scale investment, a fear of exploitation by foreign firms – typically from the colonizing countries that had previously exploited them so badly, and intellectual currents fashionable at the time (understandable in the aftermath of the Great Depression) that emphasized the limitations of markets. Interestingly, it was in the same period that economic theory came to better understand "market failures," the many instances in which profit-maximizing firms do not lead to economic efficiency or societal well-being.

It was hoped that these state-owned firms would be profitable; would reinvest their proceeds – thus closing the resource gap that separated developed from developing countries; and would also narrow the technological gap with advanced economies.

The record of the early industrial policies is mixed. While some countries were able to record high growth rates, mostly in Latin America (Ocampo and Ros, 2011), the results of these early-generation industrial policies were often disappointing: instead of converging to the developed countries' income levels, many developing countries where industrial policies were implemented stagnated or even recorded a deterioration of their income gap with developed countries. While industrial policies were often blamed for these disappointing outcomes, failures in macroeconomic policies and governance often played a role—and were often the real source of the problem.

But critics of the industrial policies implemented in many of the countries argued that they had introduced profound distortions: limited public resources were used to pursue unsustainable import-substitution policies. To reduce the burden of public subsidies, governments sometimes resorted to administrative measures – granting the non-viable enterprises in prioritized industries a market monopoly, suppressing interest rates, overvaluing domestic currency and controlling prices for raw materials. Such interventions themselves introduced further distortions, sometimes even causing shortages in foreign exchange and raw materials. Preferential access to credit deprived others of resources meaning that there was a high opportunity cost (Lin and Monga, 2013).

In the 1980s, with the rise of market fundamentalism (with President Ronald Reagan in the USA and Prime Minister Margaret Thatcher in the UK, and with international financial institutions reflecting the prevalent ideologies), the pendulum shifted from market failures to government failures: with the rise of the rational expectations in economics, the faith in the rationality of agents operating in free markets became the new intellectual gospel for development economics. It became fashionable to dismiss any proactive attempt by the government to foster structural transformation, and attribute economic success only to liberalization, privatization, and deregulation. Industrial policy took a backseat to Washington Consensus policies.

Even in the period of the ascendency of the Washington Consensus, this orthodoxy was being questioned by both academics and policymakers. In East Asia, there was historically unprecedented growth. They had active industrial policies – though they did many other things well in addition. Just as there has been controversy concerning to what extent it was sensible to ascribe disappointing results in some countries to industrial policies, so too there was in relation to the successes. But what was clear was that these countries did not subscribe to the doctrines of the Washington Consensus (World Bank, 1993; Stiglitz, 1996).

At the same time, in some developed countries, like the United States, there was growing recognition of the role that industrial policies – especially in the form of the promotion of new technologies – had played in their success.

The successes in East Asia were inevitably contrasted with the failures in the rest of the developing world, where Washington Consensus policies often dominated. Sub-Saharan Africa saw not only a decline in per capita income, but also a process of deindustrialization (Noman and Stiglitz, 2012).

Simultaneously, academic research was highlighting a deeper set of market failures. The presumption that markets were efficient was reversed, when it was shown that whenever there was imperfect and asymmetric information, and/or imperfect risk markets, the market equilibrium was not efficient (Greenwald and Stiglitz, 1986). These new theories helped explain the problems that developing countries had in capital and financial markets and in entrepreneurship.

Equally important, it was recognized that what separated developed from developing countries was a gap in knowledge (World Bank, 1998), and that markets for the production and transfer of knowledge were inherently imperfect.

Many years earlier, Solow (1957) had shown that most increases in standard of living are related to the acquisition of knowledge, to "learning." It followed that understanding how economies best learn – how economies can best be organized to increase the production and dissemination of productivity-enhancing knowledge – should be a central part of the study of development and growth. But markets on their own fail to "maximize" learning. They ignore important knowledge spillovers. Sectors where knowledge is important tend to be imperfectly competitive, with the result that output is restrained. In fact, the production of knowledge is often a joint product with the production of goods, which means that the production of goods themselves will not in general be (intertemporally) efficient. Yet, surprisingly, development economists had typically not focused on this issue, nor on the implications for the desirability of government intervention.

The 2008–09 global crisis painfully forced many economists and policy-makers to face reality: they had to acknowledge that the issues of market failures are pervasive, even in high-income countries with fairly well-developed financial markets.

Some of the most important national and global policy objectives (equality of opportunity for all citizens, pollution control, climate change, and so on) are simply often not reflected in market prices. The successful experiences of countries that did not follow the dominant Washington Consensus policy framework and their importance as new global players on the international economic scene (from China to Brazil) make the rethinking of macroeconomic strategies and industrial policy unavoidable.

There is another reason for a renewed focus on industrial policy: it has become obvious that all governments are engaged in various forms of industrial policies – even those that advocate horizontal or "neutral" policies end up taking actions that favor certain industries more than others and therefore shape the sectoral allocation of the economy. In all countries, some industries, sectors, and even firms are favored within the legal framework and heavily subsidized, often in non-transparent ways. A case in point is that of the banking sector in the United States: the Federal Reserve (a branch of the government) lends money to banks at a 1 percent interest rate, which is then used by these banks to buy Treasury bills (from the same government) at, say, 4 percent (that represents about $30 billion in subsidies a year, more than any developing country governments will ever grant to one industry). Bankruptcy laws that put derivatives first in line in the event of bankruptcy effectively give preference to the financial sector. Most countries' tax codes are riddled with tax expenditures that provide hidden subsidies to particular industries. But even in the absence of such "special" provisions, the design of depreciation allowances will affect industries with different capital lifespans differently. Budget policies also inevitably have impacts on industrial structure: where governments locate roads and ports affects different industries and firms differently. In short, one cannot escape thinking about the differential impacts of different policies on different sectors.

Even economists who oppose sectoral industrial policy (the so-called "vertical" policies to support specific industries) acknowledge the need for broad, neutral, "horizontal" industrial policy (one that does not target specific industries). Yet the lines between the two could be blurry. Everything governments do or choose not to do benefits or can be captured by vested interests. A particular exchange rate policy could be presented as "neutral" and "broad-based." Yet, we know that some sectors, industries, social groups, and even regions are always favored or penalized by any stance on exchange rates. Even when there is no change, some benefit while others lose out. Likewise, infrastructure development is often presented as a suitable tool of economic policy because of its perceived "neutrality." Yet there is nothing neutral about the choice of infrastructure that a country needs at any given time, or where and when it should be built. These decisions always involve some political judgment about priorities, and therefore represent industrial policies. The same is true for education, which is often mistakenly presented as "neutral."

Therefore, the question is not *whether* any government should use industrial policy but rather *how* to use industrial policy in the best way. True, industrial policy still carries a somewhat blemished reputation in mainstream economics and still generates controversy. However, things have changed considerably in the aftermath of the Great Recession: it is no longer associated systematically with loss-making nationalized industries. This is reflected in the public discourse of political leaders from advanced and developing countries alike, liberal and conservative. Even the import-substitution policies of Latin America have been re-examined in this new light – and appear to have been far more successful, *on average,* than critics alleged (Ocampo and Ros, 2011). Even when they imposed budgetary costs, there may have been society wide benefits; and even if these budgetary costs had adverse effects, the lesson may not be to abandon such policies, but to redesign them in ways that preserve as much of, say, the learning benefits as possible, without the financial burden that has been associated with them.

But just like the excited Chinua Achebe critics who celebrate his work for the wrong reasons, the wrong justifications are still often being made to support industrial policy. The profound changes in the distribution of power in the world economy (the rise of large middle-income economies such as China, Brazil, India, or Indonesia) and the fear of globalization (increased competition from emerging economies even in high-technology goods, deindustrialization, migration of workers) are still being offered in advanced countries to justify the granting of financial aid and protection to some industries for "strategic or national security" purposes. Similar arguments are also made in low-income countries to advocate inward-looking policies that are unsustainable. It is therefore useful to briefly take stock of intellectual progress on industrial policy, and highlight some of the lessons that the global crisis has brought to the debate.

Emerging consensus and remaining challenges

On the conceptual front, the justification for industrial policy has always been well grounded in economic theory, in particular in the theories of market failure alluded to earlier. In the development context, there are a few aspects of these "failures" that are particularly salient.

Modern economic growth is a process of continuous technological innovation, industrial upgrading and economic diversification. No country in the world has been able to move from low- to middle- and high-income status without undergoing the process of industrialization. Structural transformation is always taking place because of changes in technology, in comparative advantage, and in the global economy. There is a need for some guiding principles on how "best" any society should move its human, capital, and financial resources from low- to high-productivity sectors. For the process to be efficient, coordination issues and externalities issues must be addressed. On their own markets typically do not manage such structural transformations well.

Moreover, as we noted earlier, most increases in per capita income arise from advances in technology – about 70 percent of growth comes from sources other than factor accumulation. In developing countries, a substantial part of the growth in developing countries arises from closing the "knowledge" gap between themselves and those at the frontier. Within any country, there is enormous scope for productivity improvement simply by closing the gap between best practices and average practices. If improvements in standards of living come mainly from the diffusion of knowledge, learning strategies must be at the heart of the development strategies.

These elements of a new intellectual consensus provide further justification for industrial policy – well beyond the traditional theoretical discussion of market failures based on coordination and conventional externalities. This new theoretical perspective focuses on the reasons that markets, by themselves, are not likely to produce sufficient growth-enhancing investments, such as those associated with learning, knowledge accumulation, and research. Yet the issues of diffusion of learning throughout society to equip and empower all private agents have received little attention, in marked contrast to those of resource allocation. Indeed, much of the focus has been on narrow conceptions of industrial policy and its suspicious connotation of "picking winners" and generating private rents without social rewards.

Externalities in learning and discovery support an infant economy argument for government intervention that Greenwald and Stiglitz (this volume) argue is far more robust than the conventional infant industry argument.

The consensus among economists and policymakers has grown wider on the need for governments to focus on issues of learning, of infant industries and economies, of promoting exports and the private sector, not only in manufacturing but also in agriculture and in services like health, information technology, or finance. Industrial policy is therefore not just about manufacturing. As President Obama argued, "[E]very dollar we invested to map the human genome returned $140 to our economy. Today, our scientists are mapping the human brain to unlock the answers to Alzheimer's; developing drugs to regenerate damaged organs; devising new material to make batteries ten times more powerful. Now is not the time to gut these job-creating investments in science and innovation. Now is the time to reach a level of research and development not seen since the height of the Space Race. And today, no area holds more promise than our investments in American energy."[6]

The production of knowledge is different from the production of ordinary goods. Arrow (1962b), for instance, highlighted the non-rivalrous nature of knowledge and the associated disclosure problem, which makes the innovative projects that ignite and sustain technological developments quite different from traditional capital investments. The information problems surrounding projects that require research and development (R&D) make them difficult to finance: if one discloses enough information to a potential investor about an idea that one would like to develop to make him willing to finance it, he can often "steal" the idea.

True, inventors can try to limit these problems by requiring potential buyers to sign confidentiality agreements. However, these documents frequently prove to be difficult to enforce and ultimately ineffective. As a result, firms with the kind of promising projects that spur growth and economic development may be unable to pursue them for a lack of resources.

While industrial policies that promote the structural transformation of the economy and help create a learning economy are two of the central objectives of modern economic development, industrial policies may be used to pursue a number of other social objectives, especially in developing countries.

Industrial policy has, for instance, been used to correct not only market failures but also government failures. In some countries and contrary to popular belief, state enterprises have been islands of relatively good governance, even when the economy suffered from massive government failure. A case in point discussed in this book is Brazil's *Banco Nacional de Desenvolvimento Econômico e Social* (BNDES, development bank), which has resisted political pressures rather well through decades of poor political governance. It is credited with having helped a substantial number of industries to take off.

Other new economic functions of industrial policy include addressing distributional issues effectively and promoting employment. Despite a wide convergence of views on these new theoretical underpinnings of industrial policy, there are still some important issues up for debate – especially regarding the scope, instruments, and implementation challenges in the often weak institutional context of developing countries. The competencies of government should affect the choice of instruments, and perhaps the "ambition" of industrial policy. Limited competencies suggest that broad-based measures – like those associated with maintaining an undervalued exchange rate – may be preferable to more targeted measures. The articles in this book hopefully will shed light on such questions as: If industrial policy is inevitable anyway, what should be done differently to avoid past mistakes? What institutional context is needed to mitigate the risks of state capture and rent-seeking? Is there a fine line between state capture versus most types of public–private partnerships? What is the optimal way of designing and implementing industrial policy the context of fragile/unstable states where there are pervasive governance/rent-seeking problems?

The new thinking about industrial policy has important implications for international agreements. The World Trade Organization attempts to circumscribe subsidies and trade practices that are deemed "unfair." But what is the appropriate restraint on state–business relations within countries, especially developing countries that are striving to catch up with the more advanced? Are these trade agreements effectively "kicking away the ladder" upon which the advanced industrial countries themselves climbed, as Chang (2002) has suggested?

The papers in this volume debate these questions, identifying some basic principles that successful industrial policy arrangements have in common, but also highlighting the difficulties of moving from theory to practice.

Contents of this volume

The papers presented in this volume are organized into four sections. The first one deals with conceptual issues and principles of industrial policy. In "Comparative Advantage: The Silver Bullet of Industrial Policy," Lin and Monga identify the conditions under which industrial policy – and, more broadly, government interventions in the economy – are likely to fail or succeed. They argue that industrial policy has often failed because of the strategic mistake of setting goals inconsistent with the level of development of the country and the structure of its endowments at a given time. Deriving lessons from the experience of unrealistic development goals, they recommend that economic strategies be consistent with comparative advantage determined by the *existing* endowment structure. Such industrial policies set the stage for continuous growth, shared prosperity, and social cohesion.

Greenwald and Stiglitz, in "Industrial Policies, the Creation of a Learning Society, and Economic Development," note that market forces do not exist in a vacuum. Development economics routinely emphasizes the study of institutions as being central to growth. All the rules and regulations, the legal frameworks and how they are enforced, affect the structure of the economy, meaning that government is always, albeit often unwittingly, engaged in industrial policy. They are concerned with one particular reason for industrial policies – helping create a "learning society," one which will be marked by higher rates of technological progress and lower disparities between best and average practices. Markets, on their own, are not efficient in the production and dissemination of knowledge (learning). Sectors in which learning (research) is important are typically characterized by a wide variety of market failures. Most importantly, knowledge is different from conventional goods; it is, in a sense, a public good – the marginal cost of another person or firm enjoying the benefit of knowledge (beyond the cost of transmission) is zero; usage is non-rivalrous. Markets are not efficient in the production and distribution of public goods. It is inevitable that there be, or that there ought to be, a role for government. In a world with mobile factors, they suggest that a major determinant of a country's development strategy – of its long-term dynamic comparative advantage – is its learning capabilities. By paying careful attention to learning spillovers and the extent to which productivity is affected by production (that is, the extent to which there is learning-by-doing), Greenwald and Stiglitz are able to derive precise prescriptions for the design of industrial policies.

The second section discusses some of the special issues that developing countries face when designing and implementing industrial policy. In "Technology Policies and Learning with Imperfect Governance," Khan starts from the observation that developing countries can grow rapidly by absorbing known technologies from more advanced countries. Yet these countries often find it difficult to absorb even relatively simple technologies even when they have the resources to buy the relevant machines and have workers with the appropriate levels of formal education who are willing to work for relatively low wages. The reasons, he contends, are often contracting problems that impede critical investments being made. He argues that is it therefore important to identify the precise contracting failures that are most important to address and to design policies that have the greatest chance of being implemented given existing governance capabilities and the feasible improvements in these capabilities. The fit between problems, policies, and capabilities can explain why some countries or sectors can do well even when overall governance capabilities are weak.

In the next chapter, "The Boulevard of Broken Dreams: Industrial Policy and Entrepreneurship," Lerner assesses the long-run consequences of public policies that facilitate or hinder the development of a venture capital sector, a sector which can be vital for establishing innovative entrepreneurship. He notes that in many cases, there is likely to be a role for the government in stimulating a vibrant entrepreneurial sector, given the early stage of maturity of these activities in most nations. But at the same time, it is easy for the government to overstep its bounds and squander its investments in this arena. He concludes that only by designing a program that reflects an understanding of the entrepreneurial process can government efforts be effective.

The third section of the book is devoted to the instruments of industrial policy. In "Financing Development: The Case of BNDES," Ferraz, Coelho Leal, Silveira Marques, and Trinidade Miterhof analyze the multiple roles played by Brazil's development bank, as well as its recent participation in the federal government's anti-cyclical efforts to ward off the detrimental effects of the international financial crisis on the economic growth of the country. They show how the institution has managed, often quite successfully, to establish and employ a wide array of instruments to contend with a variety of challenges in Brazilian development.

In "Growth and the Quality of Foreign Direct Investment," Alfaro and Charlton directly address the ability of countries to correctly identify attractive industrial policy targets and then tests whether the outcomes are superior when governments intervene. They assess the possibility that the effects of foreign direct investment (FDI) on growth differ by sector. They also differentiate FDI based on objective qualitative industry characteristics, including the average skill intensity and reliance on external capital. Using a new dataset on industry-level and a two-stage least squares methodology to control for measurement error and endogeneity, they find that the effects of FDI on growth are more pronounced when the quality of FDI is taken into account.

Monga's paper on "Theories of Agglomeration: A Critical Analysis from the Policy Perspective" re-examines the notion that the concentration of production in a particular geographic area brings major external benefits for firms in that location through knowledge spillovers, labor pooling, and the close proximity of specialized suppliers – a notion that has long been enshrined in economic theory. Monga notes that the eruption of new clusters in the most unlikely places in countries like China does not just occur randomly (as suggested by some devotees of cluster analysis) but is the result of strong and deliberate government action. His paper explains why the standard theories of agglomeration can be misleading and why many attempts at building industrial clusters have not delivered the expected outcomes. It highlights the key issues to be addressed by policymakers and provides a framework for proactively building competitive clusters in a way that defies traditional prescriptions.

The final section of this volume presents a few regional and country case studies of successful and unsuccessful industrial policies. Following Monga's contribution from the previous section, Zhang's paper on "Clusters as an Instrument for Industrial Policy: The Case of China" discusses how entrepreneurs in a large emerging economy organize themselves to overcome constraints on industrial production. Clustering reduces reliance on external finances because a finer division of labor allows each business to work on a smaller portion of the production process with a corresponding lower starting capital. Easy access to trade credit from customers and suppliers also alleviates working capital constraints. Moreover, the nature of repeated transactions in a narrowly defined region creates pressures for entrepreneurs to restrain opportunistic behavior, making it easier for small business to thrive in an environment with imperfect external institutions. Local governments can play an instrumental role in facilitating cluster development by providing the necessary public goods and by coordinating collective actions.

In "Capability Failure and Industrial Policy to Move beyond the Middle-Income Trap: From Trade-based to Technology-based Specialization," Lee argues that capability failures (rather than market failures) are the most serious justification for industrial policy in developing countries, and the source of the middle-income trap. He suggests a three-stage implementation strategy to build technological capabilities: first, the assimilation of foreign technology (operational skills and production technology) and know-how through licensing, FDI, or technology transfer from public research agencies; second, learning via co-development contracts and public–private consortia once the latecomer firms establish their own in-house R&D labs as a physical basis for more indigenous learning; and third, the leapfrogging to emerging technologies which involve public–private R&D consortia and/or exclusive standard policy, procurement, and user subsidies for initial market provision.

The evolution of industrial policy in Korea is discussed in "The *Chaebol* and Industrial Policy in Korea" by Lim. Although the degree of sectoral targeting changed dramatically from the 1960s to the 1970s and then the 1980s onward, Korea maintained an outward-oriented, bottom-up, and integrated approach to industrial policy, relying on close public–private consultation and international benchmarking. The government and the *chaebol* systematically studied what had to be done to fill the missing links in the domestic value chain and move up the quality ladder, through technology acquisition, human resource development, and the construction of optimal-scale plants aimed for the global market. As the capacity of the private sector increased and sectoral targeting became a more difficult proposition, Korea shifted to a more sector-neutral approach, which provided support for industry rationalization and R&D regardless of sectors.

In "What's New in the New Industrial Policy in Latin America?" Devlin and Moguillansky shift the focus of analysis to a region of the world where there has been a long history of government intervention. During much of the period from 1950 to 1980 the general practice there was in line with the then mainstream thinking in development economics. Significant growth and some level of industrialization and modernization were recorded in many countries. However serious flaws in the design and execution of the industrial policy led to failure in caching up with advanced countries. The external debt crisis of the 1980s and the advent of Washington Consensus policies led to the dominance of the market paradigm, with even less success. In recent years, however, there has been a renaissance of industrial policy in the region. The chapter highlights the nature of the shift to a more proactive state promotion of industrial and services upgrading, as well as the important new characteristics of industrial policy, which are different from those of the past and offer more hope of success. That same general argument is made by Kupfer, Ferraz, and Silveira Marques in "New Thinking on Industrial Policy: Country Case Studies of Successful and Unsuccessful Industrial Policies." Focusing specifically on Brazil, they analyze three recent industrial policies enacted during the 2000s (the Industrial, Technological and Foreign Trade Policy, the Productive Development Policy, and the Brasil Maior Plan), and discuss their connections with the macro environment.

These papers by economists from different backgrounds offer a diversity of perspectives on industrial policy. They are accompanied by enlightening comments and even some robust challenges by discussants (Ha-Joon Chang, Josh Lerner, Pranab Bardhan, Célestin Monga, Ann Harrison, Indermit Gill, Robert Cull, Ariel Fiszbein, Shahid Yusuf, and Carlos Alvarez). Beyond the debates, there is a general recognition that successful economies have always relied on government policies that promote growth by accelerating structural transformation. The blind faith in the magic virtues of market forces in which rational agents would naturally create an optimal environment for growth and economic development has been disproved by the enormity of the Great Recession—and the swift policy responses that governments around the world adopted to weather the crisis. Still, much work remains to be done to identify the specific policy levers and institutional framework that can generate optimal industrial policy results in different contexts. This volume is a contribution to that important task.

Notes

1. President B. H. Obama, *State of the Union Address*, February 12, 2013.
2. Prime Minister D. Cameron, *Speech at the Confederation of British Industry's Annual Conference*, November 2012.
3. The roundtable was organized jointly by the International Economic Association and the World Bank and held in Washington on May 22–23, 2012.
4. See Cimoli, Dosi, and Stiglitz (2009); Griffith-Jones, Ocampo, and Stiglitz (2009); Lin (2012a, 2012b); Rodrik (2012); Rodrik and McMillan (2011).

5. The very definition of industrial policy has been source of debate and confusion. Two broad and competing conceptions can be found in the literature – and in this volume: the sector-specific one by the US International Trade Commission, according to which industrial policy involves "coordinated government action aimed at directing production resources to domestic producers in certain industries to help them become more competitive" (Tyson 1992); and the "horizontal" approach popularized by the Lisbon Agenda of the EU states, for which "the main role of industrial policy [...] is to proactively provide the right framework conditions for enterprise development and innovation in order to make the EU an attractive place for industrial development and job creation, taking account of the fact that most businesses are small and medium-sized enterprises (SMEs)" (EC 2007). The definition used in this introduction is closer to the former, though we consider industrial policy to be justified mainly for industries that are potentially competitive already.

6. *State of the Union Address*, op. cit.

References

Arrow, Kenneth J. (1962a) "The Economic Implications of Learning by Doing," *Review of Economic Studies*, vol. 29, no. 3, pp. 155–173.

Arrow, Kenneth J. (1962b) "Economic Welfare and the Allocation of Resources for Invention," in Richard R. Nelson (ed.), *The Rate and Direction of Inventive Activity: Economic and Social Factors* (Princeton, NJ: Princeton University Press for the National Bureau of Economic Research), pp. 609–626.

Cable, Vincent (2012) *Industry Policy: Letter to the Prime Minister and Deputy Prime Minister*, London, Department for Business Innovation & Skills, February 8.

Chang, Ha-Joon (2002) *Kicking Away the Ladder: Development Strategy in Historical Perspective* (London: Anthem).

Cimoli, Mario, Dosi, Giovanni, and Stiglitz, Joseph E. (eds) (2009) *Industrial Policy and Development: The Political Economy of Capabilities Accumulation* (New York: Oxford University Press).

European Commission (EC) (2010) *Communication from the Commission to the European Parliament, the Council, the European Econmic and Social Committee, and the Committee for Regions: An Integrated Industrial Policy for the Globalisation Era – Putting Competitiveness and Sustainability at Centre Stage*, SEC (2010) 1272–1276, Brussels, Com (2010) 614.

European Commission (EC) (2007) *Report – State Aid Scoreboard*, COM (2007), 347, Final.

European Commission (EC) (2005) *Implementing the Community Lisbon Programme: A Policy Framework to Strengthen EU Manufacturing – Towards a More Integrated Approach for Industrial Policy*, COM (2005) 474, Final.

Greenwald, B. and Stiglitz, J.E. (1986) "Externalities in Economies with Imperfect Information and Incomplete Markets," *Quarterly Journal of Economics*, vol. 101, no. 2, pp. 229–264.

Greenwald, B. and J.E. Stiglitz (2014) "Industrial Policies, the Creation of a Learning Society, and Economic Development," in this volume.

Griffith-Jones, Stephany, Ocampo, José Antonio, and Stiglitz, Joseph E. (eds) (2010) *Time for a Visible Hand: Lessons from the 2008 World Financial Crisis* (New York: Oxford University Press).

Lin, Justin Yifu (2012a) *The New Structural Economics: A Framework for Rethinking Development and Policy* (Washington, DC: World Bank).

Lin, Justin Yifu (2012b) *The Quest for Prosperity: How Developing Countries Can Take Off* (Princeton, NJ: Princeton University Press).

Lin, Justin Yifu, and Monga, Célestin (2013) "The Evolving Paradigms of Structural Change," in: David M. Malone, Rohinton Medhora, Bruce Currie-Alder, and Ravi Kanbur (eds), *Development: Ideas and Experiences* (New York: Oxford University Press).

Noman, A. and Stiglitz, J.E. (2012) "Strategies for African Development," in A. Noman, K. Botchwey, H. Stein, and J.E. Stiglitz (eds), *Good Growth and Governance for Africa: Rethinking Development Strategies* (New York: Oxford University Press), pp. 3–47.

Ocampo, Jose Antonio, and Jaime Ros (eds) (2011) *The Oxford Handbook of Latin American Economics* (New York: Oxford University Press).

Rodrik, D. (2012) "Do We Need to Rethink Growth Policies?," in Olivier J. Blanchard, David Romer, Michael Spence, and Joseph E. Stiglitz (eds), *In the Wake of the Crisis: Leading Economists Reassess Economic Policy* (Cambridge, MA and London: MIT Press), pp. 157–167.

Rodrik, D. and McMillan, M. (2011) "Globalization, Structural Change, and Economic Growth," in M. Bachetta and M. Jansen (eds), *Making Globalization Socially Sustainable* (Geneva: International Labor Organization and World Trade Organization), pp. 49–80.

Solow, R. (1957) "Technical Change and the Aggregate Production Function," *The Review of Economics and Statistics*,vol. 39, no. 3, pp. 312–320.

Stiglitz, J. E. (1996) "Some Lessons from the East Asian Miracle," *World Bank Research Observer*, vol. 11, no. 2, pp. 151–177.

Tyson, Laura d'Andrea (1992) *Who Is Bashing Whom? Trade Conflicts in High-Technology Industries* (Washington, DC: Institute for International Economics).

World Bank (1993) *The East Asian Miracle: Economic Growth and Public Policy*, World Bank Policy Research Report (New York: Oxford University Press).

World Bank (1998) *Global Economic Prospects and the Developing Countries 1998/1999: Beyond Financial Crisis* (Washington, DC: World Bank).

Part I
Conceptual Issues and Principles of Industrial Policy

1.1
Comparative Advantage: The Silver Bullet of Industrial Policy

Justin Yifu Lin
Peking University
Célestin Monga
World Bank

1.1.1 Introduction

Throughout human history, people have held their political leaders responsible for the general social and economic conditions of their nations. Fairly or unfairly, some leaders have been hailed as national heroes while others have been thrown out of power or even punished more harshly depending on the level of collective happiness or anger. But never in modern history has the leader of an industrialized country been convicted by courts for his stewardship of the national economy. Yet, that is what happened recently when former Iceland Prime Minister Geir Haarde was prosecuted and found guilty of failing to manage his country's economy appropriately prior to and during the 2008 global crisis. While he was cleared for the most serious charges and barely escaped jail sentence, his reputation and political legacy were forever tarnished. The irony of the story is that he had long been viewed as instrumental in transforming Iceland from a fishing and whaling backwater into an international financial powerhouse before the global crisis.[1]

Former American President John F. Kennedy famously observed that "life is unfair." Many political leaders across the world have come to embrace those words, especially in this new era of slow growth in high-income countries, high unemployment, uncertainty, and social vulnerability. The Geir Haarde trial, has been seen as a sign of growing economic malaise in the era of globalization, even in rich countries. It is also an illustration of the tense debate over the appropriate role of government in economic policy, and the ultimate responsibility of policymakers who are expected to create the optimal conditions for social welfare maximization.

Questions about the nature of political leadership in difficult times raise the fundamental issue of the scope of government intervention in economic policy. While the debates are often framed over the narrow issues of financial and macroeconomic management policies (as was the case in Iceland) and unemployment and social safety nets (as seen in both industrialized and developing countries), the reality is that they cover much broader problems about the pace, quality, and inclusiveness of growth. Sustained economic growth is a process of constant industrial and technological upgrading, associated with parallel and consistent social and institutional changes that guarantee shared prosperity.

In an interlinked world economy, the main challenge for policymakers and economists is to constantly find the appropriate formula for governments and private agents to continually anticipate their country's evolving needs, or adjust to and manage change. The specifics of such a formula are likely to differ in each country context depending on its level of development, initial conditions, and endowment structure. But regardless of their economic philosophies, almost all political leaders in the world have always tried to use the power of the state to avert the risk for their national economies of Iceland-types of crises. Following a long tradition of government support to firms in specific sectors, industries, or location,[2] the US federal and local governments constantly implement ambitious programs that can be assimilated to industrial policy.[3] The same is true for countries as diverse as the United Kingdom, Germany, Switzerland, Singapore, Japan, China, or Sweden.

But industrial policy remains highly controversial, not least because of the many failed attempts recorded across the world over the past century. The controversies stem partly from the fuzziness of its definition, scope, and instruments, which often differ from a country to another depending on levels of development. This paper contributes to the debate and tries to sort out the conditions under which industrial policy – and more broadly, government interventions in the economy – are likely to fail or succeed. While the paper focuses on industrial policy from the perspective of developing countries whose economies are still within the global technological frontier, its main conclusions are relevant for all countries regardless of their level of development.

Section 1.1.2 discusses some of the conceptual issues associated with industrial policy and its theoretical foundations, which are now part of various strands of the mainstream economic literature. Section 1.1.3 analyzes the reasons why industrial policy has often failed and stresses the fact that the mistakes were not in the design or implementation of the strategies followed by many governments but in the very development goals set by policymakers – goals inconsistent with the level of development of their countries and the structure of their endowments at that time. Deriving lessons from the experience of unrealistic development goals, it sketches an economic analysis of why economic strategies in Iceland or elsewhere should always aim at consistency with comparative advantage determined by the existing endowment structure, which is the condition for continuous growth, shared prosperity, and social cohesion. Section 1.1.4 concludes that industrial policy is a central and indispensible feature of any successful development and sustained growth strategy.

1.1.2 Theoretical rationale for industrial policy

Historically, except for a few oil-exporting economies, no country has ever become rich without industrializing. Yet the distribution of roles between governments and the private sector in the process of industrialization and economic development remains controversial. It is therefore useful to start with a brief discussion of the definition and scope of industrial policy, and a presentation of the strong theoretical grounds for government intervention in the economy.

1.1.2.1 Beyond the semantic controversies

The first and perhaps biggest source of confusion about industrial policy is the fuzziness of its definition in the economic literature, which reflects the debate over its scope, objectives, and instruments. Harrison and Rodríguez-Clare (2009) have suggested that government decisions aiming at tilting incentives in favor of some particular groups of investors, which means abandoning policy neutrality, can be considered "industrial policies."[4] The presence of externalities is then viewed as the main theoretical justification for deviating from policy neutrality. That definition is broadly consistent with Cohen's, which asserts that "industrial policy in the strict sense is a sectoral policy; it seeks to promote sectors where intervention should take place for reasons of national independence, technological autonomy, failure of private initiative, decline in traditional activities, and geographical or political balance" (2006: 85). That sector- or industry-specific approach (often labeled as "vertical") is defined in contrast to an economy-wide ("horizontal") approach to policymaking, which consists of general business environment policies that have an indirect impact on industry – including macroeconomic and social policies, as well as capital equipment and national defense policies.

In practice, however, the delineation between policy areas that are affected exclusively by a particular set of government measures is difficult to establish, as rules always have indirect, unintended, and sometimes even unobservable effects. That may explain why some authors define "industrial policy" as any form of selective intervention not just that favors manufacturing. The term then refers to all "policies for economic restructuring [...] in favor of more dynamic activities generally, regardless of whether those are located within industry or manufacturing per se" (Rodrik, 2004: 2). Because there is no evidence that the types of market failures that call for industrial policy are located predominantly in industry, he suggests specific illustrations of industrial policies that concern non-traditional activities in sectors such as agriculture or services. That broad definition of industrial policy is then used to cover functional and selective and market-based as well as direct policy measures.

Still, many researchers continue to advocate a minimalist approach to industrial policy. Weiss, for instance, argues that broadening the term too far makes it not very useful conceptually. He also suggests that it focuses exclusively on manufacturing industry, which has a special role in growth due to its greater scope for generating high levels of and growth in productivity (at least at relatively early stages of development) and externalities. In that sense, industrial policy refers to

> policy interventions designed to affect the allocation of resources in favor of industry (principally manufacturing) as distinct other sectors. Such interventions may also affect resource allocation within industry in favor of either particular branches or sub-sectors or particular firms (so they may be "selective" rather than "functional"). Interventions can involve either the price mechanism or direct controls and be focused on export as well as the domestic market. Industrial policy in this definition is thus much wider than import substitution trade policies with which it is often associated. (2011: 1)

Such semantic controversies do not really help address the challenges faced by policymakers around the world. While the rationale for narrowing the definition and scope of industrial policy may be useful from a purely conceptual standpoint, it is difficult to implement in practice, as most state interventions cannot be restricted neatly to specific policy areas. Moreover, the role of all governments is to design and implement a range of policies to foster business creation in some locations, support specific sectors of the economy, encourage exports, attract foreign direct investment, promote innovation, all of which amount to favoring some industries over others. In fact, one can even argue that the whole budget preparation and execution exercise carried out often through political debates every year by governments and parliaments around the world is mainly about industrial policy. As Nester observes, "every nation has industrial policy whether they are comprehensive or fragmented, or whether officials admit the practice or not." His research shows that "every major industry in America is deeply involved with and dependent on government. The competitive position of every American firm is affected by government policy. No sharp distinction can validly be drawn between private and public sectors within this or any other industrialized country; the economic effects of public policies and corporate decisions are completely intertwined" (1997). These observations about a country often presented as the most successful free market economy in history invalidate the semantic controversies and the proposition that industrial policy is necessarily a misguided development strategy.

Most countries, intentionally or not, pursue an industrial policy in one form or other, which broadly refers to any government decision, regulation, or law that encourages ongoing activity or investment in an industry. After all, economic development and sustained growth are the result of continual industrial and technological change, a process that requires collaboration between the public and private sectors. Historical evidence shows that in countries that successfully transformed from an agrarian to a modern economy – including those in Western Europe, North America, and, more recently, in East Asia – governments coordinated key investments by private firms that helped to launch new industries, and often provided incentives to pioneering firms (Gerschenkron, 1962; Amsden, 1989; Wade, 1990; Chang, 2003).

Even before the recent global financial crisis and subsequent recession, governments around the world provided support to the private sector through direct subsidies, tax credits, or loans from development banks in order to bolster growth and support job creation. Discussions at many high-level summits sought to strengthen other features of economic policy that eventually favor specific industries or locations, including the public financing of airports, highways, ports, electricity grids, telecommunications, and other infrastructure, improvements in institutional effectiveness, an emphasis on education and skills, and a clearer legal framework. The recent global crisis has led to a rethinking of governments' economic role. The challenge for industrial policy is greater, because it should assist the design of efficient, government-sponsored programs in which the public and private sectors coordinate their efforts to develop new technologies and industries.

The case for industrial policy is even stronger in low-income countries where there is strong theoretical justification for it – and where governments actively engage in it, unfortunately often with disappointing results. Modern economic development in nature is a process of continuous structural changes in technology, industry, socioeconomic and political institutions. It did not appear until the 18th century – before that time every country in the world was poor and agrarian. But since then it has profoundly changed the world, especially those successful high-income industrialized countries. That process is essentially one of dynamic changes and upgrades in factor endowments.

Infrastructure endowments determine firm transaction costs and how close the economy is, with its given factor endowments, to its production-possibility frontier. Although firms generally can control some of their production costs, they have little latitude over most of their transaction costs, which are largely determined by the quality of soft and hard infrastructure, mostly provided by the state. Therefore, a crucial observation in the analysis of development dynamics is the fact that most hard (or physical) infrastructure and almost all soft (or institutional) infrastructure are exogenously provided to individual firms and cannot be internalized in their production decision.

Yet with the upgrade in factor endowment and industrial structure, infrastructure must be improved in parallel for the economy to achieve x- efficiency. This is not an easy process to design and implement. Governments often fail to play their role in the provision, coordination, and improvement of infrastructure. In such situations, infrastructure becomes a bottleneck to economic development. In fact, economic growth tends to render existing institutional arrangements obsolete, as it induces constant shifts in the demand for institutional services. Institutional services are by nature public goods. Changes in institutions require collective action, which often fails because they run into the free-rider problem (Lin, 1989). Therefore, governments need to play a proactive role in the process of economic development so as to facilitate timely improvements in hard and soft infrastructure to meet the changing needs arising from industrial upgrading.

1.1.2.2   The theoretical case for industrial policy

Despite the debates and controversies over the proper scope, instruments, and conditions of effectiveness of industrial policy, there is widespread consensus among economists on its theoretical foundations. In fact, the legitimacy of government intervention has been established since Hamilton, and Adam Smith, and well described by List et al. (1856). But just as macroeconomics has evolved in two main directions in recent decades (the neoclassical and neo-Keynesian paths), two broad groups of theorists have emphasized very different types of rationales for industrial policy too.

Neoclassical theory acknowledges the need for government intervention only in situations of market failures – when market mechanisms let alone do not allocate resources efficiently. These situations arise from three major sources: the first and most widely accepted case of market failure arises from positive externalities, generally defined as opportunities that are generated by investment or risk taken by one agent and yet benefiting others in the economy. The typical case is that of research and development (R&D), which is costly to pioneer firms that pay for it and sometimes generates free new knowledge for other firms. In a free market system, risk-taking companies are not systematically rewarded for producing technological externalities and generating such social benefits. Therefore, R&D activity tends to be lower than what would be optimal from the society's perspective. For pioneer firms, the cost of scientific research and technological discovery can be high. The difficulties in appropriating the knowledge they create (typically after incurring substantial sunk costs) lower their incentives for research – unless the government values the potential social benefits of new knowledge and steps in to change the incentives by subsidizing R&D, by redefining property rights in a way that limit information and transaction costs, or by granting firms various forms of support and protection (Arrow, 1962).[5]

A second case of market failure stems from Marshallian externalities exhibited by some sectors or industries, which give rise to geographic agglomeration. These particular types of externalities can arise through local-ized industry-level knowledge spillovers, input–output linkages together with transportation costs and labor pooling (Marshall, 1920; Krugman, 1991; Harrison and Rodríguez-Clare, 2009). In some variations they can lead to monopolies or oligopolies and thus market power. In industries that are characterized by high entry barriers or high fixed costs (and thus, economies of scale) pioneer firms can enjoy the protection of first-mover advantages that prevent potential competitors to enter the market. Government inter-vention may then be required to allow other entrants and limit the rent capture by one firm, which is always detrimental to consumers (Brander and Spencer, 1986).

Another rationale for public intervention is the need to address issues of coordination. Economic growth is a process of continuous industrial and technological upgrading that requires evolving institutions. As a country climbs up the industrial and technological ladder, many economic, insti-tutional and social changes take place: the technology used by its firms becomes increasingly sophisticated, physical and human capital require-ments increase, as well as the scale of production and the size of markets. Market transactions are also more complex, as they involve agents from various parts of the economy. A flexible and smooth industrial and techno-logical upgrading process therefore requires simultaneous improvements in educational, financial, and legal institutions, and physical infrastructure so that firms in the newly upgraded industries can produce sufficient amounts to reach economies of scale and become the lowest cost producers. Clearly, individual firms or households cannot internalize all these changes cost-effectively, and spontaneous coordination among many private agents to meet these new challenges is often impossible. Changes in physical infra-structure, institutions, and regulations require collective action or at least coordination between the provider of infrastructure services and industrial firms. For this reason, it falls to the government either to introduce such changes itself or to coordinate them proactively.

A fourth case of market failure emerges from information asymmetries and incomplete markets – that is, in situations where goods or services demanded are not available even when consumers are ready to pay a higher price. Furthermore, consumers cannot assess the quality of goods on offer because the markets are characterized by asymmetric information, which can lead to adverse selection (when quality cannot be evaluated on individual goods but only on an average for comparable goods) and moral hazard (which occurs when one party to a transaction does not enter into a contract in good faith, provides misleading information about the value of its assets, or has an incentive to take unusual risks). In such situations, firms do not have equal access to information and competition can be severely restricted. When some businesses develop strategies that create imperfections in market conditions, the government has two options to intervene: either by formulating a strong competition policy in order to restore a level playing field, or by adopting a strategic industrial policy through which it plays an active role in encouraging non-opportunistic behavior (Cohen, 2006).

Theoretical justifications of industrial policy are also offered by economists who do not belong to the neoclassical tradition. Evolutionary theorists, for instance, stress the importance of innovation and technological change in the growth process. Because national economies are constantly evolving, static levels of R&D and innovation are less revealing determinants of performance than the institutional framework in place to ensure constant production of knowledge and its diffusion among private agents. It is argued that governments must play an important role in building the capacity of domestic institutions to anticipate major economic trends and cope with systemic change (Nelson, 1995).

Other theorists have focused on incentives for cooperation between businesses in sectors of industrial innovation, and in particular the need to pool financial resources and complementary competences for research in areas where strong cooperation is required as new technologies become more complex and more expensive. Since firms' cooperation in R&D reduces costs, saves them time, and spreads the risk of failure, the case can be made for governments to encourage information transfer and collaboration among companies. A well-known mechanism for achieving that objective is a financial incentive for cooperation such as the granting of public funding contingent on collaboration between firms.[6] Government interventions that help disseminate new knowledge or share existing information can increase the likelihood of producing more efficient technical solutions by firms. Cooperative research among private firms but sponsored by governments can also lead to positive information sharing and innovation, which are crucial for a knowledge-based economy (Spence, 1984; Katz, 1986).

1.1.3   Policy challenges and recipe for success

While the theoretical corpus in support of industrial policies has long existed in various strands of the economic literature, the practical difficulties of implementation have often led to disappointing outcomes. After acquiring power in the second half of the 20th century and setting big goals for their people and their nation, many developing countries' leaders across Latin America, Africa, and Asia focused on the nobility of their ambitions and adopted bold economic development goals without carefully considering their specific country conditions, endowment structure, and capabilities, and the challenges and opportunities in the global context. The many examples of failures have led to strong skepticism about it by many researchers. In fact, most analysts have focused on the symptoms or consequences of the problems, rather than the true origins. This section explains why the capital-intensive projects selected by developing country governments with the laudable goal of catching up with the industries in advanced countries often ended up as costly mistakes. It points to the notion of firm viability, and highlights the key criterion for success, which is the consistency of industrial development strategies with a country's comparative advantage.

1.1.3.1 Pervasive failures of industrial policy

The experience of industrial policy, especially in developing countries, has mostly been one of failure. Governments adopted various policy measures to promote industrialization throughout the developing world (Chenery, 1961). In Asia and the Middle East, and later in Africa, the transformation of territories previously considered colonies or semi-colonies into independent states was accompanied by strong nationalist sentiments. Lack of industrialization – especially the possession of large heavy industries, which were the basis of military strength and economic power – had forced China, India and other areas in the developing world to yield to the colonial powers. In the 1950s and 1960s, many political leaders there – especially the first-generation leaders who led their people to political and economic independence after long periods of revolution or struggle – were motivated by the desire to modernize their nations and reclaim their dignity on the international scene.[7] That mindset often led them to give priority to the development of large, advanced heavy industries, which they considered prerequisites and symbols of nation-building and modernization (Lal and Myint, 1996: chapter 7).

Ideological motivations were reinforced by the early structuralist approach to economic development, which centered on the elimination of market failures and argued that industrialization and growth could not take place spontaneously in developing countries because of structural rigidities and coordination problems. That view seemed to be supported by the Prebisch–Singer thesis of a secular decline in terms of trade of primary commodities.[8] In order to free their economies from the diktat of continuously low export prices which resulted in the transfer of income from resource-rich developing countries to capital-intensive developed countries, many nationalist leaders chose to launch domestic manufacturing industries through a process known as import substitution. But that strategy Often failed to deliver the promise of making these countries as successful as developed countries, and caused stagnations, frequent crises and even disastrous consequences for many economies.

The motivation to target modern, advanced capital-intensive industries was understandable. Unfortunately, the bold plan for developing ambitious new industries that were prevailing in advanced European countries was not rooted in any analysis of the economic fundamentals of these poor countries. The many Development Plans adopted by low-income countries (often on the model of the former Soviet Union's Gosplan) typically included the creation of state-owned companies in advanced industries where they had neither the technical capability nor the competitive cost structure or the financing to achieve their ambitious goals.

Despite the optimism of the assumptions and macroeconomic projections, these plans usually estimated that domestic resources would be sufficient to meet only a fraction of the projected financial requirements. So, foreign borrowing by the public sector had to be a big part of the financial framework. Pressing ahead with bold capital-intensive projects, some of these developing countries achieved high investment rates, often during long periods. The scale of production capacity in heavy industries was large, and the newly created capital-intensive industries had large economies of scale. But their products faced insufficient demand in the domestic market and were not competitive in international markets. As a result, they eventually ended up with excess capacity and severe losses. To survive, they needed continuous protection and subsidies from the government, which created distortions and other macroeconomic problems: the cumulated financial losses by public enterprises aggravated the country's savings deficit and contributed to balance-of-payments disequilibria, high inflation, and severe macroeconomic crises. In the end, virtually no developing country that launched industrial policies in the immediate post-World War II era was able to substantially reduce the income gap with that of the United States.

In trying to understand the reasons behind developing countries' poor development performance, many neoclassical economists have pointed out the weaknesses of the development strategies advocated by early structuralists. The obsession on market failures led to inward-looking sectoral strategies, inefficient investment policies, and many distortions that crippled poor economies: the existence of state-owned enterprises with monopolies; the provision of large subsidies to certain industries; the high frequency of political capture and rent-seeking; the pervasiveness of financial repression, often accompanied by the overvaluation of domestic currency and the rationing of capital and foreign exchange; and so on. As Cohen notes,

> the standard criticism leveled against sectoral industrial policies is that the state has neither the necessary information nor adequate incentives to make better choices than the market. Since it also obeys a political rationale, it tends to prefer spectacular and demonstrative actions to effective and selective ones. As it follows a sequential logic, it tends to misestimate the aggregate effects of its action, and in particular the negative long-term effects of the protection granted to certain firms and the negative impacts of the benefits granted to promoted sectors on other sectors. (2006: 88)

Other researchers looked for political economy-type explanations, focusing on the power and dynamics of interest groups. Some argued that the magnitude of the economic, social, or political benefits to particular interest groups often lead them to garner enough political influence to force the government to adopt distortionary arrangements that are favorable to them. The logical consequence of such an argument has been to recommend changes in the incentive system in developing countries as ways of getting rid of distortions: privatization, stronger property rights, and more intrasectoral and intersectoral competition.

Researchers have thus often relied on political-economy analyses, with explanations varying from the suggestion that politicians tend to discount the future too much (North, 1981), to the idea that they are mostly interested in redistributive taxation (Alesina and Rodrik, 1994; Persson and Tabelini, 1994), or on the impact of investment on the future political equilibrium (Acemoglu and Robinson, 2002), or simply the low implementation capacity. Because many developing countries like Ghana seem to be plagued not simply by underinvestment, but by investment in the wrong industries, more recent analyses have argued that the construction of "white elephants" should be seen as redistribution aimed at influencing the outcomes of elections. Robinson and Torvik (2005), for instance, offer a political-economy model showing that the "white elephants" are a particular type of inefficient redistribution, which are politically attractive when politicians find it difficult to make credible promises to supporters. They suggest that it is the very inefficiency of such projects that makes them politically appealing. Why? Because it allows only some politicians to credibly promise to build them and thus enter into credible redistribution. The fact that not all politicians can credibly undertake such projects gives those who can a strategic advantage.

Such political-economy conjectures seem plausible at face value. It is often the case that powerful interest groups in developing countries are associated with advanced capital-intensive sectors, which tend to gain the most from government protection. But historical evidence suggests that when the protectionist policy measures that created distortions were first introduced in many developing countries, the most powerful interest group would paradoxically lose the most from them – that is, the landowners. And although the powerful urban industrialists often gained from protectionist policies, they also lost from the many other distortions necessary to make the economic system work. For instance, they often suffered from the dominance of pervasive state ownership in advanced industries. It is therefore necessary to look for more convincing explanations.

1.1.3.2 Comparative advantage and economic viability

Past development thinking failed to decipher the true reasons of the failure of industrial policies because they got either the nature or causes of modern economic growth wrong. Early structuralists were right to try to close the structural gaps between low-income and high-income countries. But they identified the wrong causes of the problem. They attributed the low-income countries' inability to establish high-income countries' advanced industries to market rigidities. Based on this assumption, they advocated inward-looking policies to build industries that in fact were not viable in open, competitive environments. While subsidies and protection allowed some countries to achieve high investment-led growth for a period of time, that strategy came with costly distortions and was not sustainable in the medium to long term. Certainly the approach could not help them converge to high-income country levels.

The "Washington Consensus" shifted the policy pendulum toward market fundamentalism. By focusing obsessively on government failures and ignoring the structural issues It assumed that free markets will automatically create spontaneous forces to correct structural differences among countries. Yet market failures from externality and coordination are inherent in the process of structural change. Without the government's facilitation, the spontaneous process that ignites the change is either too slow or never even happens in any country. Unfortunately, the "Washington Consensus" neglected this. It also neglected many existing distortions in a developing country are typically second-best arrangements to protect nonviable firms operating in the priority sectors that were selected during the structuralist era. Without addressing the firms' viability, the attempt to eliminate those distortions could cause their collapse, large unemployment, and social and political instability. For fear of such dire consequences, many governments reintroduced disguised protections and subsidies which were even less efficient than the old subsidies and protections.

Looking carefully at the causes of the failures of industrial policy, one can see that they were in reality the consequences of misguided strategic choices in industry selection – and the necessity for keeping afloat public and private firms that were inherently not viable given the prevailing country circumstances. They were endogenous to the strategic choices made with a noble development goal. But most economists did not observe the true causes of this development failure. It is no surprise, then, that their subsequent policy recommendations – and their hope that changes in the incentive system would suffice to spur sustainable growth – were either inaccurate or insufficient to help policymakers in poor countries get out of the poverty trap.

A developing country is by nature endowed with relatively abundant labor or natural resources but has relatively scarce capital. Its labor and natural resource costs are relatively lower than the cost of capital. Therefore, a developing country will have a natural disadvantage in heavy manufacturing industry, which requires large capital inputs and small labor inputs, because its costs of production will be inherently higher than in an advanced country. This is the notion of comparative advantage, which prescribes that countries produce goods and services requiring their relatively abundant factors as inputs, thus incurring lower costs than anyone else.[9]

Going back to the historical and intellectual context of the post-World War II era, one can understand why rapid industrialization and modernization strategies advocated by early structuralists failed: they ignored the single most important determinant of a country's long-term performance, which is firm viability. They rightly focused on the structural difference between developed and developing countries and the need to solve the coordination and externalities issue in structural change. But they chose to use state resources and various forms of public interventions to build or support firms in industries that were selected without regard to economic viability.[10] Because developing countries are relatively rich in labor and natural resources but not in capital, advanced capital-intensive industries were not well-suited to the endowment structures of these poor countries at the time – or aligned with their comparative advantage. Firms created in those industries could not compete with firms in capital-abundant developed countries. Therefore, they were nonviable in open competitive markets and could not survive without government subsidies or protection.

The biggest mistake of many developing and former socialist countries was their attempt to defy the comparative advantage determined by their endowment structures: in countries where factor endowments were characterized by the abundance of labor and the scarcity of capital, government policy aimed at building modern, advanced capital-intensive heavy industries.[11] By implementing the heavy industry-oriented development strategy, they could not build firms capable of surviving in open competitive markets. Because of their high capital needs and their structurally high production costs in a developing country, these enterprises were not viable in open competitive markets. Even when they were well managed, they could not earn a socially acceptable profit in an undistorted and competitive market.

In order to mobilize resources to make investments and maintain operations in advanced capital-intensive sectors, it was necessary for developing country governments to subsidize and protect the firms in those priority industries. However, limited tax-collection capacities and large-scale protection and subsidies could not be sustained. So, to reduce the costs of investment and continue the operation of their nonviable enterprises, governments resorted to administrative measures – granting market monopolies to firms in the priority sectors, suppressing interest rates, overvaluing domestic currencies, and controlling the prices of raw materials (Lin, 2009). Such distortions enabled some poor countries to set up advanced capital-intensive industries in the early stage of their development, at least temporarily. Eventually, they also led to the suppression of incentives, the misallocation of resources, and economic inefficiencies (Lin and Li, 2009).

Once such distortions were introduced in the economy, it became politically hard to eliminate them – for three reasons. First, development strategies that defied comparative advantage created industrial elites, who generally were rich and politically well connected, especially in the nonsocialist countries. Second, the industries were considered the backbone of the countries' modernization program. Eliminating subsidies and protection would have led to their collapse, a result not acceptable to society. Third, their collapse would create large unemployment and social and political instability. That is why governments continued to subsidize large, old industries in Eastern Europe and in countries of the former Soviet Union,[12] even after their privatization (Lin, 2009; Lin and Tan, 1999).

By shielding unsustainable industries from import competition, developing countries inevitably imposed various types of other costs on their economies. Protection typically led to an increase in the price of imports and import-substituting goods relative to the world price, as well as distortions in incentives, pushing the economy to consume the wrong mix of goods from the point of view of economic efficiency. It fragmented markets, with the economy producing too many small-scale goods, again resulting in losses of efficiency. It lessened competition from foreign firms and encouraged the monopoly power of domestic firms whose owners were politically well connected. And it created opportunities for rents and corruption, raising input and transaction costs (Krueger, 1974; Krugman, 1993). The initial distortions due to misguided economic development strategies were subsequently compounded with "white elephants" and the politics that accompanied them. Development strategies inconsistent with comparative advantage also led to a bureaucratic establishment that itself became an impediment to progress in some low- and middle-income countries (World Bank, 1995).

Summing up, it can be said that the decision by developing country leaders to target sophisticated modern capital-intensive industries in advanced economies was generally unsustainable. Therefore, the problem that impeded many of the ambitious industrial ventures initiated by developing country leaders and eventually hurt their economies was the viability of these development projects in the first place. Even if they were entrusted with the best managerial capacities, the most effective institutional arrangements, and the optimal incentive system for good performance, they could not have competed with firms from advanced countries in an open market or generated acceptable rates of return.

The crucial issue of firm viability was overlooked by development economists perhaps because of the influence of neoclassical economics, which, in addition to the well-known rationality assumption, implicitly considers any firm that exists in an economy to be viable. Neoclassical theories, originating in developed countries, try mainly to explain what happens in developed countries. It is reasonable to assume that firms in those economies are viable, since the governments in advanced countries generally do not openly provide subsidies to businesses, except for a few well-known sectors such as agriculture (for jobs and political-economy reasons), defense (for national security), or very new and highly risky technological industries (for public goods). In such contexts, it is indeed reasonable to assume that business ventures in other sectors will be fully vetted by private investors, and funded with private capital only if they are viable. That is, they can be expected to earn socially acceptable normal profits with good management. Moreover, when private investors mistakenly bet on firms in industries not consistent with a country's comparative advantage and thus not viable, they will lose money and be quickly weeded out in the market.

As economies around the world struggle to maintain or restore growth, industrial policy is likely to be under a brighter spotlight than ever before. The key question is how to identify competitive industries and how to formulate and implement policies to facilitate their development. In developed countries, most industries are advanced and locate on global technology frontier, which suggests that upgrading requires new inventions. Support for basic research, and patents to protect successful innovation, may help. For developing countries, most industries locate within global frontier, their industrial upgrading and diversification can benefit from the advantage of backwardness. The challenge for them is to design and implement industrial policies that support private firms to enter industries that are the economy's latent comparative advantage.[13] Lin and Monga (2011) have recently developed an approach – called the growth identification and facilitation framework – that can help developing-country governments increase the probability of success in supporting new industries.

This framework suggests that policymakers identify tradable industries that have performed well in growing countries with similar endowment structure, and with a per capita income about double their own. If domestic private firms in these sectors are already present, policymakers should identify and remove constraints on those firms' technological upgrading or on entry by other firms. In industries where no domestic firms are present, policymakers should aim to attract foreign direct investment from the countries being emulated or organize programs for incubating new firms. The government should also pay attention to the development by private enterprises of new and competitive products, and support the scaling up of successful private-sector innovations in new industries. In countries with a poor business environment, special economic zones or industrial parks can facilitate firm entry, foreign direct investment, and the formation of industrial clusters. Finally, the government might help pioneering firms in the new industries by offering tax incentives for a limited period, co-financing investments, or providing access to land or foreign exchange. This approach provides policymakers in developing countries with a framework to tackle the daunting coordination challenges inherent in the creation of new, competitive industries. It also has the potential to nurture a business environment conducive to private-sector growth, job creation, and poverty reduction.

1.1.4   Conclusion

History tells us that while governments in almost all developing countries have attempted to play that facilitating role in fostering industrialization and economic development at some point, most have failed. The economic history of the former Soviet Union, Latin America, Africa, and Asia has been marked by inefficient public investment and misguided government interventions that have resulted in many "white elephants." Despite the good intentions of modernization that animated political leaders from developing countries – especially during the period from the 1940s through the 1970s – the projects selected to reach the goal were too capital-intensive for low-income countries characterized by relatively scarce capital. They were thus inconsistent with their comparative advantages determined by the distribution and structure of its factor endowments.

These pervasive failures were due mostly to governments' inability to align their efforts with their country's endowments and level of development. Indeed, governments' propensity to target overly ambitious industries that were misaligned with available resources and skills helps explain why their attempts to "pick winners" often resulted in "picking losers." Firms in priority sectors were not viable in an open competitive market. Their initial investments and continuous operations relied on the government's ability and willingness to mobilize a massive amount of resources for investment, on continuous protection of all sorts, and on subsidies through various distortions and direct interventions.

By contrast, governments in many successful developing countries have focused on strengthening industries that have done well in countries with comparable factor endowments. Thus, the lesson from economic history and development is straightforward: government support aimed at upgrading and diversifying industry must be anchored in the requisite endowments. That way, once constraints on new industries are removed, private firms in those industries quickly become competitive domestically and internationally. Thus, comparative advantage can be seen as the silver bullet for industrial policy.

Notes

1. Geir Haarde served as Iceland Prime Minister from June 2006 to February 2009. He fell from power after the country's three biggest banks – Glitnir, Kaupthing and Landsbanki – defaulted and collapsed within weeks of each other after the collapse of Lehman Brothers in the US sparked the 2008 credit crunch. House prices collapsed, the national currency plunged, and unemployment jumped to records levels. The government was forced to seek help from the International Monetary

Fund and borrow $10 billion to prop up its economy. The Icelandic parliament issued a "Truth Report" into the causes of the crisis and a special prosecutor was named to assess the quality of economic financial policymaking. Haarde was the first person in history to stand trial at the 15-judge court, which was created in 1905 to hear any charges brought against ministers. On April 23, 2012, he was found guilty of "gross negligence over the government's failure to prepare for the impending economic disaster."

2. The US government has always used various instruments to support private business development in specific sectors. For instance, the U.S. Department of Defense contracts played a crucial role in accelerating the early growth of Silicon Valley (Lerner, 2009).

3. According to Rodrik, "Today the U.S. federal government is the world's biggest venture capitalist by far. According to the *Wall Street Journal*, the U.S. Department of Energy (DOE) alone is planning to spend more than $40 billion in loans and grants to encourage private firms to develop green technologies, such as electric cars, new batteries, wind turbines, and solar panels. During the first three quarters on 2009, private venture capital firms invested less than $3 billion combined in this sector. The DOE invested $13 billion" (2010).

4. However, they note that "Policy neutrality does not necessarily mean free trade, or a neutral stance regarding taxation of multinational corporations, or even a common tax structure for all industries. Both optimal tax theory and practical fiscal considerations imply that countries (especially poor ones) will often want to rely on tariffs as a source of revenue or set different tax rates across industries."

5. Coase (1937) showed in his well-known theorem that when there is a conflict of property rights, the involved parties can bargain or negotiate terms that are more beneficial to both parties than the outcome of any assigned property rights. The theorem also asserts that in order for this to occur, bargaining must be costless; if there are costs associated with bargaining (such as meetings or enforcement), it will affect the outcome. Externalities may be managed by private agents not to result in an inefficient allocation of resources if they are "internalized" in situations where there are no transaction costs and when property rights are well defined.

6. A case in point is that of SEMATECH, a US association of semiconductor manufacturing firms that cooperate pre-competitively in key areas of their value chain. Similar models of cooperation among competing firms in strategic industries have been implemented in Japan under the leadership of the Ministry of International Trade and Industry, which oversees the deals and guarantees that each company acts fairly (Cohen, 2006).

7. China for instance, had been defeated repeatedly by the industrialized powers after the Opium War in 1840, and become a quasi-colony, ceding extraterritorial rights in treaty ports to 20 foreign countries; its customs revenues had been controlled by foreigners, and it surrendered territory to Britain, Japan and Russia. The Indian subcontinent, which was not significantly less developed than Britain in the 17th century and, before 1800, was a major supplier of cotton and silk textiles in international markets, including to Europe, was also reduced to be a British colony. Many countries in Asia, Africa, and Latin America had gone through similar processes.

8. See Prebisch (1950) and Singer (1950). For a discussion of the evolution of development thinking, see Lin and Monga (2012).

9. The idea of comparative advantage was initially proposed by David Ricardo in 1819 (see Ricardo, 1963). The factor endowment-based comparative advantage theory was proposed by Hechscher and Ohlin (1991).
10. A broadly well-managed firm is deemed viable if it is expected to earn a socially acceptable normal profit in a free, open, and competitive market, without any external subsidies or protection.
11. Respectable theories supported the strategy of giving priority to the capital-goods industry, such as the economic development model created by a famous Indian statistician, P.C. Mahalanobis, in 1953, which became the foundation for India's second five-year plan (Bhagwati and Chakravarty, 1969), those discussed in Amartya Sen's dissertation at Cambridge University, later published as a book (1960), and recently by Murphy, Shleifer, and Vishny (1989).
12. The Soviet Union under Stalin was able to establish advanced heavy industries and became a military superpower for more than half a century because it was the most resource-rich country in the world and could use the large resource rents to subsidize the uncompetitive industries.
13. The term latent comparative advantage refers the case that, if a country's factor cost of production in an industry is competitive globally, that is, it has comparative advantage in that industry based on its factor endowment structure. However, due to high transaction costs related to logistics, transportation, access to power, red tapes, and others, the industry has not been competitive in domestic and international markets yet.

References

Acemoglu, D. and Robinson, J.A. (2002) *Economic Backwardness in Political Perspective*, NBER Working Paper 8831 (Cambridge, MA: National Bureau of Economic Research).

Alesina, A. and Rodrik, D. (1994) "Distributive Politics and Economic Growth," *Quarterly Journal of Economics*, vol. 109, pp. 465–490.

Amsden, A.H. (1989) *Asia's Next Giant* (New York and Oxford: Oxford University Press).

Arrow, K. (1962) "Economic Welfare and the Allocation of Resources for Invention," in NBER (ed.), *The Rate and Direction of Inventive Activity, Economic and Social Factors* (Princeton, NJ: Princeton University Press).

Bhagwati, J.N. and Chakravarty, S. (1969) "Contributions to Indian Economic Analysis: A Survey," *The American Economic Review* (AER), vol. 59, no. 4, pp. 2–73.

Brander, J. and Spencer, B. (1986) "Rationales for Strategic Trade Policy and Industrial Policy," in P. Krugman (ed.), *Strategic Trade Policy and the New International Economics* (Cambridge, MA: MIT Press).

Chang, H.-J. (2003) *Kicking Away the Ladder: Development Strategy in Historical Perspective* (London: Anthem Press).

Chenery, H.B. (1961) "Comparative Advantage and Development Policy," *American Economic Review*, vol. 51, no. 1, 18–51.

Coase, R.H. (1937) "The Nature of the Firm," *Economica*, New Series, vol. 4, no. 16, pp. 386–405.

Cohen, E. (2006) "Theoretical Foundations of Industrial Policy," *EIB Papers*, vol. 11, no. 1, pp. 85–106.

Gerschenkron, A. (1962) *Economic Backwardness in Historical Perspective: A Book of Essays* (Cambridge, MA: Belknap Press of Harvard University Press).

Harrison, A. and Rodríguez-Clare, A. (2009) "Trade, Foreign Investment, and Industrial Policy for Developing Countries," in D. Rodrik (ed.), *Handbook of Economic Growth*, vol. 4 (Amsterdam: North-Holland).

Hechscher, E.F. and Ohlin, B. (1991). *Hechscher–Ohlin Trade Theory* (trans. ed. Introd. H. Flam and M.J. Flanders) (Cambridge, MA: MIT Press).

Katz, M. (1986) "An Analysis of Cooperative Research and Development," *Rand Journal of Economics*, vol. 17, no. 4, pp. 527–543.

Krueger, A. (1974) "The Political Economy of Rent-Seeking Society," *American Economic Review*, vol. 64, no. 3, pp. 291–303.

Krugman, P. (1993) "Protection in Developing Countries," in R. Dornbusch (ed.), *Policymaking in the Open Economy: Concepts and Case Studies in Economic Performance* (New York: Oxford University Press), pp. 127–148.

Krugman, P. (1991) *Geography and Trade* (Cambridge, MA: MIT Press).

Lal. D. and Myint, H. (1996) *The Political Economy of Poverty, Equity and Growth: A Comparative Study* (Oxford: Clarendon Press).

Lerner, J. (2009) *Boulevard of Broken Dreams. Why Public Efforts to Boost Entrepreneurship and Venture Capital Have Failed–and What to Do About It* (Princeton, NJ: Princeton University Press).

Lin, J.Y. (1989) "An Economic Theory of Institutional Change: Induced and Imposed Change," *Cato Journal*, vol. 9, no. 1, pp. 1–32.

Lin, J.Y. (2009) *Economic Development and Transition: Thought, Strategy, and Viability* (Cambridge, UK: Cambridge University Press).

Lin, J.Y. and Li, F. (2009) *Development Strategy, Viability, and Economic Distortions in Developing Countries*. Policy Research Working Paper 4906 (Washington, DC: World Bank).

Lin, J.Y. and Monga, C. (2011) "Growth Identification and Facilitation: The Role of the State in the Dynamics of Structural Change," Development Policy Review, vol. 29, no. 3, pp. 259–310.

Lin, J.Y. and Monga, C. (2014) "The Evolving Paradigms of Structural Change," in Bruce Currie-Alder, Ravi Kanbur, David M. Malone, and Rohinton Medhora (eds), *International Development: Ideas, Experience, and Prospects* (New York: Oxford University Press).

Lin, J.Y. and Tan, G. (1999) "Policy Burdens, Accountability, and the Soft Budget Constraint," *American Economic Review, Papers and Proceedings*, vol. 89, no. 2, pp. 426–431.

List, Friedrich, Matile, G.-A., Richelot, Henri, and Colwell, Stephen (1856) *National System of Political Economy* (Philadelphia: J.B. Lippincott & Co.).

Marshall, A. (1920) *Principles of Economics* (London: Macmillan).

Murphy, K.M., Shleifer, A. and Vishny, R.W. (1989) "Industrialization and the Big Push," *Journal of Political Economy*, vol. 97, no. 5, pp. 1003–1026.

Nelson, R. (1995) "Recent Evolutionary Theorizing about Economic Change," *Journal of Economic Literature*, vol. 33, no. 1, pp. 48–90.

Nester, W. (1997) *American Industrial Policy: Free or Managed Markets* (London: Macmillan Press Ltd).

North, D. (1981) *Structure and Change in Economic History* (New York: W.W. Norton).

Persson, T. and Tabellini, G. (1994) "Is Inequality Harmful to Growth?," *American Economic Review*, vol. 38, pp. 765–773.

Prebisch, R. (1950) *The Economic Development of Latin America and its Principal Problems* (New York: United Nations). Reprinted in *Economic Bulletin for Latin America*, vol. 7, no. 1, February 1962, pp. 1–22.

Ricardo, D. (1963) *The Principles of Political Economy and Taxation* (Homewood, IL: R.D. Irwin).

Robinson, J.A. and Torvik, R. (2005) "White Elephants," *Journal of Public Economics*, vol. 89, pp. 197–210.

Rodrik, D. (2010) "The Return of Industrial Policy," *Project* Syndicate, April 12, 2010. Available online at http://www.project-syndicate.org/commentary/the-return-of-industrial-policy.

Rodrik, D. (2004) *Industrial Policy for the Twenty-First Century*, John F. Kennedy School of Government Faculty Research Working Paper Series, Cambridge, MA.

Sen, A. (1960) *The Choice of Technique: An Aspect of the Theory of Planned Economic Development.* (Oxford: Blackwell).

Singer, H. (1950) "The Distribution of Gains between Investing and Borrowing Countries," *American Economic Review*, vol. 40, pp. 473–485.

Spence, M. (1984) "Cost Reduction, Competition, and Industry Performance," *Econometrica*, vol. 52, no. 1, pp. 101–122.

Wade, R. (1990) *Governing the Market* (Princeton, NJ: Princeton University Press).

World Bank (1995) *Bureaucrats in Business: The Economics and Politics of Government Ownership* (Washington, DC: World Bank).

1.2
Comments on "Comparative Advantage: The Silver Bullet of Industrial Policy" by Justin Lin and Célestin Monga

Ha-Joon Chang
University of Cambridge

This is an excellent paper, making a powerful and comprehensive case for what is one of the few things in economics that is more than common sense dressed up in technical language. Despite its central position in the mainstream trade theory, the concept of comparative advantage is often misunderstood. I've even occasionally heard well-established economists (hopefully in a moment of sloppiness) saying things like, "Oh, such and such poor country does not have comparative advantage in anything," which is a logical impossibility, as all countries have to have comparative advantage in *some* things. Lin and Monga make important contribution through this paper not only by reasserting the importance of this key concept but also by trying to operationalize the concept in a way that is very useful in real-world policymaking.

Lin and Monga adopts the neoclassical (Heckscher–Ohlin–Samuelson) theory of comparative advantage, which is conceptualized in terms of differences in factor endowments, but this is not the only way to theorize comparative advantage. After all, David Ricardo, the inventor of the concept, theorized comparative advantage in terms of differences in the hours of labor required to produce the same thing in different countries (based upon his labor theory of value), that is, in terms of the international differences in technological capabilities.

This alternative formulation of comparative advantage leads to a very different theory of trade and economic development from those that follow the neoclassical, or H-O-S, formulation. In the H-O-S formulation, the very thing that distinguishes the developing countries from the economically more advanced countries – that is, the differences in their technological capabilities – is assumed away, as all countries are assumed to be capable of using best-practice technologies and to differ only in terms of their factor endowments. So, in this formulation, if Guatemala is not producing things like BMWs, it is not because it cannot, but because it is too costly (in terms of opportunity costs) to do so. If you, in contrast, theorize comparative advantage in terms of differences in technological capabilities, the focus shifts to the process of accumulation of technological capabilities – an issue in explaining which neoclassical economics does not have a great record.

It may be impractical for Lin and Monga to explore this alternative formulation of comparative advantage in any depth in their paper, but it would have enriched the discussion if they had acknowledged this alternative formulation and briefly discussed its implications.

At the empirical level, Lin's and Monga's paper would have benefited from more nuanced characterizations of past development policy experiences. For example, the "comparative-advantage-defying" import-substitution industrialization (ISI) in Latin America was much more successful than what the paper acknowledges. For another example, the East Asian development strategies were less "comparative-advantage-conforming" than what the paper suggests. Korea's initial entry into the electronics industry in the 1960s may have been relatively comparative-advantage-conforming, but its entry into the steel industry later in the decade was highly comparative-advantage-defying, as the country's per capita income was less than 5 percent that of the USA at the time. Even in electronics, its entry into semiconductors in the mid-1980s was very comparative-advantage-defying, the sector being highly capital-intensive and the country still having only 14 percent of the US income per capita.

Building their theory on the basis of (factor-endowment-based) comparative advantage, Lin and Monga very much emphasize that the failure of industrial policy in many developing countries fundamentally owed to the choice of "wrong" industries, given their factor endowments. This is a welcome point, when many economists have gone overboard in acknowledging the role of non-economic factors and blamed economic failures too readily on things like neo-patrimonial politics, weak property rights, or even culture, without properly considering economic factors first. By highlighting the importance of comparative advantage, Lin and Monga has drawn our attention back to the "obvious" explanation that many industrial policy attempts may have failed because they tried to promote industries that are seriously out of line with the country's comparative advantage, rather than due to politics or institutions. This is a very powerful point.

However, is this enough? For example, in the 1960s and the 1970s, both some Latin American countries (mainly Brazil and Mexico) and South Korea tried to promote the automobile industry through protection and government subsidies. Despite all of them choosing the "wrong" industry, Korea has subsequently become one of the few countries with its own world-class carmakers while the Latin American countries have remained junior partners in the world auto industry. This spectacular divergence cannot be explained by the conformity (or otherwise) to comparative advantage, because, if anything, the initial choice was "wronger" for Korea, which had a much lower income and a smaller population (thus, less scope for achieving scale economy) than Brazil or Mexico did at the time.

I would argue that the difference between Korea, on the one hand, and Brazil and Mexico, on the other hand, was made by differences in the details of the policies, rather than differences in the conformity to comparative advantage. While Brazil and Mexico relied on the TNCs to build cars for them behind the wall of protection, the Korean government deployed a range of policies to promote the accumulation of technological capabilities by the local producers. For example, it forced, and subsidized, local car producers to start exporting early. This helped them become much more quality-conscious and achieve scale economies much earlier than what would have been possible if they relied only on the domestic market. For another example, it put conditions on FDI by TNCs in the automobile industry, such as joint venture requirements and local contents requirements, so that local partners have exposure to key technologies and management techniques. There were other differences, but the point is that it wasn't because Korea conformed more closely to its comparative advantage than did Brazil or Mexico that Korea has succeeded in the automobile industry and the others didn't.

Finally, in their paper, Lin and Monga provide a pragmatic "rule of thumb" that countries can use in choosing the comparative-advantage industries of tomorrow. They very convincingly argue that, because of various types of market failures, countries may have difficulties in moving up the value chain and therefore that the government has a role to play in identifying and promoting the comparative-advantage industries of the future. They suggest that these governments should cultivate industries that are doing well in countries with incomes that are twice (perhaps three times) higher than theirs and with endowment structures similar to theirs.

I think this is quite an important effort. The standard interpretation of comparative advantage does not really tell us how countries can move forward. It simply assumes that, as a country's factor endowment changes, industries that conform to the new comparative advantages will naturally emerge.

However, saying that we need the kind of practical guideline suggested by Lin and Monga is different from saying that their rule of thumb is the right one. Many success stories were based on moves that were far more daring than what their rule would suggest. In the late 1950s and the early 1960, Japan promoted its automobile industry when its income was just over one-sixth that of the US. As mentioned earlier, Korea entered the steel industry in the late 1960s, when its income was one-sixteenth that of the USA and entered the semiconductor industry in the mid-1980s, when its income was less than one-seventh that of the USA.

Lin and Monga are absolutely right in saying that the further you deviate from your comparative advantage, the riskier your industrial policy becomes. However, as in other things, you achieve little if you don't take risk, even though taking too much risk may leave you in a worse position. The relationship between the deviation from your comparative advantage and your economic success is, then, likely to be an inverted-U shape, in contrast to the downward-sloping line that is implicitly assumed in the standard trade theory – the more you deviate from your comparative advantage, the worse off you are. In my formulation, in the beginning, you are more likely to succeed as to deviate from your comparative, but after a while, you reach a point when further deviation lowers your chance of success. Of course, identifying the apex of this curve is the key challenge.

To sum up, Lin's and Monga's paper has made an important contribution by highlighting the crucial role that the theory of comparative advantage can, and should, play in the formulation of a viable industrial (and trade) policy. However, comparative advantage can tell us only so much. I would say that comparative advantage is less like a silver bullet, as Lin and Monga calls it in the subtitle of their paper, but more like a compass – it is absolutely necessary in finding out where you are but it does not tell you where to go or how to get there.

1.3

Industrial Policies, the Creation of a Learning Society, and Economic Development[1]

Bruce Greenwald and Joseph E. Stiglitz
Columbia University

Industrial policies – meaning policies by which governments attempt to shape the sectoral allocation of the economy – are back in fashion, and rightly so. The major insight of welfare economics of the past fifty years is that markets by themselves in general do not result in (constrained) Pareto-efficient outcomes (Greenwald and Stiglitz, 1986).

Industrial policies seek to shape the sectoral structure of the economy. This is partly because the sectoral structure that emerges from market forces, on their own, may not be that which maximizes social welfare. By now, there is a rich catalogue of market failures, circumstances in which the markets may, say, produce too little of some commodity or another, and in which industrial policies, appropriately designed, may improve matters. There can be, for instance, important coordination failures – which government action can help resolve.

But there are two further reasons for the recent interest in industrial policy: First, it has finally become recognized that market forces don't exist in a vacuum. Development economics routinely emphasizes as central to growth the study of institutions. All the rules and regulations, the legal frameworks and how they are enforced, affect the structure of the economy. So unwittingly, government is always engaged in industrial policy. For example, when the US Congress passed provisions of the bankruptcy code that gave derivatives first priority in the event of bankruptcy, but which said that student debt could almost never be discharged, even in bankruptcy, it was providing encouragement to the financial sector. Secondly, it has also been realized that when the government makes expenditure decisions – about infrastructure, education, technology, or any other category of spending – it affects the structure of the economy.

This paper is concerned with one particular distortion: that in the production and dissemination of knowledge. Markets, on their own, are not efficient in the production and dissemination of knowledge (learning). Sectors in which learning and research are important are typically characterized by a wide variety of market failures.

Both econometric and historical studies highlight the importance of learning and innovation. Maddison's (2001) research, for instance, documents that from the origins of civilization to the early 1800s, there was essentially no increase in incomes per capita. The economy was close to static. The subsequent two centuries have been highly dynamic, leading to unprecedented improvements in standards of living.

Since the work of Solow (1957), we have understood that most increases in per capita income – some 70 percent – cannot be explained by capital deepening; for the advanced developed countries most of the "Solow residual" arises from advances in technology. At least for the past quarter century, we have understood that a substantial part of the growth in developing countries arises from closing the gap in knowledge between themselves and those at the frontier. Within any country, there is enormous scope for productivity improvement simply by closing the gap between best practices and average practices (Greenwald and Stiglitz, 2014b).

Knowledge is different from conventional goods; it is, in a sense, a public good (Stiglitz, 1987a, 1999) – the marginal cost of another person or firm enjoying the benefit of knowledge (beyond the cost of transmission) is zero; usage is non-rivalrous. Markets are not efficient in the production and distribution of public goods. It is inevitable that there be, or that there ought to be, a role for government.

Moreover, as Arrow (1962a) pointed out fifty years ago, the production of knowledge is often a joint product with the production of goods, which means that the production of goods themselves will not in general be (intertemporally) efficient.

If it is the case that most increases in standard of living are related to the acquisition of knowledge, to "learning," it follows that understanding how economies best learn – how economies can best be organized to increase the production and dissemination of productivity-enhancing knowledge – should be a central part of the study of development and growth. It is, however, a subject that has been essentially neglected. That would, by itself, be bad enough. But Washington Consensus policies based on neoclassical models that ignore the endogeneity of learning often have consequences that are adverse to learning, and thus to long-term development.

Creating a learning society

Not only is the pace of learning (innovation) the most important determinant of increases in standards of living; the pace itself is almost surely partially, if not largely, endogenous. The speed of progress has differed markedly both over time and across countries, and while we may not be able to explain all of this variation, it is clear that government policies have played a role. Learning is affected by the economic and social environment and the structure of the economy, as well as public and private investments in research and education. The fact that there are high correlations across industries, firms, and functions in firms suggests that there may be common factors (environmental factors, public investments) that have systemic effects, and/or that there may be important spillovers from one learner/innovator to others. But the fact that there are large, persistent differences across countries and firms – at the microeconomic level, large discrepancies between best, average, and worst practices – implies that knowledge does not necessarily move smoothly either across borders or over firm boundaries.

All of this highlights that one of the objectives of economic policy should be to create economic policies and structures that enhance both learning and learning spillovers: creating a learning society is more likely to increase standards of living than the small, one-time improvements in economic efficiency or those that derive from the sacrifices of consumption today to deepen capital.[2]

And this is even more true for developing countries. Much of the difference in per capita income between these countries and the more advanced is attributable to differences in knowledge. Policies that transformed their economies and societies into "learning societies" would enable them to close the gap in knowledge, with marked increases in incomes.[3] Development entails learning how to learn.[4]

Market failure and learning

While the fact that knowledge is a (global) public good means that the production and dissemination of knowledge that emerges in a market economy will not, in general, be efficient, there are several other market failures that inevitably arise in an important way in the context of a learning economy.

The first set is related to the fact that those who produce innovation seldom appropriate the full value of their societal contributions. There are large externalities, and these externalities will play a pivotal role in the analysis below. Even when an innovator becomes rich as a result of his innovation, what he appropriates is sometimes but a fraction of what he has added to GDP. But even more, many of those who have made the most important discoveries – those who regularly contribute to the advances of basic science and technology – receive rewards that are substantially below their social contributions: Think of Turing, Watson and Crick, Berners-Lee or even the discovers of the laser/maser and the transistor.[5]

But externalities are more pervasive. Individuals who learn about better ways of doing business transmit that knowledge when they move from one firm to another. (We discuss these spillovers at greater length below.)

The second set is related to our imperfect attempts to provide incentives for innovation, through intellectual property. The result is that private rewards are typically not commensurate with (marginal) social returns, in some cases exceeding the social returns (me-too innovations, innovations that are designed to lead to "hold-up" patents),[6] in other cases being markedly less. The fact that the distortion which industrial policy may be attempting to partially "correct" arises from a government policy highlights an aspect of industrial policy upon which we comment further in the concluding section of this paper: it is not just market failures which lead to "distortions" in the economy, but also "government failures." (One could argue that it would make more sense to eliminate the government failure than to introduce another intervention in the market. But for one reason or another, typically related to political economy, it may not be easy to eliminate some government policies; it may be easier to introduce a new countervailing policy.)

A third source of inefficiency that industrial policies may address arises from capital market imperfections (themselves endogenous, arising from information asymmetries). But capital market imperfections can be particularly adverse to learning: Because R&D investments (or "learning investments"[7]) typically cannot be collateralized, unlike investments in buildings, machines, or inventories, it is more likely that there will be credit and equity rationing, leading to underinvestment in these areas, compared to others.[8]

There are other important interactions between traditional market failures, like imperfect competition, and learning: sectors in which innovation is important are naturally imperfectly competitive—research expenditures are fixed costs, and give rise to increasing returns. Because sectors in which competition is limited, output will be lower, and accordingly returns to cost-reducing innovations are lower (Arrow, 1962b).

Still another market failure arises from imperfections in risk markets. Innovation is highly risky – research is an exploration into the unknown. But firms cannot purchase insurance against these risks (because of well-known problems of moral hazard and adverse selection). However, because of imperfections in capital markets, firms act in a risk-averse manner, particularly in the presence of bankruptcy costs (Greenwald and Stiglitz, 1993), and this discourages investment in riskier innovation.

Problems of the appropriability of returns and imperfections of capital markets (including the absence of good risk markets) result in barriers to the entry of new firms (entrepreneurs) and the exploration of new products or processes that might be particularly appropriate for a developing country. Consider an "experiment" to discover whether conditions in a country are particularly suitable for growing a particular kind of coffee. If the experiment fails, those who conduct the experiment lose money. If it succeeds, there may be quick entry. The country benefits, but the "innovator" can't capture much of the returns. In short, an experiment that is successful will be imitated, so the firm won't be able to reap returns; but the firm bears the losses of an unsuccessful experiment. As a result, there will be underinvestment in this kind of experimentation (Hoff, 1997).

A similar argument holds for why private markets will lend too little to new entrepreneurs. The borrower who becomes successful will be poached by other lenders, so the interest rate that he can charge (after the entrepreneur has demonstrated his success) will be limited to the competitive rate. But Stiglitz-Weiss adverse selection and adverse incentive effects limit the interest rate that can be charged in the initial period, which implies that there will be limited lending to new entrepreneurs (Emran and Stiglitz, 2009).

In the absence of lump-sum (non-distortionary) taxation, there is a fundamental tension: research is a fixed cost, and there is no marginal cost to the use of an idea, so that knowledge should be freely provided. But that would imply that the producer of information (knowledge) would receive no returns. Thus, it is inevitable that there be an underproduction of knowledge (relative to the first best) and/or an underutilization of the knowledge that is produced. The patent system (in principle) attempts to balance out the dynamic gains with the short-run costs of the underutilization of knowledge and imperfections of market competition.[9] When the government finances research and disseminates it freely, there is still a static distortion (from the distortionary imposition of taxes), but no distortion in the dissemination and use of knowledge.

In light of the pervasive market failures associated with innovation and learning, the commonly heard objection to industrial policies – the mantra that government should not be involved in "picking winners"[10] – is beside the point: the objective of the government is to identify, and "correct" externalities and other market failures. While it is now widely accepted that there can be large negative externalities (for example, from pollution, or from excessive risk taking in the financial sector), we are concerned here with an equally important set of *positive* externalities.

While government may not be perfect in identifying negative externalities, there is by now consensus (except among polluters) that environmental regulations have been very beneficial; so too for positive externalities: even if government identifies such externalities imperfectly, it is wrong to assume that they are "zero": government can improve upon the market allocation. The best way of doing so is a matter of controversy, upon which we comment in the concluding section. But it is clear that many governments (both in developed and developing countries) have a credible record of industrial policy interventions.[11]

A closer look at learning spillovers

We emphasized earlier that there are important positive externalities from learning. Such spillovers are pervasive and large, and they are larger in some industries than in others. And obviously, markets will not take into account these externalities.

Spillovers occur even in the presence of a patent system. Many advances cannot be patented (advances in mathematics, for example); and the benefits of much of what is learned in the process of research cannot be appropriated. Indeed, the disclosure requirements of a patent are intended to enhance these societal benefits. We'll provide further illustration below.

There are many aspects of learning spillovers. There are direct technological spillovers: the production of any good involves many stages, and some of the stages may involve processes that are similar to those used in another seemingly distinct sector. As Atkinson and Stiglitz (1969) noted, learning is localized: it affects production processes that are similar to those for which there has been learning.[12] But the learning is not limited to a single process and related processes for a particular product. Innovations in one sector may benefit other sectors that look markedly different, but use similar processes. Sectors that are, in one way or another, more similar may, of course, benefit more. (Indeed, the same argument holds within a sector. An innovation in one technology in a given sector may have limited spillovers for other technologies – the spillovers may be greater to other products using analogous technologies.)

There are especially important spillovers in methods of production. Inventory control and cash management techniques affect virtually every firm in an economy. Just-in-time production or assembly lines are examples of production processes that affect many industries.[13]

Improvements in skills (techniques) in one sector have spillover benefits to other sectors in which analogous skills are employed. Hidalgo and colleagues (2007) characterized the product space, attempting to identify the "capabilities" that different sectors have in common. Presumably, if two products entail similar capabilities, learning that enhances a particular capability in one sector will have spillover benefits to related sectors for which that same capability is relevant.[14]

It is, as we have suggested, impossible to appropriate the benefits of much of this learning. An idea like just-in-time production, replaceable parts, or assembly lines spreads quickly throughout the economy, and can't be protected by intellectual property. Learning what grows well in a particular climate with a particular soil is information that is not patentable. The result, as we noted earlier, is that there will be insufficient investment in exploration. There are equally important economy-wide "technologies," and improvements in these have society-wide benefits. These include those that arise out of the development of institutions. A financial system developed to serve the manufacturing sector may equally serve the rural sector. Improvements in the education system, necessary for an effective industrial sector, can also have benefits for the service sector or the agricultural sector.

Knowledge is embodied in people. This is especially relevant for what is called *tacit knowledge,* understandings that are hard to codify, to articulate as simple prescriptions, that could easily be conveyed through textbooks or classroom learning. Workers move from firm to firm, and thus convey some of the learning that has occurred in one firm to those in others. But knowledge is also embodied in firms that supply inputs to multiple firms. What they learn in dealing with one firm in one industry may be relevant for another firm. There can be backward, forward, and horizontal linkages (Hirschman, 1958).

Technological knowledge is also embodied in machines, and a machine constructed for one purpose can often be adapted for quite another. It is not an accident that the Ohio Valley (stretching up to Michigan) gave rise to innovations in bicycles, airplanes, and cars: while the products were distinct, the development of these products shared some of the same technological know-how. This illustrates the principle that it may be difficult to identify *ex ante* what "nearby" products are, products such that advances in learning in one affects the other.

Knowledge, in this sense, is like a (beneficial) disease: it can spread upon contact. But some kinds of contact are more likely to lead to the transmission of knowledge than others. Some of the people who might possibly come into contact with the knowledge are "susceptible," that is, they are more likely to learn, to use the knowledge, and perhaps even develop it further. Firms, realizing that knowledge is power (or at least money), seek to limit the transmission of knowledge – it might help one's rivals, who might be able to build on it, putting oneself at a disadvantage. Thus, firms go to great lengths to maintain secrecy. While for the advancement of society, it is desirable that knowledge, once created, be transmitted as broadly and efficiently as possible, profit maximizing firms have traditionally sought to limit to the extent possible the transmission of knowledge.

The architecture of the economy – including all the rules concerning intellectual property – affects the speed and extent of transmission of knowledge.

There is, in this, however a trade-off that is fully analogous to that in the design of patents and that is at the root of the critique of the efficient markets hypothesis: if knowledge were perfectly transmitted, there would be no incentive to expend resources on gathering and producing knowledge. There would be underinvestment in knowledge creation (and in the case of developing countries, gathering knowledge from others). Hence, an optimally designed learning society does not entail the perfect transmission of knowledge (except for knowledge that is publicly provided).[15]

There are, however, natural impediments to the perfect transmission of knowledge. It is plausible that a market economy engages in excessive secrecy (relative to the social optimum). This, of course, has been the contention of the open source movement. Collaborative research in the open source movement is still economically viable, both because there are still economic returns (for example, because of the tacit knowledge that is created by the learning/innovation process itself) and because there are important non-economic returns to and incentives for innovation (Dasgupta and David, 1994).

We can thus think of the economy as a complex network of individuals interacting directly with each other and via institutions (like corporations, schools) of which they are a member, ideas (knowledge) being created at various nodes in this network, being transmitted to others with whom there is a connection, being amplified, and re-transmitted, a complex dynamic process the outcomes of which can be affected by the topography of the network, which, together with the rules of the game, affect the incentives to gather, transmit (or not to transmit), and amplify knowledge.

A sub-problem within this systemic problem is the design of the component institutions (for example, corporations). For within the institution, there may be incentives to develop knowledge and to hoard or to transmit it. The issue of the architecture of a learning firm is parallel to that of the architecture of a learning economy. In some ways, the two cannot be separated: Traditional discussions of the boundary of firms (Coase, 1937) focused on transactions costs; but equally important is the structure of learning. It may be easier to transmit information (knowledge) within a firm than across enterprises, partly because the "exchange" of knowledge is not well-mediated by prices and contracts.[16] If so, and if learning is at the heart of a successful economy, it would suggest that firms might be larger than they would be in a world in which learning is less important.[17] (On the other hand, the difficulties of developing appropriate incentives for the reward of innovation may militate against large enterprises. There is an ongoing debate over whether large or small enterprises are most conducive to innovation. Large firms may have the resources to finance innovation, typically lacking in smaller enterprises, but there is an impressive record of large firms not recognizing the value of path-breaking innovations, including Microsoft being too wedded to the keyboard, and Xerox not recognizing the important of a user-friendly interface, like Windows.)

In the discussion below, we mostly abstract from microeconomic structures, focusing on broader policies, on the principles which should guide government intervention, and on alternative instruments. Section 1.3.1 summarizes key results on the implications of learning externalities. Section 1.3.2 discusses how, in the presence of capital constraints, access to finance may be an important instrument of industrial policy. Section 1.3.3 discusses other instruments. Section 1.3.4 focuses on the role of government investment policy. We conclude, in Section 1.3.5, with a general set of remarks about industrial policy, especially as it relates to the promotion of a learning economy and society.

1.3.1 Learning externalities

A central thesis of this paper is that government should encourage industries in which there are large learning externalities. A simple two-period model in which labor is the only input to production suffices to bring out the major issues.[18] We show that government should encourage: (i) the production of goods in which there is more learning; (ii) the production of goods which generate more learning externalities; and (iii) the production of goods which enhance learning capabilities.

Assume (for simplicity) that utility is separable between goods in the two periods and between goods and labor:

$$W = U(\mathbf{x}^t) - v(L^t) + \delta[U(\mathbf{x}^{t+1}) - v(L^{t+1})],\tag{1}$$

where $\mathbf{x}^t$ is the vector of consumption $\{x_k^t\}$ at time t and L^t is aggregate labor supply at time t. The disutility of work is the same in all sectors, and L^t is aggregate labor input in period t:

$$L^t = \Sigma L_k^t \text{ and } L^{t+1} = \Sigma L_k^{t+1},$$

where L_k^i is the input of labor in sector k in period i.

Production is described by (in the appropriate choice of units)

$$x_k^t = L_k^t.\tag{2}$$

In this simple model, the more output of good j in period t, the lower the production costs in period t+1. We assume

$$x_k^{t+1} = L_k^{t+1} H^k[\mathbf{L}^t],\tag{3}$$

where $\mathbf{L}^t$ is the vector of labor inputs at time t $\{L_{ij}^t\}$.

The learning functions H^k and their properties are at the center of this analysis. In the following analysis, two properties of these learning functions will play a central role:

(a) Learning elasticity – how much sectoral productivity is increased as a result of an increase in labor input.
    We define

$$h_k = d \ln H^k / d \ln L_k^t.\tag{4}$$

h_k is the *elasticity of the learning curve in sector k.*

(b) Learning spillovers – the extent to which learning in sector i spills over to sector j.
    $\partial H^k/\partial L_j^t > 0$, $j \neq k$, if there are learning externalities,

    while

    $\partial H^k/\partial L_j^t = 0$, $j \neq k$, if there are no learning externalities.

Full learning externalities. One interesting case is that where there are full learning externalities, i.e. knowledge is a public good, so $H^k = H^j = H$.

Then we choose L^t to

$$\max U(L^t) - v(L^t) + \delta[U(L^{t+1} H[L^t]) - v(L^{t+1})$$

so

$$U_i - v' + \delta H_i[\Sigma L_k^{t+1} U_k (L_k^{t+1} H[L^t]) = 0.$$

If we assume homotheticity, $U = u(\Phi(x))$, with $\Sigma \Phi_k(x)x_k = \Phi$, then we can rewrite the above as

$$u' \Phi_i - v' + \delta h_i Uv = 0$$

where

$$v = d\ln U/d\ln \Phi$$

We can generate the optimal allocation by providing a subsidy of τ_i on the ith good, for with such a subsidy an individual

$$\text{maximizes } U(x) - v(\Sigma x_i(1 - \tau_i))$$

or

$$U_i = v' - v' \tau_i$$

We can get the optimal allocation by setting

$$\delta h_i Uv = v' \tau_i$$

or

$$\tau_i = \delta h_i Uv/v'$$

Consumption should be subsidized the more the higher the value of future consumption (the larger δ), and the higher the learning responsiveness h_i.[19]

Optimal subsidies with no cross-sectoral spillovers, full within-sector spillovers. Similar results hold in the case where there are no spillovers across sectors, but there are full spillovers within the sector. A competitive firm again will take no account of the learning benefits – learning is a sectoral public good. We illustrate with the case with separable utility. With separability of utility across goods (so $U = \Sigma u_i$), the first order condition for welfare maximization becomes

$$u_i^{t'} - v^{'t} + \delta h_i \, \eta_i \, u_i^{t+1} = 0$$

where

$$\eta_i = dln \, u_i / dln \, x_i.$$

The optimum can be achieved by setting a subsidy on the consumption of good i at

$$\tau_i = \delta h_i \, \eta_i \, u_i^{t+1} / v^{'t}$$

Again, it is apparent that, as before, *consumption should be subsidized the more the higher the value of future consumption (the larger δ), and the higher the learning responsiveness h_i.* Now, there is a third factor – the elasticity of marginal utility. If the elasticity is low, then the benefits of learning diminish rapidly.[20]

The case of full symmetry. In the case of *full* symmetry (both in consumption and in learning), the only distortion is in the *level* of output, that is, if there are n commodities, 1/nth of income will be spent on each, but in a competitive market with full spillovers within the sector, whether or not there are spillovers to other sectors, no attention is paid to the learning benefits. Hence, the market equilibrium will entail too little production (labor) the first period.

Monopolistic competition. In the case of monopolistic competition, where there is a single firm in each sector, and no learning spillovers, the firm will fully take into account the learning benefits, but now, because of imperfections of competition, output will be restricted. There is again less than the socially desirable level of learning.

Differential spillovers. The formal analysis so far abstracts from the third determinative factor – the extent of spillovers – for we have assumed that there are either no cross-sector spillovers or perfect spillovers from every sector.

There are a variety of reasons that learning may be higher in one sector than another, and why spillovers from one sector may be greater than in another. Historically, the industrial sector has been the source of innovation. The reasons for this are rooted in the nature of industrial activity. Such activity takes place in firms that (relative to firms in other sectors, such as agriculture) are (1) large; (2) long-lived; (3) stable; and (4) densely concentrated geographically. Agricultural/craft production, by contrast, typically takes place on a highly decentralized basis among many small, short-lived, unstable firms.

In the following paragraphs we describe in more detail some of the reasons for the comparative advantage of the industrial sector in learning and why that sector is more likely to give rise to learning externalities.

(1) *Large enterprises.* Since particular innovations are far more valuable to large organizations that can apply them to many units of output than

to smaller ones with lower levels of output (see Arrow, 1962b), there is far greater incentive to engage in R&D in the industrial sector than in the agricultural/craft sector. The result will be higher investments in innovation in the former sector than the latter. This can be looked at another way: Large firms can internalize more of the externalities that are generated by learning.[21] Moreover, innovation is highly uncertain, and firms and individuals are risk averse. Large enterprises are likely to be less risk averse, and thus better able to bear the risks of innovation. Moreover, because of information imperfections, capital markets are imperfect, and especially so for investments in R&D, which typically cannot be collateralized. Capital constraints are less likely to be binding on large enterprises.

(2) *Stability and continuity.* The accumulation of knowledge on which productivity growth is based is necessarily cumulative. This, in turn, greatly depends on a stable organization for preserving and disseminating the knowledge involved and on continuity in jobs and personnel to support these processes. In large organizations, with the resources to provide redundant capacity where needed, the required degree of stability and continuity is much more likely to be present than in small dispersed organizations where the loss of single individuals may completely compromise the process of knowledge accumulation. As a result, steady productivity improvement will be much more likely to arise from industrial than agricultural/craft production. There is another way of seeing why stability/continuity contributes to learning: As we noted earlier, the benefits of learning extend into the future. Long-lived firms can value these distant benefits–and because industrial firms are typically larger, longer lived, and more stable than, say, firms in other sectors, they can have access to capital at lower interest rates. They are likely to be less capital constrained, act in a less risk-averse manner, and to discount future benefits less.[22]

(3) *Human capital accumulation.* Opportunities and incentives for accumulating general human capital are likely to be far greater in large complex industrial enterprises with a wide range of interdependent activities than in small, dispersed narrowly-focused agricultural /craft enterprises. (There is, for instance, a greater likelihood of benefits from the cross-fertilization of ideas.) Long-lived stable firms may have a greater incentive to promote increased human capital that leads to greater firm productivity, better ability to finance these investments, and more willingness to bear the risks. The resulting human capital accumulation is a critical element in both developing the innovations on which productivity growth depends and in disseminating them as workers move between enterprises and across sectors.

(4) *Concentration and diffusion of knowledge across firms.* Diffusion of knowledge among densely collocated, large-scale industrial enterprises (often

producing differentiated products)[23] is likely to be far more rapid than diffusion of knowledge among dispersed small-scale agricultural/craft enterprises. (Recall that earlier we had emphasized the importance of the diffusion of knowledge, and stressed the key role that geographical proximity plays. More recent discussions of the role of clusters have re-emphasized the importance of geographical proximity. See Porter, 1990.)

(5) *Cross-border knowledge flows.* While learning is facilitated by geographical proximity, especially developing countries (where many firms are operating far below "best practices") can learn from advances in other countries. While agricultural conditions may differ markedly from one country to another, the potential for cross-border learning may be greater in the industrial sector; and the existence of large, stable enterprises with the incentives and capacities to engage in cross-border learning enhances the role of that sector in societal learning. Indeed, it is widely recognized that success in the industrial sector requires not just knowledge, but also the ability to acquire knowledge, some of which is common across borders. Again, some of this knowledge and these abilities are relevant to the agricultural sector, and disseminate to it. Learning by one firm or subsector spills over to other firms and subsectors within the industrial sector, through, for instance, the movement of skilled people and advances in technology and capital goods that have cross-sector relevance. But the benefits spill over more broadly, even to the agricultural sector, and in the following paragraphs we describe some of the ways that this occurs, especially as a result of the tax revenues that a growing industrial sector can generate. Large-scale, densely concentrated activities are by this very nature far easier to tax than small-scale dispersed activities.

(6) *The ability to support public research and development.* Thus, economies with large accessible industrial sectors will be far better able to support publicly sponsored R&D than those consisting largely of dispersed, small-scale agricultural/craft production units. This factor may be especially important in the support of agricultural research, like that undertaken by Agricultural Extension Service in the United States. These activities directly contribute to agricultural productivity growth, but could not be supported without a taxable base of industrial activity.

(7) *Public support for human capital accumulation.* Just as in the case of R&D, private capital market failures may mean that public support in the form of free primary and secondary education is a critical component of general human capital accumulation. Moreover, the high returns to education in the industrial sector lead to a greater demand for an educated labor force. Again, the greater susceptibility of concentrated industrial enterprises to taxation is key to funding. And again, as workers migrate across sectors, ultimately higher productivity growth in the agricultural/craft sector will be engendered as well.

(8) *The development of a robust financial sector.* Greater investment in the industrial sector leads to higher levels of productivity both directly through capital deepening and the embodiment of technical progress (Johansen, 1959, and Solow, 1960), and indirectly through the capital goods industry, which is often a major source of innovation. Some of the innovations here (such as those relating to mechanization) have direct spillovers to the agriculture sector. But so do the institutional developments that are necessary to make an industrial economy function. The heavy investment of a modern industrial economy requires finance. It is not surprising then that an industrial environment should be characterized by a more highly-developed financial sector than an agricultural/craft environment. Once developed, a strong financial sector facilitates capital deployment throughout the economy, even in the rural sector.[24]

The implication of this analysis is that it pays government to take actions (industrial policies) to expand sectors in which there are more learning spillovers (in the above analysis, the industrial sector; within the industrial sector, there may be subsectors for which the learning elasticity is higher and from which learning spill overs are greater).

1.3.2   Finance and industrial policy

One of the reasons that markets fail to allocate resources efficiently to "learning" are capital market constraints. R&D is hard to collateralize, and optimal learning entails expanding production beyond the point where price equals short run marginal costs.

Imperfections of information often lead, especially in developing countries, to credit and equity rationing. Interestingly, a key instrument of industrial policy in East Asia was access to finance, often not even at subsidized rates (Stiglitz and Uy, 1996).

There are several aspects of "learning" in the design of financial policy. The first, emphasized by Emran and Stiglitz, is learning about who is a good entrepreneur. The problem, as we noted earlier, is that because of "poaching" the benefits of identifying who is a good entrepreneur may not be appropriated by the lender. There will be too little lending to new entrepreneurs.

Secondly, information is local, which means foreign banks may be at a disadvantage in judging which entrepreneurs or products are most likely to be successful in the specific context of the particular less developed country. Foreign banks are accordingly more likely to lend to the government, to other multinationals, or to large domestic firms. Financial market liberalization may, accordingly, have an adverse effect on development (Rashid 2012).[25]

1.3.3   Other instruments of industrial policy

Previous sections have argued that the objective of industrial policy is to shift production toward sectors in which there is likely to be more societal learning, meaning more learning and more learning externalities. There are a variety of other instruments – indeed, as we comment in the concluding section, almost every aspect of legal and economic policy has some effect in shaping an economy.

Here, we focus on intellectual property. In a sequel (Greenwald and Stiglitz, 2012) we discuss exchange rate policy and foreign direct investment.

Intellectual property regimes are supposed to encourage innovation, by providing incentives to do research, enhancing the ability to appropriate the returns. But intellectual property interferes with the dissemination/transmission of knowledge and encourages secrecy, which impedes learning. Increasingly, there is an awareness of other adverse effects of intellectual property regimes, as developed in the advanced industrial countries, especially for developing countries (see Stiglitz, 2006). Knowledge is the most important input into the production of knowledge, and by restricting the availability of knowledge, the production of knowledge (learning) is inhibited. The patent system gives rise to monopoly power; monopolies restrict production, thereby reducing incentives to innovate. The patent system can give rise to a patent thicket, a complex web of patents, exposing any innovator to the risk of suit and holdup. Because patents "privatize" knowledge while challenging patents moves knowledge into the "commons," there will be underinvestment in challenging patents and overinvestment in patenting. No wonder then that it has been estimated that in the United States, more money is spent on patent lawyers and litigation than on research.

There are two implications of this analysis. The first is that, given the critical role of closing the knowledge gap for successful development, the appropriate intellectual property regime for developing countries and emerging markets is likely to be markedly different than that appropriate for the advanced industrial countries. In this area, more even than others, one size fits all policies are inappropriate. Secondly, there are alternative ways of designing an innovation system, with greater emphasis on prizes and on open source. Patents will play a role, but a good patent system has to pay more attention to disclosure, to problems of holdup,[26] and to designing better systems of challenging patents (see Stiglitz, 2013).

1.3.4   Government investment

In some ways, governments cannot avoid questions of industrial policy; for they have to make decisions about the direction of public investment, say in education and infrastructure, and this has to be based on beliefs about the future directions of the economy, which are in turn affected by these public decisions. But the policies with which we are concerned go well beyond this. For government can use public expenditure policies to partially compensate for deficiencies in market allocations.

To see what this implies, let's extend our earlier learning model by introducing Public Goods, denoted by **G** in the first period. For simplicity, we assume we can impose a lump-sum tax to finance them and that there are full spillovers. We focus on the "direct" control problem, where we choose the level of spending on each private and public good. Focusing on the first period, we have

$$\text{Max } U(\mathbf{L^t}, \mathbf{G}) - v(\Sigma L^t + \Sigma G) + \delta[U(\mathbf{L^{t+1}} \, H[\mathbf{L^t}, \, \mathbf{G}]) - v(\Sigma L^{t+1})$$

where the output of public good G_i is just equal to the labor input in its production. The first-order condition of G is

$$U_G - v' + \delta \Sigma U_i \, L_i^{t+1} \, H_G = 0$$

In deciding on the optimal level of investment, we look not just at the direct benefits, but also at the learning benefits.

But in the absence of subsidies on private goods that take into account the learning benefits and spillovers, the provision of the public good can have another benefit. By expanding the production of public goods which are complements to goods with high learning elasticities and large externalities, the government can help create a more dynamic economy. To see this, we reformulate our optimization as an indirect control problem (still assuming the public good is financed by a lump-sum tax)

$$\text{Max } V(\mathbf{p^t}, \, I - G^t, \, G^t) + \delta \, V(\mathbf{p^{t+1}}, I)$$

where V is the indirect utility function, giving the level of utility as a function of prices, income net of lump sum taxes, and public goods. In the absence of product subsidies, equilibrium is characterized by price equaling marginal cost, or

$$p^t = 1; \; p^{t+1} = 1/H(\mathbf{L^t}, \, G^t)$$

The set of equations can be solved simultaneously for $\{x_i^t = L_i^t\}$ as a function of the vector $\{G^t\}$.[27] An increase in G_i^t, financed by a lump-sum tax, has complex income and substitution effects on the demand for each commodity. For instance, if some public good is a close substitute for some private good, the lower spendable income as a result of the additional provision of the public good combined with the availability of a public substitute will lead to a reduction in the private demand for that good, but if the public good were a strong enough complement (a free road to a ski resort), it might increase the demand for the good (trips to the ski resort.) We denote by $\partial L_j^t/\partial G_i^t$ t the change in the demand for (consumption of) good j as a result of an increase in public good i at time t_0, standard results give

$$V_{pi}^t/V_I^t = L_i^t.$$

Hence, optimizing with respect to G_i^t yields (assuming for simplicity full spillovers)

$$V_{Gi}^t - V_I^t = \delta V_I^{t+1} [\Sigma L_k^{t+1} \{H_{Gi} + \Sigma_j(\partial L_j^t/\partial G_i^t)H_j\}/H^2]$$

The first term (H_{Gi}) on the left-hand side is the direct learning benefits, the second term $[\Sigma_j (\partial L_j^t/\partial G_i^t)(H_j/H^2)]$ is the indirect effects on learning as the composition of demand changes.

We expand the production of public goods not only to take into account the learning benefits, but also the indirect effects in inducing more consumption of some goods and less of others, taking into account the total net effect on learning.

1.3.5 Concluding comments

1.3.5.1 Theory of the second best

Industrial policies distort consumption from what it otherwise would have been. Conventional economics (such as the Washington Consensus policies) emphasized the costs of these interventions. We have emphasized that when there are market failures (as is always the case when there are learning externalities), there will be benefits. Optimal policy weighs the benefits and costs as the margin.

The economics of the second best is of particular relevance here: R&D and learning give rise to market imperfections, sometimes referred to as distortions, where resources are not allocated in a "first-best" way. Well-designed distortions in one market can partially offset distortions in others.

I use the word "distortions" with care: Common usage suggests that governments should simply do away with them. But as the term has come to be used, it simply refers to deviations from the way a classical model with, say, perfect information might function. Information is inherently imperfect, and these imperfections cannot be legislated away. Nor can the market power that arises from the returns to scale inherent in research be legislated away. That is why simultaneously endogenizing market structure and innovation is so important (see, for example, Dasgupta and Stiglitz, 1980). Similarly, the costs associated with R&D (or the "losses" associated with expanding production to "invest" in learning) cannot be ignored; they have to be paid for. Monopoly rents are one way of doing so, but – as we argue here – a far from ideal way.

As always in the modern economics of the public sector, the nature of the optimal interventions depends on the instruments and powers of government. Whether the government can abolish monopolies or undo their distortionary behavior has implications for the desirable levels of research and learning. It makes a difference, too, if the government can raise revenues to subsidize or support research or learning only through distortionary taxation rather than through lump sum taxes. There are ways to impose even distortionary taxes (that is, taxes that give rise to a loss of consumer surplus) that increase societal well-being and the speed of innovation. But the optimal investment in innovation is still likely to be less with distortionary taxation than with lump sum taxation.

1.3.5.2　Industrial policies and comparative advantage

Justin Lin (2012) has distinguished between industrial policies that defy comparative advantage, which he argues are likely to be unsuccessful, and those that are consistent with comparative advantage, which can be an important component of successful development. While there is considerable insight in this distinction, the key question is, what are the endowments of a country, that determine its comparative advantage? This is equivalent to asking, what are the relevant *state* variables? And what is the "ecology" against which the country's endowments are to be compared; that is, what are the *relevant* endowments of other countries?

It has become conventional wisdom to emphasize that what matters is not static comparative advantage but dynamic comparative advantage. Korea did not have a comparative advantage in producing computer chips when it embarked on its transition. Its static comparative advantage was in the production of rice. Had it followed its static comparative advantage (as many neoclassical economists had recommended), then rice might still be its comparative advantage; it might be the best rice grower in the world, but it would still be poor.

Ascertaining a country's static comparative advantage is difficult; ascertaining its dynamic comparative advantage is ever harder. Standard comparative advantage (cf. Heckscher–Ohlin) focused on *factor* endowments (capital–labor ratios).[28] But with capital highly mobile, capital endowments should matter little for determining comparative advantage. Still, capital (or, more accurately, the knowledge of the various factors that affect returns, and what is required to use capital efficiently) doesn't move perfectly across borders: that means that the resident of country j may demand a higher return for investing in country i. There is, in practice, far less than perfect mobility.

Thus the "state" variables that determine comparative advantage relate to those "factors" that are not mobile, which, in varying degrees, include knowledge, labor, and institutions.

Multinationals can, however, convey knowledge across borders. Highly skilled people move too. Migration has resulted in large movements in unskilled labor, but in most cases, not enough to change endowments of the home or host country significantly. Even institutions can sometimes effectively move across borders, as when parties to a contract may agree that disputes will be adjudicated in London and under British law. Still, there are numerous aspects of tacit knowledge, about how individuals and organizations interact with each other, and norms of behavior that affect economic performance, and, most particularly from our perspective, how (and whether) they learn and adapt; and these do not move easily across.

The "endowment" from our perspective which is most important is a society's learning capacities (which in turn is affected by the knowledge that it has and its knowledge about learning itself) which may be specific to learning about some things rather than others. The spirit of this paper is that industrial policy has to be shaped to take advantage of its comparative learning and learning abilities (including its ability to learn to learn) in relation to its competitors. Even if it has capacity to learn how to make computer chips, if a country's learning capacity is less than its competitors, it will fall behind in the race. But each country makes, effectively, decisions about what it will learn about. There are natural non-convexities in learning, benefits to specialization. If a country decides to learn about producing chips, it is less likely that it will learn about some other things. There will be some close spillovers, perhaps say to nano-technology. The areas to which there are spillovers may not lie near in conventional product space. There may, for instance, be similarities in production technologies (as in the case of just-in-time production or the assembly line). That is why the evolution of comparative advantage may be so hard to predict.

But while standard economic analysis may provide guidance to a country about its current (static) comparative advantage (given current technology, what are the unskilled-labor-intensive goods), guidance about its comparative advantage defined in this way (dynamic learning capacities) is much more difficult, partially because it depends on judgments made by other countries about their dynamic comparative advantage and their willingness to invest resources to enhance those advantages. Whether *ex ante* the USA, Japan, or Korea initially had a dynamic comparative advantage in producing chips, once Korea had invested enough in learning about certain kinds of chip production, it would be difficult for another country to displace it.

Looking at what other countries at similar levels of per capita income did in the past or what countries with slightly higher levels of per capita income are doing today may be helpful, but only to a limited extent. For the world today (both global geo-economics and geo-politics, and technology) is different than it was in the past. Competing in textiles today requires different skills and knowledge than in even the recent past; it may (or may not) be able to displace a country that currently has a comparative advantage in some product; the country may (or may not) be in the process of attempting to establish a comparative advantage in some other area.

1.3.5.3   Industrial strategies

A key issue of industrial strategy is not only the direction (should Korea have attempted to reinforce its comparative advantage in rice, or to create a comparative advantage in some other area?), but also the size of the step. Should it try a nearby technology (product), nudging along a gradual, evolutionary process that might eventually have occurred anyway? Or should it take a big leap? The latter is riskier: perhaps greater returns if successful, but a higher probability of failure.

We have not formally modeled this critical decision, so the following remarks are only meant to be suggestive: The ability to learn and the costs of learning increase significantly the bigger the leap; but so may the benefits. There are natural non-convexities in the value of information/knowledge (Radner and Stiglitz, 1984), implying that it pays to take a *moderate* step: small incrementalism is not optimal.

By the same token, using another analogy, to corporate strategic policy, it pays to move to a part of the product space where there are rents which can be sustained (for example, as a result of entry barriers, arising, for instance, out of returns to scale and/or specific knowledge). This almost surely entails not doing what others are or have been doing.

1.3.5.4   The inevitability of industrial policy

We have argued that government cannot escape thinking about its industrial structure. It is necessary as it makes decisions about public investments (in education, technology, and infrastructure). But the legal framework of a society also inevitably shapes industrial structure. If, as in the United States, derivatives are given seniority in bankruptcy, while student debts cannot be discharged, and large banks are effectively allowed to undertake high risks, with governments bearing the downside, and speculators are taxed at lower rates than those in manufacturing, the financial sector is encouraged at the expense of other sectors. This is an industrial policy.

Developing countries have to think carefully about every aspect of their economic policy, to make sure that they shape their economy in a way which maximizes learning. But their learning challenge is markedly different from that of the advanced industrial countries, where one of the main objectives is moving out the knowledge frontier. The focus of developing countries should be to close the knowledge gap between them and the more advanced countries (though for some of the more advanced among the emerging markets, one of the challenges it to be at the forefront, at least in some particular areas, something at which both China and Brazil have succeeded).

But this in turn has one important implication: legal frameworks and institutional arrangements (such as for intellectual property) that are appropriate for developed countries are not likely to be appropriate for developing countries and emerging markets.

1.3.5.5 Industrial policies and government failures

We began the discussion of this paper arguing that industrial policies are, in part, a response to market failures. The sectoral allocations resulting from unfettered markets are not in general optimal. But some of the inefficiencies in markets arise, as well, from government policies. A natural response is to remove the government distortions, rather than to create a new, offsetting distortion. But such an approach ignores the complexity of political economy and the difficulty of fine-tuning public policies. For instance, earlier, we referred to the impact of intellectual property. But a country's intellectual property regime is greatly affected by TRIPS, the WTO agreement, in ways which may not accord with the country's own best interests. It may, accordingly, attempt to undo or "correct" the distortions arising from that intellectual property regime.

1.3.5.6 The objectives of industrial policy

Industrial policy is usually conceived of as promoting growth, but it should be seen more broadly, as any policy redirecting an economy's sectoral allocation where market incentives (as shaped by rules and regulations) are misaligned with public objectives. Governments are concerned about employment, distribution, and the environment in ways in which the market is often not. Thus, in those countries with persistent high levels of employment, it is clear that something is wrong with market processes: labor markets are not clearing. Whether the explanation has to do with inherent limitations in markets (for example, imperfect information giving rise to efficiency wages), unions, or government (for example, excessively high minimum wages), the persistence implies that "correcting" the underlying failures may not be easy. The social costs of unemployment can be very high, and it is appropriate for government to attempt to induce the economy to move towards more labor intensive sectors or to use more labor intensive processes.

In each of these instances, shadow prices differ from market prices. This is evidently the case in many areas of the environment, where firms typically do not pay for the full consequences of their action. The consequences for investment—including investments in R&D—are obvious. Firms in many countries are searching for labor-saving innovations, even in countries with high unemployment, when from a social perspective, there are high returns to innovations that protect the environment.

1.3.5.7 Political economy

A persistent criticism of industrial policies is that, even if market allocations are inefficient, even if market prices differ from shadow prices, government attempts to correct these failures will simply make matters worse. There is neither theory nor evidence in support of this conclusion. To be sure, there are instances of government failure, but none on the scale of the losses resulting from the failures of America's financial market failure before and during the Great Recession. Virtually every successful economy has employed, successfully, at one time or another, industrial policies. And this is most notable in the case of East Asia (Stiglitz, Wade, Amsden, Chang).

In the sequel to this paper (Greenwald and Stiglitz, 2014b) we explain that limitations in government capacity ("political economy problems") should play an important role in shaping the design of industrial policies – what kinds of instruments should be employed.

In short, the debate today should not be about whether governments should pursue policies that shape the industrial structure of the economy. Inevitably, they will and do. The debate today should center around the directions in which it should attempt to shape the economy and the best way of doing so, given a country's current institutions and how they will evolve – recognizing that the evolution of the institutions themselves will be affected by the industrial policies chosen.

Appendix: A simple model of investment in R & D

In the text of this paper, we focused on how learning spillovers affected the optimal production structure—leading to an industrial structure that might be markedly different from that which might emerge in an unfettered market economy. Here, we extend this work by looking at how knowledge spill-overs affect the optimal pattern of R & D.

Assume there are two products, produced by a linear technology

$$Q_i = A_i(R_1, R_2) \, L_i$$

where R_i is the amount of research on product i and L_i is the labor devoted to production, L_i^r to research

$$E_i = L_i + L_i^r.$$

Total employment in sector i F_i is the sum of production and research workers. If $A_{ij} > 0$ (i ≠ j) implies there are spillover benefits for product i from research on product j. For simplicity, we assume $R_i = L_i^r$, the amount of labor devoted to research in sector i.

Social welfare maximization entails

$$\text{Max } U(Q_1, Q_2) - (E_1 + E_2)$$

After some manipulation, the first-order conditions can be written

$$\alpha_i^1 (L_1 / L_i^r) + \alpha_i^2 (L_2 / L_i^r) = 1$$

$$\alpha_1^2 (L_1 / L_1^r) + \alpha_2^2 (L_2 / L_2^r) = 1,$$

where $\partial \ln A_i / \partial \ln L_j^r = \alpha_j^i$.

Role of spillovers

With no spillovers $\alpha_i^j = \alpha_j^i = 0$, so

$$(L_i^r / L_i) = \alpha_i^i.$$

The ratio of employment in research in sector i to production labor is directly related to the own elasticity of productivity. If the elasticity is high – research increases productivity a lot – then a large fraction of labor should be devoted to research.

It is easy to see that if there are externalities (i.e. $\alpha_i^j > 0$), research is increased. Consider the symmetric case, where $L_1 = L_2$ in equilibrium. Then

$$L_i^r / L_1 = \alpha_1^i + \alpha_1^2.$$

With perfect spillovers,

$$\alpha_1^i = \alpha_1^2,$$

so the effect is to double the ratio of research workers to production workers.

Comparison with a market economy

In a perfectly competitive economy with a large number of firms and perfect within-industry spillovers, there would be no research, as each would try to free ride on others: $L_i^r = 0$ – clearly an underinvestment in research.

At the other extreme, assume that there were no spillovers. Then each firm would engage in some research. It would maximize output for any given input, that is,

$$\text{Max } A_i (L_i^r)(E_i - L_i^r),$$

generating

$$A'_i (E_i - L_i^r) = A_i$$

or

$$\alpha_i^i = L_i^r / L_i,$$

an equation that is identical to that derived earlier for the optimal allocation, in the case of no spillovers – highlighting the crucial role of spillovers
in industrial policies. (The overall level of employment may, however, differ
in the two situations.)

But there is another critical issue: whether there are spill overs or not is,
in part, a matter of industrial policy, for example, concerning compulsory
licensing, cooperative research efforts, and disclosure policies.

Thus, assume there are n firms in the industry, and that $A_i = A_{ii} + \beta \Sigma A_j$.
Government policy can increase β (the spillovers from sector j to sector i)
and thus the optimal amount of research. Moreover, if sector i has learning
as well as research potential, and the other sector does not, then L_i will be
much greater with $\beta \gg 0$, and hence so will L_i^r.

More typically, sectors in which research is important are imperfectly
competitive. Assume that again there is no knowledge spillover, and that
each sector faces an elasticity of demand of ε. Then, as before, we can show
that $L_i^r / L_i = \alpha_i^l$.

But now, with monopoly

$$p_i = A_i / (1 - 1/ \varepsilon),$$

where p_i is the price of the ith good (taking labor as the numeraire); while
in the competitive case

$$p_i = A_i.$$

Production (output) is lower, that is, for any given level of productivity
(A_i), L_i is smaller; and hence L_i^r is correspondingly smaller. The exploitation
of market power results in under production, and thus underinvestment in
research, since the value of research is related to the cost savings – that is,
the level of production.

In the case with identical learning functions but differences in demand
elasticities, interestingly, the percentage reduction in output is the same,
and hence relative increases in productivity stay the same. The monopoly
engages in less than optimal research[29] – but more than the competitive
market (with full within-sector spillovers, where there is no research.)

The long-term growth and structure of the economy depends critically
on the nature of competition (which itself is endogenous) and spillovers.
A Cournot duopoly may, for instance, result in more R&D spending
than a monopoly with a similar R&D function. But the pace of innovation may be lower. Over time, the effects can be cumulative, that is, the
less monopolized sector has lower productivity growth. Its scale is, as a
result, diminished, with resulting diminution in incentives to engage in
research.

Notes

1. Paper presented to the International Economic Association/World Bank Industrial Policy Roundtable in Washington, DC, May 22–23, 2012. The authors would like to thank the participants in the seminar for their helpful comments. This paper is based on Greenwald and Stiglitz (2006, 2014b) and Stiglitz (forthcoming). Greenwald and Stiglitz (2014a) provides a sequel to this paper, focusing on the implications of learning for industrial policy in the context of Africa.
2. As Solow (1956) pointed out, an increase in the savings rate simply leads to an increase in per capita income, not to a (permanently) higher rate of growth.
3. See Stiglitz (1998), which describes development as a "transformation" into a society which recognizes that change is possible, and that learns how to effect such change.
4. Stiglitz (1987b).
5. One should, perhaps, not put too much emphasis on the fact that these individuals did not appropriate the full benefits of their innovations: there is little evidence that they would have worked any harder with fuller appropriability. Discussions among economists focus on economic incentives; these may be far from the most important determinants of learning/innovation.
6. The social return is related to the arrival of an innovation earlier than would otherwise be the case. For a more extended discussion of these issues, see Stiglitz (2006, 2008, 2013).
7. Optimal learning may involve producing at a loss, necessitating borrowing. See Dasgupta and Stiglitz (1988).
8. This is an explanation of the high observed average returns to investment in technology. See Council of Economic Advisers (1995).
9. Inappropriately designed intellectual property regimes can actually inhibit innovation. (See the references cited earlier in footnote 6.)
10. In this view, it makes no difference whether the economy produces potato chips or computer chips. Let the market make the decision – not some government bureaucrat.
11. The returns on US government investments in technology and science are even higher than those of the private sector (which in turn are far higher than private sector returns elsewhere). See Council of Economic Advisers (1995).
12. Because countries differ, too, some learning that may be relevant in one country may be of limited benefit in other countries. Most changes in technology, however, *could* confer benefits across borders. The extent to which that is the case may depend on the level of skills (human capital) and the institutional arrangements.
13. They are also examples of ideas that are hard to be protected by patents, though in some cases, America's business process patents attempt to do.
14. We do not comment here whether their empirical approach really does fully capture the set of related capabilities. The effects of an improvement in one sector on other sectors depend not just on the similarity of those sectors, but on the institutional arrangements, e.g. providing scope for exploiting linkages. Thus, the fact that natural resource sectors have traditionally not been closely linked to other sectors may be partly a result of the absence of effective industrial policies, and the exploitive relationships often evidenced in that sector.
15. And indeed, this is one of the advantages of public support for the creation of knowledge.
16. That is, it is hard to write good incentive compatible innovation contracts, to know, for instance, when a firm fails to produce a promised innovation whether it was

because of lack of effort or because of the intrinsic difficulty of the task. Cost plus contracts, designed to share the risk of the unknown costs required to make an innovation, have their own problems. See, for example, Nalebuff and Stiglitz (1983).

17. An alleged major disadvantage of firms is that transactions within firms are typically not mediated by prices, with all of the benefits that accrue from the use of a price system. But if the benefits of using prices exceeded the costs, firms presumably could use prices to guide internal resource allocations, and some enterprises do so, at least to some extent. There is another perspective on these issues, related to accountability and control. See Stiglitz (1994).

18. Similar results obtain if learning is related to investment, as in Arrow's original 1962 paper. See Greenwald and Stiglitz (2014b).

19. The sensitivity of the subsidy to the learning elasticity or to δ depends on the proportionality variable $U\upsilon/v'$. Later discussions in the case of separable utility functions will provide some sense of the factors that determine that variable. See also Greenwald and Stiglitz (2014a).

20. There is a complicated fourth factor $u_i^{t+1}/v'^t = (u_i^{t+1}/u_i^t)/(v'^t/u_i^t) = (u_i^{t+1}/u_i^t)(1-\tau_i)$, so $\tau_i/(1-\tau_i) = \delta h_i \, \eta_i \, (u_i^{t+1}/u_i^t)$. u_i^{t+1}/u_i^t reflects the diminution of marginal utility as a result of increased consumption of good i over time. See Stiglitz (forthcoming).

21. As we noted earlier, it is these learning benefits that help explain an economies industrial structure – the boundaries of what goes on inside firms. In general, the diseconomies of scale and scope (related, for instance, to oversight) are greater in agriculture than in industry. In the case of modern hi-tech agriculture, there are increased benefits of learning, and that will affect the optimal size of establishments.

22. The importance of these factors has clear implications for the conduct of macroeconomic policy, which we discuss later in this paper.

23. The fact that they are producing different products enhances the likelihood that they will make different discoveries. The fact that they are producing similar products enhances the likelihood that a discovery relevant to one product will be relevant to another.

24. Exploitation by money lenders in the rural sector led to the development of rural cooperatives, for example, in the United States and in Scandinavia.

25. The extent to which this is true may vary, for example, if the foreign bank buys a local bank, it may, at least for a while, provide it with some autonomy.

26. For example, through the use of the "liability system." The US Supreme Court, in its decision for *eBay Inc.* v. *MercExchange, L.L.C.* in 2006, recognized the adverse consequences of the patent system and its enforcement as it had developed in the United States.

27. With stronger assumptions about separability, it is possible to solve for L_i^t as a function of G^t, but we consider here the more general case.

28. Krugman's research made it clear that something besides factor endowments mattered: he observed that most trade today is between countries that have similar factor endowments.

29. We note, however, that we have implicitly assumed the ability to impose lump sum taxation. With distortionary taxation, the optimal amount of research will obviously be less than with lump-sum taxation. See Stiglitz (1986).

References

Amsden, Alice (1989) *Asia's Next Giant: South Korea and Late Industrialization* (Oxford, UK: Oxford University Press).

Arrow, K.J. (1951) "An Extension of the Basic Theorems of Classical Welfare Economics," In J. Neyman (ed.), *Proceedings of the Second Berkeley Symposium on Mathematical Statistics and Probability* (Berkeley: University of California Press), pp. 507–532.

Arrow, K.J. (1962a) "The Economic Implications of Learning by Doing," *Review of Economic Studies*, vol. 29, no. 3, pp. 155–173.

Arrow, K.J. (1962b) "Economic Welfare and the Allocation of Resources for Invention," in R. Nelson (ed.), *The Rate and Direction of Inventive Activity: Economic and Social Factors*, National Bureau of Economic Research (NBER) (Princeton, NJ: Princeton University Press).

Atkinson, A.B., and Stiglitz, J.E. (1969) "A New View of Technological Change," *Economic Journal*, vol. 79, no. 315, pp. 573–578.

Chang, H.-J. (2002) *Kicking Away the Ladder: Development Strategy in Historical Perspective* (London, UK: Anthem Press).

Coase, R. (1937) "The Nature of the Firm," *Economica*, vol. 4, no. 16, pp. 386–405.

Council of Economic Advisers (1995) "Supporting Research and Development to Promote Economic Growth: The Federal Government's Role," Washington, DC: Council of Economic Advisers.

Dasgupta, P. and David, P.A. (1994) "Toward a New Economics of Science," *Research Policy, Elsevier*, vol. 23, no. 5, pp. 487–521.

Dasgupta, P. and Stiglitz, J.E. (1980) "Industrial Structure and the Nature of Innovative Activity," *Economic Journal*, vol. 90, no. 358, pp. 266–293.

Dasgupta, P. and J.E. Stiglitz (1988) "Learning by Doing, Market Structure, and Industrial and Trade Policies," *Oxford Economic Papers*, vol. 40, no. 2, pp. 246–268.

Emran, M.S. and Stiglitz, J.E. (2009) "Financial Liberalization, Financial Restraint and Entrepreneurial Development," working paper. Available at http://www.gwu.edu/~iiep/assets/docs/papers/Emran_IIEPWP20.pdf.

Greenwald, B. and Kahn, J. (2009) *Globalization: The Irrational Fear that Someone in China will Take Your Job*, Hoboken, NJ: John Wiley & Sons.

Greenwald, B. and Stiglitz, J.E. (1986) "Externalities in Economies with Imperfect Information and Incomplete Markets," *Quarterly Journal of Economics*, vol. 1, no. 2, pp. 229–264.

Greenwald, B. and Stiglitz, J.E. (1993) "Financial Market Imperfections and Business Cycles," *Quarterly Journal of Economics*, vol. 108, no. 1, pp. 77–114.

Greenwald, B. and Stiglitz, J.E. (2003) *Towards a New Paradigm in Monetary Economics* (Cambridge, UK: Cambridge University Press).

Greenwald, B. and Stiglitz, J.E. (2006) 'Helping Infant Economies Grow: Foundations of Trade Policies for Developing Countries'. *American Economic Review: AEA Papers and Proceedings*, vol. 96, no. 2, pp. 141–146.

Greenwald, B. and Stiglitz, J.E. (2014a) "Learning and Industrial Policy: Implications for Africa," in J.E Stiglitz, J.Y. Lin, and E. Patel (eds.), The Industrial Policy Revolution II: Africa in the 21st Century, London: Palgrave Macmillan and New Yark: St. Martin's press, pp. 25–49.

Greenwald, B. and Stiglitz, J.E. (2014b) *Creating a Learning Society: A New Approach to Growth, Development and Social Progress*, New York: Columbia University Press.

Hidalgo, C.A., Klinger, B., Barabási, A.-L., and Hausmann, R. (2007). 'The Product Space Conditions the Development of Nations'. *Science,* vol. 317, no. 5837, pp. 482–487.

Hirschman, A. (1958) *The Strategy of Economic Development* (New Haven, CT: Yale University Press).

Hoff, K. (1997) 'Bayesian Learning in an Infant Industry Model'. *Journal of International Economics*, vol. 43, nos 3–4, pp. 409–436.

Johansen, L. (1959) "Substitution Versus Fixed Production Coefficients in the Theory of Economic Growth," *Econometrica*, vol. 27, pp. 157–176.

Lin, J. (2012) *New Structural Economics: A Framework for Rethinking Development and Policy* (Washington, DC: World Bank).

Maddison, A. (2001) *The World Economy: A Millennial Perspective* (Paris: Development Center of the Organization for Economic Co-operation and Development).

Nalebuff, B. and Stiglitz, J.E. (1983) "Information, Competition and Markets,", *American Economic Review*, vol. 73, no. 2, pp. 278–284.

Porter, M.E. (1990) *The Competitive Advantage of Nations* (New York: Free Press).

Radner, R. and J. E. Stiglitz (1984), A Nonconcavity in the Value of Information," in Marcel Boyer and Richard Khilstrom (eds), *Bayesian Models in Economic Theory* (Amsterdam: Elsevier Science Publications), pp. 33–52.

Rashid, H. (2012) "Foreign Banks, Competition for Deposits and Terms and Availability of Credit in Developing Countries," working paper.

Simon, H.A. (1991) "Organizations and Markets," *Journal of Economic Perspectives*, vol. 5, no. 2, pp. 25–44.

Solow, R.M. (1956) "A Contribution to the Theory of Economic Growth," *Quarterly Journal of Economics*, vol. 70, no. 1, pp. 65–94.

Solow, R.M. (1957) "Technical Change and the Aggregate Production Function," *Review of Economics and Statistics*, vol. 39, no. 3, pp. 312–320.

Solow, R.M. (1960) "Investment and Technical Progress," in K. Arrow, S. Karlin, and P. Suppes (eds), *Mathematical Methods in the Social Sciences* (Stanford: Stanford University Press), pp. 89–104.

Stiglitz, J.E. (1986) "Theory of Competition, Incentives and Risk," in J.E. Stiglitz and F. Mathewson (eds), *New Developments in the Analysis of Market Structure* (London: MacMillan/MIT Press), pp. 399–449.

Stiglitz, J.E. (1987a). "On the Microeconomics of Technical Progress," in Jorge M. Katz (ed.), *Technology Generation in Latin American Manufacturing Industries* (London: Macmillan Press Ltd), pp. 56–77. (Presented to IDB-CEPAL Meetings, Buenos Aires, November 1978.)

Stiglitz, J.E. (1987b) "Learning to Learn, Localized Learning and Technological Progress," in P. Dasgupta and P. Stoneman (eds), *Economic Policy and Technological Performance* (New York: Cambridge University Press), pp. 125–153.

Stiglitz, J.E. (1994) *Whither Socialism* (Cambridge, MA: MIT Press).

Stiglitz, J.E. (1996) "Some Lessons from the East Asian Miracle," *World Bank Research Observer*, vol. 11, no. 2, pp. 151–177.

Stiglitz, J.E. (1998) "Towards a New Paradigm for Development: Strategies, Policies and Processes," 9th Raul Prebisch Lecture delivered at the Palais des Nations, Geneva, October 19, 1998, UNCTAD. Chapter 2 in Ha-Joon Chang (ed.), *The Rebel Within* (London: Wimbledon Publishing Company), pp. 57–93.

Stiglitz, J.E. (1999) "Knowledge As a Global Public Good," in Inge Kaul, Isabelle Grunberg, and Marc A. Stern (eds), *Global Public Goods: International Cooperation in the 21st Century*, United Nations Development Programme (New York: Oxford University Press), pp. 308–325.

Stiglitz, J.E. (2006). *Making Globalization Work* (New York: W.W. Norton).

Stiglitz, J.E. (2008) "The Economic Foundations of Intellectual Property," sixth annual Frey Lecture in Intellectual Property, Duke University, February 16, 2007, *Duke Law Journal*, vol. 57, no. 6, pp. 1693–1724.

Stiglitz, J.E. (2013) "Institutional Design for China's Innovation System," in , J.E. Stiglitz and D. Kennedy (eds), *Law and Economic Development with Chinese*

Characteristics: Institutions for the 21st Century (New York and Oxford: Oxford University Press), pp. 247–277.

Stiglitz, J.E. (forthcoming) "Learning, Growth, and Development: A Lecture in Honor of Sir Partha Dasgupta," publication of the World Bank's Annual Bank Conference on Development Economics 2010: Development Challenges in a Post-Crisis World.

Stiglitz, J.E. and Kennedy, D, (eds) (2013) *Law and Economic Development with Chinese Characteristics: Institutions for the 21st Century.* (Oxford: Oxford University Press).

Stiglitz, J.E. and Uy, M. (1996) "Financial Markets, Public Policy, and the East Asian Miracle," *World Bank Research Observer,* vol. 11, no. 2, pp. 249–276.

Stiglitz, J.E. and Weiss, A. (1981) "Credit Rationing in Markets with Imperfect Information," *American Economic Review,* vol. 71, no. 3, pp. 393–411.

Wade, R. (1990) *Governing the Market: Economic Theory and the Role of Government in East Asia's Industrialization* (Princeton, NJ: Princeton University Press).

1.4

Discussion of Bruce Greenwald and Joseph Stiglitz, "Industrial Policies, the Creation of a Learning Society, and Economic Development"

Josh Lerner[1]
Harvard University and National Bureau of Economic Research

This fascinating paper looks at one of the most important issues in the economics of technological change: the wedge between the social and private returns from innovation. The authors explore the implications of this important gap – often ignored in discussions of industrial policy – for the promotion of firms and technologies.

In his famous 1962 essay, Kenneth Arrow focused economists' attention on the non-rival nature of knowledge and the attendant disclosure problem. The substantial information problems surrounding R&D projects make them difficult to finance: an idea about a new innovation, unless protected by a patent or other legal means, can be readily taken and used by competitors, thereby rendering it much less valuable.[2] As a result, an inventor seeking to sell a new idea faces a real dilemma. Unless he or she reveals key details about the invention, no one is likely to offer the inventor a substantial payment for the idea. But once the details of the breakthrough are revealed, the potential buyer has every incentive to express a lack of interest, and then exploit the idea illicitly. While inventors attempt to limit these problems by requiring potential buyers to sign confidentiality agreements, these documents frequently prove to be ineffective, as the long and sad list of lawsuits between inventors and potential licensees illustrates. As a result, firms with promising projects may be unable to pursue them.

The sensitivity of innovation to capital constraints has been corroborated in a number of studies. For instance, Himmelberg and Petersen look at a panel of small firms and show that the sensitivity of R&D investment to cash flow seems to be considerably greater than that of physical investment.[3] This suggests that the problems discussed above are if anything more severe in affecting innovation as opposed to more traditional capital investments.

Dwelling on this fundamental challenge, the authors highlight several key implications for industrial policy. In particular, policymakers must not just focus on "picking winners." Rather, a major challenge should be addressing externalities, particularly those which make innovation difficult.

These policy measures, they suggest, should take several forms. On the one hand, it is important that firms can take advantage of ideas that have developed earlier. Thus, a stable environment to encourage cumulative learning is critical, as is support for human capital accumulation. Other steps are designed to make sure that once a firm develops a crucial idea, it will be able to finance it. In particular, the authors promote the public funding of R&D and the promotion of financial intermediaries as strategies that can address these issues.

These points are undoubtedly critical ones. The focus on creating an environment where firms can learn from their predecessors and protect their ideas is absolutely critical, as is often neglected in discussions of industrial policy. At the same time – as the authors acknowledge – the design and implementation of policies to effect these ends are complex, and often face substantial challenges.

We could discuss many topics here, from intellectual property policy to the enforceability of non-competition agreements. I will just focus on one illustrative area, the optimal scale and scope of firms. The authors in the paper seem to be enthusiastic about the benefits of size when it comes to innovation: as they state, "in large organizations ... the required degree of stability and continuity is much more likely to be present ... Long-lived firms can value these distant benefits." This recommendation suggests that policymakers subsidize or otherwise encourage innovation in larger concerns.

At first glance, this recommendation seems reasonable. Indeed, the lion's share of R&D spending takes place today in industrial laboratories: in 2008, for instance, corporations accounted for 74 percent of US research spending. And corporate research today is dominated by the very largest of firms.[4] The very largest firms still have the dominant share: firms with over 10,000 employees still represent over half the research spending. Those with fewer than 500 employees, a traditional definition of small business, account for under one-fifth of the total expenditures.[5]

These same patterns hold globally.[6] These patterns also hold when we look at aggregate R&D spending globally. The USA alone accounts for 35 percent of world R&D spending, towering above the amount invested in such nations as China, Germany, and Japan. As in the US, the private sector drives R&D elsewhere For instance, in Japan, business enterprises perform 76 percent of the R&D; in China, 73 percent; and across the European Union, 61 percent.

These data suggest a key question: why has the corporate lab been so central for innovation? Part of the answer lies in the sheer difficulty of developing new technologies. Many of the most important technological discoveries do not simply involve just one expert in a given area working alone. Rather, they entail insights from a variety of disciplines being combined. The process of innovation frequently draws together individuals from a variety of perspectives, who must share information and combine ideas.

Having a diverse team at these laboratories might also have a plethora of benefits after the discovery is made. A diverse team within a laboratory is likely to be more effective in identifying new applications for recently developed technologies, or complementary ideas developed elsewhere to purchase or license. If these kinds of discoveries really do need multiple experts, it makes sense to locate them in a single lab. Having them dispersed would raise too many complicating issues because trade in ideas among free agents is a challenging matter, as the Arrow argument above highlights. By bringing all the experts together under the umbrella of a single organization, the free flow of ideas can be greatly enhanced.

Another reason to bring the scientists together is the benefits of proximity in encouraging knowledge flows. Ever since the Alfred Marshall's pioneering 1890 economics textbook,[7] there has been an appreciation of the benefit from locating innovators near to each other. In particular, he highlighted the importance of "knowledge spillovers": transfers of insights in a myriad of different ways between nearby researchers.

But in recent decades, large companies have begun rethinking their commitments to large R&D expenditures, as they sought to take stock of their central lab's achievements. As David Hounshell put it, "Du Pont had no new nylons. Kodak had no radically new system of photography."[8] Even at the most successful laboratories from a scientific viewpoint, such as IBM, questions regarding the returns from these substantial investments were increasingly raised: these facilities were often seen as producing top-class science, but having limited relevance to the firms' commercial needs. And, more specifically, critics wondered about the effectiveness with which research laboratories were organized and managed. In a prescient 1964 essay, Joseph Baily wrote, "We are largely fumbling in the dark as we try to insure [researchers'] motivation, or to 'manage' the creative talents we have hired them to contribute."[9]

And indeed, the weight of the empirical economic evidence – for instance, Mike Jensen's comparisons of the stock of firms' R&D and new capital expenditures to their market value[10] and Bronwyn Hall's[11] computations of the return for firms from their investments in R&D relative to to more traditional capital expenditures (for example, in new machine tools or factories) – have suggested that the returns to innovation expenditures in large, public firms have not been high. Agency problems in the management of these projects and difficulties in designing appropriate incentives schemes have each taken their toll. As a result, firms have been pulling back from many of the ambitious visions as to what central research facilities could accomplish in the face of repeated disappointments. Instead, there has been much greater emphasis on "open innovation": investments in young firms, the opening up of technology development through contests and open source projects, and joint venture with universities.

The problems with innovation in large firms have also affected industrial policies. Consider, for instance, efforts to promote the electronics industry in the 1980s.[12] Following the ascension of François Mitterrand and the Socialist Party in 1981, the government spent about $6 billion to acquire a number of lumbering electronics giants, including CII Honeywell Bull and Thomson. Meanwhile, a number of promising smaller firms in the industries were either acquired directly by the government or pressured into merging with the giants.

The results were an unmitigated disaster. At the existing firms, once the government subsidies were in place, a tide of red ink turned into a torrent, with annual subsidies for annual losses growing from $226 million in 1980 to $4.6 billion in 1982. The vast majority of the ideas championed by young firms were extinguished as they became part of stultifying bureaucracies. Nor did the government put any real pressure on the established firms to develop their younger partners' ideas: the public bureaucrats' single-minded focus was on preserving employment at the large factories already in existence. The contrast with Taiwan's successful efforts to stimulate its computer industry in the 1990s, where numerous subsidies were given to small firms with the expectation that many would fail but a few succeed brilliantly, could not be more stark.[13]

Even if we look just at the primary goal of the French government, their efforts to preserve jobs at existing French computing employers were essentially futile. The government was forced to sell off many firms, with attendant job losses, in the face of a political uproar over the size of the subsidies. This affected even those companies that it continued to hold, such as Bull (in which the government held a majority stake until 1997), where employment fell to 8,000 from a peak of 44,000 in 1991.

Thus, undoubtedly, the issues raised in this paper are important ones. Capturing knowledge spillovers, and overcoming the Arrow information problems, are undoubtedly critical. Policymakers, as the authors argue, must pay more attention to these issues. But at the same time, the implementation of these broad goals poses numerous tricky issues.

Notes

1. I thank workshop participants for helpful comments. Research support was provided by Harvard Business School's Division of Research. This essay was drawn in part from my two books, *The Architecture of Innovation* (Boston and London: Harvard Business Press and Oxford University Press, 2012), and *Boulevard of Broken Dreams: Why Public Efforts to Boost Entrepreneurship and Venture Capital Have Failed – and What to Do About It* (Princeton: Princeton University Press, 2009).

2. "Economic Welfare and the Allocation of Resources for Invention," in Richard R. Nelson (ed.), *The Rate and Direction of Inventive Activity: Economic and Social Factors* (Princeton, NJ: Princeton University Press for the National Bureau of Economic Research, 1962), pp. 609–626.
3. Charles P. Himmelberg and Bruce C. Petersen, "R&D and Internal Finance: A Panel Study of Small Firms in High-Tech Industries," *Review of Economics and Statistics*, vol. 76 (1994), pp. 38–51.
4. This analysis is based on US National Science Board, *Science and Engineering Indicators* (Washington: National Science Board, 2011), Appendix Table 4-12, and similar tables in earlier editions.
5. This analysis includes only at the spending of non-Federal funds.
6. This analysis is based on National Science Board, *Science and Engineering Indicators*.
7. *Principles of Economics* (London: Macmillan, 1890).
8. David A. Hounshell, "The Evolution of Industrial Research in the United States," in Richard S. Rosenbloom and William J. Spencer (eds), *Engines of Innovation: U.S. Industrial Research at the End of an Era* (Boston, MA: Harvard Business School Press, 1996), p. 50.
9. "General Introduction," in Charles D. Orth, III, Joseph C. Bailey, and Francis W. Wolek (eds), *Administering Research and Development: The Behavior of Scientists and Engineers in Organizations* (Homewood, IL: Richard D. Irwin, 1964). The quote is from page 5.
10. "The Modern Industrial Revolution, Exit, and the Failure of Internal Control Systems," *Journal of Finance*, vol. 48 (1993), pp. 831–880. These numbers are taken from the updated and corrected version posted at http://courses.essex.ac.uk/ac/ac928/jensenfailureinternal%20control.pdf.
11. Bronwyn H. Hall, "The Stock Market's Valuation of R&D Investment During the 1980's," *American Economic Review Papers and Proceedings*, vol. 83 (May 1993), pp. 259–264.
12. This account is based in part on Eli Noam, "Telecommunications in Transition," in Robert W. Crandall and Kenneth Flamm (eds), *Changing the Rules: Technological Change, International Competition, and Regulation in Telecommunications* (Washington, DC: Brookings Institution Press, 1989); and Victoria Shannon, "Bull S.A., the Computer Company, Aims to Emerge from Dependence on France," *New York Times*, August 25, 2003.
13. For more about the Taiwanese incentive programs, see Kenneth L. Kraemer, Jason Dedrick, Chin-Yeong Hwang, Tze-Chen Tu, and Chee-Sing Yap, "Entrepreneurship, Flexibility, and Policy Coordination: Taiwan's Computer Industry," *Information Society*, vol. 12 (1996), pp. 215–249; and Fu-Lai T. Yu, Ho-Don Yan, and Shen-Yu Chen, "Adaptive Entrepreneurship and Taiwan's Economic Dynamics," *Laissez-Faire (Universidad Francisco Marroquin)*, vol. 24–25 (2006), pp. 57–74.

Part II
Special Issues for Developing Countries

2.1
Technology Policies and Learning with Imperfect Governance

*Mushtaq H. Khan**
Department of Economics, SOAS, University of London

Developing countries can grow rapidly by absorbing known technologies from more advanced countries. Yet developing countries often find it difficult to absorb even relatively simple technologies even when they have the resources to buy the relevant machines and have workers with the appropriate levels of formal education who are willing to work for relatively low wages. The reasons are often contracting problems that prevent critical investments being organized. A number of potentially relevant contracting failures are well known but a particularly important one is underemphasized. Developing countries typically lack the *organizational and technological capabilities* embedded in firms that are necessary for using new technologies to produce competitive products. Building organizations that can competitively use the new technologies is a difficult task that is subject to significant contracting failures. Developing the appropriate organizational capabilities involves the exertion of significant effort in the acquisition of tacit knowledge, a process that is difficult to observe and control. This exposes financiers to significant contracting risks that can result in non-investment or the failure to achieve competitiveness. In general, solutions to contracting failures require properly designed corrective policies and appropriate governance capabilities on the part of the state. Developing countries typically have limited governance capabilities and limited potential of developing these capabilities in every direction. It is therefore important to identify the precise contracting failures that are most important to address and to design policies that have the greatest chance of being implemented given existing governance capabilities and the feasible improvements in these capabilities. The fit between problems, policies and capabilities can explain why some countries or sectors can do well even when overall governance capabilities are weak.

---

*I would like to thank Pranab Bardhan and Joe Stiglitz for comments on an earlier version of the paper.

Technology policies (often also described as industrial policies) describe a range of policies that could in principle address a wide variety of contracting failures using instruments that assist the parties involved to move closer to desirable outcomes. However, the problem is that while private contracting in developing countries is subject to many contracting failures, their states also lack many of the critical enforcement and governance capabilities required to effectively implement many corrective policies. The general observation is that developing countries have weak or imperfect governance, and this often leads to the policy advice that they should steer clear of industrial policies. This avoids the problem of government failures but it obviously does not make the underlying market failures disappear. However, the historical evidence makes it painfully obvious that given imperfect governance, not all technology policies are likely to achieve the desired results. To be effective, technology policies have to be designed to be effective given the institutions and governance capabilities of particular states. This implies that the relevant contracting failures have to be properly identified to determine the problems policies have to address. Secondly, there are usually many possible responses to any particular contracting problem, and not all of them may be equally enforceable in every context. The second step is therefore to select the response that is most likely to be effective given the relative power of the interests affected by the policy in the local context. Finally, for policies to be successful, some governance capabilities may also need to be developed in critical agencies to monitor and enforce particular policies.

Understanding the interrelationships between these factors can help to explain why some countries have done rather better with industrial policies than others in contexts of weak governance. While all developing countries are far removed from the textbook requirements of "good governance" (strong enforcement of a rule of law, government accountability and well-defined property rights), some have been better or luckier in adopting policies that were more effective in the context of their governance, and better at developing the capabilities of critical agencies that enabled these strategies to be effectively implemented. These insights can help us to design better technology policies in countries that have performed less well. Although the policy solutions for addressing many technology-adoption problems can appear to be quite similar (for instance, providing temporary subsidies to firms), the governance conditions for ensuring their success can be quite different depending on the underlying contractual problem that the subsidy aims to resolve and the specific policy solutions adopted in response.

The literature on technology and industrial policies identifies a number of different contracting problems affecting technology adoption. It is likely that a country faces more than one problem at any one time. However, policy needs to ensure that the most general problems (the ones that affect all or most cases of technology acquisition) are addressed first. Unfortunately, the most general problem is not necessarily the easiest to solve in terms of appropriate policy design and the requisite governance capabilities. At the heart of the technology acquisition problem is the paradox that low-wage countries are unable to achieve competitiveness using freely-available technologies that they should in principle be able to use. The reason for this is that competitiveness depends not just on wages but also on the productivities of labor, input usage and capital equipment. The productivity of all factors depends not just on the formal technical knowledge of workers and managers but also and primarily on the *tacit knowledge* of organizational and technological capabilities that is embedded in the routines of the production team as a whole.

The *technological capabilities* of workers and managers refer to their abilities to use machines and technologies properly. These capabilities are partly based on formal education and training but can also depend on on-the-job learning-by-doing. In addition, the productivity of workers, the productivity of input usage and that of capital equipment depends on the organization as a whole working effectively as a team. This is why *organizational capabilities* are possibly even more important for the overall productivity and competitiveness of the firm. Organizational capabilities are embedded in the routines of the organization, and these organizational structures are a form of tacit knowledge that the organization acquires, again often through learning-by-doing and experimentation. Without these technological and organizational capabilities, productivity levels are typically too low for the developing country to competitively engage in production, even if it acquires the machines and has workers and managers who have the formal knowledge that is required for the use of the technology. This is true even for relatively low-technology production processes. The acquisition of tacit knowledge through learning-by-doing is one of the most general problems affecting almost all areas of technology acquisition in developing countries and is subject to important contracting failures. In the absence of solutions to these problems, a new firm or an entire country can find its technology acquisition strategies blocked.

It is widely recognized that the acquisition of tacit knowledge requires learning-by-doing. However, the problem is that "doing" without a large element of effort is not likely to generate much learning. Effort is obviously important in the learning-by-doing processes through which individual workers improve their productivity. But effort is particularly important in developing organizational capabilities because the learning that is involved here involves the organization and reorganization of firms as complex organizations that can work smoothly to produce competitive products. When infant industries fail to graduate into productive enterprises despite decades of "doing" financed by different types of implicit subsidies, it is almost always because there was a failure of organizational learning. The continuous restructuring and fine-tuning of organizations to achieve high levels of productivity and competitiveness is a high effort activity that involves risks and costs for managers and other stakeholders. Change is painful and has distributive implications that are likely to be resisted. Without pressure and even compulsion, doing can continue indefinitely without any organizational learning happening.

The obvious conclusion is that successful learning requires the exertion of a high level of effort *in the learning process*, particularly by management. The effort here refers to the effort in experimenting with and achieving the organizational design and work practices that achieve the required levels of productivity. Effort here does not refer to the effort exerted in the normal production process. The problem is that the appropriate incentives and compulsions for ensuring high levels of learning effort are difficult to enforce. This is the contracting failure that constrains private money flooding in to finance investments in learning-by-doing. But public financing is also likely to be largely wasted if it does not address the underlying contracting problem in ways that can be effectively enforced. This is likely to be the most general contracting problem affecting technology adoption. Even when developing countries succeed in acquiring and installing production facilities using technologies that are theoretically appropriate, they often find their levels of productivity are too low to achieve competitiveness. Missing tacit knowledge about *how to organize the relevant production processes* is usually at the heart of the problem. If the problems constraining the acquisition of technological and organizational capabilities are not solved, solutions to other aspects of the technology adoption problem are not likely to be effective.

Financing learning-by-doing strategies effectively requires appropriate governance capabilities on the part of the state. Discussions about the governance conditions required for effective technology policies used to be dominated by the experiences of East Asian countries, and particularly South Korea. In South Korea, high levels of effort in the learning supported by its industrial policy in the decades after the 1960s were ensured by credible state sanctions on non-performing enterprises. This required bureaucratic capabilities to monitor performance and withdraw support from non-performers and it also required a business sector that could not make political alliances to protect their temporary "learning rents" (Khan, 2000b). This combination of bureaucratic and political conditions is typically lacking in most developing countries. If the South Korean instruments for financing learning were the only ones available, we would have to reach the conclusion that technology policies were not feasible in most developing countries. However, the experience of successful sectors in developing countries with relatively weak governance capabilities shows that other types of financing can be effective in apparently adverse governance conditions. The critical requirement is that institutional and political conditions have to be appropriate for creating credible incentives and compulsions for high levels of effort during the learning process given specific financing instruments. This is illustrated with reference to examples of successful learning-by-doing and technology adoption in India and Bangladesh. The policy conclusion is that technology policy is possible in countries with "imperfect" governance conditions, but only if the financing instruments and sectors supported are compatible with the institutional and political conditions in the country.

Section 2.1.1 sets out a simple model showing how effort in learning determines the likelihood of acquiring the tacit knowledge embedded in organizations that achieve high levels of productivity and competitiveness. For investments in learning to achieve these results, a set of specific contracting failures have to be solved. Attempts to solve other contracting failures that can also plausibly constrain technology acquisition are unlikely to be effective without solutions to this fundamental problem. Section 2.2.2 discusses the variables that affect the likelihood of high levels of effort in the learning process. This part of the analysis draws on the concept of the *political settlement* that describes an equilibrium distribution of power between organizations of different types (Khan, 2010, 2012). Section 2.1.3 summarizes two cases of successful catching up from India and Bangladesh to demonstrate the general argument. The conclusion summarizes the policy messages implied by the analysis.

2.1.1 Tacit knowledge, organizational capabilities and competitiveness

Developing countries trying to absorb new technologies are attempting to produce products that already have a global price for different qualities set by the leading countries using these technologies. The machines and technologies for producing these products are likely to be well known but there may be many variants of competitive organizations using these technologies in different leading countries. These organizational variants reflect differences in local conditions, habits of work of the workforce, infrastructural constraints that have to be dealt with and so on, but in every case, the existing organizations define levels of quality and price that the catching-up country has to match. Protecting domestic markets, granting export subsidies or implicit subsidies of different types can provide infant industries in developing countries with the "loss-financing" to engage in production and learning-by-doing, but unless competitiveness catches up, these strategies become unsustainable in terms of the accumulating subsidy cost.

Competitiveness depends on both price and quality. For a catching-up firm to graduate out of subsidies, it has to achieve a price–quality mix that is globally competitive. Once this is achieved, explicit or implicit subsidies are no longer required. Products can be defined as combinations of characteristics. Broad clusters of characteristics define a particular type of product, but any product also has detailed characteristics of reliability, performance, attractiveness, design and a range of other functions that can distinguish the "quality" of particular products within a broad group (Lancaster 1966; Sutton 2005, 2007). Products can therefore be indexed by quality, with higher-quality cars (for instance) being (in general) more difficult and more expensive to produce, but also attracting a higher price that is high enough to make it worthwhile for producers to always seek to improve product quality.

Developing countries are generally not in the business of innovating new products. This is a relatively small part of the growth process even in middle-income developing countries. Rather, the most important problem for developing countries is to learn how to produce an improving range of products from the qualities that already exist, at a price that is equal to or lower than the ones already available. If a country can produce an existing product of a particular quality at a price lower than that currently prevailing it has a chance of capturing markets from already established producers or extending the market to new consumers. Lower-quality products are generally easier to produce, but for any quality level a maximum price is defined in global markets and a new entrant will not be able to sell its products without a subsidy if it cannot match this price. The problem for developing countries is that they are often unable to produce products of the requisite price–quality combination even when their wages are lower than their competitors and even when they aim at relatively low qualities and technologies.

Higher-quality products have, by definition, a higher selling price, so in general they allow either a higher wage or a higher profit mark-up or both. Improving the quality of products is therefore a way of achieving wage and profit growth. Secondly, productivity growth is likely to be higher in higher-quality products to the extent that these are still the subject of innovation in advanced countries. Developing countries that shift to higher qualities and build the organizations that can effectively produce these qualities are therefore likely to enjoy faster incremental productivity growth by being able to copy or adapt these innovations. At the same time, lower-quality products can become inferior goods as world incomes increase, and global consumers are likely to gradually shift away from goods of lower quality. Finally, lower- quality products are more likely to be targeted as entry points by even poorer countries creating gradual downward pressure on prices. It is therefore both socially and privately desirable to produce the highest quality products that are feasible.

The catching-up problem can therefore be defined as (a) entering globally competitive production for a variety of products at the highest feasible levels of quality, (b) spreading these organizational capabilities broadly to create jobs across the working population and (c) systematically moving up the quality ladder across product categories to achieve wage growth and sustained productivity growth. In reality, many developing countries struggle to produce anything competitively. Some produce a very limited range of competitive products but of low quality and find it difficult to move up the product and quality ladder. A few more advanced developing countries produce a range of competitive products, some of higher quality, but face challenges in achieving quality improvements and even greater challenges in entering new product ranges.

The essential features of the catching-up problem can be described using a simple mark-up pricing model for products of a given quality. The current global price of a particular product of quality Q is set by its cost of production in the country that is currently the global production leader. The unit price can be arithmetically broken down into the unit labor cost plus the unit input cost plus the unit amortized capital cost representing the unit cost of machinery and buildings. This is shown in eq. [1]:

$$P_Q^{global} = \left[\frac{W_Q^{leader}}{\Pi_Q^{leader}} + \sum_i \frac{P_{Qi}}{\alpha_{Qi}^{leader}} + \sum_k \frac{P_{Qk}}{\beta_{Qk}^{leader}} \right] \left(1 + m_Q \right) \quad [1]$$

$$\text{(unit labor cost)} \qquad \text{(unit input cost)} \qquad \text{(unit capital cost)} \qquad \text{(mark-up)}$$

To simplify the notation we do not denote products and simply refer to a particular quality indexed by Q, so Q+1 represents a higher-quality product compared to Q. P_Q^{global} is the international price of a particular product of quality Q. W_Q^{leader} is the wage level in the leading country producing the product of quality Q. Π_Q^{leader} is the productivity of labor in this activity in the leading country, measured by the output per person in this activity. The first term on the right hand side is therefore the unit labor cost.

The second term is the unit input cost. The production of the product requires i inputs as raw materials or semi-manufactured inputs. To simplify, we assume these inputs are globally traded, each with a global price of P_{Qi}. The efficiency with which inputs are used is measured by the productivity of input use (output per unit input). In the leading country, the input productivities of each of the i inputs are represented by α_{Qi}^{leader}. Input productivity primarily measures wastage and input loss due to rejected final products. In many production processes this is a critical determinant of competitiveness.

The third term refers to the unit "capital" cost attributable to the cost of machinery and buildings. There are k inputs of this type, and the most important elements are usually machines, which have a globally traded price, though land and buildings can also be significant cost components in some cases. The unit cost of capital is determined by the fraction of each component of these capital costs attributed to the particular period of production, represented by P_{Qk} divided by the output-capital ratio for each type of capital (the productivity of capital) measured by β_{Qk}^{leader}. As the capital stock that is available in each period is fixed, the output–capital ratio depends critically on the scale of production that determines capacity utilization. The higher the output achieved with any given capital stock, the higher the productivity of capital measured by each β_{Qk}^{leader}. Low capital productivity could therefore be the result of a lack of technological capabilities on the part of the workforce resulting in improper use of machinery but it could also reflect spare capacity if machines and fixed assets are underused because of a suboptimal scale of production. Finally, the mark-up determining price is set at m_Q.

In the same way, the cost of production (in a common currency) in the developing country is the domestic cost $C_Q^{domestic}$ for the product of quality Q, given by an exactly equivalent equation but with the appropriate domestic productivities and prices:

$$C_Q^{domestic} = \left[\frac{W_Q^{domestic}}{\Pi_Q^{domestic}} + \sum_i \frac{P_{Qi}}{\alpha_{Qi}^{domestic}} + \sum_k \frac{P_{Qk}}{\beta_{Qk}^{domestic}} \right] (1 + m_Q) \qquad [2]$$

The follower country achieves competitiveness when its $C_Q^{domestic} \leq P_Q^{global}$. The globally traded prices of inputs and machinery are typically similar in the follower and leader countries but wages and some input costs are likely to be lower in the former. The cost of borrowing, which affects the amortized cost of capital, may be higher in the follower (reflecting a higher risk premium), but the difference may not be very significant. It may therefore appear that the developing country should be able to achieve competitiveness for many simple technologies for which the appropriate formal skills exist since its wage level is lower: $W_Q^{domestic} < W_Q^{leader}$, and most other prices are either similar (globally tradable inputs and machinery) or lower (possibly for some non-tradable inputs like land and buildings). But in fact developing countries usually cannot break into the production even of relatively low technology (low quality) products because they typically suffer from significant productivity disadvantages that more than negate their wage and other cost advantages. Output per person is generally much lower, $\Pi_Q^{domestic} < \Pi_Q^{leader}$, as are many input and capital productivities, $\alpha_{Qi}^{domestic} < \alpha_{Qi}^{leader}$ and $\beta_{Qk}^{domestic} < \beta_{Qk}^{leader}$. These productivity differentials explain why despite low wages, the follower country typically has a higher cost of production than the global price even for relatively low technology products.

It may appear that a low wage could compensate for these productivity differentials, but in reality that wage may have to be much lower than is feasible. A more profound problem is that in many cases, even *zero* wages may not be able to compensate for a lower efficiency of input and capital productivity. This is because inputs and capital equipment have global prices that have to be paid. If $\alpha_{Qi}^{domestic} < \alpha_{Qi}^{leader}$ for expensive globally traded inputs, the greater wastage of inputs alone could result in a higher domestic cost of production *even if the domestic unit labor cost could be pushed to zero*. This is why efficiency in controlling the wastage of inputs and reducing product rejection is often a critical variable in achieving competitiveness. In addition, the productivity of critical capital equipment is often lower, with $\beta_{Qk}^{domestic} < \beta_{Qk}^{leader}$ as a result of machinery not being properly set up, or the optimal scale of production not being achieved. Indeed, a small disadvantage in these productivity variables across a number of inputs and types of capital could mean that even with *zero* wages, the cost of production in the developing country may be higher. In fact, wages are typically a relatively small part of the cost of production even in labor-intensive manufacturing processes. Competitiveness, even in low technology products, therefore depends more on the level and growth of productivity rather than on cost advantages.

While it is conceptually useful to distinguish between labor, input and capital productivity, all of these productivity measures are affected by the ways in which production is set up and organized by the management and workers operating machinery of a specific type. The productivity of all inputs including labor depends on how effectively the production process is *organized*. Output per person, Π_Q, depends on a variety of economy-wide and firm-level factors. The economy-wide determinants of firm labor productivity include the quality of public goods and utilities including the quality of education, infrastructure and the reliability of utility supplies. Firm labor productivity is also determined by firm-level variables like the capital equipment used by labor and the skill and experience of the workforce and management. The technological capabilities of workers are important determinants of firm-level productivity. These depend on their formal training and education but also on their tacit knowledge of operating equipment effectively as a result of learning-by-doing. However, an even more important determinant of firm-level labor productivity is the *organization* of the firm: how teams are set up to ensure a smooth flow of production, how machinery is set up to reduce bottlenecks, how management systems are set up to solve problems and so on. These organizational capabilities are also the result of effective learning-by-doing that results in the evolution of a work organization that achieves high labor productivity.

In the same way, the efficiency of input use, α_{Qi} depends on the same economy-level variables determining the skills and education of the workforce, as well as firm-level variables like the type and sophistication of the capital equipment used and the technological skills of the workforce using this equipment, based on both formal skills and tacit knowledge. In addition, the firm-level organization of production is again often of critical significance. Organizational design is critical for limiting the wastage of raw materials and for maintaining quality so that final products are not rejected, thereby maintaining input productivity at a high level. Finally capital productivity also varies significantly across countries and firms even for machinery of exactly the same type. This too reflects differences in the organization of production and the skills and capabilities of the workers and managers. However, in addition capital productivity is also a function of the scale of production. For firms entering new lines of production, the scale of production can be constrained by the low competitiveness of the firm. This is because as long as a firm suffers from low labor and input productivity, it can only sell its products at a lower profit margin or at a loss. This can prevent it from expanding the scale of production, and the low capital productivity that results can further damage its competitiveness.

Thus, competitiveness and the underlying productivities that determine competitiveness are not just determined by having the right machinery for producing products of a particular quality and having workers and managers with the right levels of formal education and training. It depends more critically on the technological and organizational capabilities of the teams using the machines to produce products, and both sets of capabilities depend on the successful outcomes of difficult learning-by-doing processes. Early development theory and practice emphasized investment in modern machinery but we now know this is not sufficient without strategies for achieving competitiveness. Crippling differences in productivity persist across countries using identical machinery (Clark and Wolcott, 2002; Sutton, 2007). While the economy-level constraints on productivity are widely recognized, the firm-level *technological and organizational capabilities* of workers and management are probably much more important in explaining why some countries take off when they do. Take-offs are rarely triggered by prior improvements in economy-wide infrastructural conditions, though sustaining growth clearly requires an improving efficiency in the delivery of education and infrastructure.

The importance of firm-level organizational capabilities as the critical determinant of competitiveness is based on two interrelated observations. First, there is the observation from observers of technological capabilities that much of the technological and organizational knowledge necessary for competitiveness is *tacit knowledge* embedded in routines (Nelson and Winter, 1982; Dosi, 1988; Pelikan, 1988; Perez and Soete, 1988). Engaging in effective productive activity requires a mix of formal or codifiable knowledge (knowledge that can be communicated in words or symbols) and uncodifiable "knowing-how-to" knowledge that is embedded in unconscious and often complex routines. The latter is defined as tacit knowledge and the significance of its non-codified form is that acquiring this knowledge requires learning-by-doing rather than attending formal courses (Polanyi, 1967). The process of learning efficient routines inevitably involves practice and the adaptation of practice to local conditions rather than reading off blueprints from a manual. Compared to the difficulty of "acquiring" this tacit knowledge, buying the machines and setting up the factory are often much the easier parts of the process of technology acquisition and growth.

The difference between technological and organizational capabilities is often difficult to distinguish in practice because the former can depend on the latter. Technological capabilities refer to the productivity of individual workers which can depend on their tacit knowledge of how to use particular machines effectively. Organizational capabilities refer to the design of the organization that determines the productivity of each individual worker, and this also determines input and capital productivity. The organization of production refers to things such as setting up the layout of the machines so that production bottlenecks are avoided given the pace of work that can be achieved with local conditions, implementing effective quality control routines with incentives that are appropriate for local conditions, managing inventories taking into account local infrastructural constraints, meeting orders on time and so on.

The importance of the organizational capabilities of a production team as a whole becomes obvious when workers migrate from developing countries to more advanced ones. Their individual productivity jumps when they join a modern organization. In migrating to join an already efficient organization, an individual worker rapidly slots into existing routines and thereby rapidly improves their individual productivity, even in terms of the learning-by-doing that improves their individual technological capabilities. In contrast, if the whole team is operating with the routines of an inefficient organization or still experimenting with new routines, the individual productivity of each worker is likely to remain low. Evolving these routines takes effort from all the stakeholders as it involves experimentation and reallocation of duties and responsibilities until the organization as a whole achieves competitiveness. Even relatively low-technology production of relatively low-quality products like garments requires acquiring a huge amount of tacit organizational knowledge embedded in the routines of interaction between the hundreds or even thousands of workers and managers in the organization.

Secondly, the literature on technological and organizational capability also points out that tacit knowledge is largely acquired through processes of *learning-by-doing* (Lall, 1992, 2000a, 2000b, 2003). If a firm has to engage in learning-by-doing to achieve competitiveness, the implication is that it has to begin production *before* it achieves competitiveness. This is very significant. Investment in a firm using new technologies in a developing country therefore requires some implicit or explicit form of loss-financing as the organization cannot *by definition* achieve competitiveness for some considerable time. This marks a very significant difference between advanced and developing countries. In the former, the financing of machinery and buildings to set up production may face uncertainties in terms of markets and prices if the product is a new one, but the organizational capabilities of the firm and its workers are typically not in question. In developing countries, the markets and prices are well known by definition because the product is a well-known one, the uncertainty is about the organizational capabilities of the team attempting to produce the product. While the uncertainty faced by innovating firms in advanced countries is well understood, the uncertainty faced by learning firms in developing countries is often ignored in economic theory and policy.

In principle, the lower profits or even losses that firms face during their period of organizational capability development could be privately financed as there is the potential of future profits. The absence of significant private engagement in investments in learning-by-doing in developing countries suggests the presence of important contracting failures that keeps private investors away from this difficult task. The difficulty is not surprising given that a locally specific organizational design is required to achieve competitiveness. External investors who may finance the learning have neither a blueprint of the organizational design that may work nor can they easily observe the effort the production team is putting in to achieve the competitive organization rapidly. In practice, governments in the past have therefore played a significant role in financing infant industry strategies. However, the relative paucity of successful infant industry programmes demonstrates the difficulty of getting the governance capabilities right for ensuring successful outcomes in these public financing strategies. Clearly, ensuring high levels of effort in these learning processes is by no means a simple affair.

The loss-financing required to engage in learning-by-doing depends on the gap between the domestic cost of production and the global price at that quality. The loss financing that would allow production (and learning-by-doing) to commence can be measured as a per unit "subsidy," s_Q, which brings the initially higher domestic cost of production $C_Q^{domestic}$ into line with the global price P_Q^{global}. The "subsidy" does not have to be a transfer from government and could be private loss financing in the form of investors accepting a lower mark-up or putting in additional cash to cover a period of loss-making. When the loss-financing involves a public subsidy, this can also be delivered in a variety of ways, some explicit, others more subtle. The possibilities include export subsidies, import protection, subsidized interest rates, subsidized inputs or infrastructure, or a cash subsidy. Thus a variety of financing instruments are available to enable learning-by-doing to commence, and in general we can describe these instruments as ways of providing "rents for learning" (Khan, 2000a).

The essential features of the problem can be described by focusing on the situation where the domestic firm can produce products of quality Q, but at a higher cost than the current global price. The required effective rate of subsidy, s_Q, is given by the equality:

$$C_Q^{domestic}\left(1-s_Q\right)=P_Q^{global} \qquad [3]$$

Inserting eq. [2] that defines $C_Q^{domestic}$ into this gives the required s_Q:

$$s_Q = 1 - \frac{P_Q^{global}}{(1+m_Q)} \left[\frac{W_Q^{domestic}}{\Pi_Q^{domestic}} + \sum_i \frac{P_{Qi}}{\alpha_{Qi}^{domestic}} + \sum_k \frac{P_{Qk}}{\beta_{Qk}^{domestic}} \right]^{-1} \qquad [4]$$

If follows from [4] that:

$$\frac{\partial s_Q}{\partial P_Q^{global}}, \frac{\partial s_Q}{\partial \Pi_Q^{domestic}}, \frac{\partial s_Q}{\partial \alpha_{Qi}^{domestic}}, \frac{\partial s_Q}{\partial \beta_{Qk}^{domestic}} < 0$$

The required rate of subsidy declines if the global price rises, or if domestic labor productivity, input productivity or capital productivity rise. It follows that the more rapidly domestic labor, input and capital productivities grow, the sooner the subsidy can be removed. The subsidy per unit required for entering production is also likely to be higher for higher quality levels. Lower and higher quality versions of the same product are indexed by Q and Q+1. Using [3], the per-unit subsidy required in each case is shown in equations [5] and [6].

$$s_Q = 1 - \frac{P_Q^{global}}{C_Q^{domestic}} \qquad [5]$$

And

$$s_{Q+1} = 1 - \frac{P_{Q+1}^{global}}{C_{Q+1}^{domestic}} \qquad [6]$$

Under plausible assumptions $s_{Q+1} > s_Q$, meaning a higher subsidy is required if a firm wants to engage in producing higher-quality products. The organization required to produce a more complex product is generally also more complex. The gap in tacit knowledge is therefore likely to be greater for constructing the more complex organization. Both the gap in labor productivity and gaps in input productivities are likely to be greater in higher-quality products because the latter typically require more sophisticated production routines and more sophisticated management of inputs. The greater labor and input productivity gaps between the two countries in quality Q+1 compared to quality Q can be represented as a set of inequalities:

$$\frac{\Pi_{Q+1}^{leader}}{\Pi_{Q+1}^{domestic}} > \frac{\Pi_Q^{leader}}{\Pi_Q^{domestic}} \quad and \quad \frac{\alpha_{Q+1}^{leader}}{\alpha_{Q+1}^{domestic}} > \frac{\alpha_Q^{leader}}{\alpha_Q^{domestic}} \quad for\ some\ or\ all\ i \qquad [7]$$

The bigger gap in organizational knowledge for higher-quality products is also likely to show up in lower initial capital productivity for higher-quality products. In addition, capital productivity in higher qualities is likely to be further affected by the fact that higher-quality production often requires more expensive machinery and is therefore likely to require a larger scale of production to become competitive. The low initial competitiveness of the firm can therefore create a further problem because the firm may find it difficult to achieve the scale economies to raise its output–capital ratio, implying a greater gap in capital productivity in higher quality products:

$$\frac{\beta_{Q+1}^{leader}}{\beta_{Q+1}^{domestic}} > \frac{\beta_{Q}^{leader}}{\beta_{Q}^{domestic}} \text{ for some or all } k \tag{8}$$

Returning to equations [1] and [2] we know that the costs of production in both countries are inversely proportional to their labor, input and capital productivities. Given the likelihood that some or all of the inequalities in [7] and [8] are likely to hold, it must be the case that

$$\frac{P_{Q+1}^{global}}{C_{Q+1}^{domestic}} < \frac{P_{Q}^{global}}{C_{Q}^{domestic}} \tag{9}$$

The inequality in [9] says that the cost of production in the developing country is greater (relative to the global price) for the higher-quality product compared to the lower-quality product. Using inequality [9] and comparing equations [5] and [6] it follows that a greater subsidy per unit will be required to overcome the initial competitiveness gap in the higher-quality product compared to the lower quality product.

$$s_{Q+1} > s_Q \tag{10}$$

These results suggest a number of propositions.

Proposition 1. *The loss-financing required to begin production is in general higher the higher the quality of the product and, moreover, the subsidy will be required for longer as more complex organizational capabilities have to be developed.*

As against this, the development of more complex organizational capabilities has a number of advantages.

Proposition 2. *The production of higher-quality products is desirable simply because their production adds more value relative to lower quality products.*

A further proposition is plausible. Economics textbooks often show tech-nical progress as an outward shift of a production frontier for a country. In reality, this is misleading because improvements in technological capa-bilities are likely to be localized around specific technologies (Atkinson and Stiglitz, 1969; Stiglitz, 1987). The localization of productivity improvements is even more likely if competitiveness is embedded in the routines of par-ticular organizations. In this case successful learning is likely to benefit the future adoption of technologies that are similar or closely related, rather than raising potential productivity across all technologies. Thus, we are likely to see "bumpy" improvements in productivity clustered around par-ticular technologies. This can explain why countries specialize in clusters of related products, possibly triggered by the random success of learning-by- doing in particular sectors. This is why it can be advantageous to acquire organizational capabilities in more advanced technologies producing higher quality products. Innovation in advanced countries is also more likely in higher quality products like electronics than lower quality products like garments. A follower country that has organizations capable of producing higher quality products is therefore more likely to benefit from further pro-ductivity growth by adopting incremental improvements in these products as innovation happens in more advanced countries.

Proposition 3. *Learning-by-doing improves organizational capabilities for pro-ducing related products and if future productivity growth is likely to be faster in higher quality products, it is beneficial to develop more complex organizational capabilities.*

The development challenge is therefore to accelerate the movement up the quality ladder subject to feasibility defined by the loss-financing capa-bilities of the society and its ability to solve the contracting failures that result in adverse outcomes for loss financing strategies.

Figure 2.1.1 summarizes some of the fundamental issues facing catching up and technology acquisition in developing countries. The competitiveness curve for a country summarizes its distance from global competitiveness across different quality products. The x-axis measures the quality of the product, and the y-axis the follower's competitiveness in producing that quality. Competitiveness is measured by the ratio $\frac{P_Q^{global}}{C_Q^{domestic}}$. A higher ratio therefore implies greater competitiveness of our country given the prices set by the leader. When this ratio is 1 or higher our country can sell a product of this quality in global markets and therefore the horizontal line at 1 can be read as the global competitiveness frontier for our country. When the ratio is less than 1 for a particular quality, our country will either not be able to produce that quality or will require (temporary) loss-financing to allow pro-duction. The required rate of "subsidy," s_Q, equals $1-\frac{P_Q^{global}}{C_Q^{domestic}}$ in eq. [5], and is

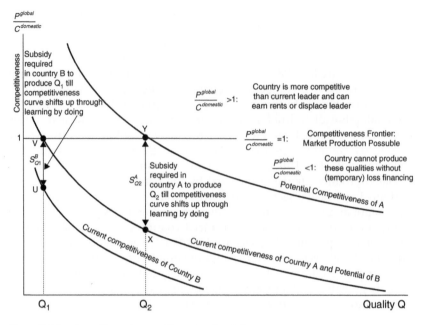

Figure 2.1.1   Loss-financing and learning-by-doing

shown in Figure 2.1.1 as the gap between the global competitiveness frontier (the horizontal line at $P/C = 1$) and current competitiveness at quality Q defined by the current competitiveness curve.

The competitiveness curve is downward sloping because although the world prices of higher-quality products are higher (which is why they are more desirable to produce), the cost of production in the follower country is even higher, giving it a greater disadvantage in higher-quality products. The greater productivity gap in higher qualities will force market-reliant developing countries to specialize in low-quality products. This may have nothing to do with the relative price of labor and capital as in standard neoclassical theory. Consistent with proposition 1, it is possible to imagine a developing country like B in Figure 2.1.1 where current organizational capabilities are so low that it cannot even produce the lowest quality of the product. In extreme cases, some developing countries may struggle to produce competitive qualities of any product. The competitiveness curve can be extended to apply to related products of different complexity. For instance, we could see different "qualities" as parts of a vertically organized value chain. Low qualities could be low value-added parts of the value chain (like packing and assembling), medium qualities could be the production of intermediate products going into the assembly and higher qualities could be design, product development and marketing. Once again, the typical developing country would struggle to locate itself at the lower ends of the value chain where the organizational gap was less challenging, and many may not even succeed in that. At an even more general level, we could use the capability curve to think about choices across all products ranked by production complexity for which "quality" is a proxy.

Figure 2.1.1 suggests that a country like B will need loss-financing of s_{Q1}^B from the outset to begin production even of low-quality products Q_1 at point U. The success of a strategy of loss-financing would be measured by the pace at which productivity increased as a result of learning-by-doing. Successful learning-by-doing should result in the competitiveness curve moving upward till the loss-financing was no longer required at V. Note that this does not necessarily require achieving levels of productivity equal to the leader country because the follower is likely to have a wage and cost advantage for some inputs. Sustained productivity growth is therefore likely to raise the follower's competitiveness to more than 1, in which case the follower could either earn a rent (a mark-up higher than m_Q) at the global price or it could bid down the global price in these qualities to below a price acceptable to the leader, thereby displacing the leader from these segments of the market and achieving more sales. If the latter is the more profitable option, the developing country becomes the leader for that quality and the global price is eventually defined by the cost of production and market power of the new leader.

Finally, proposition 3 tells us that if future technological progress is localized around higher qualities and technologies, it may be desirable to further accelerate the move up the quality ladder to the points where innovation is still happening in more advanced countries. In Figure 2.1.1 the potential future productivity growth at quality Q_1 may be relatively low because the technology is already mature and no further product and process innovations may happen at this quality level. Thus, for country A, which can produce Q_1 competitively, the imperative may be to move to a higher quality not only to prepare for future competition from country B, but also to enjoy faster productivity growth clustered around quality Q_2. Thus, for country A, there may be a policy justification to assist learning-by-doing around quality Q_2 by organizing temporary loss-financing of $s_{Q_2}^A$. The challenge for A would be to go from point X to point Y to achieve competitiveness at this higher quality level. This would not only allow the country to raise its domestic value-added and living standards, it may also ensure faster productivity growth in the future.

But if temporary loss-financing can assist a country to raise its productivity through learning-by-doing, how high should a country aim? Proposition 1 tells us that given existing capabilities, the higher the quality level that the country tries to achieve, the greater the financing cost measured by s_Q. Moreover, the greater the gap with leading countries at that quality, the longer is the catching up likely to take to reach the global competitiveness frontier. As a result, trying to aim too high may involve excessively long periods of subsidization. Moreover, the competitiveness gap is only partially due to the absence of tacit knowledge. Some of the gap could also be due to levels of formal education and skills and the poor quality of economy-level public goods. If the initial gap is too big no amount of firm-level experience and learning-by-doing may remove it entirely. As both the social time preference and the cost of finance in poor countries are likely to be high, there is a limit to how high up the quality ladder it is feasible to go.

2.1.2   Learning, effort and governance

Investments in new sectors can be constrained by a variety of contracting failures. However, the contracting failures that affect learning are different from other contracting failures that can constrain investments for other reasons. These include several different types of appropriability problems limiting future profits in the presence of externalities and the costs of coordinating complementary investments. The solutions to different contracting failures can appear to be deceptively similar, for instance many of them can involve some form of subsidy or assistance. In principle, several contracting failures may also be operating simultaneously to constrain investments in technology acquisition. Nevertheless, distinguishing different contracting failures is important because the governance requirements for effectively addressing them can be markedly different. Policies supporting technology acquisition in the past often yielded poor results because the relevant contracting failures were not properly identified and understood. As a result, policies were not designed to be effective in solving these contracting problems with existing governance capabilities, nor were the governance capabilities necessary for the success of specific policies identified and developed.

Table 2.1.1 outlines a number of critical contracting failures affecting technology acquisition, the likely policy responses and the governance capabilities required to make the policies effective. Most of these contracting failures have been discussed in the literature but the differences in the governance capabilities required to address them have not received sufficient attention (Khan, 2009). The positive externalities of investments in skills can result in an appropriability problem for investors and underinvestment in skills (Dosi, 1988; Khan, 2000a). Corrective policy involves subsidizing skills development and the required governance capabilities are to monitor outcomes and withdraw public funding if expected outcomes are not achieved. Spillovers can also affect investments in innovation, which requires the temporary protection of technology rents. While this is primarily a concern for advanced countries that rely on innovation for growth, developing countries may have to protect the intellectual property rights of multinationals

Table 2.1.1 Major contracting failures affecting technology acquisition

Contracting failures affecting investment	Likely policy instruments	Governance capabilities required for implementation
Appropriability problems facing investments in skills: investors cannot capture full benefits of training	Public co-financing of labor training and investments in skills	Capabilities in relevant agencies to ensure financing for training is not misallocated or wasted
Appropriability problems facing innovators: Poor protection of innovation rents can discourage advanced technology investors	Protection of IPRs. But TRIPS may be too restrictive and MNCs may have weak incentives to transfer technologies	Enforcement capabilities for IPRs but also policies and strategies to encourage technology transfer by MNCs
Appropriability problems facing "discovery": First movers do not capture full benefits of discovering comparative advantage	Subsidies for first mover start-up companies in new sectors	Capability to make subsidies time limited
Failures of Coordination: Complementary supporting sectors do not develop, constraining investment	Indicative or incentivized strategies for coordinating investments	Significant governance capabilities required to coordinate and discipline investments across sectors
Problem of Contracting High Effort in Learning: Financing technological-organizational learning fails because of low effort	Public co-financing or sharing of risks of financing the learning of tacit technological and organizational capabilities	Financing instruments must be compatible with governance capabilities to ensure credible compulsions for high effort learning-by-doing

Source: Author.

in order to attract advanced technology investments (Hoekman et al., 2004). Apart from a capability to protect intellectual property rights, technology transfer also requires significant negotiating skills on the part of policymakers in developing countries to negotiate technology transfer strategies with multinationals (Khan, 2000a; Stiglitz, 2007).

A further set of spillovers affect investments in "discovering" new areas of comparative advantage (Hausmann and Rodrik, 2003). Although the proposition that countries have hidden comparative advantages that need to be discovered is not particularly convincing, the possibility that first movers may not be able to capture the full benefits of their investment can justify subsidizing investments in new sectors. One reason that first movers may fail to get the full benefit of their discovery is that profits may be bid down by imitators whose entry pushes up wages. To the extent that this problem dampens investment in discovery, the appropriate policy response is to subsidize investments in new sectors and the governance capability required is to ensure that the subsidies are only available to reduce the costs of the start-up phase.

A further problem is that of coordination failures affecting investments across sectors (Rosenstein-Rodan, 1943; Nurkse, 1953; Scitovsky, 1954; Murphy et al., 1989). This problem is well known in the development literature, but solving it is difficult and requires significant capabilities in information gathering, understanding demand and supply complementarities and implementing the coordination effectively. These capabilities are typically missing in developing countries and development planning efforts therefore usually achieve very little. Our focus is on the last of the contracting problems in Table 2.1.1, the problem of contracting high-effort learning. Solutions to all the other problems in the table presume that the technological and organizational capabilities to set up competitive organizations already exist. In reality, developing countries lack the capabilities to use modern technologies and without this, attempted solutions to other problems are unlikely to have any effect. Unfortunately, this too is a particularly difficult problem to solve. Strategies of subsidization without incentives and compulsions to induce high effort in the learning process are likely to fail.

Private investment in financing learning may be motivated by the following type of calculation: An investment of s_Q in loss-financing has the prospect of achieving a competitiveness of $\frac{P_Q^{global}}{c_Q^{domestic}} \geq 1$ after n years. As the follower country has lower wages, productivity growth could eventually result in a cost of production lower than the world price. If productivity improves sufficiently, the investor can earn a normal profit of m_Q or even a rent in the form of a higher mark-up of $m_Q' > m_Q$ (after n years) with an expectation that the rent $m_Q' - m_Q$ will last for x years. The mark-up can decline over time for a number of reasons including the entry of new firms in the sector that bids up wages. The magnitudes of s_Q, n, and if relevant, $m_Q' - m_Q$ and x, and the discount rate or cost of finance facing the entrepreneur will determine whether the investment in learning-by-doing is privately profitable. Private investments in learning may happen even without the prospect of rents because the normal mark-up m_Q may be attractive enough given the alternative opportunities of the investor even taking into account the extra investment in loss-financing. This is therefore a different problem from the discovery problem where a private investor in a new sector will not invest without a subsidy because the social benefit from discovery is always greater than the private benefit, which may even be negative.

In the learning problem, the contracting failure is internal to the firm and its investors as the latter find it difficult to ensure effort in learning. If this problem can be solved then private investments may happen. If the contracting problem of ensuring high effort cannot be solved, public policy has to co-finance or share the risk of financing learning. However, in some cases the configuration of costs and benefits may require a higher return to justify the investment in learning than the return that is achievable even with high effort. The required higher return may not be achievable because it may not be feasible to achieve a low enough cost of production to generate the required private rents even with feasibly high effort *or* it may not be possible to achieve the rents for long enough because new entrants reduce the returns of the first mover by raising wages rapidly (as in the discovery model). In these cases there may be a second reason why public policy should co-finance learning and that is that the social return on learning may be higher than the feasible private return. This provides additional justification for subsidizing first-movers investing in learning in a particular sector. But even in cases where investments in learning have positive spillovers for society, if the public support for learning does not solve the problem of ensuring high levels of effort the exercise as a whole is likely to fail. This is what makes the solution of the learning problem different from the solution of the pure discovery problem and other positive externality problems which only require the provision of time-bound subsidies.

Effort is important for the learning problem because the development of technological and organizational capabilities requires both time and effort. Time and effort are inversely related: the lower the effort, the longer the learning takes. In Figure 2.1.1 firms in country B may be unable to begin production at point U without loss-financing, but the feasibility of the financing depends on *how long* firms take to go from U to V, or even whether V will ever be reached. The rate at which the competitiveness curve rises depends on the degree of effort that is put into the learning process once loss financing allows learning-by-doing to commence. Unfortunately, disciplining the learning process is a difficult problem to solve. Without incentives and compulsions, a production team can keep on repeating procedures without the innovations and experiments that improve its productivity. This is particularly the case if the firm can make a political case for continuing with the subsidy. The political alliances of firms can make subsidy withdrawal too costly for many governments. The institutional and political background can therefore set constraints on what can be done. The "learning" process can then continue indefinitely, as countries with infant industries that refused to grow up have discovered. Indeed, even if the learning process is just a little too slow, financing may become unviable in terms of opportunity costs. Moreover, if the public or private investors who may have financed the learning suspect its viability, they are unlikely to engage in the financing in the first place.

The time required for achieving competitiveness, defined as the break-even period B_t, can plausibly be determined by a number of variables. First, it depends on the initial gap between the country and the global leader which we can measure by the initial competitiveness gap that the subsidy s_Q is required to cover. The greater the initial gap, the longer it will take to catch up. Second, the time required for learning depends on the *effort* of the participants in the learning process. This includes both the individual efforts in acquiring technological capabilities, but even more so the management effort in acquiring organizational capabilities. Whatever the initial gap, a higher effort is likely to result in faster convergence. Effort can be measured by the intensity of application of workers and managers to continually improve productivity. This can be observed as the rate at which managers and workers experiment with and adapt production processes to achieve improvements in productivity. As experimentation and trials impose costs on individuals, the result can be conflicts as there may be distributive implications in redefining jobs. Thus, higher levels of effort imply costs for participants and particularly for managers. As already noted, the effort referred to here is *not* the intensity of the work process in general, but the effort expended in learning to raise productivity. Typically, low productivity is not the effect of laziness or low effort in general on the part of the work-force (though that may be a marginal contributor) but rather of a failure of effort on the part of the production team as a whole to evolve routines and organizational structures that raise individual productivity, improve quality control, reduce the wastage of inputs, reduce bottlenecks in production and improve capacity utilization.

Finally, the break-even period can also depend on country- and firm-specific factors. Country-specific factors refer to general levels of education, exposure to technology, the prior history of organized modern production, infrastructural quality and so on. If a country is significantly behind in its formal technological capabilities it may fail to approach required levels of competitiveness within any feasible time period. An example of this would be the absence of a sufficient number of formally trained engineers of a particular type required in the production process. Firm-level factors refer to idiosyncratic differences in the quality of entrepreneurship, the quality of technicians and managers inherited by a firm and so on. These variables are summarized in eq. [11]:

$$B_t = f(s_Q, e, C, F) \tag{11}$$

The break-even period B_t is likely to be longer the higher the initial gap in competitiveness measured by s_Q, the lower the level of effort, e, and if C and F, which describe country-specific and firm-specific factors respectively are adverse. Figure 2.1.2 tracks the pace at which the competitiveness curves in Figure 2.1.1 move up as a result of different levels of effort. To simplify, we assume that the value of other variables is such that it is potentially possible for the country to achieve competitiveness in quality Q. At time $t = 1$ country A's competitiveness is too low for it to begin the production of quality Q without loss-financing. The initial loss-financing is s_Q in Figure 2.1.2. If effort levels are high, the break-even period $B_t = n$ periods. At that point, loss-financing can be abandoned and indeed if improvements in productivity continue, the country may even be in a position to earn rents in subsequent periods.

The problem for the successful firm is that its reward for success is the loss of the rent it was getting in the form of loss-financing. The firm will have substituted a future of uncertain market profits and rents based on continuing efforts at productivity growth for a subsidy that allowed it to perform with low productivity. There is obviously an incentive compatibility problem here that can result in *"satisficing"* behavior on the part of management. The existing routines of production within the firm may be difficult and costly to change and it may be easier to spend management effort in protecting the subsidy. Not surprisingly, managers typically put a lot of effort into developing organizational capability and competitiveness when there are credible compulsions and pressures on them from outside the firm, possibly from the financing agencies. Otherwise a satisficing strategy may emerge that puts low effort into learning and more effort into protecting the subsidy. Competitiveness may never be achieved even with some productivity growth as productivity is also increasing in the leader. The infant

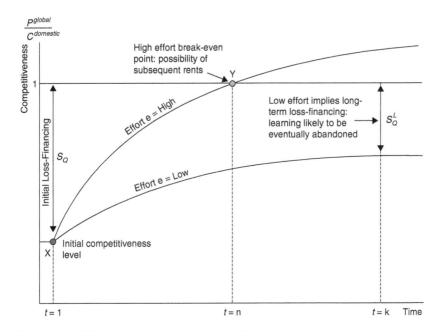

Figure 2.1.2   Effort levels and the viability of the learning process

industry will fail to grow up and eventually the catching-up strategies will have to be abandoned, but this may be many years later and managers and workers may not be too concerned about this right away.

Owner-managers financing learning-by-doing in their own organizations would not have to subcontract the management of the learning effort. However, it is unlikely that a single owner-manager will be able to finance a period of loss-making for any organization of substantial size. When external financiers are involved, they have to contract with the owner and managers of the firm to ensure high levels of effort since their returns depend on the achievement of competitiveness. The contracting problem is that the enforcement of complex contingent contracts is usually ruled out in a developing country given the weakness of contract enforcement. The overall loss-financing s_Q is therefore likely to be partly or entirely from public sources, particularly in cases where a significant organizational gap exists between the country and the market leader. The financing instruments can however vary widely, including import protection, export subsidies, subsidized credit and other forms of interventions that change relative prices and reduce or remove the losses of the learning company. However, while some level of public co-financing may be necessary, appropriate governance conditions are also required to ensure high effort. The outcome depends on the details of the financing instrument and the enforceability of the conditions critical for the success of that instrument. Enforceability depends on the governance capabilities of the relevant public agencies and the holding power of the organizations involved in the financing arrangement to resist enforcement. An important determinant of enforceability is therefore the macro-level distribution of power between firms, political organizations and enforcement agencies of different types, and we call this the *political settlement* (Khan, 1995, 2010).

Our understanding of industrial policy has been influenced by the experience of countries such as South Korea where centrally allocated learning rents achieved the rapid development of technological and organizational capabilities in the 1960s and 1970s. For a variety of historical reasons, East Asian states were untypical because their political settlements allowed the enforcement of tough conditions on domestic firms receiving support (Khan, 2009; Khan and Blankenburg, 2009). The financing provided to the *chaebol* through low-interest loans, protected domestic markets and export subsidies came with conditions, for instance for achieving export targets. These conditions ensured high levels of effort because the enforcement of these conditions was credible. The state could not only withdraw subsidies; it could also reallocate plants to different owners if they were more likely to enhance competitiveness.

Note that it was not "good governance" that enabled the South Korean state to achieve rapid learning with its centralized industrial policy. The enforcement of performance conditions was not based on the enforcement of detailed formal contracts. Moreover, the withdrawal of subsidies or the reallocation of plants usually did not respect property rights and the rule of law. Nor was corruption low in South Korea in the 1960s and 1970s. What mattered was that state agencies had the capacity to enforce conditions that it was in their interest to enforce, and that had the effect of ensuring high-effort learning (Khan, 1996, 2000b). The conditions themselves were subject to negotiation and the industrial policy system as a whole evolved as state agencies discovered and developed their enforcement capabilities. What is distinctive here is that firms discovered that subsidies could be withdrawn and even their plants could be re-allocated if they failed to raise their productivity. In contrast, in Pakistan at around the same period a similar system of centrally directed subsidies could not be matched with equivalent enforcement capabilities. The greater dispersion of power across political and bureaucratic organizations in this political settlement allowed firms to make alliances and satisficing rent-sharing agreements with particular political and state organizations to protect their rents (Khan, 1999). Not surprisingly policy did not evolve in the direction of enforcing conditions on firms receiving support as state agencies and firms knew that setting such conditions would not be credible. As a result, technological and organizational capabilities developed much more slowly and many sectors did not achieve competitiveness at all.

2.1.3 Financing learning with imperfect governance: two case studies

Fortunately, the South Korean model of centralized subsidy allocation is not the only one available for addressing the contracting failures affecting learning (Khan 2000a, 2000b). In political settlements less conducive for centralized monitoring and enforcement, other types of financing have proven successful in driving capability development. In the two cases examined here, learning and capability development succeeded because the design of the financing created incentives and compulsions for effort without requiring centralized monitoring and enforcement by state agencies. Nevertheless, state agencies played a critical role in setting up the financing arrangements, and the enforcement capabilities of some agencies were important in making the arrangements effective overall.

The Indian subcontinent did not perform very well with centralized industrial policy instruments in the 1960s and 1970s. In the 1980s the centralized policies started to unravel and exactly around that time a number of competitive sectors began to emerge. These instances of success are therefore often presented as success stories of liberalization, but the reality is more complex. We look at two sectors: automobiles in India and garments in Bangladesh. The transformation of these sectors into competitive ones involved new responses to contracting failures and in particular, new financing instruments emerged that created incentives and compulsions for high levels of learning effort that were credible in the political settlements of these countries.

The Indian automobile industry

In the 1950s and 1960s, centralized Indian industrial policy helped to build up a car industry that produced around 40,000 cars annually but of generally low quality. A protected domestic market and other implicit subsidies provided the loss-financing to low-competitiveness producers that enabled them to produce Indian cars. However, low levels of compulsion for effort meant that the low-tech Ambassador never became a globally competitive product. In the 1980s, the apparatus of centralized industrial policy began to unwind, and, at the same time, the sector went through dramatic changes. Quality and competitiveness began to rapidly improve and by 2009 Indian producers were producing 1.8 million cars, many of them of export quality (around 330,000 units that year), making India the fourth-largest global exporter. It appeared that market opening had forced quality and productivity growth exactly as liberal economists had predicted. However, a closer look tells us that learning still faced contracting failures and the state played an important though different role in co-financing a new and much more successful phase of high-effort learning.

Indian industrial policy had been supporting capability development in cars from the 1950s with the Ambassador produced by Hindustan Motors (part of the Birla group) and the Indian version of a Fiat called the Premier Padmini. Industrial policy was also assisting the manufacture of trucks and buses by Tata and tractors and jeeps by Mahindra and Mahindra. India was also developing tier one and two component producers even if they were not competitive relative to market leaders. The acceleration in the development of competitiveness in the 1980s came about as a result of an accidental train of events set off by Sanjay Gandhi (the prime minister's younger son) who decided in the 1970s to build a "People's Car": the Maruti. Early attempts to interest Volkswagen in the joint venture were not successful and the project was floundering when Sanjay died in an air crash in 1980, leaving a factory with no immediate prospects of producing anything. The potential loss of prestige for the Gandhi name made Indira's government look for effective policies that in effect created new financing instruments for the transfer of technological and organizational capabilities to India. In 1980, the government of India took over the initially private Gandhi family venture and incorporated it in 1981 as a public sector company called Maruti Udyog Ltd. After a long and committed search by top Indian bureaucrats for a foreign technology provider, an agreement was signed with Suzuki in 1982, with the latter taking a 26 percent equity stake in the company.

Suzuki, then principally a motorcycle manufacturer with a relatively minor interest in automobiles, had the advantage of knowing the Indian market and political system as they had been scouting for business in the motorcycle sector for some time. They recognized that the Indian government was serious about making this project work. The Indian government was effectively willing to open up the protected domestic market with the large rents that had previously been available for domestic learners to a foreign investor if the latter was willing to make a significant investment in transferring capabilities. The domestic market rents were a significant prize for Suzuki and this allowed the Indian government to insist on significant domestic content along the lines required by its Phased Manufacturing Programme, which required 95 per cent local content in five years (Becker-Ritterspach, 2007: 9). The joint venture agreement with Suzuki specified 70 per cent non-company value addition of which at least 60 per cent would be locally procured. On the other hand the government's commitment to make the project work was critical for Suzuki. This ensured that the policy changes that were required to make the project succeed could be pushed through. For instance, Suzuki managed to get permission to import gear boxes at low tariffs despite the opposition of the Indian machine tool industry. This made the pace of indigenization feasible while maintaining quality.

The result was a new type of arrangement for financing learning. Suzuki was expected to make significant upfront investments in learning and put in the effort to transfer organizational and technological capabilities to its Indian factory and to the Indian supplier chain. But given the risks and costs Suzuki would almost certainly not have made these significant investments without the implicit public co-financing in the form of the very substantial *ex post* rents available in the protected domestic market. These potential rewards were great enough to cover Suzuki's investments and risks in financing the learning. The result was incentive compatibility between the state and the recipient of the rent without the necessity of centralized monitoring and enforcement. This was achieved because Suzuki's ability to recover its investments in learning depended on its success in producing the higher-quality car to capture the domestic market from existing producers and meeting the domestic content requirements, a condition that was easy to monitor and within the capabilities of the Indian state to enforce. Its effort in managing the learning process was therefore assured and did not have to be monitored in terms of effort or quality of outcomes.

The result was a remarkable transformation of the competitiveness of the Indian automobile sector based on a significant transfer of technological and organizational capabilities. As Maruti's plant at Gurgaon was virtually an empty shell, the Japanese used the organizational structure of their plant at Kosai as the template around which to develop an appropriate Indian organizational structure. The relatively flat Japanese organizational structure could not be replicated in its entirety as Indian managerial hierarchies were resistant to change. But a high-effort learning-by-doing process resulted in the evolution of a new hybrid organizational structure that was much more efficient than previous Indian organizations. Even more remarkable was the success of Suzuki's supplier development program, which worked with initially technologically weak and suspicious suppliers to improve *their* organizational and technological capabilities in order to meet domestic content requirements and reduce input costs for the planned low-cost car. The organizational evolution in Gurgaon and throughout the supplier chain involved considerable investments of effort and resources by Suzuki but the results were very positive. By 1983 Maruti–Suzuki had captured 50 percent of the lucrative protected domestic market as a result of rapid improvements in quality, displacing the slumbering Ambassador from its dominant position in the market. By the late 1990s, Indian tier one component producers began to win international prizes for quality such as the Japanese Deming Prize.

Several aspects of the financing instruments and governance capabilities are important in explaining these outcomes. First, the *ex post* rent was clearly a big enough prize for Suzuki to justify its risky investments in building new capabilities. The prize was access to the large protected domestic market, which remained protected even a decade later in the 1990s and even after India began to formally liberalize. In 1993–94, three years after liberalization began, the nominal rate of tariffs on automobiles was still 85 per cent, and this only declined to 60 per cent in 2006–07. The effective rate of protection was even higher and actually increased over this period from 88 per cent to 183 per cent because of a decline in the rate of protection for components (Badri and Vashisht, 2008: 84–5). If the *ex post* prize was small, it may not have justified the significant investments and effort in improving technological and organizational capabilities right through the supply chain. Secondly, high *ex post* rents alone would not have ensured that Suzuki would spend so much effort in transforming the domestic supply chain rather than importing the required inputs. This required enforceable domestic content requirements. Fortunately, the agencies monitoring these outcomes were credible in India and the political settlement was such that foreign companies (even if they wanted to) would have found it difficult to buy political protection if they had failed to deliver on their contractual commitments. India was also lucky in that in the 1980s it was still not constrained by WTO rules (India only joined the WTO in 1995) and it could therefore set domestic content requirements for foreign investors.

The Maruti–Suzuki partnership transformed automobile production in India, even though the company did not remain in Indian hands for long. By 1987 Suzuki had increased its equity stake to 40 percent and it increased it again in 1992 – to 50 percent. After a protracted conflict over the appointment of the managing director in 1997, the Indian government began to divest its holdings and Suzuki rapidly became the dominant shareholder. However, by then Suzuki had transformed the Indian automobile industry by enhancing the competitiveness of Indian-owned tier one and tier two producers. The increasingly competitive supplier network began to attract foreign and Indian car manufacturers who continued to benefit from the financing arrangement that co-financed learning based on the formula of steep domestic content requirements combined with access to the protected domestic market. In the 1990s, DaimlerChrysler, Fiat, Ford, GM, Honda, Hyundai, Toyota and others followed Suzuki in similar deals. Domestic content requirements made successive technology providers invest further in technology transfer to the supply chain. By 2004, the development of domestically owned tier one capabilities allowed Indian producers like Tata and Mahindra and Mahindra to produce Indian branded cars with domestic content ranging from 20 to 100 per cent depending on the model.

The Bangladeshi garments industry

The dramatic growth of the labor-intensive garment industry in Bangladesh in the 1980s and beyond is another interesting story of how the financing of learning matters, particularly because it is often assumed that learning is not particularly important in low-technology industries like garments. Like automobiles in India, the garments industry in Bangladesh is often portrayed in the popular press as a success story of liberalization. The problem with the comparative advantage narrative is that low wages in Bangladesh did not result in the rapid growth of any other labor-intensive sector, and other developing countries with low wages and liberal economic policies have not experienced the dramatic growth observed in the garments sector in Bangladesh.

The answer to these puzzles is the importance of learning even in apparently low technology sectors and the specific ways in which the learning problem was solved in the Bangladeshi garments industry. As in the Indian automobile sector, the growth of the garments industry was associated with the emergence of a successful financing mechanism that created incentives for high-effort learning. One part of the "instrument" financing learning in the Bangladeshi garment sector was the lucky accident of the Multi-Fibre Arrangement (or MFA). This was set up in 1974 to protect US garments and textile manufactures from competition coming from established producers in countries like South Korea and Turkey. The established garment and textile countries were allocated quotas for US imports and as a way of getting the support of other developing countries, quota-free access was offered to less developed countries like Bangladesh that had no garments industry at all. Quota-free access created "quota rents" for these countries because they could effectively sell at a higher price in US markets after the established exporters had exhausted their quotas. The quota rent was an intended policy outcome, but the intention was to primarily benefit US garments producers who were being threatened by cheaper imports from established producers. The unintended effect was that it potentially provided loss-financing for learning in the garments sectors in countries like Bangladesh which were not competitive even though their wages were lower than the established garments exporters and much lower compared to the USA.

The quota rent helped to artificially raise Bangladeshi competitiveness for a while but so great was the productivity gap between countries like Bangladesh and more advanced exporters that the MFA on its own would not have been sufficient to enable Bangladesh to produce for exports and engage in learning-by-doing. Indeed, the necessity of additional loss-financing and of appropriate incentives and compulsions for effort is demonstrated by the fact that there were other countries in Africa and Asia that were quota free but did not experience any explosive growth in this sector. However, the MFA raised world prices and reduced the competitiveness gap for Bangladesh and thereby created incentives for Bangladeshi and foreign technology providers to find additional financing for learning in order to scale the remaining competitiveness gap. Fortunately for Bangladesh, it had just begun to acquire a broad-based group of potential investors appropriate for the development of a garments industry. Opportunities for primitive accumulation over the previous decade had helped to create a base of entrepreneurs who could potentially drive growth in the sector provided the learning problem could be solved. The solution came in the form of a collaborative agreement between a Bangladeshi company, Desh Garments and the South Korean *chaebol* Daewoo in 1979. Daewoo had both textile and garments interests, but after its garment production was limited by the MFA it needed to sell its textiles to an offshore partner making garments. This made Daewoo able and willing to transfer the know-how of garments production to an offshore partner.

The founder of Desh was Nurul Quader Khan, an ex-bureaucrat who had clearly benefited from the primitive accumulation of the 1970s and he had become a very rich man with substantial cash to invest. In the 1980s the military-backed government of Zia-ur-Rahman wanted industrialization and the president took the lead in underwriting the collaboration between Desh and Daewoo. As in India, the political commitment of the highest leadership to a particular project was more important than a general policy commitment to industrialization. It signalled to investors that small but specific problems that may otherwise have held up progress would be solved. Desh was responsible for all the physical investments in land and machinery in a modern garment factory in Bangladesh. The agreement with Daewoo was about financing the learning that would transform the factory and its workers into a competitive *organization*. Desh would literally purchase the requisite know-how from Daewoo, but as in the Suzuki case in India, Daewoo would invest in the learning *first* and would recover its investment when Desh became competitive. Daewoo did this by hosting at its own expense around 130 mid-level production managers from Bangladesh at its state-of-the-art garments factory in Busan (formerly Pusan). Their learning-by- doing in Busan was critical for acquiring the appropriate organizational and technological capabilities for modern garment manufacturing. Daewoo's investment in financing this learning-by-doing would be paid back in the form of an 8% royalty on the eventual sales of Desh. The composite financing of the learning thus came from a combination of the MFA quota rents (which reduced the competitiveness gap that Bangladesh had to climb) and further upfront investments by Daewoo that would be repaid by actual sales when Desh achieved competitiveness.

The details of the financing structure help to explain why the stakeholders had strong incentives and compulsions to put in high levels of effort in rapidly transferring the tacit knowledge, particularly about the organization of production. Daewoo had a strong incentive to put in high levels of effort because it needed to sell textiles to Bangladesh, and it needed to recover its investments in learning through royalties from Desh as quickly as possible. With the teachers strongly incentivized, the learning by the students was already half ensured. At the same time, the Bangladeshis who went to Busan had a strong incentive to learn because they had nothing to gain by prolonging their stay in Busan. Moreover, these future managers may already have known that the organizational know-how they were acquiring could also be personally lucrative for them as potential garments entrepreneurs in their own right. Indeed, of the 130 mid-level managers who went to Busan for Desh, 115 eventually set up their own garment factories!

The rate at which learning happened surprised all the participants. Desh had estimated that it would take five years of collaboration with Daewoo to achieve international competitiveness. But so successful was the learning at Busan and subsequently that the deal for cooperation on learning was terminated after less than two years. Desh's growth and that of the Bangladesh garment industry was explosive: Desh grew at around 90 percent a year from 1981 to 1987. The Bangladesh garment industry grew from an almost zero base in 1980 to around 3,500 medium-sized firms in 2005 employing more than three million workers and accounting for 70 percent of Bangladesh's exports. One of the ways in which Desh continued to create incentives for the learning effort of its managers was to allow them to leave and set up their own plants if they wished to do so. With large pools of labor, there was no threat of profits being squeezed by wage increases caused by a growing demand for labor in the garments industry as it grew. Moreover, as a critical part of the learning was evolving *organizational* design, the departure of individual managers was not a critical loss. On the contrary, the growth of an industrial cluster had many advantages in attracting buyers to Bangladesh. Fortunately for Bangladesh, Desh understood its basic economics and it did not create obstacles for managers who wanted to leave. Indeed, this created strong incentives for its managers to continue to experiment and develop organizational and technological capabilities and the company benefited from this ongoing learning and productivity enhancement. By 2010, Bangladesh had become the world's third biggest garments exporter and continued to enjoy double-digit growth in 2010 despite the global slowdown.

The critical features of the financing instruments and the reasons for their success in financing learning were different in the Bangladeshi garments industry compared to the automobile sector in India. The public rent component here did not come from a protected domestic market but from the MFA, with its sources entirely outside Bangladesh. Bangladeshi producers had no credible mechanism to negotiate its allocation or extension. They rightly saw the MFA as a temporary arrangement and this too supported incentives for effort. The complementary private part of the financing instrument was the collaborative agreement between Desh and Daewoo where the investment in learning was made upfront by the South Korean partner with repayment from the sales of the Bangladeshi firm. This again created strong incentives for the rapid transmission and absorption of the relevant tacit knowledge. The role of the Bangladeshi government was limited but not negligible. The introductions between Desh and Daewoo took place through the direct intervention of President Zia. In developing countries informal government support that is perceived to be based on genuine commitment is often more credible than formal support. Daewoo, like Suzuki in India, found the commitment credible. It assured the foreign partner that administrative problems would be ironed out – as indeed they were. Zia's government and its successor pushed through critical institutional innovations like the back-to- back letter of credit (which allowed garments manufactures to finance raw material imports by using their export orders as collateral) and bonded warehouses, both of which reduced the financing cost of importing raw materials and fabrics. Indeed, so successful was the sector that Ronald Reagan imposed quotas on Bangladesh as early as 1985, just a few years after Desh began exporting.

Bangladesh's manufacturing sector now accounts for a similar share of GDP as India, largely because of the garments and textiles industry. The challenge for Bangladesh is to move up the value chain in the garment and textile industry and beyond. However, policymakers do not generally see the success of the garments sector as an application of technology policy and there has been little progress in designing the types of financing instruments for high-effort learning that is required in other sectors. Upgrading within the garments industry is happening as a result of individual entrepreneurs with deep pockets investing in backward linkages. Bangladesh has moved into fabrics and accessories, but the absence of policies to finance learning has constrained upgrading and the development of new sectors like electronics. As in India, the dominant public perception is that competition and comparative advantage explain the success of growth sectors. But the economics of comparative advantage cannot explain why other competitive labor-intensive sectors are not emerging, or why other poor countries that stood to gain from the MFA did not in fact do so. The examination of the garments take-off shows that learning and tacit knowledge transfer were financed by a combination of private investments and public rents, and that the financing instruments were structured to create strong incentives for effort. The challenge is to design similarly effective learning processes in other sectors in Bangladesh and elsewhere.

2.1.4 Conclusion

An examination of successful growth sectors in the Indian subcontinent shows the importance of addressing the contracting failures affecting learning. The standard instruments of centralized industrial policy performed weakly in the past because they could not ensure high levels of effort given the political settlements in these countries. The ability of South Asian states (and perhaps states in developing countries in general) to withdraw targeted rents from domestic firms was too weak to be a credible threat that could induce sustained effort in learning. The examples from India and Bangladesh suggest that alternative mechanisms of financing that are credible in the context of their political settlements have to be sought and that in principle such financing instruments do exist. Sector-specific financing instruments have fared much better in the period after 1980, and explain the success of critical sectors.

In both our sectors publicly created rents were important complements to private investment in learning. At the same time, private investments were necessary to create the incentives and compulsions for effort in contexts where the political settlement limited the state's disciplining capabilities. In the Indian automobile industry, public policy created rents in the protected domestic market that indirectly financed learning. In the Bangladeshi garment industry, the public policy creating rents was located in the international trade architecture in the form of the MFA. Neither set of rents would necessarily play a positive role in inducing learning if they existed on their own. Indeed, India's protected domestic market for automobiles did not induce anyone to aspire to global competitiveness. However, combined with the right type of private co-financing and some additional enforceable conditions, the public rents achieved remarkable results. Sadly, the public policies that created these particular rents in automobiles and garments would now be precluded by WTO rules. However, in the absence of any public rents for learners, the competitiveness gap in most sectors in South Asia and contracting difficulties would be likely to preclude purely private solutions to learning. One set of policy challenges is therefore to create public rents within WTO rules for sharing the costs of learning when private investors are unwilling to undertake the entire investment in learning on their own. If WTO rules prove to be too constraining for financing learning in developing countries, the rules need to be re-examined.

Given the political settlements in South Asian countries, centralized public strategies of financing learning failed in the past because high levels of
effort could not be enforced. The second feature of our successful learning
cases was therefore the critical role of private investments complementing
the public financing of learning. The design of the financing instruments
ensured high levels of effort because those responsible for organizing the
learning were investing their own money first. Prolonging the learning
process through *satisficing* strategies was unlikely to be a dominant strategy
in this case. Instead, strong incentives and compulsions were created for
high levels of effort in transferring the tacit knowledge quickly. Public co-
financing enhanced the *ex post* rewards and thereby reduced the risk facing
these investors, inducing them to invest in financing learning in the presence of contracting failures. In both cases, the private investors who were
financing the learning were also providing the organizational and technological know-how. The investors therefore had a good idea of the knowledge
that needed to be transferred and it was their assessment that the *ex post*
rewards including the public rents promised satisfactory returns on their
investments of resources and effort in ensuring the transfer.

Thus, by combining public and private financing and structuring the
private investments appropriately, the centralized monitoring and disciplining of learning rents was no longer necessary. The public rents succeeded
in ensuring that private investments in learning were forthcoming and
private pre-commitment ensured high levels of effort. The evidence from
other sectors in India and Bangladesh suggests that capability development
and growth has generally been slow in sectors that did not enjoy this combination of public co-financing of private learning. Clearly, the contracting
failures affecting learning remain important. In these two sectors and a
number of others, serendipitous combinations of public rents and private
investments were sufficient to develop the organizational and technological
capabilities necessary for achieving competitiveness. One challenge facing
the construction of deliberate policy for other sectors is to calibrate the public support so that the *ex post* reward does not give too many free handouts
to private investors who may have invested with lower incentives, but at the
same time provide sufficient incentives for a successful outcome.

Finally, some political and governance conditions were important in both
cases, highlighting that every response to a contracting failure has specific
enforcement and governance requirements. A common feature of both our
cases was that for different reasons the top political leaderships were committed to the success of the particular project. This is likely to be a particularly
important condition in developing countries where the overall governance
environment is weak and success may depend on political leaders supporting particular projects. The political commitment may make more credible
the monitoring and enforcement of critical contracts. In the Indian case the
monitoring and enforcement of domestic content requirements was never

doubted by Suzuki. In Bangladesh Daewoo and Desh were confident that back-to-back letters of credit and bonded warehouses would come through and that their specific profit-sharing contract would be enforceable. These requirements are much less demanding than the expectation that some central agency will monitor performance and reallocate resources, but nonetheless they are governance requirements. The specific details of the financing instruments, political conditions and governance requirements in our two cases are obviously not directly replicable for other sectors or countries. Nevertheless, they suggest that in principle learning can be financed using instruments that generate incentives for effort that are credible even in political settlements where centralized industrial policy instruments are not likely to be effective.

References

Atkinson, Anthony B. and Stiglitz, Joseph E. (1969) "A New View of Technological Change," *The Economic Journal*, vol. 79, no. 315, pp. 573–578.

Badri, Narayanan G. and Vashisht, Pankaj (2008) *Determinants of Competitiveness of the Indian Auto Industry*. Working Paper No. 201 (New Delhi: Indian Council for Research on International Economic Relations).

Becker-Ritterspach, Florian (2007) *Maruti–Suzuki's Trajectory: From a Public Sector Enterprise to a Japanese Owned Subsidiary*, 15th GERPISA International Colloquium, June 20–2 (Paris: GERPISA International Network). Available online at www.becker-ritterspach.de/pdf/Gerpisa%20Becker-Ritterspach.pdf.

Clark, Gregory and Wolcott, Susan (2002) "One Polity, Many Countries: Economic Growth in India, 1873–2000," in Dani Rodrik (ed.), *Institutions, Integration, and Geography: In Search of the Deep Determinants of Economic Growth* (Princeton, NJ: Princeton University Press).

Dosi, Giovanni (1988) "The Nature of the Innovative Process," in Giovanni Dosi, Christopher Freeman, Richard R. Nelson, Gerald Silverberg, and Luc Soete (eds), *Technical Change and Economic Theory* (London: Pinter Publishers).

Hausmann, Ricardo and Rodrik, Dani (2003) "Economic Development as Self Discovery," *Journal of Development Economics*, vol. 72, no. 2, pp. 603–633. Available online at http://ksghome.harvard.edu/~drodrik/selfdisc.pdf.

Hoekman, Bernard M., Maskus, Keith E. and Saggi, Kamal (2004) *Transfer of Technology to Developing Countries: Unilateral and Multilateral Policy Options*. World Bank Policy Research Working Paper No. 3332 (Washington, DC: World Bank).

Khan, Mushtaq Husain (1995) "State Failure in Weak States: A Critique of New Institutionalist Explanations," in John Harriss, Janet Hunter, and Colin M. Lewis (eds), *The New Institutional Economics and Third World Development* (London: Routledge).

Khan, Mushtaq Husain (1996) "The Efficiency Implications of Corruption," *Journal of International Development*, vol. 8, no. 5, pp. 683–696.

Khan, Mushtaq Husain (1999) *The Political Economy of Industrial Policy in Pakistan 1947–1971*, SOAS Department of Economics Working Paper No. 98 (London: School of Oriental and African Studies, University of London).

Khan, Mushtaq Husain (2000a) "Rents, Efficiency and Growth," in Mushtaq H. Khan and K.S. Jomo (eds), *Rents, Rent-Seeking and Economic Development: Theory and Evidence in Asia* (Cambridge: Cambridge University Press).

Khan, Mushtaq Husain (2000b) "Rent-seeking as Process," in Mushtaq H. Khan and K.S. Jomo (eds), *Rents, Rent-Seeking and Economic Development: Theory and Evidence in Asia* (Cambridge: Cambridge University Press).

Khan, Mushtaq Husain (2009) *Learning, Technology Acquisition and Governance Challenges in Developing Countries*, Research Paper Series on Governance for Growth (London: School of Oriental and African Studies, University of London). Available online at https://eprints.soas.ac.uk/9967/1/Learning_and_Technology_Acquisition_internet.pdf.

Khan, Mushtaq Husain (2010) *Political Settlements and the Governance of Growth-Enhancing Institutions*, Research Paper Series on Governance for Growth (London: School of Oriental and African Studies, University of London). Available online at http://eprints.soas.ac.uk/9968/1/Political_Settlements_internet.pdf.

Khan, Mushtaq Husain (2012) "The Political Economy of Inclusive Growth," in Luiz de Mello and Mark A. Dutz (eds), *Promoting Inclusive Growth: Challenges and Policies* (Paris: OECD Publishing). Available online at http://www.oecd-ilibrary.org/economics/promoting-inclusive-growth/the-political-economy-of-inclusive-growth_9789264168305-3-en;jsessionid=4rg80c1r7eqch.delta.

Khan, Mushtaq Husain and Blankenburg, Stephanie (2009) "The Political Economy of Industrial Policy in Asia and Latin America," in Giovanni Dosi, Mario Cimoli, and Joseph E. Stiglitz (eds), *Industrial Policy and Development: The Political Economy of Capabilities Accumulation* (Oxford: Oxford University Press).

Lall, Sanjaya (1992) "Technological Capabilities and Industrialization," *World Development*, vol. 20, no. 2, pp. 165–186.

Lall, Sanjaya (2000a) *Selective Industrial and Trade Policies in Developing Countries: Theoretical and Empirical Issues*, Working Paper Series No. 48 (Oqford: Queen Elizabeth House).

Lall, Sanjaya (2000b) *Skills, Competitiveness and Policy in Developing Countries*, Working Paper Series No. 46 (Oxford: Queen Elizabeth House).

Lall, Sanjaya (2003) *Reinventing Industrial Strategy: The Role of Government Policy in Building Industrial Competitiveness*, Working Paper Series No. 111 (Oxford: Queen Elizabeth House).

Lancaster, Kelvin J. (1966) "A New Approach to Consumer Theory," *Journal of Political Economy*, vol. 74, no. 2, pp. 132–157.

Murphy, Kevin M., Shleifer, Andrei, and Vishny, Robert W. (1989) "Industrialization and the Big Push," *Journal of Political Economy*, vol. 97, no. 5, pp. 1003–1026.

Nelson, Richard R. and Winter, Sidney G. (1982) *An Evolutionary Theory of Economic Change* (Cambridge, MA: Belknap Press of Harvard University Press).

Nurkse, Ragnar (1953) *Problems of Capital Formation in Underdeveloped Countries* (Oxford: Oxford University Press).

Pelikan, Pavel (1988) "Can the Imperfect Innovation Systems of Capitalism be Outperformed?," in Giovanni Dosi, Christopher Freeman, Richard R. Nelson, Gerald Silverberg, and Luc Soete (eds), *Technical Change and Economic Theory* (London: Pinter Publishers).

Perez, Carlota and Soete, Luc (1988) "Catching Up in Technology: Entry Barriers and Windows of Opportunity," in Giovanni Dosi, Christopher Freeman, Richard R. Nelson, Gerald Silverberg, and Luc Soete (eds), *Technical Change and Economic Theory* (London: Pinter Publishers).

Polanyi, Michael (1967) *The Tacit Dimension* (Garden City, NY: Doubleday Anchor).

Rosenstein-Rodan, Paul N. (1943) "Problems of Industrialisation of Eastern and South-Eastern Europe," *The Economic Journal*, vol. 53, nos 210/211, pp. 202–211.

Scitovsky, Tibor (1954) "Two Concepts of External Economies," *Journal of Political Economy*, vol. 62, no. 2, pp. 143–151.

Stiglitz, Joseph E. (1987) "Learning to Learn, Localized Learning and Technological Progress," in Partha Dasgupta and Paul Stoneman (eds), *Economic Policy and Technological Development* (Cambridge: Cambridge University Press).

Stiglitz, Joseph E. (2007) *Making Globalization Work* (London: Penguin).

Sutton, John (2005) *Competing in Capabilities: An Informal Overview* London: London School of Economics). Available online at http://personal.lse.ac.uk/SUTTON/com peting_capabilities_informal_washington.pdf.

Sutton, John (2007) "Quality, Trade and the Moving Window: The Globalization Process," *The Economic Journal*, vol. 117, no. 524, pp. F469–498.

2.2
Comments on "Technology Policies and Learning with Imperfect Governance" by Mushtaq H. Khan

Pranab Bardhan
University of California, Berkeley

1. The paper rightly emphasizes the key problems of technological, and particularly organizational, capabilities in the acquisition of tacit knowledge and organizing the relevant production and learning processes and their financing in the early stages of development. It gives illustrations from two successful cases of sector-specific financing mechanisms from countries otherwise quite deficient in economic governance—one from the car industry in India and the other from the garment industry in Bangladesh.

2. The contrast with the East Asian cases of industrial policy has been drawn in terms of state capacity, which is often missing in South Asia. But the concept of state capacity is a little circular; one often measures state capacity ultimately in terms of some outcome variables, and, thus defined, capacity cannot explain those outcomes. The East Asian state often carried out a policy of contingent rents which induced private agents to act in certain ways. But the successful cases from South Asia cited in the paper are also linked to some arrangements of rents (largely generated by content protection in the case of the Indian car industry and quota rents in the case of the Bangladeshi garment industry), though clearly those rents were not by themselves sufficient in generating the private efforts and investment in learning.

3. There are other cases in India where some kind of centralized industrial policy did succeed. For example, the Indian patent policy of protecting processes but not products, until the World Trade Organization (WTO) rules started biting in the last decade, helped nurture the generic pharmaceutical industry. The policy of promoting high-powered engineering institutes (like the Indian Institutes of Technology (IITs)) and that of driving out IBM in the 1970s played some role in encouraging the blossoming of the software and business processing industry. In these cases, unlike in the two cases discussed in the paper, learning was achieved without any major input from foreign investors.

4. The paper ignores the issues of labor institutions altogether. Labor repression in East Asia, and, to some extent in Bangladesh, facilitated profit-making. For some historical reasons industrial relations were relatively healthy in the early years of Maruti–Suzuki (in contrast to the militant trade unionism that afflicted some other industries in India); only very recently have labor-repressive methods by Suzuki damaged labor peace in their factories in India.
5. The model and the equations in the paper do not provide any additional insights beyond what had already been said in the text. The paper could have profitably referred to some of the dynamic quality ladder models in the growth literature (summarized in the textbooks of Grossman and Helpman, Aghion, etc.), which, of course, need to be adapted to the case of learning in developing countries.

2.3

The Boulevard of Broken Dreams: Industrial Policy and Entrepreneurship[1]

Josh Lerner
Harvard University and National Bureau of Economic Research

The financial crisis and recession that began in 2008 opened the door to massive public interventions in the western economies. In many nations, governments responded to the threats of illiquidity and insolvency by making huge investments into troubled firms, frequently taking large ownership stakes.

The magnitude of these investments boggles the imagination. Consider, for instance, the over $150 billion invested by the US government in AIG in September and November 2008 in exchange for 81 percent of the firm's stock, without any assurances that the ailing insurer will not need more funds. Or the Swiss government's infusion of $60 billion into UBS in exchange for just under 10 percent of the firm's equity: this capital represented about 20 percent of the nation's gross domestic product.[2]

Many concerns can be raised about these investments, from the hurried way in which they were designed by a few people behind closed doors to the design flaws that many experts anticipate will limit their effectiveness. But one question has been lost in the discussion. If these extraordinary times call for massive public funds to be used for economic interventions, should they be entirely devoted to propping up troubled entities, or at least partially devoted to promoting new enterprises? In some sense, 2008 saw the initiation of a massive global experiment in the government as venture capitalist, but as a very peculiar type of venture capitalist: one that focuses on the most troubled and poorly managed firms in the economy, some of which may be beyond salvation.

A two-sided picture frames the basic puzzle at work here. When we look at the regions of the world that are, or are emerging as, the great hubs of entrepreneurial and activity in the world – places such as Silicon Valley, Singapore, Tel Aviv, Shanghai, Bangalore, and Dubai – the stamp of the public sector is unmistakable. Enlightened government intervention played a key role in creating each of these regions. But for each effective government intervention, there have been dozens, even hundreds, of disappointments, where substantial public expenditures bore no fruit.

This scenario might lead the reader to conclude that the pursuit of entrepreneurial growth by the public sector is a massive casino. The public sector is simply making bets, with few guarantees of an attractive return. Perhaps there are no lessons to be garnered from the experiences of the programs that did and did not meet their goals of stimulating entrepreneurial activity.

The truth, however, is very different. When we look at the abandoned efforts by governments to promote venture and entrepreneurial activity, in many, many cases, the fact that the programs did not meet their goals were completely predictable. These efforts have featured a shared set of flaws in their design, which an objective observer might conclude doomed them virtually from the start. In many corners of the world, from Europe and the United States to the newest emerging economies, the same classes of problems have reappeared.

Fast-growing entrepreneurs have attracted increasing attention both in the popular press and from policymakers. These business creators and the investors who fund them have been seen as having played a dramatic role in creating new industries and revitalizing economies. Many nations have launched efforts to encourage this activity. Such attention is only likely to intensify as nations seek to overcome the deleterious effects of the credit crunch and its recessionary aftereffects.

This article is an effort to shed light on the evidence regarding the ways which governments can avoid making mistakes in an attempt to stimulate entrepreneurship. One limitation is that we won't be looking at all efforts to boost entrepreneurship. In recent decades, there has been an explosion in the number of efforts to provide financing and other forms of assistance to the poorest of the world's poor, in order to facilitate their entry into entrepreneurship or the growth of the small ventures they already have. Typically, these are "subsistence" businesses, offering services such as snack preparation or clothing repair. Such businesses typically allow the business owner and his or her family to get by, but little else. The public policy literature – and indeed academic studies of new ventures – often have not been very careful in making this distinction between which types of businesses are being studied.

Our focus here will be exclusively on high-potential new ventures and the policies that enhance them. This choice is not intended to diminish the importance or relevance of efforts to boost micro-enterprises, but rather reflects the complexity of this field: the dynamics and issues involving micro-firms are quite different from their high-potential counterparts.[3] As we'll see, a substantial literature suggests that promising entrepreneurial firms can have a powerful effect in transforming industries and promoting innovation.

It might be obvious to the reader why governments would want to promote entrepreneurship, but why the frequent emphasis on venture funds as well? The answer lies in the challenges facing many start-up firms, which often require substantial capital. A firm's founder may not have sufficient funds to finance these projects alone, and therefore must seek outside financing. Entrepreneurial firms that are characterized by significant intangible assets, expect years of negative earnings, have uncertain prospects, and are unlikely to receive bank loans or other debt financing. Venture capital – as independently managed, dedicated pools of capital that focus on equity or equity-linked investments in privately held, high-growth companies – can help alleviate these problems.

Typically, these investors do not primarily invest their own capital, but rather raise the bulk of their funds from institutions and individuals. Large institutional investors, such as pension funds and university endowments, are likely to want investments in their portfolio that have the potential to generate high yields, such as venture capital, and typically do not mind placing a substantial amount of capital in investments that cannot be liquidated for extended periods. Often, these groups have neither the staff nor the expertise to make such investments themselves. Thus, they invest in partnerships sponsored by venture capital funds, which in turn provide the funds to young firms.

Instead, we will explore efforts that seek to promote the growth of high-potential entrepreneurial ventures, as well as the venture funds that fund them. We'll highlight that while the public sector role is important in stimulating these activities, far more often than not public programs have not met their goals. Many of these disappointments could have been avoided, however, if the leaders had taken some relatively simple steps in designing and implementing these efforts.

It is also important to note that the focus of this article is on new ventures, rather than restructurings, leveraged buyouts, and other later-stage private equity investments. Later-stage private equity resembles venture capital in a number of respects, sharing similar legal structures, incentive schemes, and investors. Those funds also invest in entities that often find external financing difficult to raise: troubled firms that need to undergo restructurings. Similar to venture capitalists, buyout funds protect the value of their equity stakes by undertaking careful due diligence before making the investments and retaining powerful oversight rights afterwards. But the organizations that finance these high-risk, potentially high-reward projects in mature firms pose an interesting – but quite different – set of issues. They are thus the topic for another work!

I also shy away from the answer to the often-asked question of what makes a good industry for a given nation to promote at a particular time. These questions have, of course, no "one size fits all" answer, but are very specific to the individual circumstances. While the industrial organization and strategy analyses needed to answer these questions are fascinating, they would take us too far afield.

2.3.1 The Boulevard of Broken Dreams

Our understanding of the ideal policies to promote new ventures is still at an early stage. But the desire for information on how to encourage entrepreneurial activity is very real. Particularly in an era of economic turmoil and recession, governments are looking to entrepreneurial ventures to serve as an economic spark plug that will reignite growth.

If we have heard too many pronouncements of Silicon Valley patriarchs, we might begin with the view of new ventures as an activity where the government has nothing to contribute.[4] Isn't this the realm of heroic entrepreneurs and investors, as far removed from pointy-headed government bureaucrats as imaginable?

A review of the history of Silicon Valley and several of the pioneering venture capital groups suggests that reality is far more complex than some of our more libertarian entrepreneur friends might have us believe. In each case we consider the role of the government as an initial catalyst was critical in stimulating the growth of the region, sector, or firm.

This is not to minimize that miscues were made along the way. There were any number of challenges with these efforts:

- Silicon Valley's pioneers labored with a "stop-and start" pattern of government funding: wartimes would see a surge of funding for research and procurement, which would frequently disappear upon the cessation of hostilities.[5]
- The founders of pioneering venture groups, such as American Research and Development and 3i, did not clearly distinguish in their early years between social goals and financial objectives, which led to a muddled mission and confused investors.[6]
- The Small Business Investment Company program initially had problematic features, with numerous counterproductive requirements, and then implemented inconsistently, which led to the incompetent and even outright crooked funds.[7]

Despite these caveats, it seems clear from these mini-cases that the role of the public sector – or in the case of American Research and Development, individuals operating with a broader social framework in mind – proved to be a critical component in catalyzing growth.

Rationales for government efforts to stimulate entrepreneurship rest on two pillars. First, the role of technological innovation as a spur for economic growth is now widely recognized. Indeed, policy statements by governments worldwide highlight the importance of encouraging innovation as a key to meeting goals to sustain economic growth and prosperity.

Second, academic research has highlighted the role of entrepreneurship and venture capital in stimulating innovation.[8] These financiers and firms have developed a set of tools that are very well suited to the challenging task of nurturing high-risk but promising new ideas. One study estimates that because of these approaches, a single dollar of venture capital is as powerful in generating innovation as three dollars of traditional corporate research and development. Venture capital and the entrepreneurs they fund will never supplant other wellsprings of innovation, such as vibrant universities and corporate research laboratories (in an ideal world, these will all feed on each other). But in an innovative system, a healthy entrepreneurial sector and venture capital industry will be important contributors.

If that were all there was to it, there would be a pretty compelling case for public involvement. And there probably would be no need for this essay! But the case for public intervention also rests on a third leg: the argument that governments can effectively promote entrepreneurship and venture capital. And this is a much shakier assumption.

To be sure, the characteristics of entrepreneurial markets have features that allow us to make a credible intellectual case that there is a natural role for government in encouraging their evolution. Entrepreneurship is a business where there are increasing returns. Put another way, it is far easier being a start-up founder if there are ten other entrepreneurs nearby than if one is alone. In many respects, firm founders and venture capitalists benefit from their peers. For instance, if entrepreneurs are already active in the market, investors, employees, intermediaries such as lawyers, data providers, and the wider capital markets are likely to be knowledgeable about the venturing process and what it requires in terms of strategy, financing, support, and exit mechanisms. In the language of economics, entrepreneurship and venture capital are activities where the actions of any one group are likely to have positive spillovers – or "externalities" – for their peers. It is in these types of settings where the government can often play a very positive role as a catalyst.

Reflecting this observation, there are numerous examples where government intervention has triggered the growth of a venture capital sector. For instance, the Small Business Investment Company (SBIC) program in the United States led to the formation of the infrastructure for much of the modern venture capital industry. Many of the early venture capital funds and leading intermediaries in the industry – such as lawyers and data providers – began as organizations oriented to the SBIC funds, and then gradually shifted their focus to independent venture capitalists. Similarly, public programs played an important role in triggering the explosive growth of virtually every other major venture market around the globe.

But there are reasons to be cautious about the efficacy of government intervention. In particular, I highlight two well-documented problems that can derail these programs. First, government programs can simply get it wrong: allocating funds and support in an inept or, even worse, a counter-productive manner. An extensive literature has examined the factors that affect the quality of governmental efforts in general, and suggests that more competent programs are likelier in nations that are wealthier, with more heterogeneous populations, and an English legal tradition.

Economists have also focused on a second problem, delineated in the theory of regulatory capture.[9] These writings suggest private and public sector entities will organize to capture direct and indirect subsidies that the public sector hands out. For instance, programs geared towards boosting nascent entrepreneurs may instead end up boosting cronies of the nation's rulers or legislators. Among the annals of government venturing programs, examples abound of ways in which these efforts have been hijacked in such a manner.

Unfortunately, even without delving into the much-discussed misadventures of the Obama administration with cleantech investing, there is no shortage of examples of both problems in the history of public venturing programs:

- In its haste to roll out the Small Business Investment Company program in the early 1960s, the U.S. Small Business Administration chartered – and funded – hundreds of funds whose managers were incompetent or crooked.
- The incubators taking part in Australia's 1999 BITS program frequently captured the lion's share of the subsidies aimed toward entrepreneurs, by forcing the young firms to purchase their own overpriced services.
- Malaysia opened a massive BioValley complex in 2005 with little forethought as to whether there would be any demand for the facility. The facility soon became known as the "Valley of the Bio-Ghosts."
- Britain's Labour and Conservative governments subsidized and gave exclusive rights in the 1980s to the biotechnology firm Celltech, whose management team was manifestly incapable of exploiting those resources.
- Norway squandered much of its oil wealth in the 1970s and 1980s propping up failing ventures and funding ill-conceived new businesses begun by relatives of parliamentarians and bureaucrats.

2.3.2 Strategies and their limitations

Policies that governments employ to encourage venture capital and entrepreneurial activities take two forms: those that ensure that the economic environment is conducive to entrepreneurial activity and venture capital investments; and those that directly invest in companies and funds.

First, it is necessary to ensure that entrepreneurship itself is an attractive option. Often, in their eagerness to get to the "fun stuff" of handing out money, public leaders neglect the importance of setting the table, or creating a favorable environment.

Such efforts are likely to have several dimensions. Ensuring that creative ideas can move easily from universities and government laboratories is critically important. But many entrepreneurs come not from academia, but rather from corporate positions, and studies have documented that the attractiveness of entrepreneurial activity for these individuals is very sensitive to tax policy. Also important is ensuring that the law allows firms to enter into the needed contracts – for instance, with a potential financier or a source of technology – and that these contracts can be enforced. Finally, education is likely to be critical. Ensuring that business and technology students are exposed to entrepreneurship classes will allow them to make more informed decisions; and creating training opportunities in entrepreneurship for mid-career professionals is also likely to pay dividends.

Second, it is important to ensure that international investors find the nation or province an attractive one in which to invest. In most entrepreneurial hubs that have emerged in the past two decades, the critical early investments have not been made by domestic institutions, but rather by sophisticated international investors. These investors are likely to have the depth of knowledge and experience that enables them to make substantial bets on the most promising organizations. But these players are likely to be very reluctant to take part if regulatory conditions are not up to global standards, or if there are substantial concerns about the ability of investors to exit investments. Reaching out to interested and skilled individuals overseas – most often, expatriate entrepreneurs – can also provide a source of capital and expertise.

A final important – though very challenging – role for government is to intervene directly in the entrepreneurial process. As noted above, these programs must be designed thoughtfully, so as to be sensitive to the private sector's needs and to the market's dictates. Because of the "increasing returns" nature of entrepreneurship, these efforts can play an important role in the industry's early days.

At the same time, governments must avoid the common pitfalls that befall public venture initiatives. I divide these pitfalls into two categories: conceptual issues, which doom a program from its very start, and implementation issues, which create problems as the programs enter operation.

One common conceptual problem is to ignore the realities of the entrepreneurial process. For instance, many public venture capital initiatives have been abandoned after a few years: the programs' authors have apparently not understood that these initiatives take many years to bear fruit. Others have added requirements – such as the stipulation that portfolio companies focus only on explicitly "pre-commercial" research – that while seemingly reasonable from a public policy perspective, run counter to the nature of the entrepreneurial process. In other cases, reasonable programs have been created that are too tiny to have any impact or so large that they swamp the already existing funds.

A second frequently encountered conceptual problem is the creation of programs that ignore the market's dictates. Far too often, government officials have sought to encourage funding in industries or geographic regions where private interest simply was not there. Whether driven by political considerations or hubris, the result has been wasted resources. Effective programs address this problem by demanding that credible private sector players provide matching funds.

These broad design problems can ensure that a program will not meet its goals even before it is started. But there are plenty of pitfalls once programs begin. One frequently encountered implementation problem is not worrying about incentives. Far too often, participants in public schemes to promote entrepreneurship do well, no matter whether the program meets the public sector's objectives. In fact, in many instances, they do well even if the companies go belly-up! The contrast with the best practices among private investors, where a scrupulous attention to incentives is commonplace, could not be more striking. It would be desirable if public initiative managers paid more attention to what will happen in various scenarios, and how incentives can lead to problematic behavior.

Another implementation pitfall is the absence of appropriate evaluative mechanisms. Ideally, programs will undergo careful scrutiny at two levels. First, each program will be carefully analyzed. While recognizing that any initiative will take time to bear fruit, it is important to periodically take stock as to what aspects appear to be working well and which are problematic. Second, fund managers and firms participating in the programs should be scrutinized. It is important to ensure that the groups benefiting from these programs are the most promising in the industry in terms of market performance and can benefit the most from public investment, rather than simply being those most adept at garnering public funds.

A final frequent implementation issue is to ignore the international nature of the entrepreneurial process. Today's venture industry is a global one on many levels. Limited partners' capital commitments, venture capitalists' investments, and entrepreneurial firms' spending increasingly flow across borders and continents. To attempt to build a local entrepreneurial sector and venture capital industry without strong global ties is a recipe for an irrelevant sector without much economic impact. Yet in many instances, international participation is actively discouraged.

2.3.3 Research and case study findings re program outcomes

Many policymakers suggest that they are primarily interested in enhancing the growth and dynamism of entrepreneurial companies in their region as a lever for overall regional or national economic performance. Our research suggests a few policy levers consistent with achieving that objective:

- *Remember that entrepreneurial activity does not exist in a vacuum.* Entrepreneurs are tremendously dependent on their partners. Without experienced lawyers able to negotiate agreements, skilled marketing gurus and engineers who are willing to work for low wages and a handful of stock options, and customers who are willing to take a chance on young firms, new ventures are unlikely to be able to grow. But despite the importance of the entrepreneurial environment, in many cases government officials gravitate straight to handing out money without thinking about the other barriers that entrepreneurs face. This behavior is unlikely to address the problems of these firms. In some cases, crucial aspects of the entrepreneurial environment may initially seem somewhat tangential: for instance, the importance of robust public markets for young firms as a spur to venture investment. Singapore provides a great example of a nation which took a broader view, and sought not just to address deficiencies in the availability of capital, but also the many other barriers that limited the creation of a productive arena in which entrepreneurs could operate.

- *Leverage the local academic scientific and research base more effectively.* One particular precondition to entrepreneurship deserves special mention: in many regions of the world, there is a mismatch between the low level of entrepreneurial activity and venture capital financing on the one hand and the strength of the scientific and research base on the other. The role of technology transfer offices is absolutely critical here. Effective offices do far more than simply license technologies; they also work closely to educate nascent academic entrepreneurs and facilitate introductions to venture investors. Building the capabilities of local technology transfer offices, and ensuring that both potential academic entrepreneurs and technology transfer personnel have opportunities for training about the nature and mechanics of the new firm formation process, is critically important. In particular, all too often, technology transfer offices are encouraged to maximize the short-run return from licensing transactions. This leads to an emphasis on transactions with established corporations that can make substantial upfront payments, even though considerable evidence suggests that licensing new technologies to start-ups can yield substantial returns in the long run, both to the institution and to the region as a whole. If policymakers are earnest about developing an entrepreneurial sector, it is important that they think seriously about the way in which technology transfer is being undertaken, the incentives being offered, and their consequences.

- *Respect the need for conformity to global standards.* It is natural to want to hold onto long-standing approaches in matters such as securities regulation and taxes. In many cases, these approaches have evolved to address specific problems, and have proven to be effective responses. Despite this understandable reluctance to change, there is a strong case for adopting the de facto global standards if a nation is serious about promoting entrepreneurship and venture capital. Global institutional investors and venture funds are likely to be discouraged if the customary partnership and preferred stock structures cannot be employed in a given nation. Even if a perfectly good alternative exists, they may be unwilling to devote the time and resources to explore this option. Unless one is located in a nation such as China – where global investors will feel compelled to master the system, no matter how complex, owing to the size of the market opportunity – there is much to be said for allowing transactions that conform to the models widely accepted as best practice.

- *Be sure to let the market provide direction when providing subsidies to stimulate entrepreneurial and venture activity.* As noted above, two efforts which largely have met their goals (at least to date) have been the Israeli Yozma program and the New Zealand Seed Investment Fund. While these programs differed in their details – the former was geared toward attracting foreign venture investors, the latter encouraged locally-based, early-stage funds – they shared a central element: each used matching funds to direct where public subsidies should go. In undertaking these efforts, it should be kept in mind:

  o The identification of appropriate firms or funds is not likely to take place overnight. Rather than starting with the expectation of funding dozens of groups immediately, it typically makes sense to first fund a handful of entities. As feedback is received from the early participants, it may be appropriate to launch a second and third batch, or instead to supplement the capital of the pioneering firms and funds.

  o It is important that these initiatives not become competitors with independent venture funds or engage in the protracted financing of sub-standard firms that cannot raise private financing. Thus, it would be helpful if these efforts, emulating initiatives that have met their goals in the past, required a substantial amount of funds to be raised from non-public sources.

  o In selecting venture funds to which to provide capital, it is important to realize that it may be a challenge to interest top-tier venture groups. Rather, the expectation should be that a given region can attract solid groups with a particular interest in industries where there is already real local strength.

  o In the same spirit, policymakers may wish to cast their net broadly in terms of the types of firms and funds that they seek to attract. In addition to traditional stand-alone start-up venture funds, they may wish to consider encouraging corporate spinouts and venture funds as well.

  o In encouraging seed companies and groups, leaders should be aware that in many cases, extensive intervention may be needed before they are "fund-able." This may entail working closely with the organizations to refine strategies, recruit additional partners (perhaps even from other regions), and identify potential investors. Moreover, it is important that the firms and groups understand that they need to retain enough "dry powder" so that they do not go "belly-up" once the government subsidies run out. Having the right leader for this program is critical if these interventions are to be effective.

o If the goal is to promote success, it would be helpful if policymakers publicized in advance their evaluation criteria for assessing prospective firms and funds, and that these evaluation standards were close to those employed in the private sector for assessing entrepreneurs and venture funds.

- *Resist the temptation to "over-engineer" entrepreneurship and venture capital initiatives.* In many instances, government requirements that limit the flexibility of entrepreneurs and venture investors have been very detrimental. It is tempting for policymakers to add restrictions on several dimensions: for instance, the locations in which the firms can operate, the type of securities venture investors can use, and the evolution of the firms going forward (for example, restrictions on acquisitions or secondary sales of stock). It would be desirable for the government to eschew such efforts to "micro-manage" the nature of the entrepreneurial process. While it is natural to expect that firms and groups receiving subsidies will retain a local presence or continue to target the local region for investments, it is helpful if these requirements are as minimal as possible.

- *Recognize the long lead times associated with public venture initiatives.* One of the common challenges of public entrepreneurship and venture capital initiatives has been excessive impatience. Building an entrepreneurial sector is a long-run endeavor, which will not take place overnight. It is important that the programs that appear to have some initial promise be given enough time to prove their merits. Far too often, promising initiatives have been abandoned on the basis of partial (and often, not the most critical) indicators: for instance, low interim rates of return of initial program participants. Moreover, in many cases politicians have very unrealistic expectations about the likelihood of job growth in the short and medium term from these efforts. On the one hand, there is no doubt that high-impact young firms are an engine of overall job creation for the economy, and that this is particularly true at the regional level.[10] At the same time, even a substantial amount of innovation-driven entrepreneurship may not overcome a "jobs" problem at a very great speed: as the last few years have illustrated, massive layoffs from automobile manufacturing and construction are not going to be solved with even an extremely well-run biotech incubator. Having unrealistic expectations and too much impatience – and consequently creating rules that force program participants to focus on short-run returns – is a recipe for disappointment.

- *Avoid either too large or too small initiatives.* Policymakers must walk a tightrope in finding the appropriate size for venture initiatives. Too small a program will be unlikely to have much of an impact in addressing the challenging environment facing pioneering entrepreneurs and venture funds. Moreover, inflated expectations may create a backlash that makes future efforts difficult. But too substantial efforts run the risk of swamping the local markets. The imbalance between plentiful capital and limited opportunities may introduce any number of pathologies. Consider the experience of the Canadian labor fund program. Not only did it end up backing mostly incompetent groups that did little to spur entrepreneurship, but it had the effect of crowding out some of the most knowledgeable local investors.

- *Understand the importance of global interconnections.* As this piece has repeatedly emphasized, entrepreneurship and venture capital are increasingly emerging as global enterprises. This evolution has two important consequences. First, no matter how eager policymakers are to encourage activity in their own backyard, they must realize that to meet their goals, firms must increasingly have a multinational presence. Efforts to restrict firms to hiring and manufacturing locally are likely to be profoundly self-defeating. Second, in the interests of promoting successful firms, it is helpful to involve overseas investors as much as feasible. The benefits to local companies of relationships with funds based elsewhere but investing capital locally can be substantial. Moreover, initial investments which do well will attract more overseas capital. In addition, local affiliates of a fund based elsewhere – having developed an attractive track record – will gain the credibility they need to raise their own funds. That being said, when using public funds to subsidize activities by overseas parties, it is important to carefully question and obtain commitments from these entrepreneurs and groups about their intentions to recruit personnel to be resident locally and the extent to which the partners based elsewhere will be involved with the management of the local groups.

- *Institutionalize careful evaluations of these initiatives.* All too often, in the rush to "do something," policymakers make no provision for the evaluation of these efforts. The future of these initiatives should be determined by the extent that they meet their goals, rather than other considerations (such as the vehemence with which program supporters argue for their continuation). The design of careful program evaluations will help insure better decisions. It is helpful if these evaluations consider just the individual funds and companies participating in the programs, but also the broader context, such as:
    - o Gathering and publicizing accurate data on the extent of high-potential entrepreneurship and formal and informal venture capital activity. Some of this information can be collected beginning immediately; other information can only be gathered after some activity. These data will be important not only for the program evaluations, but also to publicize the growing size and dynamism of the local venture market to prospective investors.

○ Comparing publicly supported firms and venture groups to their peers to infer the difference the program has made.

○ Carefully tracking the performance of the companies that are and are not participating in the program, including not just financial returns but also such elements as sales and employment growth.

The evaluators may also wish to consider whether it would be feasible to randomize at least some awards, or explore the use of regression discontinuity analysis in the evaluations.

- *Realize that the programs to promote entrepreneurship and innovation need creativity and flexibility.* Too often, public venturing initiatives are like the pock-faced villain in a horror film – as much as one tries, they cannot be killed off! Their seeming immortality reflects the capture problem discussed above: powerful vested interests soon coalesce behind these initiatives, which makes them impossible to get rid of. The nations that have had the public programs with the greatest impact, on the other hand, have been willing to end programs that are not doing well, and substitute other incentives. Even more powerfully, they have been willing to end programs on the grounds that they are *too* successful – they have met their goals and hence no longer in need of public funding. Moreover, program rules may have to evolve and change, even if it means eliminating important classes of participants. If government is going to be in the business of promoting entrepreneurship, it needs some of the same qualities itself.

- *Recognize that "agency problems" are universal, and take steps to minimize their danger.* The temptations to direct public subsidies in problematic ways are not confined to any region, political system, or ethnicity. While we might wish that humanity everywhere would simply confine themselves to maximizing the public welfare, more selfish interests all too often rear their ugly heads. In designing public programs to promote venture capital and entrepreneurship, limiting the possibilities for such behavior is clearly essential. As we have seen, approaches such as defining and adhering to clear strategies and procedures for venture initiatives, creating a "firewall" between elected officials and program administrators, and careful assessments of the programs can help limit these problems.

- *Make education an important part of the mixture.* It is helpful if there is an emphasis on education with at least three dimensions:

○ The first is building the understanding of outsiders about the local market's potential. One of the critical barriers to the willingness of venture investors to invest in a given nation is a lack of information. If one visits a racetrack for the first time, it's always nice to know whether the track favors front-runners or late closers, and who the hot local jockeys are. In the same way, institutions often feel much more comfortable investing if they can access information about the level of entrepreneurial activity in local markets, the outcomes of the investments, and so forth. An important role that government can play is directly gathering this information, or else encouraging (and perhaps funding) a local trade association to do so.

o Second, educating entrepreneurs is a critical process. In many emerging venture markets, entrepreneurs may have a great deal of confidence, but relatively little understanding of the expectations of top-tier private investors, potential strategic partners, and investment bankers. The more that can be done to fill these gaps, the better.

o Finally, a broad-based understanding in the public sector of the challenges of entrepreneurial and venture capital development is very helpful. As we have repeatedly highlighted, in many instances, policymakers have made expensive errors in promoting these activities out of a lack of understanding of how these markets really work.

2.3.4 Less consistent approaches

But not all suggestions are good ones. Some ideas which are frequently heard – indeed, often touted by consultants and intermediaries of various types – are inconsistent with the global evidence on appropriate steps to build an entrepreneurial sector or venture capital.

Local entrepreneurs and venture investors frequently demand that local pools of government funds – whether sovereign funds owned by the states or pension funds for public employees – be mandated to devote a large allocation of their general investment pool to domestic entrepreneurs or venture funds. This suggestion, while initially plausible, is problematic for several reasons.

First, as discussed above, the creation of dynamic markets appear to be largely driven by the engagement of global private equity limited partners, rather than local players. Early-stage venture funds – assuming that they can develop a reasonable track record – are likely to attract considerable interest from institutional investors. By directing funds to local groups that cannot raise money, governments are likely to be rewarding precisely the groups that don't deserve funds.

Moreover, as highlighted above, a real danger with public programs is that they end up flooding the market with far more capital than they can reasonably deploy. Such well-intentioned steps can actually end up hurting entrepreneurs and venture capitalists.

Finally, it flies in the face of the principle that public venture capital funds should rely on the market to identify where attractive opportunities are, rather than mandating activity. While it would be hoped that local pension and investment funds will eventually play an important role here, it should be at a pace that they are comfortable with.

A second, less helpful idea is the commonly heard demand for provisions that would give investors an immediate tax deduction when a venture capital investment is made. A frequently cited model is the CAPCO program pioneered in Louisiana and adopted by a number of American states. Unfortunately, these efforts have been largely not met their goals.

This suggestion, while initially appealing, raises concerns for two reasons. First, the evidence suggests that the primary way in which tax policy encourages venture capital is through the demand side: the incentive that the entrepreneur has to (typically) quit his salaried job and begin a new firm instead. Little evidence suggests that tax policy can dramatically affect the supply of venture capital by the types of sophisticated institutional investors that provide capital to the world's leading venture industries. (Indeed, many dominant venture capital investors – such as pension funds and endowments – are exempt from taxes in most nations.)

Second, one of the powerful features of the venture capital process is the alignment of incentives. Everyone – whether limited partner, venture capitalist, or entrepreneur – does not get substantial gains until the company is sold or goes public. Economists argue that such an alignment keeps everyone focused and minimizes the danger of strategic behavior that benefits one party but hurts the firm.[11] Giving substantial tax incentives at the time of the investment could distort this alignment of incentives.

A third idea which raises concerns is relying on an outside investment firm to manage a fund-of-funds for that locale. Such an effort that has been tried in a number of American states. These efforts seem problematic for several reasons. First, the fees charged by these intermediaries are frequently substantial. These services, while they may appear small (only one percent of capital under management!), often end up eating up a huge fraction of the returns.

Second, it is by no means clear that the investments by the intermediary will be primarily driven by the local government's priorities. These fees can also create incentives to do deals for their own sake, rather than taking the steps that advance the mission of the fund. Thus, a financial institution may be tempted to put the money to work quickly, so it can raise another fund (and generate more fees). Alternatively, there may be funds that the intermediary has a "special relationship" with (for instance, an investment bank's fundraising group may be gathering capital for that group). In these instances, divided loyalties will come into play, and the best interests of the government may not be served. Thus, it is not surprising that US states that have tried such efforts, such as Oklahoma, have seen only very limited growth in their venture industries.

Another persistent theme – perhaps the hardest to resist – is the desirability of blindly duplicating programs and incentives provided elsewhere. For instance, many Persian Gulf states have borrowed concepts from Dubai, even if the very fact that the strategies worked for Dubai means that they are less likely to work elsewhere (such as the creation of a major air travel hub).

Moreover, in many cases, there has been a strong temptation to emulate even programs that have proved to be ill-considered elsewhere. For instance, incentive schemes in other regions that gave large tax benefits for those who invest in entrepreneurial firms have typically not met policymakers' goals in promoting entrepreneurship, yet have been widely emulated. Similarly, we have seen that the widely adopted strategy of instructing local pension fund managers to make economically targeted investments with employees' funds has had a very mixed and troubled legacy.

It is important to remember the adage that "two wrongs do not make a right." Ill- considered steps to promote entrepreneurship and venture capital can be profoundly distorting, attracting inexperienced operators and leading to ill-fated investments. The poisonous legacy that results can discourage other legitimate investors from participating in the market for years to come and set back the creation of a healthy industry. Thus, tempting as it is to match these investment incentives offered by others, if a strategy appears ill considered, it is best avoided.

2.3.5 Final thoughts

As we acknowledged in the introduction, the quest to encourage venture activity can seem like a side-show among the many responsibilities of government, from waging war to ensuring the stability of major financial institutions. Certainly, the dollars spent each year on these programs – while significant on an absolute basis – pale when compared to defense and healthcare expenditures. But the picture changes when we consider the long-run consequences of policies that facilitate or hinder the development of a venture sector: that is, the impact on national prosperity that a vital entrepreneurial climate can have. In the long run, the significance of these policies looms much larger.

In many cases, there is likely to be a role for the government in stimulating a vibrant entrepreneurial sector, given the early stage of maturity of these activities in most nations. But at the same time, it is easy for the government to overstep its bounds and squander its investments in this arena. Only by designing a program that reflects an understanding of, and a willingness to listen to, the entrepreneurial process can government efforts be effective.

There is also a great need for more academic research in this area. This topic has not attracted the attention it really deserves. In part, this paucity reflects the fact that these programs are difficult to evaluate: In undertaking these assessments, one has to ask what would have happened without the subsidies. This may seem pretty daunting: we need to look inside a crystal ball, and figure out what would have happened in the parallel universe in which the program did not exist.

Of course, this is a familiar problem in many settings, whether evaluating new pedagogical approaches or novel pharmaceuticals. By undertaking randomized trials, in which some entities are selected for awards that would not otherwise "make the cut," while not choosing some entities that would be chosen otherwise, the impact of the program can be understood. The entrepreneurs who received awards that are below the cut-off score, and those who are above the line but did not get awards, are compared to their peers to get a sense of the program's impact. In this way, any unobserved differences between the awardees and the controls are eliminated. Just because those entrepreneurs who take part in a government program do better than their peers doesn't mean the program has made a difference. Rather, the applicants could have been disproportionately the best and the brightest entrepreneurs, who were smart enough to learn about the program and find the time to fill out the application. Moreover, if there was a competition for the rewards, the screening process should have picked out the better groups.

Yet such trials – however widely adopted in other areas – remain quite rare when assessing public efforts to promote entrepreneurship. A frequent objection to randomization is that it's wrong to knowingly give public money to an inferior entrepreneur. While we have long been comfortable with the use of randomized trials in medical research, where one set of cancer patients gets the experimental drug and the others get the traditional treatment, the introduction of random choices in economic development settings make many leaders profoundly nervous. Whatever the merits of their reluctance, it has blocked attempts to use randomization while assessing public venturing programs.

Fortunately, there is an alternative: the use of an approach called "regression discontinuity" analyses. Essentially, this type of analysis exploits the fact that when program managers do their assessment of potential participants, there are always going to be some applications that fall just above or just below the cut-off line. By comparing these entrepreneurs or venture funds, which are likely to be very similar to each other in everything except for the fact that some were chosen for the program and others not, one can get a good sense of the program's impact without a randomization procedure. As Adam Jaffe, one of the most vocal advocates of better evaluation approaches, has observed: "I and others have previously harped on randomization as the "gold standard" for program evaluation. I now believe that [regression discontinuity] design represents a better trade-off between statistical benefits and resistance to implementation."[12] But even getting access to data about rejected applicants can be a sensitive process. In part, getting better research will require policymakers who are willing to be more open to policy experiments; but it will also take academics who are willing to engage in reaching out to and working with government officials to overcome their natural concerns.

These are issues of critical importance to all of us. While these issues may sometimes seem arcane and technical, well-considered – or misguided – policies are likely to have a profound influence on our opportunities, as well as those of our children and grandchildren. However challenging the encouragement of entrepreneurship may occasionally seem, these issues are truly too important to be left to the policy specialists!

Notes

1. This is based on *Boulevard of Broken Dreams: Why Public Efforts to Boost Entrepreneurship and Venture Capital Have Failed – and What to Do About It* (Princeton, NJ: Princeton University Press, 2009). I thank Harvard Business School's Division of Research for financial support. All errors are my own.

2. "AIG Gets $150 Billion Government Bailout; Posts Huge Loss," *Reuters News Service*, November 10, 2008, and Nelson D. Schwartz, "UBS Given an Infusion of Capital," *New York Times*, October 16, 2008.

3. For a discussion of these issues, see Antoinette Schoar, "The Divide between Subsistence and Transformational Entrepreneurship," *Innovation Policy and the Economy*, vol. 10 (2010), pp. 57–81.

4. See, for instance, T.J. Rodgers, *Why Silicon Valley Should Not Normalize Relations with Washington D.C.* (Washington, DC: Cato Institute, 2000), pp. 2–9.

5. See Stuart W. Leslie and Robert H. Kargon, "Selling Silicon Valley: Frederick Terman's Model for Regional Advantage," *Business History Review*, vol. 70 (1996), pp. 435–472; Annalee Saxenian, *Regional Advantage: Culture and Competition in Silicon Valley and Route 128* (Cambridge, MA: Harvard University Press, 1994); and especially Timothy J. Sturgeon, "How Silicon Valley Came to Be," in Martin Kenney (ed.), *Understanding the Silicon Valley: Anatomy of an Entrepreneurial Region* (Stanford: Stanford University Press, 2000), pp. 15–47.

6. Spencer Ante, *Creative Capital: Georges Doriot and the Birth of Venture Capital* (Boston, MA: Harvard Business School Press, 2008); and Patrick R. Liles, *Sustaining the Venture Capital Firm* (Cambridge, MA.: Management Analysis Center, 1978).

7. C.M. Noone and S.M. Rubel, *SBICs: Pioneers in Organized Venture Capital* (Chicago: Capital Publishing, 1970); Jonathan J. Bean, *Big Government and Affirmative Action: The Scandalous History of the Small Business Administration* (Lexington: University Press of Kentucky, 2001); and Liles, *Venture Capital Firm*.

8. Thomas Hellmann and Manju Puri, "The Interaction between Product Market and Financing Strategy: The Role of Venture Capital," *Review of Financial Studies*, vol. 13 (2000), pp. 959–984; and Samuel S. Kortum and Josh Lerner, "Assessing the Contribution of Venture Capital to Innovation," *Rand Journal of Economics*, vol. 31 (2000), pp. 674–692.

9. The articulation of this model in the economics literature is frequently attributed to Mancur Olson, *The Logic of Collective Action* (Cambridge, MA: Harvard University Press, 1965); and George Stigler, "The Economic Theory of Regulation," *Bell Journal of Economics*, vol. 2 (1971), pp. 3–21; its formal modeling to Sam Peltzman, "Towards a More General Theory of Regulation," *Journal of Law and Economics*, vol. 19 (1976), pp. 211–240; and Gary S. Becker, "A Theory of Competition among Pressure Groups for Political Influence," *Quarterly Journal of Economics*, vol. 98 (1983), pp. 371–400.

10. See several of the earlier papers in this series, most recently John Haltiwanger, "Job Creation and Firm Dynamics in the U.S.," *Innovation Policy and the Economy*, vol. 12 (2012) forthcoming.

11. For a detailed review of the academic literature, see Paul Gompers and Josh Lerner, *The Venture Capital Cycle* (Cambridge, MA: MIT Press, 2004), volume 2.

12. Adam B. Jaffe, "Building Program Evaluation into the Design of Public Research Support Programs," *Oxford Review of Economic Policy*, vol. 18 (2002), pp. 22–34 (33).

2.4

Comment on "The Boulevard of Broken Dreams: Industrial Policy and Entrepreneurship" by Josh Lerner

Indermit Gill
Chief Economist for Europe and Central Asia, World Bank

2.4.1   Industrial policy as stone soup

It is a pleasure to comment on this paper, which is essentially chapter 1 of the 2009 book by Josh called *The Boulevard of Broken Dreams*. I liked the book very much when I read it, and I have recommended it to many people. And I recommend it to all of you today, if you haven't already read it.

In preparing for this comment, I did some research on the subject on industrial policy. I came across a piece by Dani Rodrik called "The Return of Industrial Policy," though Dani contradicts his own headline by asserting (correctly) that industrial policy never went out of fashion. Dani writes:

> British Prime Minister Gordon Brown promotes it as a vehicle for creating high-skill jobs. French President Nicolas Sarkozy talks about using it to keep industrial jobs in France. The World Bank's chief economist, Justin Lin, openly supports it to speed up structural change in developing nations. McKinsey is advising governments on how to do it right.

I have a feeling that McKinsey will be in this business for a long time, because it will take a lot to get governments to do this right. And that brings me to my comment.

As I read the paper, especially the parts where Josh lists his lessons, I was reminded of the old folk tale popularly known as "Stone Soup." Hence the title of this commentary.

I am sure you know the story. One version has a young smart traveler who is hungry. He comes to a village, starts a fire, puts a pot full of water on top of it, and puts a bright-looking stone in it. Soon a villager comes by and asks what he's cooking. He says its stone soup, which will be delicious, but he could use some garnish. The villager says he has some carrots that he could spare. Another brings turnips, another onions, another a chicken and so on. At the end they all enjoy delicious soup.

136

The moral of the story, of course, is that it's not the stone that helped to make good soup, but all the other naturally good stuff. A bright villager would have taken notes, jotting down the list of ingredients that went into the cauldron.

Replace the clever traveler with Josh or McKinsey—indeed, one version of the story has a group of travelers rather than just one fellow—and you have successful industrial policy as stone soup.

Josh writes:

> If we have heard too many pronouncements of Silicon Valley patriarchs, we might begin with the view of new ventures as an activity where the government has nothing to contribute. A review of the history of Silicon Valley and several of the pioneering venture capital groups suggests that reality is far more complex than some of our more libertarian entrepreneur friends might have us believe. In each case we look at, the role of the government as an initial catalyst was critical in stimulating the growth of the region, sector, or firm.

The reader is led to believe that Josh will tell us the magic ingredient – a new industrial policy that works. He starts making soup, and the villagers gather around. Josh lists the things he needs the villagers to put into the pot. I will abuse his work a bit to summarize the "policy levers" he identifies, which are essentially a set of reminders for governments who want to do successful industrial policy:

1. **Remember that entrepreneurial activity does not exist in a vacuum.** You need experienced lawyers, skilled marketers and engineers, and investors. And robust public markets. And capital for investment. Essentially, Josh concludes, you have also to get rid of all "other barriers that limit the creation of a productive arena in which entrepreneurs could operate."
2. **Leverage the local academic scientific and research base more effectively.** Technology transfers, and so on.
3. **Respect the need for conformity to global standards.** Unless you are as big as China.
4. **Be sure to let the market provide direction.** When providing subsidies, make sure you do this in a way that the funded agencies don't compete with independent venture funds. Use the same evaluation criteria as what the market uses. Cast the net widely. Pick good leaders. Best of luck.
5. **Resist the temptation to overengineer initiatives.** Like specifying the location of firms.
6. **Recognize long lead times associated with public ventures.** Don't be impatient (it takes time to make soup).
7. **Avoid either too large or too small initiatives.** Whatever that takes to decide.

8. **Understand the importance of global interconnections.**
9. **Realize that these programs need creativity and flexibility.** These are not two things that government agencies have in abundance, I imagine.
10. **Recognize that agency problems are universal, and take steps to minimize their danger.**
11. **Make education of everybody an important part of the policy package.**
12. **Institutionalize careful evaluations of these initiatives.**

If you do all this, industrial policy works. You can have sector-specific interventions, and they will do no harm. They might even make policymakers hurry up a bit to get the other ingredients into the pot.

I could not possibly object to these lessons. But it is a difficult list to remember. The question is: is there another that is easier to remember, but which still provides the necessary ingredients for making good soup?

It turns out that there is. It is based on the things that an enterprise needs for doing business, things that help a government to create a good investment climate. Here is the list of ten things that we have good information about, with a couple of examples for each:

1. **Make it easy to start a business.** Put procedures online, have a one-stop shop, etc.
2. **Make it easy to register property.** Set time limits for registration, have fixed transfer fees.
3. **Make it easy to pay taxes.** Allow electronic filing and payment, have one tax per tax base.
4. **Make it easy to get electricity and to hire the right workers.** Doing things electronically will require having power...
5. **Realize that getting credit can be made easier.** Through things like allowing out-of-court enforcement, and distributing both positive and negative credit information.
6. **Make it easier to deal with construction permits.** Have an organized set of building rules, and using risk-based building approvals.
7. **Make it easier to trade across borders.** Using electronic data interchange, using risk-based inspections.
8. **Remember to protect investors.** Even if you are as big as China. Allow access to all corporate documents, require detailed disclosure.
9. **Make it easier to enforce contracts.** Have a specialized commercial court or judge, and make judgments publicly available.
10. **Recognize that insolvency is part of healthy business.** Provide a legal framework for out-of-court settlements...

Of course, you will recognize that this is the list from the World Bank's *Doing Business* report. I think it should be in the toolkit of every policymaker charged with industrial policy. It is a relatively easy list to remember, and even easier to look up. If you have managed to get governments to add these ingredients to the mix, you can add the magic stone of industrial policy. It won't make much of a difference.

Josh has a telling comparison in his paper between Jamaica and Singapore. In the early 1960s, when Singapore and Jamaica became independent, their per capita incomes were slightly less than $3,000, in 2006 US dollars. By 2006, Singapore's per capita GDP was more than $30,000, whereas Jamaica's was less than $5,000.

How do these countries do in facilitating business? Singapore is the best in the world: it tops the World Bank's *Doing Business* ratings. Jamaica ranks 88th out of 180 countries. Both must have got better over time, but Singapore is clearly outstanding. By the way, Spain is 44th, Italy is 87th, and Greece is 100th.

You could say that India is doing fine, and it is 132nd, so these rankings don't mean too much. Brazil is 126th. Russia is 120th. China is doing fantastically, and it is 91st. Actually, the only "policy implication" of these rankings is that it pays to be a big country. I won't say more.

So what is the difference between Josh and Justin?

Josh appears to know that the stone is a just a good way to get the attention of policymakers, so that they make it easier to do business. The stone is optional. I read in his CV that he has an undergraduate degree from Yale University. That should tip you off, since Yalies are usually very bright people. Dani and Justin have tasted delicious soup often enough to believe that they've found a magic stone, and the carrots and onions and the other naturally good stuff are optional. Go with the Yalie.

Part III
Instruments of Industrial Policy

3.1

Financing Development:
The Case of BNDES[1]

João Carlos Ferraz, Claudio Figueiredo Coelho Leal,
Felipe Silveira Marques and Marcelo Trindade Miterhof

3.1.1 Introduction

The 2009–11 period revealed Brazil's capacity to stay on the growth path, which had characterized the national economic performance from 2005 up to the first hint of damaging effects of the international financial crisis on the country in the second half of 2008. Not only was it possible for the country, by means of incisive anti-cyclical initiatives, to diminish the severity of the crisis, but the government's determination and the array of instruments available were also reinforced to prioritize the long-term nature and maintain the growth of investment ahead of GDP. In fact, the proportion of Gross Fixed Capital Formation (GFCF) in GDP rose from 17.4 percent in 2007 to 19.3 percent in 2011, despite the fall posted at the end of 2009. From the perspective of sustainable development, however, this level is clearly insufficient. It is essential to further raise the rate of investment in Brazil, without which it will be difficult to maintain the recent growth trajectory and to strengthen the competitiveness of Brazilian firms.

BNDES' recent operations have combined support for investment projects with anti-cyclical intervention when the private credit crunch was at its bleakest in 2009 and 2010. This was only possible because of four combined factors: (1) the accumulated experience in dealing with long term financing: (2) the availability of a wide range of financial instruments; (3) the solidity of its financial performance and equity structure; (4) the political decision taken by the Lula administration, through the National Treasury, to provide the Bank with the necessary resources to face an increasing demand and to avoid a lack of credit for those interested in investing in Brazil.

The aim of this article is to discuss the Bank's operations when facing long-standing and emerging challenges in the country, such as productive development, infrastructure and socio-environmental sustainability. The paper is divided into four sections besides the introduction and conclusion: (1) a discussion of the role of development banks in the contemporary world is carried out; (2) an account of the history and profile of the institution; (3) the recent performance and, (4) the upcoming challenges BNDES is dealing with.

3.1.2   Development banks in the contemporary world

Long term financing is strategic and serves the purposes of more and better work opportunities, infrastructure, and competitive capabilities. To reach sustainable development, investment must grow ahead of production to mitigate inflationary pressures. In the external side, however, investment tends to stress balance of payments since in emerging economies capital goods are usually imported. In order to mitigate this pressure, it is important to have minimum local content requirements in capital goods in public financed investments, government procurement and public concession as oil and gas and telecommunications.

Investment growth, however, can be susceptible by the pro-cyclicity of financial markets. A development bank (DB), can in this context, be an instrument of systemic stability, providing investment funding and working capital in times of financial markets retraction.

As markets are shallow, incomplete or "fail", a DB is an essential instrument to foster sustainability, investment and accumulation of competences. However, these banks must have the necessary resources and instruments to face this challenge.

Historically, DBs have been an important instrument used by governments to promote economic development in practically all countries around the world, regardless of their stage of development. DBs have been established in former socialist economies, advanced capitalist countries and emerging economies to finance the construction of roads, highways, energy plants, dams, and telecommunication infrastructure; foster incipient industries and small and medium enterprises (SMEs); and provide financial services to low-income households (World Bank, 2012). In emerging market economies, for instance, DBs usually constitute the main source of long term credit, loan guarantees, and other financial services in the infrastructure, housing and agriculture sectors. Even in some advanced economies, where private financial institutions and capital markets satisfy the financial needs of firms and individuals, several DBs continue to play an active role in providing financial services to so called strategic sectors of the economy.

The World Bank Survey[2] reveals that the universe of DBs is heterogeneous and, as a result, they cannot and should not be treated as a uniform group of institutions. DBs differ among themselves in various areas, such as:

- Ownership structure (fully vs partially owned by government)
- Policy mandates (narrow vs broad mandates)

- Funding mechanisms (deposit-taking vs non-deposit-taking institutions)
- Target sectors and clients (narrow vs wide focus)
- Lending models (first-tier vs second-tier)
- Pricing of lending products (subsidized vs market interest rates)
- Regulation and supervision (special regime vs same regime applicable to private banks)
- Corporate governance (independent vs government-controlled boards)
- Transparency standards (wide vs limited disclosure)

There might be a role for DBs to play again as turbulence in financial markets continues and the ability and cost of borrowing of firms is seriously affected. During the current financial crisis, most development banks in Latin America, followed by Asia, Africa, and Europe, have assumed a countercyclical role by scaling up their lending operations exactly when private banks experienced temporary difficulties in granting credit to the private sector. Thus, in the short or medium terms, there are strong reasons for governments to continue modernizing their DBs and giving them tools to become more effective and successful in fulfilling their policy mandates. Scale and scope, however, matters as Brazilian Development Bank, BNDES, presented in the following sections shows.

3.1.3   The history and the profile of BNDES

BNDES is the main provider of long-term financing in Brazil, holding two-thirds of bank loans over five years. It is a 100 percent state-owned company under private law, with institutional funding[3] and 2,500 employees. BNDES is among the biggest development banks of the world in terms of assets, equity and disbursement (Table 3.1.1).

However, more important than its absolute size is: (1) the accumulated experience in dealing with long term financing: (2) the availability of a wide

Table 3.1.1   Development banks statistics, 2010

Development Banks	US$ billion			
	Assets	**Equity**	**Disbursement**	**ROE**
BNDES	329.5	39.6	96.3	21.2%
World Bank	282.8	37.4	28.9	−2.3%
IADB	87.2	21	10.3	1.6%
CAF	18.6	5.8	4.6	3.7%
China DB	665.2	55.5	93	8.8%

Sources: BNDES (Dec 31. 2010), IADB (Dec 31. 2010), WB (Jun 30. 2010), CAF (Dec 31. 2010)e CDB (Dec 31. 2010)

range of financial instruments; and (3) the solidity of its financial performance and equity structure.

As a financial institution wholly-controlled by the federal government and with stable sources of funding to carry out its mission, the BNDES, throughout its history, has managed to rise to the challenges in fostering economic and social development in the country.[4] This role is carried out via an extensive range of credit lines and programs, capable of offering: (i) traditional support for large-scale industrial and infrastructure projects, (ii) efforts to foster the commercialization of machinery and equipment via Finame, (iii) support for exports of engineering-intensive goods and services, (iv) assistance for micro and small companies by means of the BNDES Card, (v) and support for the capital market as well as for corporate governance of companies through BNDESPAR, BNDES equity arm. It operates directly and using other banks in credit operations, equity investments, project finance and grants concession.

Taking into account the nature of the funding composition, the BNDES can be considered the main source of long-term, third-party resources available for companies to finance their investments, as Figure 3.1.1 shows.

This large scope of products enables BNDES to follow the rise of investments in Brazilian economy and act counter-cyclically when GFCF fells. This way BNDES helps the continuous improvement of the investment rate, with significant job creation (Figure 3.1.2 and 3.1.3).

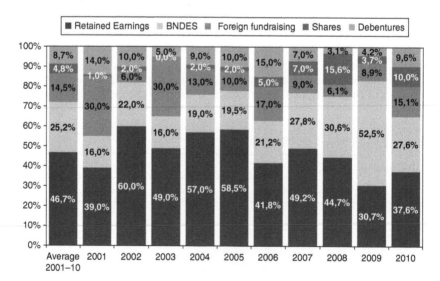

Figure 3.1.1   Sources of financing for investment (in %)
Source: BNDES.

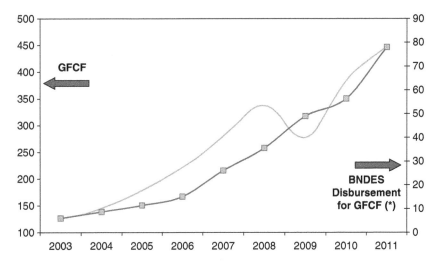

Figure 3.1.2 GFCF and BNDES disbursement for GFCF, 2003–2011 (in R$ billion)
*exc. BNDES Exim; working capital, M&A and Equity Financing.
Sources: BNDES and IBGE.

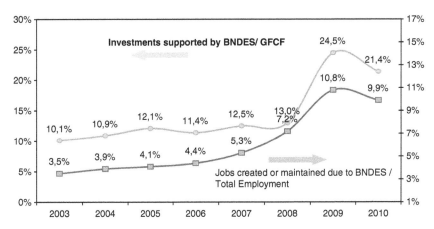

Figure 3.1.3 BNDES contribution to investment and employment, 2003–2010 (in %)
Sources: BNDES, IBGE and MTE/RAIS.

3.1.4 Fostering investment and mitigating crisis: the recent performance

One of the most important results from the institutional aspect of its sources is that the BNDES is able to operate anti-cyclically at times when private financial institutions are highly opposed to risk. The severity of the international financial crisis that affected the Brazilian economy as of the second half of 2008, and whose more critical effects dragged on until the first quarter of 2009, meant that the federal government had to employ a variety of anti-cyclical tools aimed at reestablishing credit. Two of these efforts were specifically relevant to the BNDES' operations – the creation of the Investment Maintenance Program (PSI), in June 2009, and the launch of extraordinary programs to support companies' working capital. With these two pillars, which indicate the decision to simultaneously alleviate the short-term credit crunch and pursue the return to investment, it was possible for the country to safely navigate the crisis.

The PSI, currently in its fourth edition, consists of a financing line to acquire machinery and equipment at a price set by the National Monetary Council (CMN, in Portuguese). The program is earmarked for both the isolated equipment financed by the BNDES' network of financial agents within the scope of the Finame product and the sub-credit for capital goods in large-scale investment projects.[5] The program began in June 2009, which sheds an important light on the right moment to react to express challenges. The strength of the program may not have been so readily evident had the launch taken place in the second half of 2008, when there was a strong recoil in investment. This idea is presented in the following chart, which shows the inversion of the path of Finame disbursements after the launch of the

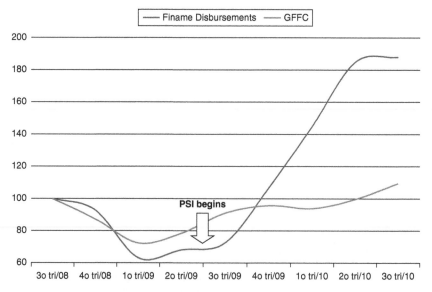

Figure 3.1.4   BNDES' Finame disbursements and GFFC (3Q08 = 100)
Sources: IBGE and the BNDES.

PSI and the behavior of the Gross Formation of Fixed Capital (GFFC) (see Figure 3.1.4).

Parallel to efforts aimed at sustaining investments throughout a clearly adverse environment between the end of 2008 and over the entire year of 2009, the efforts of public banks were also decisive in strengthening short-term credit for companies. Going beyond its traditional role, on this particular occasion, the BNDES, in this period, was required to create extraordinary lines of credit for working capital – even though not associated to investment projects. These programs not only had shorter terms and higher costs than the Bank's regular lines of credit, but were also limited to the size of the borrowing companies, and, in the case of some programs, earmarked for specific sectors. Table 3.1.2 lists some of the BNDES' initiatives related to efforts to supply working capital and maintain investments, which were later discontinued in light of the improving domestic scenario.

3.1.5   Long standing and emerging challenges

Beyond its anti-cyclical efforts, the BNDES, a public bank aimed at long-term financing, has the mission of supporting investments deemed as a priority for the Brazilian economy. The Bank's history has shown a constant inclusion of new concerns.[6] Some matters have been part of its efforts for several decades, such as expanding investments and financing infrastructure projects. The creation of basic infrastructure, especially energy and transport, marked the 1950s. The intermediate goods industry was a highlight in the 1960s, while basic inputs and capital goods were the main areas incorporated in the 1970s. In the same vein, new aims have been included on the BNDES' priority agenda over the last few decades, namely financing for innovation, fostering socio-environmental sustainability, support for

Table 3.1.2 Measures chosen by the BNDES to combat the crisis

Oct. '08	Opening access to the Pre-shipment line
Nov. '08	Creation of BNDES PEC (Special Credit Program)
Jan. '09	Expansion of REFIN
Feb. '09	Creation of Used Capital Goods Program
April '09	Creation of BNDES PEF (Emergency Financing Program)
April '09	Creation of BNDES PROCER (Special Rural Credit Program)
April '09	Improvement to conditions in BNDES Pre-shipment Product
April '09	Improvement to conditions in BNDES Bridge-loan Product
June '09	Creation of BNDES Refin – Capital goods

Source: BNDES.

modernizing public administration, as well as stimulus for local development, production inclusion, and opening up access to credit.

These matters illustrate the classical concept of development, which associates economic growth with social well-being, innovation and competitiveness. Contemporary concerns have expanded the meaning of this concept, under the insignia of sustainability, in such a way as to incorporate issues, such as environmental preservation and more efficient use of natural resources, which can also be called the green economy.

In this way, it is worth mentioning the BNDES' recent performance in three areas or activities: productive development, infrastructure and socio-environmental sustainability (or the green economy).

3.1.5.1   Productive development

The Bank's efforts to stimulate industrial growth in the country are aimed at three significant challenges: expanding the production capacity in the industrial and services sectors; increasing exports; and raising the capacity for innovation, an essential factor for growth in a globalized world. Since 2006, the BNDES has expanded its efforts in these areas, in keeping with the industrial policies elaborated at that time: Industrial, Technological and Foreign Trade Policy (PITCE, 2004–07), Productive Development Policy

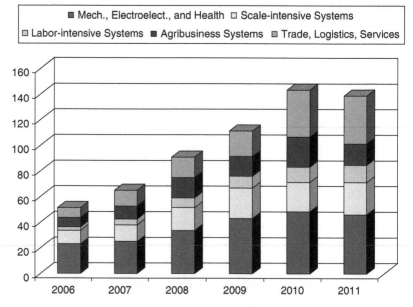

Figure 3.1.5   BNDES' disbursements to production systems (in R$ billion)
Source: BNDES.

(PDP, 2008–10), and the *Brasil Maior* Plan (PBM, 2011–14). Such growth has not sacrificed priority sectors (Mechanics, Electro-electronic and Health systems[7]), whose participation remained at close to one-third of total disbursements, a number which increases to 55 percent when calculating support for acquisition of capital goods through other production systems. The most considerable effect of the international crisis on the BNDES' disbursements to productive sectors was a small reduction in the participation related to scale-intensive systems[8] and agribusiness, which focus more on the foreign market. The counterpart was the increased participation of Trade, Logistics and Services, segments aimed at the domestic market, which led growth in the period.

Over the period, several programs were created and altered in favor of aggregating value locally. Among them, we detach the PSI, as mentioned earlier, support for innovation projects (FUNTEC, Criatec, Innovative Capital, Innovation Production, Pro-engineering, BNDES Card and so on[9]) and the BNDES' sectorial programs, which offer special credit conditions to knowledge-intensive sectors, such as Pro-P&G (Oil & Gas supply sector), Prosoft (Software and Information Technology Services), Profarma (Industrial Health Sector), Proplastico (Plastic Production Sector) and Proaeronautics (Aeronautics Production Sector) (see Table 3.1.3).

3.1.5.2   Infrastructure

While the meaning of causality is not always clear, there are no doubts as to the strong correlation between economic development and the supply of infrastructure, which in general mutually feed of each other. Solving infrastructure problems is necessary to improve the well-being of the population, allowing universal access to basic services, such as electric energy, communications, urban transport and sanitation. At the same time, expanding infrastructure brings about a drop in costs, an increase in productivity, improvements in the quality of goods and services in the production framework, and consolidation of regional integration.

The BNDES has always worked in the area. Over the last few years, however, there has been an expressive increase in the BNDES' disbursements, owing to economic growth and to the Bank's participation in the Growth Acceleration Program (PAC) (see Figure 3.1.6).

Over the period, several programs were created and altered to foster investments in infrastructure. Among them, highlights include the creation, in February 2008, of the Project Structuring Fund (FEP) – which provides non-reimbursable financing for studies, widely advertised to the general public, that contribute to making public policy or to generating projects related to the economic and social development of Brazil and Latin America –, as well as the creation, in November 2009, of the BNDES Financing Line for States, aimed at designing and implementing development programs across Brazilian states (see Table 3.1.4).

Table 3.1.3 Select measures to support productive and technology development (Jan. '06–Jan. '12)

Dec. '06	Creation of the Machinery and Equipment Modernization Program (FINAME MODERNIZA BK); and the creation of the FINAME Program for manufacturers of capital goods to acquire locally-manufactured pieces, parts and components (FINAME-COMPONENTES)
Dec. '06	Creation of CRIATEC, an investment fund for start-ups aimed at innovation
June '07	Creation of Support Program for Automotive Engineering
Aug. '07	Creation of PRO-AERONÁUTICA
Sept. '07	Expansion of the Support Program for Development of the Pharmaceutical Production Sector (PROFARMA), renamed the Support Program for Development of the Industrial Health Sector (PROFARMA)
Jan. '08	Creation of the line of credit Innovation Capital
June '09	Creation of the Support Program for Engineering (PROENGENHARIA)
July '09	Creation of the BNDES' Investment Maintenance Program (BNDES PSI)
Sept. '09	Expansion of the BNDES PROSOFT, with an increase in budget and support for investment in ITES-BPO.
Dec. '09	Creation of the Innovation-Production Line
June '10	Creation of the BNDES' Support Program for Development of the Plastic Production Sector (BNDES Proplastico)
Nov. '10	Support for Research, Development and Innovation projects within the scope of the BNDES Automatic.
Mar. '11	Launch of the BNDES-Finep joint plan aimed at Support Industrial Technological Innovation in the Sugar-based Energy and Sugar-based Chemical Sectors (PAISS)
Mar. '11	R$ 1 billion loan to support Finep's innovation portfolio
May '11	Creation of the BNDES' Support Program for Development of the Goods and Services Supply Sector related to the Oil & Natural Gas sector (BNDES P&G)
Oct. '11	Alteration of the BNDES' Operational Policies favoring local content and innovation
Oct. '11	Creation of the BNDES' Support Program for Professional Qualification (BNDES Qualification)
Nov. '11	R$ 2 billion loan to support Finep's innovation portfolio

Source: BNDES.

3.1.5.3   Socio-environmental sustainability

Socio-environmental development is a corporate priority which is reflected in the Bank's financing policy. Nevertheless, concerning the importance of recent efforts to put together lines of credit focusing specifically on the environment, most disbursements related to reducing carbon emissions

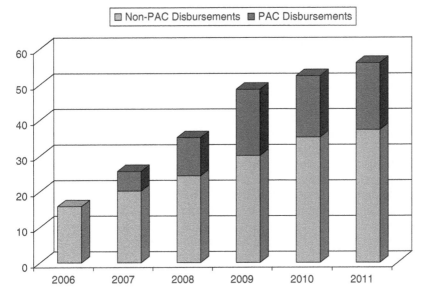

Figure 3.1.6 The BNDES' disbursements to infrastructure (in R$ billion)
Source: BNDES.

Table 3.1.4 Select measures to support infrastructure (Jan. '06–Jan. '12)

Mar. '06	Creation of the BNDES Financing Program for Self-employed Truck Drivers (BNDES PROCAMINHONEIRO)
April '06	Creation of the Highway Intervention Program (PROVIAS)
Dec. '06	Creation of the Support Program for Implementation of the Brazilian Land-based Digital TV System (PROTVD)
Mar. '07	Creation of the Credit Line for Modernization of Management of Revenue, Tax, Finances and Equity in State Administration
Mar. '07	Creation of the Commuting-to-School Program
May '07	Creation of the Financing Program for Acquisition of School Transport Vehicles (PROESCOLAR)
Feb. '08	Creation of the Project Structuring Fund (BNDES FEP)
Mar. '09	Creation of the Special Program for Support in the Oil & Gas Sector; Creation of the BNDES Civil Construction Program, and the inclusion of inputs for civil construction on the BNDES Card
Nov. '09	Creation of the BNDES Financing Line for States
July '10	Support for the A Computer for Every Student Program (PROUCA)
Aug. '10	Alteration to the conditions in the lines of credit "Electric Energy" and "Renewable Energy," increasing the BNDES' participation and expanding the amortization term
Oct. '11	Creation of the BNDES' Emergency Program for Reconstruction Municipalities Affected by Natural Disaster (BNDES PER)

Source: BNDES.

are in the energy and transport sectors, which have become the main motivation behind the BNDES' operations. The recent increase in green disbursements is, for the most part, related to sectors such as hydroelectric and wind power,[10] benefited by the PAC. Implementing PAC's Large City Mobility Program, concentrated on host-cities for the 2014 World Cup, is expected to boost disbursements related to urban transport significantly (see Figure 3.1.7).

Employing several different initiatives, the BNDES stimulates its clients to transform their attitude when taking into consideration the matter of sustainability, whether they are private companies or the government. Highlights include the Bank being chosen as the manager of the Amazon Fund, since 2008, and, more recently, the Ministry of the Environment (MMA) opting for the Bank to manage the National Climate Change Fund (Fundo Clima). In both cases, even more so with the creation of the Bank's Environmental Division, focus turns to the BNDES' skills in developing its role as manager of the external funds related to the green economy – a competence that BNDESPAR had already shown when it conceived several funds aimed at sustainable investments, and when it, together with the BM& F-Bovespa, spearheaded the creation of the carbon-efficiency index in 2010.

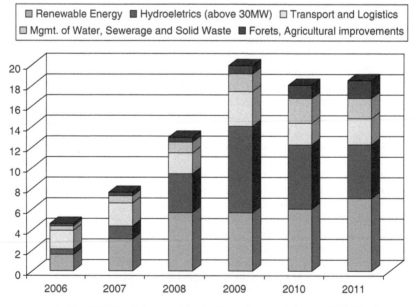

Figure 3.1.7   The BNDES' disbursements to the green economy (in R$ billion)
Source: BNDES.

Table 3.1.5 Select measures to support the green economy (Jan. '06–Jan. '12)

May '06	Creation of the Environmental line of credit
May '06	Creation of the line of credit to support Energy Efficient Projects (PROESCO)
June '07	Creation of the BNDES' Clean Development Program
Aug. '08	Creation of the Incentive Program for Sustainable Agricultural and Cattle-raising Production (PRODUSA)
Sept. '08	Creation of the Amazon Fund
April '09	Constitution of the Mata Atlântica Initiative
July '09	Creation of the BNDES' Support Program for Forest Compensation (BNDES Forest Compensation); and the alteration to the Environmental line of credit – Support for Carajás Forest Recovery (REFLORESTA), which is to be called the Support Line for Reforestation, Recovery and Sustainable Use of Forests (BNDES Forest).
July '10	Creation of the Incentive Program for Sustainable Agriculture and Cattle-raising Production (PRODUSA)
Oct. '11	Creation of the Program to Reduce Greenhouse Gas Emissions in Agriculture (Program ABC)
June '11	Creation of the BNDES' Fund Program for Innovation in the Environment
Nov. '11	Creation of the Climate Fund Program

Source: BNDES.

3.1.6 Conclusion

The path taken by the BNDES over the last few years has shown a substantial jump in its capacity to disburse funds due to resources coming for the National Treasury. The Bank is expected to stabilize the growth of its disbursements in R$140 billion. This level indicates the Bank's increased operational capacity both in taking on specific challenges, as happened in the recent international crisis, and in seeking out the structural challenges associated with development, intensifying support in sectors that have always been a priority for the Bank, such as infrastructure, while making efforts to reach new goals, as in the case of environmental sustainability and incorporating new concerns in productive development (innovation and regional development).

As one of the most important Brazilian institutions in fostering development, it is assuring to note that the BNDES, today, has operational capacity that is substantially higher than four of five years ago. However, perspectives and challenges for national development are not evidently limited solely to the Bank. On the contrary, they require dialog with several players. It is evident, for example, that the country is facing robust investment blocs that require systems and financing structures on a scale that exceeds the capacities of the BNDES.

In this way, among the developing uncertainties related to the international economic crisis, the Bank has a double challenge: to continue on its mission to assure financing for the multiple concerns and sectors associated with Brazil's development; and, at the same time, to encourage private sources of long-term resources, which can add to the efforts being taken to increase the rate of investment in the country. This has always been the BNDES' aim, but which requires a new and decisive stimulus with the domestic interest rate being adjusted to match the international rate.

Besides this, Brazil's success in the extraction industry and in agribusiness, a fundamental leverage for development, has become a benchmark for the transformation industry. With this, some challenges to productive development will feature on the BNDES' priority agenda over the coming years. One of these will be support for foreign sales of engineering-intensive goods and services aimed at diversifying exports. Another is to reinforce the competitiveness of suppliers of pieces, parts and components in the transformation industry, especially in the Oil & Gas sector. Also relevant are the new projects linked to industries, such as pharmaceutical and information and communication technologies (ICTs).

Faced with these new (and old) challenges, the BNDES will continue supporting investments that are a priority for the Brazilian economy. This mission has been the core of its long-term vision over the 60 years of its existence.

Notes

1. This article is an English version of Ferraz et al. (2012).
2. The Global Survey of Development Banks, conducted by the World Bank, got responses from 90 DBs in 61 countries. At the end of 2009, the DBs in the survey reported total assets in the amount of US$2.01 trillion and a combined loan portfolio of US$1.59 trillion. Most of the DBs examined in the survey were established between 1946 (after the end of World War II) and 1989 (49 percent), 39 percent between 1990 and 2011 and 12 percent before 1946.
3. The FAT, Workers' Assistance Fund, is a government-established fund based on social tax contribution over all Brazilian enterprises net operating revenues (1988). FAT transfer to BNDES independent of Federal Budget and as an undermined term, resulting in a quasi-equity funding mechanism.
4. For an insight into the recent path of the BNDES, see Além and Giambiagi (2010).
5. In the first edition of the PSI, the final cost to companies was 4.5 percent. Successive revisions of the program, in addition to extending the scope of the original operations to incorporate other objectives, especially support for innovation, raised the cost to almost 9 percent p.a. At this level, there is no need for the National Treasury to equalize.

6. For an historical account of the BNDES' operations, see BNDES (2013).
7. The Mechanics, Electro-electronic and Health systems are equivalent to Bloc 1 in the *Brasil Maior* Plan and account for the following sectors: Oil & Gas and Shipping (supply sector); Health Sector (pharmaceuticals, medicine, medical and hospital equipment as well as health services); Automotive; Aeronautics as well as Defense and Aerospace Sector; Capital Goods; besides Electro-electronic and Information and Communication Technologies (ICTs).
8. These include: Chemicals; Renewable Energy; Personal Hygiene, Perfume and Cosmetics (HPPC); Mining; Metals; as well as Pulp and Paper.
9. In general, the Bank's support for innovation, defined as a priority within the scope of its corporate planning, lies in the three-prongs: reimbursable credit lines, non-reimbursable support within the scope of FUNTEC, and the subscription of shares and debentures directly convertible or by means of funds. More recently, loan contracts were signed and a credit limit was opened for on-lending from Finep's innovation lines of credit. The concerted efforts of these three areas is fundamental to potentializing the efficiency in using public resources, seeking to combine, on the one hand, the challenge of expanding the number of innovative companies and, on the other hand, supporting structuring projects that engage technical and corporate capacities in areas in which the country has or can build competitive advantages. Concerning this, it is worth mentioning the combined initiatives of the BNDES and Finep with the Support Program for Sugar-based Ethanol (PAISS), which, through a public call-to-bid, sought to select business plans to develop the production of second-generation sugar-based ethanol (also known as cellulosic ethanol). For a reflection on the BNDES' support for innovation, see Kickinger and Veiga de Almeida (2010).
10. In 2011, for the first time, the BNDES' disbursements for wind-power projects surpassed those for hydroelectric power generation.

References

Além, A.C. and Giambiagi, F. (eds), *O BNDES em um Brasil em Transição* (Rio de Janeiro: BNDES).

BNDES (2013) BNDES: a bank of history and of the future (São Paulo: Museu da Pessoa).

Ferraz, J.C., Leal, C., Marques, F., and Miterhof, M. (2012) "O BNDES e o financiamento do desenvolvimento," *Revista da USP,* no. 93, Dossiê Especial: Desenvolvimento: uma corrida de longa distância (São Paulo: USP).

Kickinger, F.C. and Veiga de Almeida, H.T. (2010) "Reflexões sobre a inovação no Brasil e o papel do BNDES," in Além and Giambiagi (eds), *O BNDES em um Brasil em Transição* (Rio de Janeiro: BNDES).

World Bank (2012) *Global Survey of Development Banks,* Policy Research Working Paper no. 5969 (Washington, DC: World Bank).

3.2
Comment on "Financing Development: The Case of BNDES" by João Carlos Ferraz, Claudio Figueiredo Coelho Leal, Felipe Silveira Marques and Marcelo Trindade Miterhof

Robert Cull
World Bank, Development Economics Research Group

Clearly one cannot deny the influence of BNDES on the Brazilian economy, its fundamental contribution in the provision of longer-term finance, and its pronounced counter-cyclical lending during the recent global financial crisis, and all of those points are well made in the paper. What is less clear is whether this model is replicable and advisable for other developing countries, whether BNDES' size and influence will adversely affect (or has adversely affected) the provision of long-term finance by private financial institutions, and whether counter-cyclical lending by state banks reaches the borrowers who are most worthy of credit.

As shown in the paper, BNDES is large – very large by the standards of development banks. In fact, its $330 billion in assets is substantially larger than the World Bank's $283 billion, and its $96 billion in loan disbursements in 2010 far outstrips the World Bank's $29 billion. While many state-owned banks in Latin America stepped up lending during the crisis, those in other regions (notably in Eastern Europe) did not.[1] Even by the standards of government-owned banks in Latin America, BNDES' lending during the recent crisis was enormous. Few government-owned banks have the accumulated experience and financial resources to have played such a role during the crisis, and it is likely unwise for other developing countries to try to emulate BNDES, at least not for the sole purpose of having a large state-owned bank to lend counter-cyclically in times of crisis.

And lending on this scale is not cost-free. Substantial government funds are required. Although there are few specifics about the scale of such support in the paper, it is acknowledged that BNDES receives transfers from the

Workers' Assistance Fund (the FAT), a government-established fund that draws social tax contributions from Brazilian enterprises based on their net operating revenues, funds which are independent of the federal budget. From 2008 onward BNDES also received a series of long-term, low-interest rate loans totaling a remarkable $140 billion from the National Treasury. These funds were used to support companies' working capital needs by providing credit lines during the crisis and to subsidize interest rates on loans for large capital investment purchases via the Investment Support Program, which began in June 2009.

While these may have been very sensible uses of those government funds, it is difficult to know just how sensible without some comparison to potential alternative uses (on which the paper is silent). It is still too early to ascertain the quality of lending during the crisis, and only time will tell whether repayment rates on those loans remain high. From the description in the text, it seems that much of lending support during the crisis went to large-scale enterprises. This may or may not be the most efficient allocation of funds during a crisis, but it suggests that small-scale businesses and the poorer segments of the Brazilian population received little assistance from BNDES during the crisis. And indeed, recent evidence from the Pesquisa de Orçamentos Familiares, the primary survey of household income and expenditure in Brazil, indicates that usage of financial services (especially credit) declined sharply among the poor, those located in less populated areas, and households headed by self-employed individuals.[2] Only larger employers were able to offset losses in income by borrowing from formal lenders. Perhaps other government programs were designed to assist these groups through the crisis, but the data indicate that many groups suffered.

Another interesting aspect of the paper is the view that the expansion of BNDES into multiple financial services is a virtue. These services include traditional support for large-scale industrial and infrastructure projects, fostering sales and acquisition of machinery and equipment, support for the export of engineering-intensive goods and services, financial access for micro and small companies, and support for the development of the capital market as well as the corporate governance of individual firms through BNDESPAR, the equity arm of BNDES. The argument in the paper is that the diversification of products enables BNDES "to follow the rise of investments in the Brazilian economy and act counter-cyclically when gross fixed capital formation falls," thus enabling "continuous improvement of the investment rate, with significant job creation." It is difficult to understand why diversification necessarily provides such benefits. Certainly there is a large literature on the performance of state-owned banks, highlighting their inefficiency and poor financial performance due to the politicization of their lending, a literature which is ignored in the paper.[3] Mission creep on the part of a large state-owned financial institution would seem to be at least as likely to breed such problems as it would the benefits espoused in the paper.

BNDES was created to address failures in the market for long-term finance. As described by the authors, in developing countries these markets tend to be shallow and incomplete, and they fail to respond adequately to investment needs. In principle, state-owned development banks could help to resolve those failures while also helping to counteract the "pro-cyclical nature of financial markets that can impede development processes." And BNDES has been successful, as it holds two-thirds of all Brazilian bank loans of duration greater than five years. One wonders, however, whether BNDES has been too successful, and whether its dominance and potential funding and pricing advantages have impeded the entry of private institutions into the market for long-term finance. The authors are sensitive to this concern, noting in their conclusion that: "It is evident that the Brazilian investment frontier is so vast and the challenges of development so complex that a strong BNDES dependence will be counterproductive to the very development process. The time has come for the "crowding in" of the private finance industry to actively engage in long term financing." A laudable goal, but which policies can help achieve it? And do BNDES' size, scope, history, and experience make it less likely that such a transition will occur?

Ultimately, understanding the effects of mission creep and the dominance of long-term financing by a state-owned financial institution requires empirical analyses that facilitate comparisons between banks (both private and state-owned). To that end, the authors describe a new database for state-owned development banks that could be helpful. This is the Global Survey of Development Banks, conducted by the World Bank, which summarizes information from 90 banks in 61 countries on their ownership structures, policy mandates, funding mechanisms and structures, target sectors and clients, lending models, pricing of lending products, regulation and supervision, corporate governance, and disclosure standards.[4] With luck, that data collection exercise will be repeated in future years and expanded to include a wider set of banks.

While I commend the paper for raising a set of issues worthy of testing and describing a dataset that could begin to be used for such purposes, much research still needs to be completed to better understand when and where state-owned development banks are most likely to be effective, what their mandates should be, and how they should organize and govern themselves to achieve their objectives.

Notes

1. See Cull and Martinez Peria (2012), for example.
2. See Cull, Leite, and Scott (2011).
3. See World Bank (2001, 2008) for overviews of that literature.
4. De Luna-Martínez and Vicente (2012).

References

Cull, Robert, Leite, Philippe G., and Scott, Kinnon (2011) "Coping with the Financial Crisis: Household Evidence from Brazil," Chapter 3 of *Poverty and Social Protection in Brazil during the Twin Crises of 2008/09*, report prepared for the Brazil country unit of the World Bank (Washington, DC: World Bank).

Cull, Robert J. and Martínez Pería, María Soledad (2012) "Bank Ownership and Lending Patterns during the 2008–2009 Financial Crisis: Evidence from Latin America and Eastern Europe," mimeo (Washington, DC: World Bank).

De Luna-Martínez, José and Carlos Leonardo Vicente (2012) *Global Survey of Development Banks*, World Bank Policy Research Working Paper 5969 (Washington, DC: World Bank).

World Bank (2001) *Finance for Growth (Policy Choices in a Volatile World)*, World Bank Policy Research Report (New York: Oxford University Press).

World Bank (2008) *Finance for All? (Policies and Pitfalls in Expanding Access)*, World Bank Policy Research Report (Washington, DC: World Bank).

3.3

Growth and the Quality of Foreign Direct Investment*

Laura Alfaro
Harvard Business School and NBER
Andrew Charlton
London School of Economics

3.3.1 Introduction

Policymakers and academics often maintain that foreign direct investment (FDI) can help in the development efforts of host countries. In addition to supplying capital, FDI can be a source of valuable technology and know-how and foster linkages with local firms that can help to jumpstart an economy.[1] While academics tend to treat FDI as a homogenous capital flow, policy makers, on the other hand, seem to believe that some FDI projects are better than others. National policies toward foreign direct investment (FDI) seek to attract some types of FDI and regulate other types in a pattern which seems to reflect a belief among policymakers that FDI projects differ greatly in terms of the national benefits to be derived from them. UNCTAD's World Investment Report 2006 for instance describes "quality FDI" as "the kind that would significantly increase employment, enhance skills and boost the competitiveness of local enterprises." Policymakers from Dublin to Beijing have implemented complex FDI regimes with a view to influencing the nature of the FDI projects attracted to their shores. Sean Dorgan, Chief Executive of Ireland's Industrial Development Agency, for example, claims that "the value of inward investment must now be judged on its nature and quality rather than in quantitative measures or job numbers alone."[2] Chinese officials have openly stated that the new challenge for the country is to attract more "high quality foreign direct investment."[3]

In this paper we attempt to distinguish different qualities of FDI to re- examine the relationship between FDI and growth. We use "quality" to mean the effect of a unit of FDI on economic growth. Precisely establishing what a quality project is a complicated task because it is a function of

---

* We thank Garrick Blalock, Gordon Hanson, Ann Harrison, Lakshmi Iyer, Beata Javorcik, Ethan Kapstein, John van Reenen, Alessandra Tucci, Lou Wells, and Eric Werker for comments and suggestions.

many different country and project characteristics which are often hard to measure and the data quality is generally poor or available only at an aggregate level. Hence in this paper we define and differentiate "quality FDI" in several ways, using both objective and subjective criteria. First, we look at the possibility that the effects of FDI differ by sector and industry. Second, we differentiate FDI based on objective qualitative industry characteristics including the average skill intensity and reliance on external capital. Note that we do not mean that high-skill sectors and sectors which are dependent on external finance are high-quality sectors per se, but that the effect of FDI on output is higher and hence they are "high quality FDI sectors." There are good reasons for this to be the case. Sectors characterized by high skills are likely to benefit from foreign ownership where technology and pay tends to be higher. In addition sectors which require external finance may benefit from foreign ownership since foreign owned firms tend to be more capital intensive and less capital constrained. Third, since no one characteristic of FDI can determine quality and because the quality of FDI is the interaction of investment and country characteristics, we use a new dataset on industry-level targeting to analyze quality FDI based on the subjective preferences expressed by the receiving countries themselves. Finally, we use a two-stage least squares methodology to control for measurement error and endogeneity. In order to do this, we exploit a comprehensive industry-level dataset of 29 countries between 1985 and 2000. To summarize our findings, the growth effects of FDI increase when we account for characteristics which might affect the quality of FDI.

Despite the strong case for a positive relationship between economic growth and FDI, the empirical evidence has been mixed. Firm-level studies of particular countries often find that FDI does not boost economic growth and these studies frequently do not find positive spillovers. As noted by Carkovic and Levine (2005), "[T]aken together, firm level studies not lend much support for the view that FDI accelerates overall economic growth." Evidence at the macro level also does not find exogenous positive effects of FDI on growth.[4] The macro literature that looks at the impact of FDI on host country growth has look at the direct effect of FDI on economic growth using the growth rate of output measured as the growth of real per capita GDP in constant dollars. Lipsey (2002) notes that "[I]n general, the results of these studies indicate that the size of inward FDI stocks or flows, relative to GDP, is not related in any consistent way to rates of growth."

One explanation for the ambiguity of the evidence is that the growth effects of FDI may vary across industries.[5] In particular, potential advantages derived from FDI might differ markedly across the primary, manufacturing and services sectors.[6] More generally, there might also be differences among industries within a sector. Most of the macro empirical work that has analyzed the effects of FDI on host economies, however, has not controlled for the sector in which FDI is involved, mostly due to data limitations. Indeed, we find that when we control for industry characteristics and time effects, there are important differential effects across sectors. Our results imply that an increase in FDI flows from the 25th to the 75th percentile in the distribution of flows is associated with an increase of 13 percent in growth over the different industries' sample means.

Industry level analysis also enables us to differentiate FDI according to its industry-average characteristics. The macro literature has emphasized the dependence of positive growth effects from FDI on the role of local conditions with specific reference to human capital and financial development.[7] We find that the relation between FDI at the industry level and growth in value added is stronger both for industries with higher skill requirements and for industries more reliant on external capital as defined by Rajan and Zinagles (1998).[8] These results, apart from being consistent with the existing macro literature and hypothesized benefits of FDI, are further evidence of important cross-industry differences in the effects of FDI.

There are, of course, numerous project and industry characteristics which may affect the quality of foreign direct investment such as the mode of entry (Greenfield vs M&A), the country of origin, and many others.[9] In this paper we are constrained by the availability of data at the industry level; however, we are able to include subjective measures of quality as determined by policymakers themselves. Countries presumably target industries for investment promotion because they believe them to be especially beneficial.[10] For example, while export oriented high tech manufacturing firms may be suitable for one country, labor-intensive textiles might be more appropriate for other countries. Indeed, while academics, especially those who employ national FDI statistics, might tend to treat FDI as homogenous, policymakers most surely do not. More than 160 governments have established investment promotion agencies (IPAs) to attract foreign direct investment, and more than 70 percent of these agencies report that they focus their resources on a small number of "target" industries that they deem to be of particular benefit; see Charlton et al. (2004). For example, the Czech investment promotion agency CzechInvest targets automotive manufacturing, electronics, plastics, and business services.[11] We argue that using countries' own targets to subjectively distinguish between industries is appropriate because the national benefits of an FDI project are determined by the interaction of project and country characteristics. First, policymakers' concepts of "quality FDI" are likely to be based on a complex combination of different country characteristics such as human capital skills and financial dependence. Second, for any host country, the desirability of an industry will involve an interaction between the characteristics of the industry and the characteristics of the country. We test whether the benefits of FDI are stronger in the industries to which governments accord special priority.[12] Including only these targeted industries increases the significance of our results. We find in these selected industries that increasing FDI flows from the 25th to the 75th percentile in the distribution of flows occasions an increase of 73 percent in growth over the different industries' sample means.

Of course, we are well aware that these correlations might not imply causality. An important concern in the FDI growth literature is that growth may itself spawn more FDI. Alternatively, some third variable might affect a country's growth trajectory and, thereby, its attractiveness to foreign capital.[13] In these cases, the coefficients on the estimates are likely to overstate the positive impact of foreign investment. As a result, one could find evidence of positive externalities from foreign investment where no externalities occur.

Our ideal specification in this paper would be to correlate economic growth with exogenous changes in a homogenous type of FDI. Unfortunately, as described above, we cannot do this because FDI projects, as measured through balance of payments statistics, are neither homogenous nor exogenous. In short, we may have both endogeneity and measurement problems. Either our OLS results are biased downward because FDI statistics fail to accurately capture the heterogeneous impact of different types of foreign investment, introducing a form of measurement error into our ideal specification, or our OLS results are biased upward because of some reverse causation.

This is a tough issue to deal with and almost impossible to address without good instruments at the industry level. To identify the effect of FDI on growth, we need an instrument that is correlated with the "idealized" quality-adjusted FDI volumes, but not with growth. In this paper we use a binary variable created from industry-level policy decisions to provide an instrument. Targeting an industry for investment promotion should, if it is found to be effective, lead to an increase in both the quality and quantity of FDI. Our instruments satisfy conditions of relevance and exogeneity. The exclusion restrictions implied by our instrumental variable regression is that, conditional on the controls included in the regression, FDI targeting has no effect on current industry growth. The major concerns with these exclusion restrictions is that targeting is a policy choice which might be correlated with the current environment and have a direct effect on economic performance, or that industry targets are chosen based on expectations of future growth. We perform several tests, among them, overidentification tests to analyze whether FDI targeting has a direct effect on growth. We find no evidence of a direct effect of targeting on growth. Also lagged growth has a non-significant effect on industry targeting. Recognizing the selection problem that arises from the fact that industry-targeting activity is a choice rather than a natural policy experiment, we also use propensity score matching to ensure that we have a valid control group. Our main results are robust to this specification.

In our instrumental variable (IV) strategy, we find a strong first-stage relationship between the decision to target an industry and FDI flows to that industry. Our two-stage, least square estimates of the effect of FDI flow on industry value added growth is significant. As observed above, our results imply that increasing FDI flows from the 25th to the 75th percentile in the distribution of flows results in a 59 percent increase in growth over the sample mean in our preferred specifications. There is also considerable evidence that investment promotion attempts to encourage higher quality FDI.[14]

The estimated coefficient using the IV strategy is higher than its OLS counterpart on the subsample of targeted industries. That our IV estimates are higher than their OLS counterparts for the entire sample suggests that there is some attenuation bias caused by measurement error that outweighs the bias caused by endogeneity resulting from reverse causality. These results may be evidence of measurement error in the FDI data, but they may also be evidence that the quality of FDI is heterogeneous *within* as well as between industries and when countries target an industry for FDI they increase both the quantity and quality of the projects in that industry. In the process of targeting an industry for FDI, investment promotion agencies work at the project level to identify and attempt to attract foreign investors within their target industries that are believed to be especially beneficial to the host country. Hence, if targeting industries in which FDI is expected to promote growth (high tech, high skill, greenfield, and so forth) then our IV coefficient should be higher than our OLS coefficient. Despite the limitations of the data, our instrumentation strategy yields similar results to the other exercise we conducted that attempted distinguish among the different forms and the quality of FDI. Overall, growth effects increase when we account for the "quality" of FDI. Our estimates should be interpreted with caution particularly in terms of deriving policy implications in favor of promoting FDI. An analysis of such question should consider the cost of incentives used versus the potential benefits. This kind of analysis is beyond the scope of this paper.

The rest of the paper is organized as follows. Section 3.3.2 provides an overview of the data. Section 3.3.3 explores the role of heterogeneity at the industry level. Section 3.3.4 presents empirical evidence on complementarities across sectors and analyzes differences in the quality of FDI. Section 3.3.5 discusses FDI targeting and our instrumentation strategy. Section 3.3.6 concludes.

3.3.2   Data and descriptive statistics

3.3.2.1   Foreign direct investment: industry data

Figure 3.3.1 breaks down national FDI statistics into seven sectors. The columns show the sum of inward FDI in constant 2000 US dollars over the period 1985–2000. Finance, business, and real estate account for more than half, 53 percent, of FDI, manufacturing for 27 percent. The line in Figure 3.3.1 plots the ratio of FDI flows to total value added in the sector, which varies widely across industries from almost 15 percent in finance, business services, and real estate to less than 1 percent in agriculture.

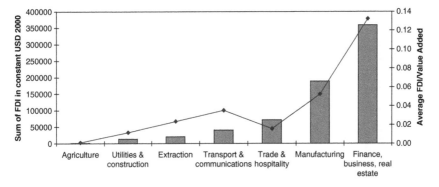

Figure 3.3.1 Foreign direct investment by sector (1985–2000)
Source: OECD's International Direct Investment database.

Annual data on FDI inflows and stocks at the industry level are available from the OECD's International Direct Investment database. The OECD data are available at the International Standard Industrial Classification (Revision 3) secondary level classification. Nineteen industries, six in manufacturing, three in the agriculture and mining sectors, and ten in services, are listed and characterized in Table 3.3.1. As we are interested in the growth effects of FDI, we use data for three five-year periods between 1985 and 2000. In the robustness section, we also use three-year averages and, from Dun & Bradstreet's WorldBase database of public and private companies, an alternative measure of industry FDI based on the number of foreign firms.

We also use an alternative specification in the robustness section using annual industry total factor productivity (TFP) growth as the dependent variable. Although our preferred dependent variable would be TFP growth, because data for industry-level capital stock are missing for many countries, the number of observations available to us is reduced significantly.

The main source of data on industry value added is the Industrial Statistics Yearbook of the United Nations Statistical Division, which reports data by industry (also using ISIC Rev. 3 classifications), but at the 3-digit level, for 29 industries. We mapped this data to the higher level of aggregation demanded by the OECD data. Our growth variable measures the growth of value added in each industry in each country for three five-year periods between 1985 and 2000, measured by the difference in the log values over the period. We derive an appropriate deflator for manufacturing value added in 1995 from the difference between constant local currency and current local currency growth in total manufacturing value added reported by the World Bank.[15] The initial share of the industry was derived by dividing the value added for each industry by the total national manufacturing value added.

Appendix A explains all data and sources in detail. Table 1 presents summary statistics for these variables. Table 2 presents the correlation matrix.

Table 3.3.1 Descriptive statistics (1985–2000)

Industry	Code	Targeted by # Countries	Growth in Value Added	FDI/ Value Added	Share of Value Added	Dep. External Finance	White High Skill	Blue and White High Skill
Agriculture and Fishing	1	4	2.617	0.001	0.055	-0.297	0.040	0.707
Mining of Metals	2	2	3.309	0.000	0.015	0.455	0.168	0.687
Extraction of Petrochemicals	3	5	1.473	0.009	0.012	0.318	0.341	0.674
Food Products	4	5	5.314	0.013	0.041	-1.717	0.074	0.427
Textile and Wood Activities	5	5	3.362	0.015	0.026	-0.946	0.145	0.594
Petroleum, Chemical, Rubber, Plastic Products	6	9	5.755	0.033	0.043	0.285	0.397	0.546
Metal and Mechanical Products	7	3	5.104	0.024	0.037	-0.796	0.181	0.615
Machinery, Computers, RTV, Communication	8	10	5.821	0.013	0.051	-0.692	0.352	0.619
Vehicles and Other Transport Equipments	9	11	5.999	0.032	0.022	-0.664	0.357	0.644
Electricity, Gas and Water	10	3	4.471	0.004	0.038	-0.359	0.257	0.599
Construction	11	0	6.563	0.001	0.087	-0.919	0.071	0.711
Trade and Repairs	12	1	6.004	0.010	0.163	-0.416	0.151	0.262
Hotels and Restaurants	13	5	7.518	0.003	0.031	-0.100	0.062	0.349
Land, Sea and Air Transport	14	1	5.733	0.002	0.071	-0.150	0.055	0.140
Telecommunications	15	12	6.762	0.007	0.031	-0.119	0.033	0.190
Monetary Intermediation	16	1	5.071	0.030	0.053	-2.445	0.820	0.827
Other Financial Intermediation	17	1	9.184	0.050	0.006	-3.613	0.714	0.737
Insurance	18	1	5.974	0.050	0.013	-3.586	0.761	0.773
Real Estate and Business Activities	19	11	8.741	0.008	0.210	-0.173	0.564	0.612

Notes: Number of industries corresponds to the 3 digit ISIC Rev. 3. FDI corresponds to Foreign Direct Investment Flows from OECD International Direct Investment Database. Dependence on external finance is the difference between investment and cash generated from operations in the U.S. following Rajan and Zingales (1998). Skill data is the ratio of high skilled workers to other workers in German Industries. Skilled workers include: White-collar high-skill (WCHS): Legislators, senior officials and managers (Group 1), Professionals (Group 2), Technicians and associate professionals (Group 3). White-collar low-skill (WCLS): Clerks, service workers (Group 4), shop & sales workers (Group 5). Blue-collar high-skill (BCHS): Skilled agricultural and fishery workers (Group 6), Craft & related trade workers (Group 7). Blue-collar low-skill (BCLS): Plant & machine operators and assemblers (Group 8), Elementary occupations (Group 9). See Appendix A for detailed explanation of all variables and sources.

Table 3.3.2 Correlation – main variables

	Growth in Value Added	Log FDI	FDI/Value Added	Log Value Added	Share of Value Added
Growth in Value Added	1.0000				
Log FDI	–0.0478	1.0000			
FDI/Value Added	0.0029	0.1333	1.0000		
Log Value Added	–0.1645	0.2671	–0.0770	1.0000	
Share of Value Added	0.0922	0.0662	–0.0433	0.4041	1.0000

Notes: FDI corresponds to Foreign Direct Investment Flows from OECD International Direct Investment Database. Log Value Added and Share of Value added correspond to the beginning of the period and are from the U.N. Industrial Statistics Yearbook. See Appendix A for detailed data description.

3.3.2.2 "Qualitative" Characteristics of Foreign Direct Investment

To test the differential effect of FDI, we divide sectors according to reliance on external finance (equity) and intensity of human capital. We use a measure of dependence on external finance (equity rather than cash generated flows) as defined by Rajan and Zingales (1998). High external finance sectors include extraction of petrochemicals, petroleum, chemical, rubber and plastic products; low external finance sectors include textiles and wood activities and food products. Our measure of skill is the ratio of high-skilled workers to other workers in German industries, following Carlin and Mayer (2003). Occupational data are based on the new version of the International Labor Office's International Standard Classification of Occupations, ISCO 88. White-collar high-skill includes financial intermediation, legislators, senior officials and managers, professionals, and technicians and associate professionals. White-collar low-skill includes clerks, service workers, and shop and sales workers. Blue-collar high-skill includes skilled agricultural and fishery workers and craft and related trade workers. Blue-collar low-skill includes plant and machine operators and assemblers and elementary occupations. Monetary intermediation has the highest skill requirements while transport has the lowest. Table 3.3.1 presents the main summary statistics by sector.

For any country, the benefits of an FDI project are, as noted earlier, determined by the interaction of project and country characteristics. Because countries presumably target for investment promotion industries they believe will be especially beneficial – for example, one country might choose export-oriented, high-tech manufacturing firms, another low-tech call centers – we use in addition to objective industry characteristics a subjective criteria determined by the host countries.

We do this by exploiting policy changes in FDI attraction that operate at the industry level. Our industry-level investment promotion variable is constructed from survey information collected directly from promotion agencies; see Charlton et al. (2004) and Charlton and Davis (2006). Investment promotion describes the set of policies governments employ to attract foreign investment. More than 160 national level, and more than 250 subnational, investment promotion agencies worldwide are tasked with performing various activities to attract foreign direct investment. Wells and Wint (1991) grouped these activities into four functional categories: national image building (for example, many IPAs disseminate favorable information about their countries through advertising campaigns, participation in investment exhibitions, and trade missions); investment generation (specific firm- or industry-specific research and sales presentations); facilitation services for potential investors (for example, assistance with identifying potential locations and meeting regulatory criteria and fast-track investment approval processes); and policy advocacy (many agencies, for example, provide feedback from foreign investors to policymakers and might lobby for pro-investment policies).

Our approach takes advantage of the fact that IPAs tend to focus their investment promotion resources on small numbers of "target industries." A survey of more than 120 national investment promotion agencies revealed that more than 70 percent report target industries; see Charlton et al. (2004). For example, CINDE, the Costa Rican Investment Board, established in 1982, initially targeted only the electronics industry. In 1994, it announced expansion into medical devices and later into a range of business service industries. Similarly the Danish IPA focuses on just a small number of target industries, reporting that its strategy is to "concentrate especially on three focus areas where Denmark has global strengths: Life Sciences, ICT, and Renewable Energy."[16] What does targeting an industry for FDI actually involve? More than half of a subgroup of survey respondents asked to describe how targeting polices were implemented in practice acknowledged their organizational structure to be designed around target industries with specialized staff responsible for specific industries. For example, Invest in Sweden Agency (ISA) reports that it focuses on the automotive, life sciences, communications and wood processing industries and these priorities are reflected in its organization structure which includes discrete management units for each target industry – staff in these units focus their efforts specifically on target industries.[17] More than 80 percent of these reported that they offered targeted industries special services such as investment incentives and investor facilitation. All reported that they give priority to potential investors in target industries.[18] In practice, this involved focusing marketing activities, as well as fiscal and financial incentives, on special audiences related to the target industries (as well as projects within targeted sectors).

Charlton et al. (2004) conducted a detailed survey of 28 OECD countries' targeting strategies in 2003.[19] IPAs were asked which industries they had targeted between 1990 and 2001 and the dates on which targeting had begun and ended.[20] Five countries that reported that they did not target specific industries were dropped from the sample.[21] In some cases, target industry choices do not neatly match the industry categories for which FDI data are available. We deal with this problem in two ways. First, if the reported industry target cuts across several industries in the OECD data, we ignore it as an observation. For example, Poland reported that it targets "automotive manufacturing, business services, and R&D" for FDI. The first two industries fit neatly into the OECD industry categories; R&D, being too broad to assign to a specific industry, is excluded from the sample. Second, if the target industry is a subset of a more aggregated industry reported in the OECD data, we include the data point. For example, Australia identi-fied "wood products" as a target for foreign investment. At the highest level of dis-aggregation, the OECD FDI data reports figures for "textiles and wood products." Although Australia targets only one of these industries, we include the observation in the sample. In most cases, the IPA industry choices correspond closely to the OECD's SIC classifications. We end up with annual FDI flow data for 19 sectors and industries in 22 countries over 12 years from 1990 to 2001.

The most popularly targeted industries in the OECD subsample are telecommunications, chemical and plastics manufacturing, and business services (see Table 3.3.1). The survey also revealed two main rationales for investor targeting. Some IPAs stated that their objective was to focus scarce promotion resources on industries in which the country had a competi-tive advantage. Other IPAs attempted to use targeting to focus investment promotion on improving the quality of FDI flows. For many IPAs, this meant using investment promotion to attract industries that diversified and brought new skills and technology to the local economy. The survey revealed the most commonly targeted industries to be high-tech manu-facturing industries. Six industries – electronics and electrical equipment, tourism and tourist amenities, industrial machinery and equipment, infor-mation and communication technologies, food and kindred products, and crop agriculture – were targeted by more than 40 percent of the countries surveyed. Several industries, including those in the wholesale and retail trade sectors, were not targeted by any countries.[22]

A concern that arises with any survey data is the potential for respondents to misreport. Surveys that require historical recollection might be biased if records are incomplete or not consulted. Staff turnover, absence of record-keeping regulations, and changes in computer systems might contribute to reporting errors, and IPAs might have an incentive to misreport in order to rationalize their behavior ex-post (e.g., capitalizing on exogenous increases in FDI by later claiming that the growth industry had been the subject of promotional efforts).

Our survey design mitigates these concerns. The first survey, of IPA websites and annual reports, yielded information on priority industries for

28 OECD IPAs, but historical records and other information was available for only 12, and often did not extend back to the beginning of our sample period. Charlton et al. (2004) followed this with a written survey followed up by several rounds of communication that achieved a 100 percent response rate among OECD IPAs. In 2003, the authors inserted questions on industry targeting into a telephone survey on various aspects of investment promotion. Respondents were presented with information gleaned from the two previous rounds of research and asked to fill in missing information. Where the three sources of information were discrepant, documented information, when available, was weighted most heavily.

3.3.3   Results: foreign direct investment and growth at the industry level

The purpose of our empirical analysis is to examine the relation between growth and FDI at the industry level. To focus on the effect of a small number of variables without incurring excessive omitted variable bias, we control for industry and country fixed effects. Our specification enables us to focus specifically on a small number of control variables without worrying about bias from unobserved country or industry characteristics. This approach can be thought of as an analysis of deviations from average growth rates, that is, it asks: is abnormal industry growth associated with abnormal industry characteristics in a particular country? Hence, we look at whether, in the same industry, growth in value added is greater in a country with higher FDI flows than in a country with lower FDI flows. We estimate the following model using OLS.

$$GROWTH_{ict} = \alpha Ln(FDI_{ict}) + \beta \log(INITIAL\ VALUE\ ADDED_{ict})$$
$$+ \phi \frac{VALUE\ ADDED_{ict}}{VALUE\ ADDED_{ct}} + \lambda X_{ict} + \delta_i + \delta_c + \delta_t + \varepsilon_{ict} \qquad (1)$$

where $GROWTH_{ict}$ is the five-year average growth in the value added of industry i in country c at time t. In the robustness section, we also use three-year average growth. FDI_{ict} is the volume of FDI inflows in industry i in country c at time t. In the regression analysis, we use the log of the FDI inflows variable. The analysis includes a full set of industry, country, and time dummies used to control for extraneous industry and country specific sources of growth: δ_i refers to industry dummies; δ_c are country dummies that capture time invariant country-specific factors that might drive cross-country differences in growth; δ_t is a vector of year dummies included to control for cross-country correlation over time due to common world shocks. As well as controlling for industry heterogeneity, another appealing feature of industry analysis is that it mitigates some of the effects of unobserved heterogeneity and model misspecification, which are difficult to control at the national level.

We also include two measures of the initial state of the industry. The industry's initial (log) level of value added, Log(*INITIAL VALUE ADDED*$_{ict}$), controls for industry mean reversion, whereby sectors that have grown rapidly in the past are less likely to continue to grow rapidly in the future.[23] The industry's initial share of total value added in the country, *VALUE ADDED*$_{ict}$ / *VALUE ADDED*$_{it}$, captures agglomeration effects, whereby industries that develop early in a particular country enjoy continued, relatively strong growth. The distinction of these variables is between the role of the industry size, and the industry share. The first is subject to mean reversion, the second is an issue about comparative advantage. X_{ict} is a set of control variables, ε_{ict} an error term. The estimation procedure uses White's correction for heteroskedasticity in the error term.[24]

Table 3.3.3 presents the main results. Column (1) shows a positive, albeit not significant, relation between FDI and growth of value added, controlling for country fixed effects.[25] The relation becomes positive and economically and statistically significant when we include a full set of country, industry, and time effects as well as additional industry characteristics, as can be seen in column (2). To get a sense of the magnitude of the effect of FDI inflows on growth of value added in the average industry, consider an increase from

Table 3.3.3 OLS regression of growth value added and FDI – Industry data dependent variable is 5-year average industry growth in value added, 1985–2000

	(1)	(2)	(3)	(4)
Log FDI	0.146	0.329	0.323	0.454
	[0.157]	[0.170]*	[0.147]**	[0.148]***
Log Value Added		−7.462	−2.066	−1.603
		[0.465]***	[0.557]***	[0.557]***
Share Value Added		75.795	7.649	4.235
		[7.984]***	[8.682]	[8.564]
Country Dummies	Y	Y	Y	Y
Industry Dummies		Y	Y	Y
Time Dummies		Y	Y	Y
Country × Time Dummies			Y	Y
Industry × Time Dummies				Y
R²	0.49	0.72	0.83	0.85
# Observations	674	674	674	674

Notes: All regression are estimated by White's correction of heteroskedasticity. Standard errors are in parenthesis denoting *** 1%, ** 5%, * 10%. The dependent variable is the growth in industry value added (5 year averges). FDI corresponds to Foreign Direct Investment Flows from OECD International Direct Investment Database. Log Value Added and Share of Value added correspond to the beginning of the period and are from the U.N. Industrial Statistics Yearbook. See Appendix A for detailed explanation of all variables and sources.

the 25th to the 75th percentile in the distribution of flows. Based on the results presented in column (2), the increase in growth of value added is, on average, 2 percent higher in the country with higher flows. This represents a 13 percent increase in growth over the sample mean. Note that our results may underestimate the effects of FDI on growth as we analyze only intra-industry effects.[26] However, since we use wide industry categories (2 digit) this effect is likely to be small. Given potential concerns about trends in the data, we modify specification (1) in columns (3) and (4) and include time dummies interacted with country and industry dummies respectively.[27] Our main results remain significant with a slightly higher estimated coefficient on the FDI variables in (4).

We present robustness tests for the OLS results in Table 3.3.4. Column (1) shows our results to be robust to a specification that does not control for the share of value added. Column (2) presents results only for the manufacturing sector. We also rerun our basic specification, using three- instead of five-year periods in column (3), and include a measure of FDI based on international firm-level data from Dun and Bradstreet in column (4). Overall, the results suggest a positive and significant relation between FDI flows and growth in value added at the industry level. Column (5) controls for industry trade (defined as imports and exports over value added) as a proxy for openness. An important concern is that the positive coefficient on FDI may be capturing other factors such as industries more open to trade being for able to attract larger inflows and FDI and thus grow faster. Our estimated coefficients are somewhat lower but they remain positive and significant. Column (6) uses the ratio of FDI to capital in the sector.

An important concern is that our specification may be simply picking up a mechanical relation between changes in value added and investment. In column (7) we use an alternative specification with industry total factor productivity (TFP) growth as the dependent variable, and the ratio of FDI to industry capital stock as the main regressor. Given data limitations in terms of the availability of capital stocks at the industry level, our estimation uses yearly data and hence growth estimates should be interpreted with caution. Our results, however, are supportive of our previous findings.

Because our methodology is subject to concerns about endogeneity and our FDI data do not describe homogenous investment projects opening the possibility for measurement biases, these results require careful analysis. We address these concerns in section 3.3.5.

3.3.4   Foreign direct investment and industry characteristics

Several recent studies have investigated the role of national characteristics in allowing countries to reap benefits from FDI such as the domestic level of level of human capital (Boreinsztein, De Gregorio, and Lee, 1998; Blomström and Kokko, 2003) and the development of local financial markets

Table 3.3.4 Robustness: OLS regression of growth value added and FDI – Industry data

	Dependent Variable:						
	Growth Value Added 5 Years	Growth Value Added 5 Years Manuf. Only	Growth Value Added 3 Years	Growth Value Added 5 Years	Growth Value Added 5 Years	Growth Value Added 5 Years	Annual TFP
	(1)	(2)	(3)	(4)	(5)	(6)	(7)
Log FDI	0.393 [0.182]**	0.620 [0.219]***	0.331 [0.173]*		0.308 [0.169]*	1.034 [0.375]***	
Log Value Added	-5.162 [0.424]***	-4.204 [1.379]***	-3.848 [0.604]***	-13.406 [0.496]***	-6.941 [0.504]***	0.577 [2.202]	0.055 [0.005]***
Share Value Added		117.227 [36.712]***	33.866 [10.622]***	66.099 [5.619]***	67.377 [8.585]***	-17.388 [29.797]	-0.169 [0.058]***
Log Gross Capital						-0.389 [1.059]	
Trade					-0.109 [0.420]	0.323 [0.149]**	
FDI/Capital							0.055 [0.027]**
Log # of Foreign Firms				1.776 [0.242]***			
Country Dummies	Y	Y	Y	Y	Y	Y	Y
Industry Dummies	Y	Y	Y	Y	Y	Y	Y
Time Dummies	Y	Y	Y	Y	Y	Y	Y
R²	0.70	0.74	0.55	0.73	0.57	0.62	0.82
Observations	674	230	958	1053	538	462	216

Notes: All regression are estimated by White's correction of heteroskedasticity. Standard errors are in parenthesis denoting *** 1%, ** 5%, * 10%. FDI corresponds to Foreign Direct Investment Flows from OECD International Direct Investment Database. Log Value Added and Share of Value added correspond to the beginning of the period and are from the U.N. Industrial Statistics Yearbook. See Appendix A for detailed explanation of variables.

(Alfaro et al., 2004, 2006). Variation in absorptive capacities between industries between countries (and countries) is a promising line of research, offering, potentially, an appealing synthesis of the conflicting results that have emerged from the literature. FDI studies have documented the dependence of positive effects on various national characteristics, but not considered how this dependence varies across industries. These national-level studies are subject to the objection that unobserved heterogeneity of countries could be correlated with the national characteristics being tested, thereby complicating interpretation of their interaction coefficients. Industry analysis is consequently an important cross check on the validity of interpretations of these studies' results. Among other benefits, FDI is presumed to bring skills, technology, and capital to the host country. We test whether the growth effects of FDI are stronger in industries that are particularly dependent on skills and external finance.

Note that we do not mean that high-skill sectors and sectors which are dependent on external finance are high-quality sectors per se, but that the effect of FDI on output is higher and hence they are "high-quality FDI sectors." There are good reasons for this to be the case. Sectors characterized by high skills are likely to benefit from foreign ownership where technology and pay tends to be higher. In addition sectors which require external finance may benefit from foreign ownership since foreign owned firms tend to be more capital intensive and less capital constrained.

3.3.4.1   Foreign direct investment and financial dependence

In this subsection, we assess whether an industry's degree of dependence on external finance affects the relationship between FDI and growth.[28] In a cross-country analysis, Alfaro et al. (2004) find that FDI benefits countries with well-developed financial markets significantly more than it does countries with weaker markets. The authors find no direct effect of FDI on growth, but obtain consistently significant results when FDI is combined in an interaction term with a range of measures of financial development.

We examine the industry-level implications of Alfaro et al.'s (2004) hypothesis. Industry analysis is motivated by recent papers that analyze the effect of financial development on economic growth at the industry level (Rajan and Zingales (1998), Cetorelli and Gambera (2001), Fisman and Love (2003, 2004), and Carlin and Mayer (2003)). These papers identify differences in the degree of financial dependence among industries, and test whether industries that are particularly dependent on external finance grow more strongly in countries with well-developed financial markets.[29] These inter-industry differences provide a convenient test for the relationship between financial development and FDI effects. We expect a stronger relationship between FDI and growth in industries dependent on external finance.

The financial dependence variable – the industry's reliance on equity financing – is taken from Rajan and Zingales (1998), who measure the ratio of net equity issues to capital expenditures for U.S. firms in each industry during the 1980s. The dependence of U.S. firms on equity finance is a good proxy for the demand for equivalent finance in other countries because the United States, being the most highly developed financial market in the world, represents the best available measure of the underlying requirements of firms operating in those industries.

We investigate whether industries that are more reliant on external finance grow faster in countries with more FDI, controlling for industry and country specific effects. Columns (1) to (7) in Table 3.3.5 present our main OLS results. We find growth in industries more reliant on external finance to be more sensitive to FDI. One additional concern is that financial dependence is correlated to sector capital intensity. Column (4) controls for the capital stock in the sector obtaining similar results. Column (5) shows the estimated effects to be higher when we restrict the sample to the manufacturing sector. To test the differential effect of FDI, we subdivide our sample into industries with high dependence on external finance and run equation (1) on each group of industries. The estimates in column (6) indicate that an interquantile movement in the distribution of the FDI variable implies for industries with low dependence on external finance 11 percent more growth over the sample mean, the estimates reported in column (7) that a similar movement implies for industries with high external finance 16 percent more growth over the sample mean.

3.3.4.2 Foreign direct investment and human capital

We also assess whether an industry's skill intensity affects the relationship between FDI and growth. Borensztein, De Gregorio, and Lee (1998), for example, in a study of 69 developing countries, found FDI to be positively associated with growth only in countries with sufficiently high levels of human capital. Industry-level analysis enables us to design a test for one aspect of this conditional relationship. If human capital does affect the capacity of the host economy to benefit from FDI, we would expect this effect to be stronger in industries in which the potential benefits are more reliant on skilled labor and hence, presumably, the more skill-reliant the industry, the larger the effect of FDI on growth.

The proxy for industry skill intensity follows Carlin and Mayer's (2003) index of skill levels in each German manufacturing industry. Germany is the country in the world with the lowest share of workers without qualifications in manufacturing industries (Machin and Van Reenen, 1998). They therefore conclude that Germany has a highly developed labor market and that German industry skill ratios are a good proxy for the underlying skill requirements of firms operating in each industry. To reduce feedback from industry growth to industry characteristics, we remove Germany from our sample of countries. We divide our sample into high- and low-skill industries and, to minimize differences in the quality of FDI. The results in Table

Table 3.3.5 OLS regression of growth value added and FDI: Financial dependence and skill intensity dependent variable is 5-year industry growth in value added, 1985–2000

	FDI and Finance				Only Manuf.	Low Financ. Dep.
	(1)	(2)	(3)	(4)	(5)	(6)
Log FDI	0.270 [0.054]***	0.278 [0.046]***	0.372 [0.055]***	0.535 [0.080]***	0.456 [0.093]***	0.271 [0.072]***
Log Value Added	−7.216 [0.153]***	−1.877 [0.182]***	−6.99 [0.148]***	−1.569 [0.290]***	−9.559 [0.216]***	−5.550 [0.239]***
Share Value Added	68.958 [2.531]***	1.682 [2.719]	67.47 [2.450]***	22.645 [3.729]***	119.230 [4.787]***	55.783 [3.659]***
Log FDI × Fin.Dep.	0.055 [0.021]***	0.055 [0.017]***	0.058 [0.033]***	0.074 [0.019]***	0.089 [0.035]**	
Log FDI × Skills						
Log Gross Capital				−0.125 [0.172]		
Country Dummies	Y	Y	Y	Y	Y	Y
Industry Dummies	Y	Y	Y	Y	Y	Y
Time Dummies	Y	Y	Y	Y	Y	Y
Country × Time Dummies		Y				
Industry × Time Dummies			Y			
R^2	0.70	0.81	0.74	0.69	0.82	0.64
# Observations	674	674	674	601	271	299

Notes: All regression are estimated by White's correction of heteroskedasticity. Standard errors are in parenthesis denoting *** 1%, ** 5%, * 10%. Industries are divided in (6) and (7) into low in and high external finance as defined by Rajan and Zingales (1998). Industries are divided in (13) and (14) into low (blue collar) and high skills (white collar). See Appendix A for detailed explanation for all variables and sources.

FDI and Skills							
High Financ. Dep.					Only Manuf.	Low Skill	High Skill
(7)	(8)	(9)	(10)	(11)	(12)	(13)	(14)
0.409	0.296	0.411	0.469	0.531	0.303	0.168	0.363
[0.075]***	[0.069]***	[0.044]***	[0.069]***	[0.098]***	[0.107]***	[0.071]**	[0.072]***
−8.790	−7.218	−2.099	−6.980	−1.774	−8.319	−7.817	−7.381
[0.188]***	[0.153]***	[0.147]***	[0.149]***	[0.296]***	[0.221]***	[0.231]***	[0.200]***
76.033	69.685	26.212	68.542	23.486	134.950	60.168	76.535
[3.612]***	[2.537]***	[1.982]***	[2.45]***	[3.885]***	[5.012]***	[3.670]***	[3.445]***
	0.019	0.199	0.253	0.077	1.372		
	[0.175]	[0.055]***	[1.173]**	[0.105]	[0.145]***		
				0.114			
				[0.161]			
Y	Y	Y	Y	Y	Y	Y	Y
Y	Y	Y	Y	Y	Y	Y	Y
Y	Y	Y	Y	Y	Y	Y	Y
		Y					
			Y				
0.79	0.70	0.76	0.71	0.67	0.79	0.77	0.70
375	674	674	674	601	271	263	411

3.35, columns (8)–(14) demonstrate that there are, indeed, substantial benefits from FDI in sectors with higher skill requirements. Column (11), in particular, controls for capital stock as skill intensity might be correlated with sector capital intensity. Column (12) shows the effects to be greater when the sample is restricted to the manufacturing sector. Comparisons of the estimated coefficients, columns (13) and (14), show the effects of FDI on industry growth to be twice for high-skill sectors what they are for low skill sectors. The estimate in column (13) and (14) indicate, respectively, that an interquantile movement in the distribution of the FDI variable implies 7 percent more growth over the sample mean for industries with low skill and 15 percent for industries with high skill.

3.3.4.3   Foreign direct investment and country targets

In this section, we use subjective criteria chosen by the host countries to distinguish between industries. This is appropriate for two reasons. First, policymakers' concepts of 'quality FDI' are likely to be based on a complex combination of different characteristics including skills, financial dependence and other characteristics. Second, for any host country, the desirability of an industry will involve an *interaction* between the characteristics of the industry and the characteristics of the country. Costa Rica's IPA, CINDE, for example reports that it currently targets medical devices, electronics and a range of services because it wishes to concentrate "its efforts in promoting Costa Rica as a competitive place for investing in sectors which can be benefited from the country's strengths."[30]

We exploit the industry-targeting variable described above to test the relationship between FDI and growth on the subset of industries targeted for foreign investment promotion. Specifically, we run equation (1) on the subsample of industries that our survey revealed to be targeted for investment promotion in each country. Table 3.3.6 presents our main OLS results. We find growth in targeted industries to be more sensitive to FDI than average. The estimates in column (1) suggest that an interquantile movement in the distribution of the FDI variable implies 73 percent more growth over the sample mean, significantly more than the average increase across all industries.

We offer three possible explanations for these results, which require careful analysis, and which we elaborate in the following section. One is that the effect of FDI on growth varies across industries, and that governments are correctly identifying the industries in which FDI is most beneficial. However, this result runs counter to the generally mixed evidence on the success of industry policy, so we consider several alternative explanations. Our results suggest that expending resources on FDI attraction increases the inflow of FDI. However we say nothing about the cost of FDI promotion, nor its net benefits (as this is not the focus of this paper), and so our results should not be interpreted as supporting industry policy.[31] A second possibility is that the act of targeting FDI in a particular industry alters the impact of FDI on growth in that industry. For example, investment promotion

Table 3.3.6 OLS regression of growth value added and FDI: Targeted industries dependent variable is 5-year industry growth in value added, 1985–2000

	(1)	(2)
Log FDI	1.838	1.687
	[0.666]**	[0.480]***
Log Value Added	–8.495	–5.019
	[3.330]**	[2.485]*
Share Value Added	40.503	24.112
	[35.880]	[25.899]
Country Dummies	Y	Y
Industry Dummies	Y	Y
Time Dummies	Y	Y
Country × Time Dummies		Y
Industry × Time Dummies		Y
R²	0.90	0.95
# Observations	58	58

Notes: All regression are estimated by White's correction of heteroskedasticity. Standard errors are in parenthesis denoting *** 1%, ** 5%, * 10%. The dependent variable is the growth in industry value added (5 year averges). FDI corresponds to Foreign Direct Investment Flows from OECD International Direct Investment Database. Log Value Added and Share of Value added correspond to the beginning of the period and are from the U.N. Industrial Statistics Yearbook. See Appendix A for detailed explanation of all variables and sources.

might have a positive effect on the quality of FDI attracted to a location if the investment promotion agency focuses its resources on especially desirable projects. A third possibility is that some endogeneity in the process is correlated with industry targeting. Perhaps foreign investors are attracted to high-growth industries and investment promotion agencies choose these as their target industries. We investigate these possibilities below.

3.3.5 IV results: endogeneity and heterogeneity

3.3.5.1 Instrumentation methodology

Due to endogeneity and measurement problem concerns, in order to identify the effect of FDI on growth we need an instrument that is correlated with the "idealized" quality-adjusted FDI volumes, but not with growth. In this section, we transform our industry-targeting information into a binary variable with industry, country, and time variation, and show that it satisfies both the validity and excludability requirements as explained below.

Table 3.3.7 highlights the strong relation between industry targeting and FDI flows. In particular, the table presents the results of the following OLS regression.

$$FDI_{ict} = \alpha_{FDI} + \beta_{FDI} IndustryTargeting_{it} + \lambda_{FDI} X_{ict} + \delta_i + \delta_c + \delta_t + \varepsilon_{FDIict} \qquad (2)$$

Table 3.3.7 Determinants of FDI – Industry data (OLS regression) dependent variable: FDI activity, 1985–2000

	(1)	(2)	(3)	(4)	(5)
Dependent Variable	Log of FDI Flows				Log # Foreign Firms
Industry Targeting	0.179 [0.065]***	0.363 [0.062]***	0.426 [0.062]***	0.154 [0.063]**	0.277 [0.131]**
Log Value Added	0.363 [0.037]***	0.177 [0.040]***	0.108 [0.039]***	0.003 [0.042]	0.194 [0.060]***
Log FDI_{-1}		0.307 [0.015]***	0.318 [0.015]***		
Comparative Advantage (Size)				0.994 [0.059]***	
Country Dummies	Y	Y	Y	Y	Y
Industry Dummies	Y	Y	Y	Y	Y
Time Dummies	Y	Y	Y	Y	Y
Country × Time Dummies			Y		
Industry × Time Dummies			Y		
R^2#	0.68	0.78	0.82	0.70	0.82
Observations	530	355	355	530	767

Notes: All regression are estimated by White's correction of heteroskedasticity. Standard errors are in parenthesis denoting *** 1%, ** 5%, * 10%. The dependent variable in (1)–(4) is the log of FDI flows which corresponds to Foreign Direct Investment Flows from OECD International Direct Investment Database; in (5) the log of the number of foreign firms from Dun & Bradstreet. See Appendix A for detailed explanation of all variables and sources.

where FDI_{ict} is the measure of FDI activity in industry i in country c at time t, targeting is a dummy equal to one in the period following the targeting of industry i by country c, and X_{ict} is a set of control variables. The regression includes a full set of country, industry and time effects. In columns (1)–(4) we use as a proxy variable for foreign activity the log of FDI flows from the *Balance of Payments*, and in column (5) the number of foreign firms.

Overall, there is a positive and significant effect of industry targeting on foreign firm activity. The results in column (1) were obtained using as main regressions the industry-targeting dummy and share of value added as well as country, industry, and time dummies. The estimates in column (1) imply 19 percent extra FDI in targeted industries. Column (2) adds lagged FDI values, there being evidence that FDI tends to be self-enforcing. Column (3) adds a full set of interacted dummies, column (4) an additional control variable for comparative advantage in industry i in country c, $(x_{ic}/x_c)/(x_i/y)$, defined as exports (x) in industry i in country c to total exports in the country relative to industry output (y). The similar results reported in the last column were obtained using number of foreign firms as a proxy for FDI activity.[32]

Evidence of strong effects of industry targeting notwithstanding, these estimates should be interpreted with caution. Testing the effectiveness of investment promotion in international data has been an elusive empirical problem. Given the myriad factors that determine the size of any nations' foreign direct investment flows, it is difficult to isolate the effect of a single (endogenous) policy variable for which there are few natural instruments. First, investment promotion might be correlated with imperfectly observed country attributes, potentially introducing bias into cross-sectional studies. We include time-varying industry covariates and time-interacted dummies to address some of these concerns. However, even the availability of panel data is unable to mitigate this endogeneity if the unobserved county attributes are time-varying (for example, other policy changes introduced concurrently with FDI promotion; countries that actively promote foreign investment might be doing so, for example, as part of a broader economic reform agenda).

An additional concern that emerges from Table 3.3.7 is the correlation between targeted sectors and growth. One might worry that some other factor correlated with growth might also affect the industry-targeting variable. If, for example, the variable used to proxy for investment promotion (for example, the establishment of a foreign investment office) is a consequence rather than a cause of increased bilateral FDI flows, the estimates might be subject to reverse causation. As a first cut, we regressed average growth rates over (pre-sample period) on industrial targeting in the sample period. There is a non-significant effect of pre-sample growth on the subsequent five years of targeting (see column 1 in Table B1). Recognizing that industry targeting is a choice rather than a natural policy experiment, we also use propensity score matching to ensure the validity of our control group.[33] As explained in Appendix B, we conduct a matching exercise following Rosenbaum and Rubin (1983) to ensure that we have a valid control group for which the distribution of the variables affecting the outcome is as similar as possible to the distribution of these variables for targeted industries.

Industry targeting is also correlated with FDI quality. There is considerable evidence that IPAs hold preferences for particular characteristics of FDI projects. Several IPAs, for example, use models that calculate rates of "economic and social" return based on the contributions of proposed FDI projects to employment, exports, and skills.[34] Further evidence that industry targeting is associated with changes in the quality of FDI is provided by OIR, a firm that sells to national investment promotion agencies data about firms intending to invest overseas. We noted earlier that OIR clients can purchase data in several categories. By mode of entry, 100 percent of OIR's clients choose to receive data on greenfield projects; 30 percent data on M&A projects. By functional category, 100 percent choose to purchase data on production facilities and R&D centers; fewer than 70 percent data on back office functions, and fewer than 50 percent data on marketing/sales facilities.

One concern with this line of reasoning is that some IPAs are widely seen to be ineffective, thus, their efforts might not produce observable results along the metric of either quantity or quality of FDI. Many such IPAs consist of little more than a website and a handful of staff whose impact on investment flows is likely to be minimal. There are, nevertheless, also examples of IPAs that are credited with being effective, among them, the Irish IPA, the Industrial Development Agency, the Czech IPA CzechInvest, and the Costa Rican IPA, CINDE. A key finding of the IPA survey, however, was that the target industries named by IPAs were determined centrally by other government agencies, most commonly the ministry of finance. Thus, in some cases, our observations of targeted industries might reflect a broader government effort to attract an industry that is merely being signaled by the IPA.

3.3.5.2   Two Stage Least Square Estimates

Table 3.3.8 presents two-stage least square (2SLS) estimates of equation (1). The FDI flows variable is treated as endogeneous and modeled as in equation (2). This identification strategy is valid as long as the *Industry Targeting* variable is uncorrelated with ε_{ict}. The exclusion restriction is that the targeting variable does not appear in (1) as discussed below.

Panel A of Table 8 presents the 2SLS estimates of equation (1). Panel B reports the associated first-stage regressions. We find a strong first-stage relationship between industry targeting and industry FDI flows. As shown in column (1) of panel A, average FDI flows, where they are instrumented by the industry-targeting variable, have a causal effect on growth. The first-stage regression shows the effect of the industry-targeting variable on FDI flows to be significant. The first-stage regression also shows the significant effect of targeting on FDI flows with an R^2 of 0.8. The estimated coefficient is higher than the OLS counterpart shown in Table 3.3.3 because the IV regression corrects for both endogeneity and the attenuation bias caused by the measurement error in the balance of payments FDI data. In fact, the results suggest that measurement error is a more serious concern than reverse causality.

A sense of the magnitude of the effect of FDI inflows on growth is provided by the results reported in column (2): if we move up from the 25th percentile to the 75th percentile in the distribution of the flows, we have, on average, 4.3 percent more growth. This represents an almost 59 percent increase in growth over the sample mean. This result warrants careful interpretation. Given the causal effect, these results imply an impressively large effect of foreign investment flows on growth. Note that the quantitative effect obtained from the IV regression is much larger than the one obtained from the OLS regression due to the attenuation bias in the latter.

Table 3.3.8 IV regression of 5-year growth value added and FDI – Industry data

	(1)	(2)
	Panel A: Two-Stage Least Squares	
Log FDI	2.010	1.468
	[1.050]**	[0.595]**
Log Value Added	−2.660	−2.771
	[0.792]	[0.864]***
Share Value Added	15.320	13.104
	[12.350]	[12.051]
Country Dummies	Y	Y
Industry Dummies	Y	Y
Time Dummies	Y	Y
Industry × Time dummies	Y	Y
Country × Time dummies	Y	Y
R²	0.74	0.74
# Observations	483	483
	Panel B: First Stage for Log FDI	
Industry Targeting	0.806	0.428
	[0.244]**	[0.210]**
Log Value Added	0.311	0.328
	[0.127]	[0.204]
Share Value Added	−2.980	−2.590
	[2.53]	[2.99]
Log FDI$_{-1}$		0.288
		[0.050]***
Sargan Test		0.68
F-statistic	13.48	23.45
R²	0.81	0.83

Notes: Panel A reports the two-stage least square estimates, instrumenting foreign direct investment flows using the industry targeting variable and other controls. The dependent variable is the growth in industry value added (5 year averges). Panel B reports the corresponding first stage. All regression are estimated by White's correction of heteroskedasticity. Standard errors are in parenthesis denoting *** 1%, ** 5%, * 10%. See Appendix A for detailed explanation of all variables and sources.

How should we interpret the IV estimate being larger than the OLS estimate? According to our theory, investment promotion agencies identify and attempt to attract specific foreign investors they believe will benefit their country.[35] Surveys of investment promotion agencies indicate that they are interested in particular types of projects such as high-tech, export, and greenfield projects, and joint ventures. According to UNCTAD, industry targeting should be explicitly linked to an increase in the quality of FDI projects.[36] Thus an increase in industry-specific promotion will be associated with an increase in the quantity and quality of FDI flows. Industry targeting is focused particularly on "good-quality" FDI sought and facilitated by investment promotion agencies. Hence, targeting is correlated with good FDI leading to an increase in the effect of FDI (instrumented by the targeting variable). Targeting is therefore a relevant instrument for identifying the good aspect of FDI, provided our results are interpreted with caution. One concern is that our results do not necessarily mean that the relation is causal; the causation might be reversed, that is, when IPAs think there is going to be an increase in FDI they target that sector.

The first stage of our 2SLS estimates the coefficient β_{FDI} on the targeting dummy. This coefficient represents the increase in industry FDI that occurs simultaneously with the IPA targeting an industry. The predicted value from the first stage, FDI_{ict}, is a linear combination of the estimated coefficient on the targeting dummy and the other first-stage controls. In the second stage, the raw FDI variable (measured by the balance of payments system) is replaced by this predicted value, which reflects, specifically, the increase in FDI consequent to targeting. As noted above, FDI is not homogeneous (given the distinction made by IPAs). The increase in predicted FDI associated with targeting is an increase in a particular kind of FDI, the kind IPAs want to attract. Hence, the predicted values from the first stage of our 2SLS specification focus on quality FDI, and our instruments will have two upward effects on the IV coefficient on FDI, which first reduces measurement errors and, second, focuses on more growth-enhancing FDI.

Are our instruments relevant? One way to check for weak instruments when there is a single endogenous regressor is to compute F-statistic testing the hypothesis that the coefficient on the instruments are all zero in the first stage of 2SLS. The F statistics are all greater than 10, the simple rule of thumb-value proposed by Staiger and Stock (1997) as validation of relevance.[37]

Another important concern is whether our instruments are uncorrelated with the error term (exogenous). We use overidentification tests to determine whether there is a direct relationship between FDI targeting and industry growth, and investigate the validity of our approach According to our theory, the decision to target an industry is associated with an increase in foreign investment, specifically, an increase in the kind of foreign investment the IPA is trying to attract. Our instrumental variable regression implies an exclusion restriction that, conditional on the controls, the industry-targeting policy exerts no effect on industry growth other than through an increase in FDI. The overidentification test presumes the other instruments to be truly exogenous, and tests for the exogeneity of investment promotion.[38] To implement this test, one needs additional potential instruments. This is not an easy task, in particular, at the industry level.[39] We use the lag of FDI as a second instrument although we note that there are important issues due to persistence of FDI flows (and its observed determinants) and so the tests should be taken as suggestive.

According to our theory, the decision to target an industry is associated with an increase in foreign investment, specifically, an increase in the kind of foreign investment the IPA is trying to attract. Our instrumental variable regression implies an exclusion restriction that, conditional on the controls, the industry-targeting policy exerts no effect on industry growth other than through an increase in FDI. The overidentification test presumes the other instruments (for example, lag FDI) to be truly exogenous, and tests for the exogeneity of investment promotion.[40] The results of the overidentification tests, and related results, are reported in Appendix Table C1. Panel A reports the 2SLS estimates of the effect of FDI on growth using a variety of instruments other than investment promotion. Panel B gives the corresponding first stages and panel C reports the p-value from the appropriate χ^2 over identification test (Sargan test) as well as additional diagnostic tests of the relevance of our instruments. Subject to the usual problems of power, the overidentification tests show the instruments to be valid. These estimates are in every case quite close to those reported in Table 3.3.7. Albeit concerns of the use of lag FDI as an instrument, the tests give some confidence that we are estimating the effect of FDI on growth with our instrumental variable strategy. In column (1), we use the industrial targeting variable as the only instrument for FDI, in column (2) the lagged value of FDI. The result in this case is an estimated effect of 1.379 (with standard error 0.229), as compared to our baseline estimate of 1.35. Using, in column (3), data from the WorldBase database on the number of foreign firms in each sector yields similar results. Finally, column (4) reports the results of an easy-to-interpret test for validity and excludability of the instrument that follows Acemoglu, Johnson, and Robinson (2001). The test adds the investment promotion as an exogenous regressor in panel A. If investment promotion had a direct effect on growth, we would expect this variable to be positive and significant. The effect, however, as seen in the table, is small and statistically insignificant.

As discussed above, one concern with our strategy is that some other factor correlated with growth might also affect the industry-targeting variable. Investment promotion agencies' industry-targeting practices are not random experiments, but rather conscious decisions by policymakers. We have to be concerned that countries choose target industries in which they believe they have some future comparative advantage. If foreign investors have similar views about future industry prospects, the evolution of industry comparative advantage could explain both growth and promotion. As a first cut, we do not find significant evidence that lagged growth rates are associated with current targeting practices. We further resolve this issue in two ways: (1) by including time-varying industry covariates that capture changes in comparative advantage; and (2) by conducting a matching exercise to ensure that we have a valid control group for which the distribution of the variables affecting the outcome is as similar as possible to the distribution of these variables for targeted industries. We use the propensity score matching method and, as explained in Appendix B, our main results remain robust to this analysis.

3.3.5.3 IV results: robustness

Overall, the results in Tables 3.3.3, 3.3.4, and 3.3.5 show FDI flows and value-added growth, when we consider industry characteristics, to be strongly correlated. An appealing feature of industry analysis is that it mitigates some of the effects of unobserved heterogeneity and model misspecification, which are difficult to control at the national level. Analyzing a cross-section of industries within a cross-section of countries enables us to include a full set of industry and country dummy variables, which control for time-invariant unobserved industry and country heterogeneity.[41] There are nevertheless a number of important reasons why the relation should not be interpreted as causal. An important concern with FDI growth regression is that fast-growing countries are likely to attract more FDI. In addition to reverse causality, many omitted time-variant determinants of growth might be correlated with FDI flows. If this is the case, the coefficients on estimates are likely to overstate the positive impact of foreign investment. As a result, one could find evidence of positive growth effects of foreign investment even in the absence of such benefits. An instrument of FDI flows at the industry level can address these issues. Such an instrument must account for the variation observed in FDI flows, but have no direct effect on economic growth. The discussion in the previous section suggested

Table 3.3.9 Robustness I: IV regression of growth value added and FDI – Industry data dependent variable is 5-year industry growth in value added, 1985–2000

	Comp. Adv. (1)	Gross Capital (2)	1995–2000 (3)	FDI/CAP only (4)
	Panel A: Two-Stage Least Squares			
Log FDI	1.279	1.078	1.716	
	[0.212]***	[0.349]***	[0.137]***	
Log Value Added	−4.926	−0.584	−3.505	0.908
	[0.377]***	[0.823]	[0.300]	[0.642]
Share Value Added	2.482	−4.417	11.801	−9.131
	[4.061]	[10.155]	[5.08]***	[10.280]
Comparative Advantage (Size)	2.039 [0.192]***			
Log Gross Capital		0.070 [0.413]		
Log FDI/Capital				1.279 [0.371]***
Country Dummies	Y	Y	Y	Y
Industry Dummies	Y	Y	Y	Y
Time Dummies	Y	Y	Y	Y
R^2	0.68	0.43	0.88	0.42
# Observations	674	186	313	186

(continued)

Table 3.3.9 Continued

	Comp. Adv. (1)	Gross Capital (2)	1995–2000 (3)	FDI/CAP only (4)
		Panel B: First Stage for Log FDI		
Industry Targeting	0.366 [0.060]***	0.466 [0.077]***	0.421 [0.068]***	0.38 [0.080]***
Log Value Added	0.686 [0.073]***	0.566 [0.142]***	0.338 [0.081]***	−0.28 [0.119]**
Share Value Added	−0.842 [0.894]	0.315 [0.069]***	−1.340 [1.146]	0.19 [1.892]
Log FDI -1	0.307 [0.015]***	0.357 [0.023]***	0.243 [0.018]***	0.34 [0.024]***
Comparative Advantage (Size)	−0.316 [0.040]***			
Log Gross Capital		−2.128 [1.830]		
R^2	0.79	0.74	0.90	0.80
		Panel C: OLS Regressions		
Log FDI	0.285 [0.163]*	0.877 [0.372]**	0.562 [0.208]***	
Log Value Added	−8.824 [0.482]***	0.331 [2.226]	−3.320 [1.034]***	1.268 [1.700]
Share Value Added	33.964 [9.486]***	−12.882 [30.078]	42.815 [11.543]***	−16.924 [29.380]
Comparative Advantage (Size)	2.837 [0.380]***			
Log Gross Capital		−0.168 [1.067]		
Log FDI/Capital				0.824 [0.363]**
R^2	0.75	0.32	0.55	0.32

Notes: Panel A reports the two-stage least square estimates, instrumenting foreign direct investment flows using the industry targeting variable. Dependent variable is the growth in industry value added (5 year averges). Panel B reports the corresponding first stage. Panel C the reports the OLS regressions. All regression are estimated by White's correction of heteroskedasticity. Standard errors are in parenthesis denoting ***1%, **5%, *10%. See Appendix A for detailed explanation of all variables and sources.

that industry targeting is a plausible candidate for such an instrument. The previous section discusses the validity of the instruments.

We performed a series of robustness and sensitivity tests, the results of some of which are reported in Table 3.3.9. Column (1) shows the robustness of the results to including a measure of comparative advantage (exports in industry *i* in country *c* to total exports in the country relative to industry output). In column (2), we add the log of gross capital flows to the list of control variables yielding some interesting results. The coefficient and significance of the FDI term increase across the different specifications, suggesting that FDI might have positive effects over and above its direct role in capital accumulation. In column (3) we restrict the sample to the period 1995–2000. In column (4) we use FDI to the capital stock as the proxy for foreign activity. Table 3.3.10 shows our results to be robust to using three-year growth rate averages. Appendix Table B2

Table 3.3.10   Robustness II: IV regression of growth value added and FDI – Industry data dependent variable is 3-year industry growth in value added, 1985–2000

	(1)	(2)	(3)	(4)	(5)
	Panel A: Two-Stage Least Squares				
Log FDI	4.441	3.251	1.642	1.296	1.468
	[1.538]***	[1.311]**	[0.272]***	[0.219]***	[0.595]**
Log Value Added	−4.893	−4.561	−3.203	−2.128	−2.771
	[0.642]***	[0.511]***	[0.289]***	[0.300]***	[0.864]***
Share Value Added	18.585	17.259	16.010	4.206	13.104
	[6.197]***	[7.127]***	[3.910]***	[3.658]	[12.051]
Country Dummies	Y	Y	Y	Y	Y
Industry Dummies	Y	Y	Y	Y	Y
Time Dummies	Y	Y	Y	Y	Y
Industry × Time dummies		Y			Y
Country × Time dummies		Y			Y
R^2	0.20	0.59	0.51	0.63	0.63
# Observations	895	675	743	675	675
	Panel B: First Stage for Log FDI				
Industry Targeting	0.294	0.354		0.091	0.058
	[0.065]***	[0.276]		[0.068]	[0.021]**
Log FDI $_{-1}$			0.220	0.247	0.324
			[0.011]***	[0.011]***	[0.025]***
Log Value Added	0.369	0.324	0.406	0.551	0.644
	[0.039]***	[0.052]***	[0.046]***	[0.051]***	[0.170]***
Share Value Added	2.992	2.312	0.392	−1.248	−1.643
	[0.634]***	[0.721]***	[0.704]	[0.713]*	[2.112]
R^2	0.69	0.77	0.73	0.77	0.76
	Panel C: Diagnostic Tests				
Sargan overid P-Value				0.69	0.88

Notes: Panel A reports the two-stage least square estimates, instrumenting foreign direct investment flows using the industry targeting variable and other controls. The dependent variable is the growth in industry value added (3 year averges). Panel B reports the corresponding first stage. Panel C resports the diagnostic tests. All regression are estimated by White's correction of heteroskedasticity. Standard errors are in parenthesis denoting *** 1%, ** 5%, * 10%. See Appendix A for detailed explanation of all variables and sources.

Table 3.3.11 IV regression of growth value added and FDI: External finance and skill dependence dependent variable is 5-year industry growth in value added, 1985–2000

	Low Financ. Dep.		High Financ. Dep.		Low Skill		High Skill	
	(1)	(2)	(3)	(4)	(5)	(6)	(7)	(8)
Panel A: Two-Stage Least Squares								
Log FDI	1.392	1.342	2.397	2.437	0.324	0.202	4.398	4.545
	[1.219]	[1.189]	[0.923]***	[0.914]***	[0.181]	[0.181]	[0.815]***	[0.815]***
Log Value Added	−2.469	−2.367	−5.112	−5.091	−0.874	−0.863	−8.127	−7.486
	[1.471]	[1.471]	[1.221]***	[1.221]***	[0.152]***	[0.256]***	[0.922]***	[0.901]***
Share Value Added	−6.235	−4.155	29.256	33.256	−5.370	−5.786	94.450	85.170
	[17.943]	[20.245]	[19.895]*	[19.675]*	[4.110]*	[3.124]*	[16.358]***	[14.528]***
Country Dummies	Y	Y	Y	Y	Y	Y	Y	Y
Industry Dummies	Y	Y	Y	Y	Y	Y	Y	Y
Time Dummies	Y	Y	Y	Y	Y	Y	Y	Y
R²	0.67	0.68	0.68	0.69	0.79	0.82	0.37	0.43
# Observations	145	144	205	202	395	430	420	418
Panel B: First Stage for Log FDI								
Log Value Added	0.497	0.397	0.501	0.487	0.291	0.331	0.566	0.530
	[0.402]	[0.342]	[0.231]**	[0.240]**	[0.790]***	[0.080]***	[0.103]***	[0.099]***
Share Value Added	−1.940	−1.944	−4.657	−3.657	−0.869	−0.161	−6.023	−6.046
	[5.454]	[5.353]	[4.568]	[4.282]	[1.011]	[1.028]	[1.811]***	[1.960]***
Industry Targeting	0.414	0.313	0.471	0.488	0.301	0.405	0.498	0.397
	[0.395]	[0.345]	[0.261]*	[0.278]*	[0.055]***	[0.068]***	[0.113]***	[0.121]***
Log FDI −1		0.274		0.291		0.283		0.248
		[0.087]***		[0.067]***		[0.018]***		[0.031]***
R²	0.61	0.64	0.60	0.63	0.75	0.80	0.77	0.79
F-statistic	3.88	5.11	10.74	12.17	18.49	141.73	21.78	39.31

(continued)

Table 3.3.11 Continued

	Low Financ. Dep.		High Financ. Dep.		Low Skill		High Skill	
	(1)	(2)	(3)	(4)	(5)	(6)	(7)	(8)
				Panel C: OLS Regressions				
Log FDI	0.279	0.279	0.474	0.473	0.168	0.168	0.464	0.363
	[0.241]	[0.241]	[0.239]*	[0.244]*	[0.071]**	[0.071]**	[0.072]***	[0.072]***
Log Value Added	-5.774	-5.774	-8.95	-8.95	-7.817	-7.817	-7.481	-7.381
	[0.761]***	[0.761]***	[0.578]***	[0.578]***	[0.241]***	[0.231]***	[0.200]***	[0.200]***
Share Value Added	61.394	61.443	82.545	82.535	60.168	60.168	76.545	76.535
	[12.456]***	[12.456]***	[11.499]***	[11.399]***	[4.670]***	[3.670]***	[4.395]***	[3.445]***
R²	0.64	0.64	0.81	0.81	0.77	0.77	0.70	0.70

Notes: Panel A reports the two-stage least square estimates, instrumenting foreign direct investment flows using the industry targeting variable. Dependent variable is the growth in industry value added (5 year averges). Panel B reports the corresponding first stage. Panel C reports the OLS regression. Industries are divided into low in (1)–(2) and high external finance in (3)–(4) as defined by Rajan and Zingales (1998); and into low (blue collar) in (5)–(6) and high skills (white collar) in (7)–(8). All regression are estimated by White's correction of heteroskedasticity. Standard errors are in parenthesis denoting *** 1%, ** 5%, * 10%. See Appendix A for detailed explanation of all variables and sources.

shows in column (1) the results of using the matched observations, and in column (2) the results of using the number of foreign firms as a proxy for foreign activity; both yield similar results. We analyze whether the complementarity that results between FDI and finance and skills is robust as well to our instrumentation strategy. Table 3.3.11, panel A reports the IV results, panel B the corresponding OLS results. In this case, we find higher effects for industries dependent on external finance and those reliant on highly skilled labor.[42] Finally, we also examined the robustness of the results of using whether FDI has an effect on total factor productivity (not reported). As mentioned in section 3.3.3, missing capital stock data reduced considerably our sample size with further limited the IV analysis. However, we contain consistent results even with the limited number of observations. In this case, our results imply an almost 43 percent increase of TFP over the sample mean which is consistent with our previous findings.

3.3.6 Conclusions

This paper exploits a comprehensive, industry level data set for the period 1985–2000 that encompasses 29 countries to examine differential effect of different "types" of FDI on growth. An appealing feature of industry analysis is that it mitigates some of the effects of unobserved heterogeneity and model misspecification, which are difficult to control at the national level. We also use as an instrument a new industry-level data set on industry targeting. We find the relation between and FDI and growth to be stronger for industries with higher skill requirements and for industries more reliant on external capital. We also use the new data set on industry targeting and two-stage least squares methodology to identify quality FDI as determined by the host countries. FDI quality is also associated with positive and economically significant growth effects.

Understanding the effect of FDI on economic growth is important for a number of reasons. It has implications for the effect of rapidly growing investment flows on the process of economic development. It also informs foreign investment policy. In 1999 alone, there were 140 changes to state or national laws related to foreign direct investment. More than 90% of these changes liberalized foreign investment policy. One fifth introduced new incentives for foreign investors including tax concessions, financial incentives, import duty exceptions, and infrastructure and training subsidies (UNCTAD, 2000). Such policies however do not guarantee realization of the potential benefits of FDI that go beyond the "capital" FDI transfers to the host country. If FDI does not exert a robust positive influence on growth, these pecuniary incentives and the active international competition for investment should be reconsidered. Local conditions in the recipient country can pose binding constraints on such spillovers. Our analysis, due to data limitation, has been restricted to OECD countries, which arguably have the local conditions to take advantage of FDI effects. More generally, studying the costs and benefits of FDI promotion are beyond the scope of this paper. More research on the consequences of FDI is warranted before advocating FDI promotion. And clearly, much more research is required to clarify the impact of MNEs on host countries.

Appendix A: Data Description

FDI Inflows and Stocks: Annual data for the period 1985–2000 on FDI inflows and stocks at the industry level. From the OECD's International Direct Investment database.

Industry Growth: Growth in real value added in each industry in each country for three- and five-year periods. From the *Industrial Statistics Yearbook* of the United Nations Statistical Division.

Share of Value Added: Share of value added in industry *i* in country *c* to the country's value added. From *Industrial Statistics Yearbook* of the United Nations Statistical Division.

Number of Foreign Firms: From the WorldBase compiled by Dun & Bradstreet.

Comparative Advantage (Size): Exports in industry *i* in country *c* to total exports in the country relative to industry output (size), $(x_{ic}/x_c)/(x_i/y)$, where x is exports and y is output.

Dependence on External Finance (Equity): Constructed by the authors for 1987–1996 following Rajan and Zingales (1998). An industry's external financial dependence is obtained by calculating the external financing of US companies. Rajan and Zingales (1998) identify an industry's need for external finance (the difference between investment and cash generated from operations) under two assumptions, (a) that U.S. capital markets, especially for the large, listed firms they analyze, are relatively frictionless, enabling us to identify an industry's technological demand for external finance, and (b) that such technological demands carry over to other countries. Following their methodology, we constructed similar data for the period 1987–1996 for all sectors for which Compustat had data. Using data from Compustat, a firm's dependence on external finance is defined as: (Capex-Cashflow)/Capex, where Capex is capital expenditures and Cashflow cash flow from operations. Industries with negative external finance measures have cash flows that are higher than their capital expenditures.

Skill Intensity Measure: Ratio of high skilled workers to other workers in German industries, following Carlin and Mayer (2003). The occupational data are based on the new version of the International Standard Classification of Occupations of the International Labour Office, ISCO 88.

The following categories and subcategories are defined. White-collar high-skill (WCHS) includes legislators, senior officials, and managers (Group 1), professionals (Group 2), technicians and associate professionals (Group 3); white-collar low-skill (WCLS) includes clerks and service workers (Group 4) and shop and sales workers (Group 5); blue-collar high-skill (BCHS) includes skilled agricultural and fishery workers (Group 6) and craft and related trade workers (Group 7); blue-collar low-skill (BCLS) includes plant and machine operators and assemblers (Group 8) and elementary occupations (Group 9).

Total Factor Productivity (TFP): We calculate $TFP = Y/(K\beta L^{(1-\beta)})$ where Y is the value added of the business sector, K the stock of the business sector capital, and L the employment in the business sector. Given the limited availability of data, TFP growth is calculated on a yearly basis. Total factor productivity growth was estimated from a constant returns to scale Cobb-Douglas production function with the capital share set at 1/3 and the labor share set at two-thirds.

List of Countries: Australia, Austria, Belgium, Canada, Switzerland, Czech Republic, Germany, Denmark, Spain, Finland, France, United Kingdom, Greece, Hungary, Ireland, Iceland, Italy, Japan, Korea, Luxembourg, Mexico, Netherlands, Norway, New Zealand, Poland, Portugal, Sweden, Turkey, USA.

Appendix B: Matching

Following Charlton and Davis (2006), we identify the probability that industry j is targeted by country i in time t using a logit model.

$$P(\Pr ob_{ij} = 1) = F(Z_{ijt}, D_{ijt})$$

where F is the normal cumulative distribution function and D_{ijt} is a full set of country, industry, and time dummies. We use the predicted probability, P_{ijt}, as a monotone function to select comparison non-targeted observations for each targeted observation. The nearest neighbor, k, to each targeted observation is selected such that $|P_{ijt} - P_{ikt}| = \min\{P_{ijt} - P_{ikt}\}$ over all k in the set of non-targeted industries. Matches are only accepted if $\min\{P_{ijt} - P_{ikt}\}$ is less than a caliper which we vary between 0.005 and 0.001.

The success of matching techniques rests on our ability to predict the probability than an industry will be targeted. A good predictive model helps to support the conditional independence assumption implicit in propensity score matching. The industry-targeting survey contained questions covering the reasons for targeting and the reasons for adopting or dropping target industries. The three highest responses were industries in which the country had some comparative advantage, a large volume of FDI, and high export propensity.

Appendix Table B1 presents the probit model of industry targeting. The dependent variable takes the value of one if industry *j* was targeted for the first time by country *i* in time *t*. We control for factors that might affect the desirability of the industry as a target for investment promotion such as the global volume of FDI in the industry (OECD countries) and measures of the country's comparative advantage. Differences between targeted and non-targeted sectors are reduced when the target group is compared with the matched counterparts. The predicted model gives us a propensity score. Nearest neighbor matching means that we can use only a subset of a sample. We matched the 85 targeting observations to the nearest four non-targeting observations and applied a caliper of 0.01. Table B2 presents results of the change in growth rate of FDI for the matched subsample.

Table B1   Logit model of industry target choice – Industry data dependent variable: Industry targeting, 1990–2000

	(1)	(2)	(3)
Log Global Industry Flows		0.585	0.494
		[0.238]**	[0.129]***
Log FDI_{-1}		−0.292	−0.193
		[0.164]*	[0.098]**
Comparative Advantage (Size)		1.511	0.910
		[0.544]***	[0.330]***
Growth Real Value Added$_{-1}$ (%)	0.019	0.037	0.028
	[0.019]	[0.026]	[0.018]
Growth Real Value Added (%)		−0.088	−0.001
		[0.075]	[0.037]
Skills			−0.609
			[0.856]
Financial Dependence			0.219
			[0.122]*
Country Dummies	Y	Y	Y
Industry Dummies	Y	Y	
Time Dummies	Y	Y	Y
Country × Time Dummies	Y	Y	Y
Industry × Time Dummies	Y	Y	
R^2	0.22	0.39	0.33
Observations	443	376	378

Notes: Logit estimation. Standard errors are in parenthesis denoting *** 1%, ** 5%, * 10%. Dependent variable takes the value of one if the country *i* targeted industry *j* for the first time in year *t*. FDI corresponds to Foreign Direct Investment Flows from OECD International Direct Investment Database. Log Value Added and Share of Value added correspond to the beginning of the period. See Appendix A for detailed explanation of all variables and sources.

Table B2 Regression of growth value added and number of foreign firms dependent variable is 5-year industry growth in value added, 1985–2000

	Matched Observations (1)	Number of Firms (2)
	Panel A: Two-Stage Least Squares	
Log FDI	1.953 [0.333]***	
Log Value Added	−2.181 [0.652]***	
Share Value Added	−8.907 [5.504]	2.087
Log # of Foreign Firms		[0.699]*** −1.478
Log # of all Firms (Start of Period)		[0.557]***
Country Dummies	Y	Y
Industry Dummies	Y	Y
Time Dummies	Y	Y
R^2	0.80	0.68
# Observations	149	793
	Panel B: First Stage for Log FDI	
Industry Targeting	0.369 [0.067]***	0.107 [0.054]***
Log Value Added	1.231 [0.120]***	
Share Value Added	−4.100 [1.471]***	1.658 [0.418]***
Log FDI_{-1}	0.220 [0.022]***	
Log # of Foreign Firms$_{-1}$		0.113 [0.008]***
Or Log # of all Firms (Start of Period)		0.723 [0.012]***
R^2	0.81	0.64
	Panel C: OLS Regression	
Log FDI	0.601 [0.331]*	
Log Value Added	0.283 [1.538]	
Share Value Added	−19.452 [19.583]	

(continued)

Table B2   Continued

	Matched Observations (1)	Number of Firms (2)
Log # of Foreign Firms$_{-1}$		0.324 [0.219]
Log # of all Firms (Start of Period)		−0.719 [0.254]***
R²	0.81	0.53

Notes: All regression are estimated by White's correction of heteroskedasticity. Standard errors are in parenthesis denoting *** 1%, ** 5%, * 10%. The dependent variable is the growth in industry value added (5 year averges). Column (1) shows matched results; column (2) uses as independent variable the number of foreign firms from Dun & Bradstreet. See Appendix A for detailed explanation of all variables and sources.

Table C1   Robustness instrument stragegy regression of 5-year growth value added and FDI – Industry data

	(1)	(2)	(3)	(4)
	Panel A: Two-Stage Least Squares			
Log FDI	1.871 [1.034]*	1.379 [0.229]***	1.307 [0.221]***	1.100 [0.288]***
Log Value Added	−2.166 [0.680]***	−2.726 [0.297]***	−4.943 [0.379]***	−3.050 [0.378]***
Share Value Added	−1.036 [3.514]	12.612 [4.074]***	2.433 [4.068]	11.616 [5.011]**
Industry Targeting			−0.128 [0.282]	
Country Dummies	Y	Y	Y	Y
Industry Dummies	Y	Y	Y	Y
Time Dummies	Y	Y	Y	Y
R²	0.62	0.66	0.68	0.72
# Observations	601	523	354	330
	Panel B: First Stage for Log FDI			
Industry Targeting	0.169 [0.064]***		0.366 [0.059]***	0.464 [0.071]***
Log Value Added	0.522 [0.056]***	0.313 [0.059]***	0.307 [0.0148]***	
Share Value Added	−3.238 [0.850]***	−2.662 [0.901]***	−0.841 [0.894]***	
Log FDI $_{-1}$		0.308 [0.015]***	0.686 [0.073]***	0.280 [0.020]***

(*continued*)

Table C1 Continued

	(1)	(2)	(3)	(4)
Foreign/Domestic Firms				0.002
				[0.001]***
R²	0.71	0.80	0.81	0.73
	Panel C: Diagnostic Tests			
Sargan overid PV				0.14

Notes: Panel A reports the two-stage least square estimates, instrumenting foreign direct investment flows using the industry targeting variable and other controls. The dependent variable is
the growth in industry value added (5 year averges). Panel B reports the corresponding first stage.
Panel C resorts the diagnostic tests. All regression are estimated by White's correction of heteroskedasticity. Standard errors are in parenthesis denoting *** 1%, ** 5%, * 10%. Column (3) add
investment promotion as an exogenous regressor. See Appendix A for detailed explanation of all
variables and sources.

Notes

1. See Blomström and Kokko (1998), Hanson (2001), Lipsey (2002), Gorg and
   Greenaway (2004), Barba-Navaretti and Venables (2004), and Alfaro and
   Rodriguez-Clare (2004) for surveys of theoretical work and empirical findings.
2. Taken from IDA Annual Report (2006).
3. See http://www.china.org.cn/english/BAT/42600.htm.
4. See Borensztein et al. (1995), Alfaro et al. (2004), Carkovik and Levine (2005).
5. In this paper, "industry" refers to the 2 digit ISIC classification level.
6. UNCTAD World Investment Report (2001:138), for instance, notes that, "[I]n the
   primary sector, the scope for linkages between foreign affiliates and local suppliers is often limited... The manufacturing sector has a broad variation of linkage
   intensive activities. [In] the tertiary sector the scope for dividing production into
   discrete stages and subcontracting out large parts to independent domestic firms
   is also limited." Girma, Greenaway and Wakelin (2001), for example, find no evidence of intra-industry effects due to MNC presence in the aggregate in the UK,
   but strong effects in high skill industries.
7. Borensztein, De Gregorio, and Lee (1998) and Xu (2000), for example, report a positive relationship only when a country has a minimum threshold of human capital.
   Alfaro, Chanda, Kalemli-Ozcan, and Sayek (2004) and Durham (2004) find that only
   countries with well developed financial markets benefit significantly from FDI.
8. In related work, Prasad, Rajan, and Subramanian (2007) find that in countries
   with weaker financial systems, foreign capital does not contribute to the growth
   of financially dependent industries.
9. Javorcik, Saggi and Spatareanu (2004), for example, find significant differences
   between effects associated with foreign investors of different origin in Romania.
   Our data, however, do not allow controlling for these differences.
10. According to UNCTAD (2001), targets are investors which: (a) Already have a
    presence in the host economy; (b) Are part of the supply chain; (c) Are users of
    countries' own resources, including raw materials and human skills; (d) Are active
    in strong production sectors with growth opportunities; (e) Help to establish new
    core competencies.

11. See Charlton et al. (2004) and www.czechinvest.org.
12. Using survey data verified by the annual reports of investment promotion agencies, we are able to identify which industries were targeted over which periods.
13. Our main specification includes fixed effects which control for time invariant effects; we also control for different industry-time varying effects in the robustness section.
14. Further evidence that IPAs consciously target "quality" FDI is provided by the FDI consultancy OIR, which sells to national investment promotion agencies data about firms intending to respond with overseas investments. OIR clients can purchase data in several categories. By mode of entry, 100 percent of clients choose data on greenfield projects; 30 percent data on M&A projects; by functional category, 100 percent choose data on production facilities and R&D centers, fewer than 70 percent data on back office functions, and fewer than 50 percent data on marketing/sales facilities.
15. Where total manufacturing value added data was unavailable, we derive a deflator from constant and current GDP data, also from the World Bank.
16. See www.investindk.com.
17. See Invest in Sweden Agency, Annual Report, 2006/07.
18. Invest in Spain, for example, lists four target sectors which qualify for incentives "(1) extractive and processing industries; (2) specific food processing and fish-farming industries; (3) industrial support services which markedly improve commercial structures; and (4) specific tourist facilities" See http://www.investinspain.org/incentives.htm.
19. More recently, Harding and Javorcik (2007) have implemented a similar methodology.
20. Prior to the 1990s, the practice of targeting FDI was not widespread (and few countries had IPAs). To test the robustness of our results, we nevertheless restrict the FDI data to 1990s in the robustness section.
21. We exclude these countries in order to be able to directly compare OLS and IV estimates.
22. For further information on targeting practices within investment promotion, see Charlton et al. (2004).
23. See Carlin and Mayer (2003) for an analysis of the extent to which relative growth rates are attributable to initial industry allocations. They find a small share of industry growth performance to be attributable to mean reversion.
24. One concern with our specification is that, to the extent that the size of the industry is related to its future growth, our value added variables are effectively lagged endogenous variables. Given that size of the sample is small, estimation by fixed effects may not be consistent. However, simulations have shown that while this may bias the lagged variables, the bias on the other variables is likely to be small. Judson and Owen (1999) estimate that under fixed effects when $t = 5$, the bias in the lagged dependent variable is over 50 percent, whereas the bias in the other coefficient is only about 3 percent. Our results remained robust to running regression (1) on the log of FDI_{ict} variable only and a full set of dummies. The estimated coefficient of the log of FDI_{ict} variable of such regression was 0.357 (s.e. 0.147).
25. The correlation matrix in Table 2 shows a negative relation between growth of value added and the log of FDI.
26. A new group of papers has explored the existence of positive externalities from FDI towards local firms in upstream industries (suppliers) with more encouraging results, see Javorcik (2004) and Alfaro and Rodríguez-Clare (2004).

27. We find manufacturing and services sector dummies to be positive and significant, suggesting that manufacturing and services have grown faster than agriculture.
28. There is considerable evidence that well-developed financial systems directly enhance growth by reducing transaction costs and improving the allocation of capital; see King and Levine (1993a, b). In addition, there are several plausible reasons to expect that financial markets might complement the spillover effects of foreign direct investment. First, the successful acquisition of new technologies introduced by foreign firms will generally involve a process of reorganization and reinvestment by domestic competitors. To the extent that this process is externally financed from domestic sources, efficient financial markets will enhance the domestic industry's competitive response. Well-developed financial markets also enable other domestic firms and entrepreneurs to capitalize on linkages with new multinationals; see Alfaro et al. (2004, 2006).
29. These papers demonstrate significant interactions between a range of measures of financial development (for example, size of the banking sectors and stock markets, accounting standards, bank concentration) and a range of industry characteristics (for example, dependence on external finance, dependence on trade credit). Carlin and Mayer (2003) also investigate the effect of these interactions on industry-level measures of fixed investment and research and development.
30. CINDE Annual Report 2006.
31. For a survey on industrial promotion practices see Pack and Saggi (2006).
32. Using data on US FDI abroad from the Bureau of Economic Analysis and IMF FDI data, Harding and Javorcik (2007) find that investment promotion appears to increase FDI inflows to developing countries. See also Morrisset and Andrews-Johnson (2004).
33. That is, there is the possibility that policy makers might have targeted certain sectors in anticipation of favorable economic outcomes. The notion that they anticipated future growth, however, gives considerable credit to policymakers.
34. IDA (2004) "Annual Report."
35. Launching a strategy document for Britain's IPA, UK Trade & Investment (UKTI), Trade and Industry Secretary Alistair Darling described the role of UKTI to "increase further the value added to the UK from inward investment through more intensive relationships with high value overseas owned companies." See Speech by Alistair Darling on July 20, 2006. Similarly, one of the performance metrics of the Irish Industrial Development Agency is the average salary offered in the investment projects they have facilitated as well as the number of "Approved Innovation Projects" by their client foreign investors. See IDA Annual report 2006.
36. The success of FDI targeting lies in devising and implementing a cohesive and coherent strategy based on extensive feedback from potential investors, outside and within the country, on the type of conditions that need to be created, and facilities provided, to ensure that a substantial flow of quality FDI is generated in the targeted sector. See UNCTAD (2003).
37. Our instruments also passed another simple rule of thumb such as the first stage R^2 being greater than 0.3. We also undertook Anderson canonical correlations likelihood ratio tests for the relevance of instruments. A rejection of the null indicates that the model is identified and that the instruments are relevant (Hall, Rudebusch and Wilcox, 1996). We obtained similar results further easing concerns that our instruments are not weak.

38. As noted by Acemoglu, Johnson, and Robinson (2001), "This approach is useful since it is a direct test of our exclusion restriction. However, such tests may not lead to a rejection if both instruments are invalid, but still highly correlated with each other. Therefore, the results have to be interpreted with caution."
39. Among the few consistently significant determinants of FDI are lagged FDI, real exchange and institutional quality. Of these variables, only lagged FDI varies at the sectoral level. Wheeler and Mody (1992) provide evidence that existing stock of foreign investment is a significant determinant of current investment decisions.
40. This approach may be useful since it is a direct test of our exclusion restriction. However, such tests may not lead to a rejection if both instruments are invalid, but still highly correlated with each other. Therefore, the results have to be interpreted with caution.
41. Since unobserved country heterogeneity might be correlated with FDI and growth, cross-sectional studies fail to establish causality and are likely to generate biased coefficients. For example, at the micro level, foreign firms might be located in high productivity industries as opposed to causing productivity externalities. At the macro level, high growth countries might attract more FDI as opposed to FDI causing this high growth.
42. Note that the F statistics for low external finance industries in columns (1) and (2) are below 10. Although this is in part due to the reduced sample size, it can also indicate that for such industries, FDI targeting is not a great predictor, which is consistent with our argument.

References

Acemoglu, D., Johnson, S., and Robinson, S. (2001) "The Colonial Origins of Comparative Development: An Empirical Investigation," *The American Economic Review*, vol. 91, pp. 1369–1401.

Alfaro, L., Chanda, A., Kalemli-Ozcan, S., and Sayek, S. (2004) "FDI and Economic Growth: The Role of Local Financial Markets," *Journal of International Economics*, vol. 64, pp. 113–134.

Alfaro, L., Chanda, A., Kalemli-Ozcan, S., and Sayek, S. "Does Foreign Direct Investment Promote Growth? Exploring the Role of Financial Markets on Linkages." *Journal of Development Economics* 91, no. 2 (March 2010): 242–256.

Alfaro, L. and Chen, M (2012) "Selection, Reallocation, and Spillover: Identifying the Sources of Gains from Multinational Production," NBER Working Papers 18207 (Cambridge, MA: NBER).

Alfaro, L. and Rodriguez-Clare, A. (2004) "Multinationals and Linkages: Evidence from Latin America," *Economia*, vol. 4, pp. 113–170.

Barba-Navaretti, G. and A. Venables (2004) *Multinational Firms in the World Economy* (Princeton, NJ: Princeton University Press).

Blomström, M. and Kokko, A. (2003) "The Economics of Foreign Direct Investment Incentives," NBER Working Paper 9489 (Cambridge, MA: NBER).

Blomström, M. and Kokko, A. (1998) "Multinational Corporations and Spillovers," *Journal of Economic Surveys*, vol. 12, pp. 247–277.

Borensztein, E., De Gregorio, J., and Lee, J.W. (1998) "How Does Foreign Direct Investment Affect Economic Growth?," *Journal of International Economics*, vol. 45, pp. 115–135.

CINDE (2006) *Annual Report* (San Jose: CINDE).

Carkovic, M. and Levine, R. (2005) "Does Foreign Direct Investment Accelerate Economic Growth?," in T. Moran, E. Grahan and M. Blomström, (eds), *Does Foreign Direct Investment Promote Development?* (Washington, DC: Institute for International Economics).

Carlin, W. and Mayer, C. (2003) "Finance, Investment, and Growth," *Journal of Financial Economics*, vol. 69, pp. 191–226.

Cetorelli, N. and Gambera, M. (2001) "Banking Market Structure, Financial Dependence and Growth: International Evidence from Industry," *Journal of Finance*, vol. 56, pp. 617–648.

Charlton, A. and Davis, N. (2006) "Does Investment Promotion Work?," London School of Economics Working Paper.

Charlton, A., Davis, N., Faye, M., Haddock, J., and Lamb, C. (2004) "Industry Targeting for Investment Promotion: A Survey of 126 IPAs," Oxford Investment Research Working Papers.

Durham, K.B. (2004) "Absorptive Capacity and the Effects of Foreign Direct Investment and Equity Foreign Portfolio Investment on Economic Growth," *European Economic Review*, vol. 48, pp. 285–306.

Fisman, R. and Love, I. (2004) "Financial Development and Inter-Sectoral Allocation: A New Approach," *Journal of Finance*, vol. 59, pp. 2785–2808.

Fisman, R. and Love, I. (2003) "Trade Credit, Financial Intermediary Development, and Industry Growth," *Journal of Finance*, vol. 58, pp. 353–374.

Girma, S., Greenaway, D., and Wakelin, K. (2001) "Who Benefits from Foreign Direct Investment in the UK?," *The Scottish Journal of Political Economy*, vol. 49, pp. 119–133.

Gorg, H. and Greenaway, D. (2004) "Much Ado About Nothing? Do Domestic Firms Really Benefit from Foreign Direct Investment?," *World Bank Research Observer*, vol. 19, pp. 171–197.

Hall, A.R., Rudebusch, G.D., and Wilcox, D.W. (1996) "Judging Instrument Relevance in Instrumental Variables Estimation," *International Economic Review*, vol. 37, pp. 283–298.

Hanson, G.H. (2001) "Should Countries Promote Foreign Direct Investment?," G-24 Discussion Paper 9.

Harding, T. and Javorcik, B. (2007) "Developing Economies and International Investors: Do Investment Promotion Agencies Bring Them Together," mimeo.

IDA Ireland (2004) *Annual Report* (Dublin: IDA Ireland).

IDA Ireland (2006) *Annual Report* (Dublin: IDA Ireland).

International Labour Office, *International Standard Classification of Occupations*, ISCO 88.

Invest in Sweden Agency (2006/07) *Annual Report* (Stockholm: Invest in Sweden Agency).

Javorcik, Beata S. (2004) "Does Foreign Direct Investment Increase the Productivity of Domestic Firms? In Search of Spillovers Through Backward Linkages," *American Economic Review*, vol. 94, pp. 605–627.

Javorcik, B.S., Saggi, K., and Spatareanue, M. (2004) "Does It Matter Where You Come From? Vertical Spillovers from Foreign Direct Investment and the Nationality of Investors," World Bank Policy Research Working Paper 3449 (Washington, DC: World Bank).

Judson, R. and Owen, A. (1999) "Estimating Dynamic Panel Data Models: A Guide for Macroeconomists," *Economic Letters*, vol. 65, pp. 9–15.

King, R. and Levine, R. (1993a) "Finance and Growth: Schumpeter Might be Right," *Quarterly Journal of Economics*, vol. 108, pp. 717–738.

King, R. and Levine, R. (1993b) "Finance, Entrepreneurship and Growth: Theory and Evidence," *Journal of Monetary Economics*, vol. 32, pp. 513–542.

Lipsey, R.E. (2002) "Home and Host Country Effects of FDI," NBER Working Paper 9293 (Cambridge, MA: NBER).

Machin, S. and Reenen, J.V. (1998) "Technology and Changes in Skill Structure: Evidence from Seven OECD Countries," *The Quarterly Journal of Economics*, vol. 113, pp. 1215–1244.

Morrisset, J. and Andrews-Johnson, K. (2004) "The Effectiveness of Promotion Agencies at Attracting Foreign Direct Investment," FIAS Occasional Paper No. 16 (Washington, DC: Foreign Investment Advisory Service).

Pack, H., and Saggi, K. (2006) "Is there a Case for Industrial Policy? A Critical Survey," *The World Bank Research Observer*, 1–33.

Prasad, E., R. Rajan, and A. Subramanian (2007) "Foreign Capital and Economic Growth," NBER Working Papers 13619 (Cambridge, MA: NBER).

Rajan, R.J. and Zingales, L. (1998) "Financial Dependence and Growth," *American Economic Review*, vol. 88, pp. 559–586.

Rosenbaum, P. and Rubin, D. (1983) "The Central Role of Propensity Score in Observational Studies for Causal Effects," *Biometrica*, vol. 70, pp. 41–55.

Staiger, D. and Stock, J.H. (1997) "Instrumental Variables Regressions with Weak Instruments," *Econometrica*, vol. 65, pp. 557–586.

United Nations (2010) *Industrial Statistics Yearbook of the United Nations Statistical Division*, 55th edn (New York: United Nations).

UNCTAD (2003) "Effectiveness of Foreign Direct Investment Policy Measures," Note TD/B-COM.2/EM.13/2.

UNCTAD (2001) *World Investment Report: Promoting Linkages* (New York: United Nations).

UNCTAD (2006) *World Investment Report: FDI from Development and Transition Economies: Implications for Development* (New York: United Nations).

Wells, L.T. Jr. and Wint, A.G. (1991) "Marketing a Country: Promotion as a Tool for Attracting Foreign Investment," Foreign Investment Advisory Service Occasional Paper No. 1 (Washington, DC: International Finance Corporation/Multilateral Investment Guarantee Agency).

Wheeler, D. and A. Mody (1992) "International Investment Location Decisions: The Case of US Firms," *Journal of International Economics* 33, 57–76.

Xu, B. (2000) "Multinational Enterprises, Technology Diffusion, and Host Country Productivity Growth," *Journal of Development Economics* 62, 477–493.

3.4
Comments on "Growth and the Quality of Foreign Direct Investment" by Laura Alfaro and Andrew Charlton

Ann Harrison
The Wharton School and NBER

This paper explores the notion that not all types of foreign direct investment are created equal. In particular, the paper makes two important contributions. First, the authors document a persistent use of industrial policy in targeting certain forms of incoming foreign investment. Countries favor some types of foreign investment over others through tax holidays, regulations, investment promotion, and facilitation of entry. Second, the authors then identify whether targeted foreign direct investment (FDI) results in higher growth. They find that it does. They also find that FDI in credit-constrained sectors or sectors with more human capital leads to higher growth. These results are robust to correcting for endogeneity of FDI.

I really like the focus of this paper, which directly addresses the ability of countries to correctly identify attractive industrial policy targets and then tests whether the outcomes are superior when governments intervene. The authors convincingly show that most countries do in fact prefer some forms of FDI over others, and deliberately target them. In particular, their Table 3.4.1 shows that the most popular sectors targeted by countries are machinery, computers, telecommunications, and the transport sector. Documenting the clear non-neutral stance of different countries is excellent support for Dani Rodrik's claim that we are "doomed to choose."

The next question the authors address is whether governments that are choosing some sectors over others make choices which result in higher growth. Alfaro and Charlton first document that more FDI in a sector is associated with higher growth in value added for that sector. They then show that the gains from incoming FDI are higher in sectors which are more financially constrained or where there is a higher share of skilled labor. The idea here is that FDI will lead to higher benefits for the host country either when the right preconditions are in placed (skilled labor) or in sectors which are starved of additional capital.

Finally, Alfaro and Charlton attack the most challenging problem in this literature: how to identify whether FDI promotion has *causally* resulted in higher-quality FDI inflows and led to higher sectoral growth. They use an arsenal of weapons to attack this difficult problem. One approach they adopt is to use propensity score matching, whereby they statistically select a control group which is the best match for their treatment. Another approach is the use of instrumental variables (IV) estimation. They create an instrument for FDI inflows, which is a binary variable indicating likelihood of selection for industrial policy, which is used to predict FDI inflows in the first stage.

I was initially skeptical of the IV approach used by the authors, as it did not seem a priori evident to me that the instrument would pass overidentification tests. However, Alfaro and Charlton proved me wrong. They show that their instrument persuasively predicts FDI inflows. The typical F-test in the first stage is greater than 10 (refuting a weak instrument problem), and their evidence suggests that there is 19 percent more FDI in targeted industries. When they test whether the instrument belongs in the second stage (which it shouldn't in order to pass the overidentification tests) they find that it doesn't. They also try a direct approach – introducing their instrument directly as an independent variable in the second stage – and show that their instrument does not directly affect GDP growth.

This is an excellent paper on an important area of industrial policy. I have one minor suggestion. Alfaro and Charlton show that targeting works by presenting results for the growth of value added for targeted sectors alone (Tables 3.3.6 and 3.3.7). When they do this, they show that the coefficient on FDI is significantly higher than for the sample as a whole. I would have preferred that they do this exercise in a slightly different way. I would have liked to see them report the results for both the targeted and the non-targeted sample, so that readers could compare the coefficients on both samples. They could have done a formal t-test of whether the coefficients on the log FDI variable are significantly different across the two samples. But, as stated above, this is a minor suggestion.

This paper adds to the growing literature documenting the extensive use of industrial policies to foster developed and developing country growth. Andres Rodriguez and I review this extensive literature elsewhere (Harrison and Rodríguez-Clare, 2010). In our review, we cite this paper and others showing the widespread use of FDI policies to achieve growth objectives. Any policy which tilts incentives to invest in some sectors over others is a non-neutral, industrial policy. Country efforts to succeed at these policies have resulted in a range of outcomes. India, for example, attempted to negotiate with multinational companies during the period of the "license raj" and drove away many firms. China, on the other hand, in part due to the attraction of its enormous domestic market, has negotiated more successfully with multinationals to ensure maximum technology transfer.

One of the most interesting aspects of the Alfaro and Charlton paper is their ability to "test whether the benefits of FDI are stronger in the industries to which governments accord special priority." With my co-authors Luosha Du and Gary Jefferson (2011), we also test for the effectiveness of industrial policy using a panel of firms in China. We investigate how tariff reforms, FDI promotion, income tax holidays, and China's entry into the WTO in 2002 affected the performance of manufacturing enterprises in China. The advantage of examining a range of industrial policies simultaneously is that we are able to compare the effects of different instruments of industrial policy on firm performance. This more comprehensive approach also allows us to address any possible omitted variable bias.

Du, Harrison and Jefferson (2011) suggest varied success with industrial promotion policies. We are able to "rank" the effectiveness of different kinds of industrial policies, and show that the use of tax holidays and FDI promotion led to significantly better outcomes than higher tariffs. In particular, using tax holidays as our firm-specific measure of industry promotion, we find that productivity spillovers were higher from foreign firms that paid less than the statutory corporate tax rate. Our results are consistent with Alfaro and Charlton, but also indicate that the type of *policy instrument* used to target foreign investment varies in its effectiveness.

One important conclusion from the Alfaro and Charlton paper is that there is enormous heterogeneity in effects of FDI. They focus on differences in human capital, access to credit, and targeting by governments. Other sources of heterogeneity include the degree of competition and the citizenship of the foreign investors. Aghion, Dewatripont, Du, Harrison, and Legros (2011) show that industrial policy is most effective when implemented in conjunction with greater competition. Du, Harrison and Jefferson (2012) show that in China, the source of FDI makes considerable difference in estimating vertical and horizontal spillovers. In particular, they show that FDI inflows into China from Hong Kong, Taiwan, and Macao fail to generate positive spillovers, while FDI from other locations generates significant vertical linkages.

To conclude, this is an excellent contribution documenting the effectiveness of industrial policy in the area of foreign investment. Alfaro and Charlton decompose FDI into industry-specific inflows across 29 countries and for the period 1985 through 2000 to pinpoint the differential effect of different kinds of FDI on growth. They show that incoming FDI has heterogeneous effects on growth – their measure of "quality" – depending on characteristics such as skill intensity and capital constraints in the sector. They also address the potential endogeneity of FDI using a two-stage approach that models FDI as a function of industry-specific targeting.

References

Aghion, Philippe, Dewatripont, Mathias, Du, Luosha, Harrison, Ann, and Legros, Patrick (2011) "Industrial Policy and Competition," *NBER Working Paper* (Cambridge, MA: NBER).

Du, Luosha, Harrison, Ann, and Jefferson, Gary (2012) "Testing for Horizontal and Vertical Foreign Investment Spillovers in China, 1998–2007," *Journal of Asian Economics*, vol. 23, no. 3, pp. 234–243.

Du, Luosha, Harrison, Ann, and Jefferson, Gary (2011) "Do Institutions Matter for FDI Spillovers? The Implications of China's 'Special Characteristics,'" *NBER Working Paper 16767* (Cambridge, MA: NBER).

Harrison, Ann and Rodríguez-Clare, Andres (2010) "Trade, Foreign Investment, and Industrial Policy for Developing Countries," in *Handbook of Development Economics*, vol. 5, edited by Dani Rodrik and Mark Rosenzweig (Amsterdam: North-Holland), pp. 4039–4214.

3.5
Theories of Agglomeration: Critical Analysis from a Policy Perspective

Célestin Monga
World Bank

3.5.1 Introduction

Science fiction and fantasy writer Vera Nazarian famously observed that "luck is not as random as you think. Before that lottery ticket won the jackpot someone had to buy it." Many economic theorists have neglected that wisdom and mistakenly reduced the existence of clusters (defined as geographical concentrations of interconnected companies with close supply links, specialist suppliers, service providers, and related industries and institutions) to an almost banal phenomenon that randomly occurs whenever private firms gather by accident in someplace, start trading together, and eventually realize that it is more profitable even for competitors to stick together in a specific location. Clusters have thus been viewed merely as byproducts of economic development.

The theory underlying the benefits of clusters dates back to Alfred Marshall, whose *Principles of Economics* (1890) helped think systematically about agglomeration externalities (the notion that the concentration of production in a particular geographic area brings major external benefits for firms in that location through knowledge spillovers, labor pooling, and close proximity of specialized suppliers). Just like Adam Smith before him, Marshall offered several historical examples of clusters, which all appear to emerge accidentally in various places in Britain in the 18th and 19th centuries. The story of modern examples of agglomeration, which include Silicon Valley software industry, Detroit car manufacturing, Dalton (Georgia, United States) carpets, or Massachusetts Route 128 high-tech corridor, has generally been told as evidence of randomness in the emergence of clusters – the so-called "economics of QWERTY,"[1] most notably by Krugman (1994).

It is therefore not surprising that most countries that have attempted to proactively build clusters to reap the economic benefits of agglomeration have relied on chance. Even those that have chosen to achieve that goal through the creation of free zones and other special economic zones (SEZs)[2] have largely elected to let the "invisible hand" of the market make things happen. But success has been scarce: there have been too few high-performing clusters – which generate economic growth and good employment opportunities – especially in the developing world. Luck has either been too random, or the "economics of QWERTY" has not yielded its magic.

Fortunately, the eruption of new clusters in countries like China, often in the most unlikely places, and as the result of strong and deliberate government action is challenging conventional knowledge. For instance, Qiaotou, Wenzhou and Yanbu are all relatively small regions in China that account for 60 percent of world button production, 95 percent of world cigarette lighter production, and dominate global underwear production, respectively (Lyn and Rodríguez-Clare 2011). Industrial clusters have also emerged in places such as Dongguan, Guangdong (electronic products), or Shandong (transport equipment). Thanks to these startling developments, economists and policymakers around the world are being forced to reassess the validity of theories of agglomeration. They also raise new interesting questions about clusters are why they emerge and why they matter – especially in the context of developing countries.

The remainder of this paper, which draws on Monga (2011), is organized as follows: Section 3.5.2 explains why many attempts at building industrial clusters have not delivered the expected outcomes and why theories of agglomeration can be misleading. Section 3.5.3 highlights the key issues to be addressed by developing countries and provides a policy framework for building competitive clusters. Section 3.5.4 summarizes the argument.

3.5.2   Beyond economic randomness and chaos

There is broad consensus among economists on the central role of private sector development in generating and sustaining inclusive growth. The still unanswered question is how to foster the type of dynamics that results in the creation of viable, competitive firms, in which workers (unskilled or educated) also get the right incentives and opportunities to acquire the skills that help them prepare for the constantly changing demands of the global economy. Theories of agglomeration and clusters outlined since Adam Smith and Marshall have been interpreted and developed to imply limited role for government policies. A closer look at the reasons for the problems of special economic zones (often designed to foster clustering) in the developing world suggests that reliance on randomness tends to increase the risks of failure.

3.5.2.1   Why some clusters fail: the misleading similarity with QWERTY

The story of clusters emerging entirely randomly has been analyzed in the economic literature mainly through the prism of increasing returns to scale, or economies of scale, which convert increased levels of output into downward sloping average costs curves. That insight dates back to Marshall's industrial district analysis, which showed that economies of scale may even be "external," emerging from outside the firm because of asset-sharing, such as the provision of specific goods and services by specialized suppliers or the emergence of a localized labor pool due to the concentration of production. In addition, the very proximity of firms working on similar products or competing closely against each other eventually yields collective benefits in new research, new managerial and organizational practices (Griliches 1979). Such learning dynamics and spillovers increase the stock of knowledge available for each individual firm.

The implications of all these Marshallian externalities for the patterns of international trade, the welfare gains from trade, and industrial policy, have been studied extensively, most notably by Krugman (1995, 2008), Paul and Siegel (1999), Rodríguez-Clare (2005), Aghion (2009), and Harrison and Rodriguez-Clare (2010). The topic is particularly important in an increasingly globalized world economy: recent work based on quantitative analysis and looking at the question of whether Marshallian externalities lead to additional gains from trade indicates that this is indeed the case, and that they increase overall gains from trade by around 50 percent (Lyn and Rodriguez-Clare 2011). Yet the basic question of the causes and optimal conditions for their emergence has remained a mystery, even for economic theorists who have focused their efforts on the topic.

In the 1980s and 1990s, an interesting story was told quite convincingly to explain the emergence of clusters simply as an illustration of "the economics of QWERTY." It was based primarily on the work of David (1985), who chronicled the rise to dominance of the QWERTY keyboard. While it was not the most efficient layout in terms of finger movement, it forced typists to work slowly and mitigated the risks of mistakes due to the tendency of the keys to jam on the early machines. With innovation and technical progress, the jamming problem was subsequently corrected but a path had already been set and manufacturers and typists had had been hooked to the bizarre keyboard layout. In sum, a historical accident had set the stage for a long-lasting technical standard and the development of typing keyboards. The theoretical lesson derived from that story was straightforward:

> A *path-dependent* sequence of economic changes is one of which important influences upon the eventual outcome can be exerted by temporally remote events, including happenings dominated by chance elements rather than systematic forces. Stochastic processes like that do not converge automatically to a fixed-point distribution of outcomes, and are called *non-ergodic*. In such circumstances "historical accidents" can neither be ignored, nor neatly quarantined for the purpose of economic analysis; the dynamic process itself takes on an *essentially historical* character. (David, 1985: 332)

Despite that grandiose pronouncement David was quite prudent not to draw definitive conclusions about economic phenomena from his investigation of the origins of the QWERTY keyboard rule. He wrote: "Standing alone, my story will be simply illustrative and does not establish how much of the world works this way. That is an open empirical issue and I would be presumptuous to claim to have settled it, or to instruct you in what to do about it" (1985, p. 332). In fact, the main point he drew himself from the story was that "it is sometimes not possible to uncover the logic (or illogic) of the world around us except by understanding how it got that way." Yet, some theorists were quick to infer much broader implications not only for the setting of technical standards within an industry but also for the reason why firms are sometimes forced to mimic each other and even why certain industries find themselves better off locating in clusters. That was quite a jump!

Arguing that the QWERTY keyboard was "not just a cute piece of trivia" but "a symbol for a new view about how the economy works" and "a parable that opens our eyes to a whole different way of thinking about economics," Krugman hailed it as evidence that neither the market nor the government can manufacture good economic outcomes. He wrote: "That different way of thinking rejects the idea that markets invariably lead the economy to a unique best solution; instead, it asserts that the outcome of market competition often depends crucially on historical accident... And this conclusion is fraught with political implications, because a sophisticated government may try to make sure that the accidents of history run the way it wants" (1994, p. 223). He then went on to compare the randomness of QWERTY emergence and dominance to that of the film industry in Hollywood or the concentration of banking and financial institutions in New York.

Perhaps the extensive reliance on that story was merely a stylistic device by Krugman to make the broader and theoretically valid point about the importance of clusters (increasing returns to scale and external economies of scale). However, his insistence in doubting government policy agendas that may be designed to facilitate the emergence of clusters has been unfortunate, as it endorsed the misleading notion that governments should refrain from getting involved in the emergence of clusters.

The traditional policy advice given to developing countries by most mainstream economists and development institutions is indeed to stick to minimalist government intervention, and adopt "neutral", "horizontal" economic strategies (that is, implementing prudent macroeconomic policies and improving the business environment through broad microeconomic and institutional reforms without special consideration being given to particular industries). The pertinence of such advice is questionable. In fact, evaluation studies often show that such generic prescriptions have rarely yielded sustained and inclusive growth. Not surprisingly, many successful countries (most notably China, Brazil or Vietnam in recent years) have not followed that advice, often because it typically requires trying to remove at once all the distortions that stifled the economy in the first place, and engaging at the national level some politically difficult reforms.

Economic development is a continuous process of structural transformation involving industrial and technological upgrading and diversification. It requires continuous and coordinated upgrading of physical and human capital, and institutions. For poor economies with limited financial resources and administrative capacity, it is essential that economic policies be geared toward the changing patterns of industrial structure and technology diffusion, and the choice of production bundles and modernization and innovation strategies that are consistent with their comparative advantage and level of development (Lin, 2012a, 2012b). The challenge of sustained economic growth is basically to break into global industrial markets and find their own niches, or organize their economies to take advantage of the opportunities being vacated by middle-income countries that are forced out of these niches because of rising wages, rising productivity levels, and the need for industrial upgrading.

While that general recipe has long been understood by economists and policymakers, few countries have actually managed to design and make good use of policy frameworks and instruments to achieve the goals. The recourse to special economic zones (SEZs) has long been seen as a way of circumventing the difficult challenge of reforming entire struggling economies at once, and to foster the development of clusters. The well-known rationale for SEZs in developing countries is to provide special policy incentives and infrastructure in a circumscribed geographic location to firms that can attract foreign direct investment, create jobs, develop and diversify exports (even when economy-wide business environment problems and protective barriers are not yet resolved) and foreign exchange earnings, and serve as "experimental laboratories" for new pricing, labor, financial or labor policies. The ultimate expectation is that the knowledge spillovers of these experiments eventually translate into private sector development, sustained growth, productivity increases, and other financial and economic benefits for the entire economy. Policy incentives in SEZs typically include import and export duty exemptions, streamlined customs and administrative controls and procedures, facilitated access to foreign exchange and relatively low income tax rates. Export-oriented SEZs are generally intended to "convey 'free trade status' to export manufacturers, enabling them to compete in global markets and counterbalance the anti-export bias of trade policies" (FIAS, 2008: 12).

It is clear that SEZs have often been used effectively by some latecomers such as Ireland, Korea, Mauritius, Taiwan-China, or China, to build clusters, emulate the economic development strategies of leader countries and even catch up with them in the race to economic prosperity. Unfortunately, most countries that have tried to replicate that strategy have not gained the expected benefits. Historically, poor countries typically faced two main constraints that impeded private sector development: high factor costs (skilled labor and capital) and high transaction costs often compounded by political capture and rent seeking. Thanks to globalization and free movement of labor and capital, high factor costs have generally come down even in remote places.

Moreover, factor costs can be lowered if economic development strategies are fully consistent with a country's comparative advantage so that the factor which is in relative abundance (whether it is unskilled labor, land, or natural resources) is used extensively. That constraint is therefore removed when the industries selected and attracted into SEZs are primarily those that make good use of low-skill labor, are competitive, and quickly establish effective backwards linkages with the rest of the domestic economy.

The removal of the second constraint – high transaction costs – necessitates the development of clusters with large numbers of firms in industries where economies of scale, intra-industry knowledge spillovers, "forward and backward" linkages,[3] good supply chain/logistics, and other agglomeration effects can be achieved. The reasons for that can be found in economic theory, empirical analyses and country case studies. Clusters or industrial agglomeration arise in situations where there is clear potential for industry-specific externalities and where government interventions take place facilitate the process.

Empirical studies of economic diversification also provide important insights for the development of clusters. Recent research has shown that poor economies with more diversified economies tend to have higher levels of income per capita. Sectoral *diversification* in early stages of development is generally accompanied by geographic *agglomeration*. In the words of Imbs and Wacziarg (2003), the range of industries expands and factors are allocated increasingly equally across sectors. At the same time, new sectors tend to localize in specific regions. Regions become increasingly different. Such trends typically hold until countries reach an income level of approximately US$9,000 per capita, after which higher levels of income per capita are then associated with increased specialization. In fact, sectoral concentration in later stages of development is accompanied by geographic de-agglomeration. The range of activities produced across all regions is reduced and the location of economic activities seems to matter much less. The location of production is of particular importance as it allows for (or impedes) agglomeration externalities, a key element for improving productivity and exploiting economies of scale (World Bank 2009).

3.5.2.2   Looking beyond failure and chance

The renewed enthusiasm about clusters and the use of SEZs to foster their emergence justify the need to understand why most attempts in the developing world have failed to deliver their promises.[4] In most countries, the benefit–cost ratio for setting up and running SEZs has been disappointing: personal income tax on employment, permit fees and services charges, sale and rental fees on public land to developers, import duties and taxes on products from the zones sold to the domestic customs territories, concession fees for facilities such as ports or power plants, and corporate income tax (when assessed) usually totaled only negligible amounts. In the meantime, import duties and charges lost from the smuggling opportunities created by SEZs, tax revenue forgone from firms relocating from the domestic customs territory into the zones, public investment for (often untargeted) infrastructure and recurrent expenditures (mainly the wage bill of public sector workers needed to run and regulate the zones) often represented substantial costs to governments. Even in China, some of these initiatives failed to attract competitive industries and generate employment and the authorities had to re-engineer them (Chenggang, 2011; Zhang, 2012).

Looking in retrospect at the reasons for their generally weak performance, it is clear that the general belief that they should emerge randomly (just like QWERTY keyboards) played an important role. While one can point to a variety of factors ranging from poor institutional design and management of the initial concept to ineffective macro- and microeconomic policies, which often created major distortions and led to failure, the bottom line is that government policies to support them were either insufficient or inappropriate. The objectives of these clusters were often not clearly articulated or unrealistic, and the policy instruments for achieving them inconsistent (Farole, 2011).

Too often, the industries that emerged in these clusters sometimes defied the country's comparative advantage and were therefore not viable without a strong set of protection policies. In most instances, policymakers either identified those industries that they wanted to favor for personal and political reasons, or they did not actively attempt to identify which particular industries may be most suited to their country's endowment structure (that is, labor-intensive industries). They assumed that any foreign firm that would be willing to join an SEZ or EPZ would create some employment, which would be better than nothing... One consequence of the absence of identification strategies was the random emergence of small single firms from very different types of industries. But given the limitations of state budgets and weaknesses of public investment programs, few governments could provide them with the industry-specific infrastructure support they needed.

Many SEZs were exclusively developed, regulated, and operated by governments or public entities. Beyond the obvious issues of expertise and capacity, their institutional arrangements often led to conflict of interest situations, with regulatory agencies also engaged in zone development activity, especially when public zones competed with private firms outside the zone. Privileges in the zones were generally restricted, at least in theory. Access to a generous set of benefits was often controlled by a small group of civil servants. The criteria for selecting qualifying firms were not always transparent. And when there was transparency, the criteria it seemed too restrictive, as firms typically had to export at least 80 percent of their production. Merchandises that could be introduced duty- and tax-free by registered enterprises or individuals were restricted to direct inputs for manufacturing. Such regulations were often the source of rents.

The choice of the location was not always optimal. While some zones were built in port cities that were already growth poles or near transport hubs, others were created as isolated geographic enclaves or in remote areas, not on the basis of an economic rationale but as a way of appeasing political constituencies. This resulted in increased production and transaction costs for the few firms willing to build factories there. Reducing transaction costs was not part of the strategic focus. Because of the randomness in industry selection and the limited government financial resources, even basic utilities and services were sometimes not made available in many of these zones. Governments did not proactively play their indispensable facilitating role: they did not provide some basic industry-specific infrastructure and often waited (in vain) for qualifying firms to finance investment in electricity, water, or telecommunication within the zone. They did not coordinate the design and implementation of the investment needed and used collectively by firms in their industries (storage facilities, for example).

Investment climate surveys also indicate that SEZs managers in many countries did not realize that successful integration into the world economy increasingly requires behind-border measures that fall under the heading of trade facilitation: they did not alleviate the burden of red tape, nor did they provide the type of efficient services such as customs and port efficiency. In some countries, it often took more than a year for a foreign firm to obtain necessary permits to operate. They also had to deal with heavy and complex bureaucratic rules and procedures, a very high cost of infrastructure (communications, energy, water), and constraining labor regulations. In addition, they had to commit their companies to unrealistic employment creation goals and high requirements for initial investment. In other places, qualifying firms that managed to join SEZs still had serious difficulties accessing foreign exchange and to other financial services.

In sum, the belief in the randomness of clusters emergence generally led to disappointing results. Because of their poor design, ineffective management and misguided policies, most SEZs did not attract enough firms in competitive industries. Moreover, their firms did not generate enough backward linkages and subcontracting business relationships with local enterprises. Local firms either had no interest in supplying cluster-based firms in the zones or they failed to meet world market standards for quality, price, and delivery times. SEZs-based firms themselves tended to use domestic factors and inputs only in limited extent and condemned themselves to remain small enclaves in poor economies. Given the often inappropriate strategic focus of these zones (where a few firms benefited from lucrative special deals with influential politicians and could afford to produce the wrong goods in otherwise uncompetitive factories), the fact that they remained enclaves limited exacerbation of the economy-wide distortions. However, disconnect with the domestic private sector worsened their perception by local business people. In some cases, the poor logistics and weak supply chain (both a reflection of limited clustering) led these firms to rely heavily on imports (with industries such as electronics or even apparel often showing imports ratios well over 60 percent); in such situations, currency devaluations compounded the distortion of net exports. Eventually, they faced high transaction costs. Despite the benefits of distortive protection by governments, they failed to yield enough business volume to be credible entities.

Clusters can only be successful if the issues discussed above, which led to the failure of most SEZs, are addressed effectively.

3.5.3 A policy framework to foster agglomeration

Alfred Marshall observed that many of Britain's successful industries in the late 19th century were concentrated in specific industrial districts: cotton around Manchester, ironworking in Birmingham, cutlery in Sheffield, etc. Subsequent theories of agglomeration and clustering have explained well the underlying reasons for success – and highlighted their perceived unpredictability. But the more recent success of some developing countries in defying geographic randomness and engineering clusters in specific locations provide useful lessons for policymaking.

To embark successfully on the path to the industrial and technological upgrading that leads to sustainable growth and create employment, developing countries should expand and rationalize the scope of privileges of their cluster zones, and remove the distortions and inefficiencies that have characterized them. Instead of creating generic, broad-purpose SEZs, they should consider building entities with specialized facilities that are configured to the needs of specific industries and sectors. Such cluster-based industrial parks (CBIP) could be of various sorts depending on the particular industries to be promoted, which should be consistent with the country's revealed or latent comparative advantage (Lin and Monga 2011).[5] With their specialized facilities customized to the unique needs of target industries, they may be airport-based zones to support air-based activities (fruits and vegetables or cut-flower exports, for instance), agro-processing, or even simply financial services zones aiming at promoting off-shore activities.

3.5.3.1 Good general principles

The industries undertaken in CBIPs should be carefully selected and consistent with each country's revealed or latent comparative advantage to ensure that they make the best possible use of the abundant factor (typically low-skilled labor) and can become competitive in international markets without excessive forms of government protection. At least in their initial phase, they should host in labor-intensive, assembly-oriented activities such as textiles, apparel, footwear, electrical and electronic goods. Within such industries, the scope of activities should be expanded to include not only manufacturing and processing but also commercial and professional services such as warehousing or transshipment.

All investors (foreign and local) should be treated equally. Appropriate legislation, rules, and regulation should therefore be in force to reduce the probability of distortions in incentives. Moreover, there should be a unique set of fiscal incentives for all promoted industries, regardless of their location (within the zone or outside).

Never before have political leaders around the world been confronted with the difficult sociopolitical challenges posed by increasingly large, demanding, and (often) educated crowds. In fact, it has become very costly to remain in power without delivering tangible results, especially on the employment front. With the emergence of a new, more pragmatic leadership in developing countries, policymakers are much more likely to respond to electoral politics and be more accountable for their economic policy choices.

Deliberate efforts should be made to integrate CBIPs into national economies. In order to preempt the inevitable domestic criticism, social fears and political economy issues, the strategic focus of CBIPs should be on generating manufacturing jobs and absorbing large segments of the low-skill labor force; promoting skill, industrial, and technological upgrading;[6] improving the economy's endowment structure and moving toward higher-value activities but at a realistic pace; encouraging linkages between CBIPs firms and local firms so that the zones provide demonstration effects for success and serve as catalysts to broader reforms; and compliance with ILO labor standards. It is indeed important to communicate the message that for most people in the labor force in poor countries, the alternative to employment in such CBIPs would be low-productivity, low-income informal activities, underemployment in urban areas, unprofitable and highly risky agricultural work in rural areas, unemployment, and the perpetual trap of poverty. Even with low levels of formal education, many unskilled workers could still be employed in CBIPs that specialize in basic assembly operations.

3.5.3.2   Effective institutional arrangements

Many of the basic insights from the early theoretical literature on economic agglomeration remain valid – especially the central role that the private sector should play in designing and managing clustering sites (Krugman 1994). CBIPs that are privately-owned, managed, and operated should be encouraged. But they could start as public–private partnerships, with public provision of off-site infrastructure such as roads and public–private funding of on-site facilities. Governments can provide direct financial support or guarantees to build infrastructure and facilities in the zone. Private sector participation can take many different forms: basic partnership with shared risks and rewards with governments; concession agreements; "build-own-operate," "build-operate-transfer," or "build-own-operate-transfer" arrangements (see FIAS, 2008). Successful models of CBIPs include a variety of contract types, often with public–private partnerships that evolve over time. A model that has been popular recently involves "equity-shifting" arrangements, with a private contract manager of a government zone being allows to exercise a purchase option once pre-defined levels of performance have been reached.

Even well-designed CBIPs can only succeed if they are backed by strong political commitment from the highest levels of governments to improve the business environment and quickly remove all the obstacles that may stand in the way of implementation. A good institutional framework for preparation could be an interministerial committee headed by a political "champion" who has the credibility and power to make things happen. That "champion" should also be the main interface between CBIPs developers and firms and all government entities. He/she should be able to respond quickly and effectively to the requests from the business community. But he/she should be insulated from political pressures to please any domestic political constituency.

3.5.3.3 Facilities and services

The provision of industry-specific on-site infrastructure is an important determinant of transaction costs and competitiveness. It helps attract firms and facilitate the clustering and the development of subcontracting relationships among them. Policymakers should work closely with private sector operators to fully equip and service CBIPs with purpose-built facilities, which can then be put up for sale or lease. Private zone developers should be allowed to supply utilities services (water, power, sewerage, and telecommunications) to cluster-based firms. As developing countries continue to need substantial private sector financing for infrastructure projects, attention should turn to still underdeveloped capital markets as a potential channel for fund-raising. The creation of an effective municipal bond market and other innovative public–private solutions to fund and implement key infrastructure projects should be the focus of discussion. International development institutions should also be involved, especially to provide various types of guarantees.

Building clusters will be made easier if governments are willing to find land parcels and secure titles for lease to private zone developers. In many poor countries, the legal framework allows for an enduring influence of the state bureaucracy on land distribution and land rights. Governments are reluctant to hand over the power of land distribution and state control is legitimized as historically and socially fair. Such control offers potential spaces for rents and bureaucratic arbitrariness. State ownership, and especially the power to redistribute land plots, makes citizens and business people vulnerable to arbitrary actions of local bureaucrats who decide about which individual is granted access to land. CBIPs represent a good opportunity for implementing land reforms gradually, in a way that can generate quick wins to all stakeholders and improve collective welfare. The fact that some countries such as Ethiopia or Tanzania, with a long history of strong resistance to the privatization of land property rights to individual plot holders, are willing to consider changes in their land tenure policy, may be the sign of progress – and the recognition that it may be the most viable alternative.

In expanding the range of facilities and amenities available within CBIPs, public and private partners should consider not only industry-specific factories and infrastructure but also a wide array of services such as high-speed telecommunications and Internet services, common bonded warehouse facilities, training facilities, maintenance and repair centers, product exhibition areas, on-site customs clearance and trade logistics facilities, on-site housing, on-site banking, medical clinics, shopping centers, childcare facilities, and so on. Developing a cluster zone not as on stand-alone but rather as an integrated industrial, commercial, residential, and recreational entity allows developers to diversify their potential sources of revenue and offset the potential low profitability of certain activities with higher margins in others. In many well managed private zones in East Asia, as much as half of total annual revenue is derived from business support services and other sources of income.

3.5.3.4 Political economy issues

Political economy concerns identified in the theoretical literature of agglomeration are legitimate but only for the traditional type of SEZs and EPZs which host firms in industries that defy comparative advantage. Firms in these industries are not viable in an open, competitive market. Their existence and continuous operation often depend on large subsidies and protection, which create opportunities for rent-seeking and corruption, and make it difficult for the government to abandon interventions and exit from distortions. CBIPs would promote a completely different development model: the industries that are consistent with the economy's latent comparative advantage. Firms are viable once the constraints to their entry and operation are removed. The incentives provided by the government to the first movers must be transparent, targeted, temporary and small, solely for the purpose of compensating for their information externality. In that context, the issues of pervasive rent-seeking and the persistence of government intervention beyond its initial timetable can be mitigated. Selecting labor-intensive industries with economies of scale (so that there are incentives for foreign investors to localize in lower-wage countries) and potential for upgrading (to open up future possibilities for domestic value-added creation) would generate the kind of quick wins that policymakers need to build their own domestic political capital and pursue reforms.

Not all developing countries are confronted with extreme internal political economy. In some of them, minimum wage and other labor laws rigidities are actually much less binding than they appear in the books. In such countries, especially those where basic transportation, energy, and telecommunication infrastructure could be improved quickly, CBIPs could be much bolder in their design and implementation to become "freeports." Instead of being mainly export drivers, they could be large platforms for private investment and catalysts for knowledge spillovers throughout the entire national economy and beyond, and even serve as a basis for regional hubs in specific industries. In such places, CBIPs – selected on the basis of their economic rationale and not for political considerations – could:

- Cover much larger areas, therefore allowing greater flexibility to firms in their choice of plant location and opportunities for inter-firm linkages;
- Allow full access to the domestic markets on a duty-paid basis – that is, lift the traditional requirement of exporting 80 percent or more of the production, and allow instead unrestricted sale to domestic consumers as long as all applicable import taxes and other duties are fully paid; and
- Allow firms to engage into any legal economic activity they deem profitable, including manufacturing, warehousing, transshipment, etc. Registered firms or individuals could also be offered duty-free privileges to permit the introduction of all types of merchandise, which can then be sold at the retail or wholesale level, or even consumed within the zone area.

Developing country policymakers may consider best practices from Ireland, Taiwan (China), and Korea, and allow duty-free access to inputs for local firms just as it is the case for CBIPs-based firms. Domestic producers, especially small and medium-sized enterprises, could then benefit from tax credit and rebates on duties paid on imported goods and services used in products sold to CBIPs-based firms. Local suppliers could import intermediary products and components on the basis of letters of credit initiated by CBIPs-based firms. The latter could also provide domestic firms with technical assistance or financing arrangements as part of subcontracting arrangements. Such policy measures aiming at fostering backward linkages would eventually help diffuse initial political opposition to CBIPs.

Governments could also work closely with firms in competitive industries to support training and apprenticeship for workers, promote study tours and personnel exchanges, and implement programs tailored for purchasing and technical managers of export-oriented firms based in CBIPs to help their local suppliers achieve high-quality standards and meet the required delivery times. By bringing local business leaders into the picture and creating the conditions for them to fully share the success of CBIPs, governments would foster job generation and weaken domestic sociopolitical resistance to the new policy (including from trade unions).

Finally, political commitment should be clearly signaled to potential foreign investors to convince them that all constraints on businesses in CBIPs will be removed quickly. Personal engagement by presidents, prime ministers, and other high-level government officials will be needed to convey the message that once the policy is adopted, there will be no reversal. Well-organized and well-targeted (to specific industries) visits to countries where potential investors are located (China, Thailand, India, Brazil, Qatar, etc.) would help overcome skepticism, and give credibility to the new policy.

3.5.4   Conclusion

Traditional theories of agglomeration rightly highlight the importance of clusters, where increasing returns to scale and external economies of scale. But they also suggest that policymakers refrain from interfering with the emergence of clusters, which are supposed to be efficiently generated by market forces. Yet, in an increasingly globalized world economy where sustained growth depends primarily on the diffusion of knowledge, proactive government intervention is unavoidable. Economic development and sustained growth are the result of continual industrial and technological upgrading, a process that requires strong, dynamic, and carefully orchestrated public–private collaboration. Various forms of industrial policies (decisions, regulations or laws) that encourage ongoing activity or investment in a particular industry is an integral feature of any successful strategy. By facilitating coordination and addressing externality issues, industrial policy can help build effective clusters. It can entice domestic and foreign firms to enter sectors that are consistent with the country's latent comparative advantage and turn them into overt comparative advantages, and thereby improve productivity within the industries and enhance the economy's competitiveness internationally.

The proposition that governments play a proactive role in the creation of clusters certainly entails many risks of failure. But carefully-designed cluster-based industrial parks that are privately administered provide a good framework for mitigating such risks. This paper draws lessons from experiences of cluster building around the world and provides a policy framework for success. It challenges the blind reliance on the market dynamics. It stresses the need to move from passive Marshallian externalities that may or may not emerge spontaneously from private firm cooperation, and recommend proactive strategizing by developing country governments to identify potentially competitive industries and provide the industry-specific infrastructures and services necessary for success.

Notes

1. In trying to understand why the most advanced modern computers have the same keyboard layout as 19th-century typing machines with the first line starting with the strange word "QWERTY," economists have offered various theories about the power of historical accidents and the randomness of certain dominant phenomena.
2. The International Convention on the Harmonization and Simplification of Customs defines a free zone as a specific place in a country "where any goods introduced are generally regarded, insofar as import duties and taxes are concerned, as being outside the customs territory [...] and not subject to the usual customs control" (Annex D). Free zones have existed in various parts of the world for centuries, most notably in Gibraltar (1704) and Hong Kong-China (1848). Modern special economic zones (SEZs) typically are located in a geographically delimited area (often secured), and host firms that are eligible for benefits, a separate customs area (duty free benefits) with streamlined procedures, and single management structure.
3. Backward linkages can be defined as the various channels through which money, goods, services, and information flow between a firm and its suppliers and create a network of interdependence and mutually beneficial business opportunities. Forward linkages are similar connections between a firm and its customers.
4. In 2008, there were already about 3,000 zones in 135 countries worldwide (FIAS, 2008).
5. CBIPs should not try to promote static comparative advantage. They should support for the upgrading and diversification into new industries. However, their goals should not be too ambitious as it is often the case in countries where policymakers advocate the promotion of *dynamic* comparative advantage. The nuance here is important. Theories of dynamic comparative advantage typically attempt to help firms to enter industries that are a country's *future* comparative advantage. Because of endowment constraints in the African context, firms in those industries would not yet be viable in a competitive market even if the government helped them with the co-ordination and externality compensation. By contrast, CBIPs should aim at helping firms enter industries with *latent* comparative advantage. Under that scenario, firms would be *immediately* viable and require no subsidies or protection once the government provides coordination and externality compensation.
6. It is estimated that SEZs in Sub-Saharan Africa generally contribute nearly 50 percent of exports. It can be inferred from their impact on the diversification of the region's export base that they also contribute to skill upgrading.

References

Aghion, P. (2009) *Some Thoughts on Industrial Policy and Growth*. Working Paper No. 2009–09 (Paris: OFCE-Sciences Po).

Arrow, K.J. (1962) "The Economic Implications of Learning by Doing," *Review of Economic Studies*, vol. 29, pp. 155–172.

Chenggang, X. (2011) "The Fundamental Institutions of China's Reforms and Development," *Journal of Economic Literature*, vol. 49, no. 4, pp. 1076–1151.

David, P.A. (1985) "," *The American Economic Review*, vol. 75, no. 2, Papers and Proceedings of the Ninety-Seventh Annual Meeting of the American Economic Association. (1985), pp. 332–337.

Farole, T. (2011) *Special Economic Zones in Africa: Comparing Performance and Learning from Global Experiences* (Washington, D.C.: World Bank).

FIAS (2008) *Special Economic Zones: Performance, Lessons Learned, and Implications for zone Development* (Washington, DC: IFC-World Bank).

Griliches, Z., 1979. "Issues in Assessing the Contribution of R&D to Productivity Growth," *Bell Journal of Economics*, vol. 10, pp. 92–116.

Harrison, A. and Rodríguez-Clare, A. (2010) "Trade, Foreign Investment, and Industrial Policy for Developing Countries", in D. Rodrik (ed.) *Handbook of Economic Growth*, vol. 5 (Amsterdam: North-Holland), pp. 4039–4213.

Imbs, J., and Wacziarg, R. (2003) "Stages of Diversification," *American Economic Review*, vol. 93, no. 1, 63–86.

Krugman, P. (2008) "The Increasing Returns Revolution in Trade and Geography," Nobel Prize Lecture, Oslo, December 8.

Krugman, P. (1994) *Peddling Prosperity: Economic Sense and Nonsense in the Age of Diminished Expectations* (New York: W.W. Norton and Co.).

Krugman, P.R. (1995) "Increasing Returns, Imperfect Competition, and the Positive Theory of International Trade," in G.M. Grossman and K. Rogoff (eds), *Handbook of International Economics*, vol. 3 (Amsterdam: North-Holland).

Lin, J.Y. (2012a) *New Structural Economics: A Framework for Rethinking Development and Policy* (Washington, DC: World Bank).

Lin, J.Y. (2012b) *The Quest for Prosperity: How Developing Countries Can Take Off* (Princeton, NJ: Princeton University Press).

Lin, J.Y. and Monga, C. (2011) "Growth Identification and Facilitation: The Role of the State in the Dynamics of Structural Change," *Development Policy Review*, vol. 29, no. 3, pp. 259–310.

Lyn, G., and Rodriguez-Clare, A. (2011) "Marshallian Externalities, Comparative Advantage, and International Trade," mimeo, University of California Berkeley. Available online at http://emlab.berkeley.edu/~arodeml/Papers/LR_Marshallian_Externalities_Trade.pdf.

Marshall, A. (1890) *Principles of Economics* (London: Macmillan).

Monga, C. (2011) *Cluster-Based Industrial Parks. A Practical Framework for Action*, Policy Research Working Paper no. 5900, December (Washington, DC: World Bank).

Paul, C.J. and Siegel, D.S. (1999) "Scale Economies and Industry Agglomeration Externalities: A Dynamic Cost Function Approach," *American Economic Review*, vol. 89, pp. 272–290.

Rodríguez-Clare, A. (2005) *Clusters and Comparative Advantage: Implications for Industrial Policy*, Working Paper no. 523 (Washington, DC: Inter-American Development Bank).

Stiglitz, J.E. (2001) Information and the Change in the Paradigm in Economics, Nobel Prize Lecture, December 8.

World Bank (2009) *World Development Report: Reshaping Economic Geography* (Washington, DC: World Bank).

Zhang, X. (2012) "Clusters as an Instrument for Industrial Policy: The Case of China," Paper presented at the International Economic Association (IEA) – World Bank Roundtable "New Thinking in Industrial Policy" at the World Bank, May.

Part IV
Regional Case Studies of Successful and Unsuccessful Industrial Policies

4.1
Clusters as an Instrument for Industrial Policy: The Case of China*

Xiaobo Zhang
Peking University and International Food Policy Research Institute

4.1.1 Introduction

Developing countries face a long list of seemingly insurmountable obstacles to industrialization, including but not limited to underdeveloped financial systems and a lack of formal institutions. Since pooled resources are necessary to build factories and to purchase manufacturing equipment, financial development has been widely regarded as a key instrument for industrialization (Goldsmith, 1969; Rajan and Zingales, 1998). Entrepreneurs are afraid to make business deals unless the underlying contracts are trustworthy. Thus building a sound legal system is also crucial for ensuring the functioning of market economy (North, 1990). A common view among donors and policy makers is the necessity of creating these fundamental institutions.

However, it may take a long time to develop a sound financial and legal system and the process is wrought with challenges. Microfinance institutions (MFIs) are a telling example. Formal banks normally shy away from the poor because of the high accrued monitoring and information costs as a fraction of loan size (Banerjee and Duflo, 2007). Money lenders and other informal finance institutions tend to charge exorbitant interest rates on credit to the poor. By extending loans to people en masse and making repayment an implicit social contract, MFIs have reached hundreds of millions of the poor worldwide who otherwise would lack access to small loans at reasonable interest rates. However, as recent evaluations (Banerjee, Duflo, Glennerster, and Kinnan, 2010; Karlan and Zinman, 2010) show, MFIs are not as miraculous as widely thought. Especially, because of the risk-averse nature embedded in group lending and fixed repayment schedules, MFIs are not suitable for most entrepreneurs who often need to make risky investment decisions.

---

* Helpful comments from Wonhyuk Lim, Justin Lin, Célestin Monga, Joseph Stiglitz, and other roundtable participants are gratefully acknowledged.

The rapid industrialization of China in the past several decades also challenges conventional thinking. At the inception of economic reform in the late 1970s, the state-owned banks did not extend any credit to individual entrepreneurs because private ownership was banned. MFIs have never been officially promoted at all. Private ownership was not formally recognized by the constitution until 2004 when China was already on a track of high economic growth. Despite these obvious obstacles, China has become the "world factory" in just a few decades. The Chinese example illustrates that industrialization can still occur even when facing institutional deficiencies and credit constraints. In other words, these factors may not be as binding as widely regarded in the literature.

In reality, when facing large constraints which seemingly cannot be removed in the near future, people, including the poor, are ingenious in figuring out ways to circumvent them. Clustering – or the banding together of small businesses, which are part of the same industry, to specialize in one narrowly defined stage of production – is one such instrument. China's industrial development is largely cluster-based (Long and Zhang, 2012). Thousands of firms, large and small, each specialized in a finely defined production step, lump together in a densely populated region. Many formerly rural towns in the coastal areas have become so specialized that they have acquired well-known nicknames, such as Socks City, Sweater City, Kid's Clothing City, Footwear Capital, and so on. For example, Datang Town in Zhejiang Province, previously a rice-farming village with only one thousand people in the 1970s, now produces nine billions of socks a year (more than one pair per person on the earth), and is acclaimed as the world's "Socks Capital" (*New York Times*, 2004).[1]

Clusters are a viable model of industrial production in China because it fits into China's comparative advantage – high population density and low capital/labor ratio. As shown in Long and Zhang (2011), the number of firms grows faster in clustered areas than in non-clustered areas; Firms are more productive and export more to the international market in clusters than their counterparts outside the clusters. In a word, clustering has been a key factor and distinguishing feature of China's rapid industrialization.

A question arises: are industrial clusters a phenomenon unique to China? The answer is no. Clustering appeared in many European countries during their early stages of industrialization and is still common in both developed and developing countries. In the *Wealth of Nations*, Adam Smith described the putting-out system in numerous specialty towns in the early stages of the Industrial Revolution in the UK, where traders brought designs and raw materials to sell, outsourced the production to various family workshops, collected the final products, and sold them to the market.

In specialty towns, production processes were segmented to an unbelievable extent. The following narrative on the small-arms industry in

Birmingham in the 1860s by Allen (1929) and cited in Stigler (1951:192–3) vividly illustrates the inner workings of a cluster in the UK:

> Of the 5,800 people engaged in the manufacture within the borough's boundaries in 1861 the majority worked within a small district round St Mary's Church .... The reason for the high degree of localization is not difficult to discover. The manufacture of guns, as of jewelry, was carried on by a large number of makers who specialized on particular processes, and this method of organization involved the frequent transport of parts from one workshop to another.
>
> The master gun-maker – the entrepreneur – seldom possessed a factory or workshop ... Usually he owned merely a warehouse in the gun quarter, and his function was to acquire semi-finished parts and to give these out to specialized craftsmen, who undertook the assembly and finishing of the gun. He purchased materials from the barrel-makers, lock-makers, sigh-stampers, triggers-makers, ramrod-forgers, gun-furniture makers, and, if he were engaged in the military branch, from bayonet-forgers. All of these are independent manufacturers executing the orders of several master gun makers.... Once the parts had been purchased from the "material-makers," as they were called, the next task was to hand them out to a long succession of "setters-up," each of whom performed a specific operation in connection with the assembly and finishing of the gun.

This high degree of division of labor affected not only the gun making industries, but also other trades, including jewelry, brass foundry, and saddlery and harness. Allen (1929) commented that "Perhaps the most remarkable feature of the industrial structure of the district in 1860 was the co-existence in many trades of highly subdivided processes of production and the small unit" (p. 151).

Although subsequently the factory-based mass-production system largely replaced the cluster-based putting-out system in the UK, industrial clusters are still a viable production structure in many countries, including both developing and developed ones. For example, Italy remains to be renowned for industrial districts (a synonym for cluster), for example, the city of Como is known for its silk fabric, Vicenza for its fine wool, and Veneto for its knitting. In the USA, Silicon Valley in California and Route 128 in Boston are celebrated technology clusters (Saxenian, 1994). Piore and Sabel (1984) and Porter (1990) maintain that the cluster-based production system with flexible specialization could help advanced economies form their own competitive advantages.

Clusters are widely observed in developing countries as well. For example, in Thailand, "One Tambon One Product" has been widely promoted. Under this program, each Thai Tambon (subdistrict) is encouraged to develop its industry centering around one key product. Phillips also adopts a similar

"One Town One Product" program. Sonobe and Otsuka (2006) discuss both the pattern and the mechanism of cluster-based industrialization in Asian countries. Oyelaran-Oyeyinka and McCormick (2007) present nine case studies of clusters across seven African nations, suggesting that clusters are ubiquitous across the continent. The cluster stories included in these books mimic the one cited by Stigler during the Industrial Revolution in the UK.

Cluster-based industrial production may hold great potential for industrialization in developing countries for several reasons. In *Principle of Economics* (1920), Marshall highlighted three key positive externalities of industrial districts: technology and information spillover, labor pooling, and access to markets. Within a cluster, one can easily observe and mimic what others are doing, thereby greatly lowering the costs of adopting production technologies. In clusters, workers can easily find jobs requiring the same skills among numerous similar businesses. The constant demand for skill attracts more workers to the clusters, which in turn provides firms with a stable supply of skilled labor force. Moreover, both input and output markets are frequently embedded in industrial clusters. Due to proximity to intermediate inputs and the buyers of their products, firms in clusters enjoy lower purchasing and marketing costs than those residing outside the clusters.

Apart from these three notable features, recent studies have shown that clusters play an additional role in helping entrepreneurs to bypass credit constraints and institutional deficiencies – two seemingly insurmountable road blocks to industrialization. In clusters, production processes are partitioned into fine incremental steps, reducing the capital requirement for each step and opening doors to a large pool of potential entrepreneurs with limited financial resources. The repeated transactions and easy flow of information in a cluster serves a commitment device for entrepreneurs to do business honestly. They know that if they break a contract, their reputation will be affected, ruining their business within the cluster. Since their business and social capital are attached to the particular location, they would be worthless elsewhere. Therefore, the best option for entrepreneurs is to honor their contracts, even informal ones. Clusters provide a way for firms to reduce transaction costs amid imperfect institutional environments, such as the difficult legal reality of many developing countries wherein they lack independent courts to enforce contracts. In summary, clusters can be used as an instrument for tapping into the talent of potential entrepreneurs from a wide swath of the population, including the poor, and for creating nonfarm employment opportunities in developing countries.

In the next three sections, we provide some examples to illustrate how clustering can help ameliorate financial and institutional constraints and foster entrepreneurship. Then we discuss the role of local governments in facilitating cluster development. The paper concludes with some reflections on cluster-based local industrial policy.

4.1.2 Clustering and credit constraints

4.1.2.1 Capital entry barrier[2]

Following the seminal work of Marshall (1920), a large body of literature has been devoted to testing the three Marshallian hypotheses. Hayami, Kikuchi, and Marciano (1998) and Schmitz and Nadvi (1999) are among the earliest to point out the link between clustering and financial constraints, an aspect largely neglected in the previous literature. Their idea is surprisingly simple. In clusters, production processes are often broken down into many incremental stages, which are undertaken by dispersed independent workshops. Naturally it requires much less capital to start a small business working on only one step of the production than engaging in the whole production process. Because in developing countries, many potential entrepreneurs are financially constrained, having lower entry barriers from a fine division of labor enables a greater number of entrepreneurs to set up otherwise impossible businesses in clusters.

Based on a primary survey in Puyuan, one of the largest cashmere sweater clusters in China, Ruan and Zhang (2009) provide empirical evidence in support of this hypothesis. The production of the cashmere sweaters in Puyuan consists of eight major steps: yarn purchasing, weaving, dyeing, finishing, printing, ironing, packaging, and selling. Cashmere sweaters can be produced through two modes of production. One is the modern factory system (Figure 4.1.1a), which integrates most of the production steps under one roof. This organizational chart consists of four entities: large integrated

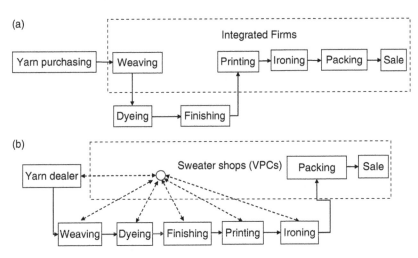

Figure 4.1.1 (a) Integrated production organization; (b) Putting-out production organization
Source: Ruan and Zhang (2009).

manufacturing factories, yarn dealers, dyeing factories, and finishing factories. Most of these integrated enterprises are located in the industrial park. They purchase yarn from marketplace yarn dealers or directly from yarn factories elsewhere, and complete the weaving process in-house. They then outsource the semi-finished goods to specialized dyeing factories and finishing factories. After this process, the products are ironed, sorted and packaged inside the factory before being ultimately shipped out to the national market through the logistics center.

The other one is the putting-out system as shown in Figure 4.1.1b. A group of master sweater merchants – similar in role to the master gunsmiths relayed in Stigler's account of the Industrial Revolution – take the place of a physical production facility and play a key role in coordinating the production of the sweaters. These merchants either rent or own shops in the township's designated sweater marketplaces, and coordinate the entire production process. More often than not, they imitate the designs of big companies or those seen in fashion magazines, using them to guide production of sample sweaters, which they display in their shops. For example, Puyuan is the largest cashmere sweater market in China, and many merchants visit the shops in its marketplaces to purchase sweaters. When the master merchants receive orders or believe that a certain style will sell well, they purchase raw materials from the marketplace and have them delivered to family weaving workshops down the production chain. The generated semi-finished goods are sent to dyeing, finishing, printing, and ironing enterprises, and master merchants perform quality inspections and package the final products in their shops. If any quality problems are identified, they are traced back to the sources of production and the master merchants resolve the issue with the responsible party. In this business model, the raw materials and intermediate products are frequently transported from one processing point to another by a number of couriers who use electric or man-powered three-wheeled vehicles. After going through this "assembly line," the final products are transported to other markets through the Puyuan logistics center. In essence, this business model is similar to the putting-out system that was widespread in the United Kingdom during the early stage of Industrial Revolution.

Table 4.1.1 lists the amount and sources of start-up capital for all surveyed enterprises, both integrated companies and those engaged in vertical division of labor. The average starting capital for an integrated enterprise is equivalent to 132 times of the annual salary of a typical worker. The average and median starting capital for several types of capital-intensive enterprises along the chain of sweater production (dyeing, finishing, and the logistical company) are also far beyond the means of ordinary workers. Not many people can afford to establish these enterprises purely out of their own pockets. Naturally, they are more likely to seek help from banks. For these capital-intensive enterprises, bank loans account for 21–50 percent of

Table 4.1.1 Amount and source of starting capital in Puyuan cluster

	Average (10,000 yuan)	Median (10,000 yuan)	Mean/ Wage	% of initial capital investment from banks
Yarn dealers	12.45	10.00	6.25	0.00
Family weaving workshops	7.31	4.50	3.65	2.90
Dyeing factories	340.07	200.00	170.05	20.63
Finishing factories	177.82	65.27	88.90	25.68
Printing workshops	10.60	10.00	5.30	0.00
Ironing workshops	3.83	4.00	1.90	0.00
Three-wheeler drivers	12.74	0.45	0.25	6.95
Sweater shops	0.54	10.00	6.35	0.00
Logistics company	4000.00	4,000.00	–	50.00
Integrated enterprises	263.84	220.38	131.90	21.13

Source: Adopted from Ruan and Zhang (2009). The value is in 2005 constant price. The exchange rate in 2005 is: $1= 8.1 yuan.

total initial capital investments. By contrast, the mean initial investment of labor-intensive enterprises (yarn dealers, family weaving workshops, printing workshops, ironing workshops, three-wheeler drivers and sweater shops) is much lower. For example, a young male migrant worker can use three months of salary to purchase a used three-wheeler (4,500 yuan) and start a local transport business. With such low capital requirements, one doesn't need to borrow much, if at all, from banks.

Using China Industrial Census 1995 and China Economic Census 2004, Long and Zhang (2011) confirm that the this pattern originally seen in Puyuan – that as a county increasingly clusters, the minimal capital requirement for entry decreases – holds true for China as a whole.

4.1.2.2 Working capital constraints

A business needs not only starting capital, but also working capital to operate. Small businesses rarely rely on bank credit as the major source of working capital for several reasons. First, banks normally require fixed assets as collaterals for loans, which small business usually do not possess. Second, the loan amount is often too small to be profitable for banks. The cost of monitoring and administrating a loan is largely independent of loan size – it is less cost-efficient to administer a small loan than a large loan. Third, the long periods of processing that loan applications require clash with businesses' urgent need for working capital. When a firm runs short of working capital, it requires credit immediately. However, it takes days, if not weeks, for a major bank in China to process a loan application. By the time that the loan is approved, it may already be too late. As a result, small and medium enterprises (SMEs) tend to seek informal sources for help despite the much higher interest rates than bank rates. The resulting high financing cost is a constraint on the development of SMEs.

Clusters provide a way to lower working capital constraints facing small enterprises through trade credit. With repeated and close interactions within a cluster, the members of upstream and downstream enterprises get to know each other very well, often building rapport. This trust forms a basis for a given enterprise to acquire trade credit support from upstream or downstream enterprises.

Take the Puyuan industrial cluster as an example (Ruan and Zhang, 2009). Capital credits emerge during the stage of yarn purchasing. When a yarn dealer makes their first purchase from a yarn manufacturer, the trade generally does not involve credit. However, after a number of transactions have occurred and mutual trust has been established, yarn dealers can often order yarn with delayed payment. The yarn manufacturers, which are usually large state-owned enterprises, often enjoy generous support from state banks.

Similarly, master sweater merchants also frequently extend trade credit to processing workshops. Through trade credit, bank loans pass through yard manufactures, yard dealers, master sweater merchants, and processing workshops. This kind of credit transfer along the production chain enables many SMEs to indirectly access formal credit. For example, 47% of family workshops, 40 percent of printing workshops, and 33% of ironing workshops report trade credit as their most importance source when facing working capital problem, while none of them list bank loans as their top choice. In this way, the trade credit arrangements among upstream and downstream enterprises can be seen alleviating the constraints of working capital.

The trade credit phenomenon observed in Puyuan is not unique. As shown by Long and Zhang (2011) based on firm-level data from national censuses, the provision trade credit among firms is widespread in clusters in China. The prevalence of trade credit is highly positively associated with the degree of clustering. State-owned enterprises are more likely to extend trade credit while private ones tend to be on the receiving end. The popularity of trade credit may go beyond Chinese clusters. A recent study (Zhang, Moorman and Ayele, 2011) reveals that trade credit is common among handloom weavers and traders in rural handloom clusters in Ethiopia.

Trade credit was also a key feature during the early stage of industrialization in the UK as shown in the following paragraph in Allen (1929: 155):

> the chief link between the divers forms of organization which were comprehended in the factor system is to be found in the financial dependence of the manufacturer and the factor. Indeed an understanding of

industrial finance during the nineteenth century is impossible between the banks and the small makers who could not then resort to them for credit. Through the factor, industry was supplied with its working capital; for though the domestic workers and shop owners might not all receive their materials from the factor, they all depended on him for weekly advances, from which they might meet their expenses of production.

Flexible payment is another way to ease out working capital constraints. Different types of business may adopt different payment methods according to their needs. For example, integrated enterprises and most production-processing enterprises settle the payment according to a fixed time period (usually monthly or quarterly). The yarn dealers and sweater shops prefer a more flexible payment schedule contingent upon their sale status, primarily because they bear the most market risk and their sales and profits are more variable than those of the production-processing workshops. For transportation services, payment most often follows the completion of the order.

Apart from trade credit and flexible payment, firms in a cluster also save marketing costs (Sonobe and Otsuka, 2006). Market developments are often in sync with cluster developments. Buyers like to go to clusters because they can find everything they need in one place. A large scale of concentration of production in one place also attracts suppliers to serve the whole cluster. When both input and output markets are around, enterprises in the cluster can call merchants in market to deliver intermediate materials to their workshops and directly sell their products in the local product markets.

Above all, several positive features of clusters – mutual financing, flexible settlements, and lower marketing costs – allow SMEs to operate normally in the production chain without fear of collapsing due to credit crunches.

4.1.3   Clusters and institutional constraints

In the last section, we have discussed the advantages of division of labor inherent in clusters. However, as division of labor deepens, production is increasingly undertaken by dispersed independent firms (or more exactly, workshops in Chinese clusters). This may involve greater coordination costs among producers (Becker and Murphy, 1992). The efficient functioning of markets requires good contract enforcement (North, 1990). However, because courts are not totally independent in China, it is often too costly to enforce contracts through formal legal means. Clusters provide an alternative way for firms to enforce contracts and control – or even reduce – coordination costs through private ordering.

One key feature of cluster-based production is that both upstream and downstream enterprises are nearby. Proximity can reduce transaction costs for several reasons. First, in a close area, it is much easier for one to learn information about upstream and downstream partners, making reputation a bigger factor in business dealings. If a producer does not honor his contract, others in the location could quickly learn about his reputation for bad business. This is a serious deterrent. It is hard to recover from a bad reputation, as it takes time and money to rebuild trust with new customers and suppliers. Among the 126 enterprises surveyed in Puyan cashmere sweaters (Ruan and Zhang, 2009), almost all the transactions were based on oral agreement. Yet, people did not act opportunistically to break oral agreements despite their informality.

Second, the clustering mode of production creates location specificity, which in turn increases the opportunity cost of committing dishonest behavior. In a town specialized in only one major production, a producer's investment and network are specific to the location. If he moves to another town specializing in another product, his investment and network would be worth much less.

Third, competitive pressure may foster long-term relationships. Given the abundance of competitors at most stages of production, enterprises have the incentive to develop long-term relationships with a few upstream and downstream firms because if they fail to do so, others who do develop business relationships could easily replace them. It is well known that repeated games create a self-disciplinary mechanism. Therefore, it is possible for private order to ensure the proper functioning of market transactions without the need for formal contracts. According to a survey on 140 enterprises in Wenzhou footwear cluster (Huang, Zhang, and Zhu, 2008), 103 explicitly expressed that they resolved contractual conflicts through out-of-court negotiation or mediations via the third party, whereas only four reported going to court.

The same pattern is also observed in handloom clusters in rural Ethiopia where the formal institution is even more lacking than in China. Among 291 handloom weavers and workshops, none of them have ever used the police or courts to resolve a quality dispute (Zhang, Moorman, Ayele, 2011). The vast majority of them talked directly with trader/buyer to work out a mutually acceptable solution.

In summary, it is possible for a dispersed production structure to occur and exist in a cluster, keeping coordination costs at bay, even in the absence of formal contractual institutions.

4.1.4   Clusters and entrepreneurship

Given that clusters facilitate technology spillover, ease credit constraints, and moderate the deficiencies of formal institutions, we would expect clusters to be a breeding ground for entrepreneurship. The lower technical, financial, and institutional barriers in clusters enable many entrepreneurs with limited means to operate their business there, which otherwise would have been impossible outside clusters.[3] There are multiple channels that clusters can foster entrepreneurship, including the three classical Marshallian agglomeration effects and an emerging set of additional drivers, such as the presence of a network of suppliers (Chinitz, 1961), supporting and related industries (Porter, 1990), and anchor firms (Agrawal and Cockburn, 2002). Putting the potential different channels aside, clusters are found to be associated with higher growth in new business establishments in the US (Delgado, Porter, and Stern, 2010).

Here we mainly focus on the additional role of clustering in ameliorating financial constraints, which are widely regarded as key obstacles to industrialization in developing countries. Let's use Figure 4.1.2 to illustrate the logic of clustering on entrepreneurship. The bell curve represents the density of potential entrepreneurs in relation to their wealth level. In the extreme case, suppose that an entrepreneur can only start up his business using his own resources. The lowest capital requirement for setting up a business is K_0 as shown by the right vertical line. Naturally, only those potential entrepreneurs whose wealth exceeds K_0 can afford to start up a business. The poor guys whose wealth is below the threshold would have to forgo their entrepreneurial dreams and work for others or stay unemployed.

As discussed earlier, clustering lowers the cost to start and run a business. In Figure 4.1.2, this is represented by a shift in the vertical line leftward from K_0 to K_1. Consequently, those potential entrepreneurs, whose wealth level lies between K_0 and K_1 and were previously too poor to start up a business, now can test their entrepreneurial talent. The impact of clustering on entrepreneurship is the area below the bell curve and between the two vertical lines (K_0 and K_1).

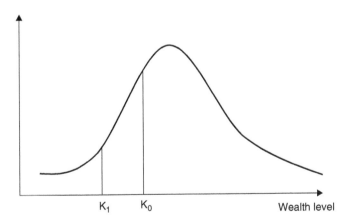

Figure 4.1.2 Illustration of capital entry barriers and entrepreneurship
Note: Drawn by the author. The vertical axis stands for the density of potential entrepreneurs corresponding to the wealth level at the horizontal axis.

Figure 4.1.3 plots the growth rate in number of enterprises from 1995 and 2004 against the initial degree of clustering in 1995 at the county level in China. It is apparent from the figure that new firms have emerged at a faster pace in more clustered areas. When a region starts from a lower level of clustering, the positive impact of clustering on the extensive firm growth is notably strong. As a region clusters to a certain threshold, the impact of clustering levels off. The pattern shown in Figure 4.1.3 is largely consistent with our hypothesis. However, this is just suggestive evidence.

Using the firm-level data from the 1995 and 2004 Censuses, Long and Zhang (2011) provide more solid empirical evidence on the positive role of clustering on both extensive and intensive firm growth. First, they confirm that clusters play a role in lowering the minimal capital requirements and fostering the provision of trade credit. Second, they show that the emergence of private firms is positively related to the initial degree of clustering. As a placebo test, the number of foreign and state-owned enterprises was found to have little to do with the initial degree of clustering largely because those firms do not face financial constraints in the first place.

Since clusters encompass a large number of similar firms, the competition is extremely fierce. Competition forces firms to improve their productivity. This is exactly what Long and Zhang (2011) find. Firms in clusters are more productive and more likely to export than their counterparts outside

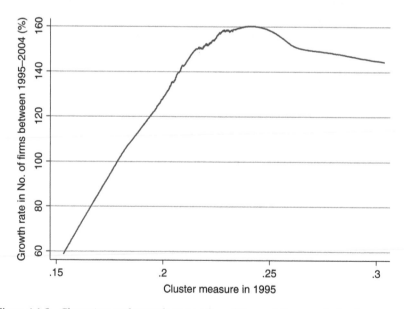

Figure 4.1.3   Clustering and growth in number of firms at the county level
Note: Drawn by the author based on China Industrial Census 1995 and China Economic Census 2004. The cluster measure is taken from Long and Zhang (2011).

clusters. This may explain why China's industrial production has become rapidly clustered in the past several decades.

4.1.5 Role of local government

Although clusters are prevalent in both developed and developing countries, why have clusters developed much faster in China than many other parts of the developing world? One key factor setting China apart is the active role of local governments in fostering cluster development (Xu and Zhang, 2009).

The functioning of clusters depends upon some key public goods and services. Without the presence of necessary public goods, such as markets and order, it would be difficult for an enterprise to keep just one step of production in house, often the case in clusters. In the Chinese context, in almost all the clusters, local governments have played a key role in setting up marketplaces, which greatly facilitate division of labor within a cluster and enhance the scale of production.[4]

Better infrastructure is perhaps another reason behind the rapid growth in Chinese clusters. Industrial production is often powered by electricity. In China, power supply from the grid is stable and robust. SMEs in Chinese clusters do not need to equip their own generators. In contrast, power is not uniformly available in certain developing countries. Even places with access to electricity may be plagued by frequent power outages, such as Bangladesh and India. To ensure normal production, some firms have to prepare a power generator, incurring additional capital and fuel costs. Power supply can greatly shape production structure and firm performance. By comparing areas with and without access to electricity, Zhang, Moorman, and Ayele (2011) show clearly that labor productivity in rural handloom clusters in Ethiopia is much higher in areas with electricity because producers work longer hours by sharing lit workspaces at lower rental costs.

The centrally provided heating system in Puyuan sweater cluster is another telling example. It is costly for each ironing workshop to provide its own heating system. If the heating system is centrally operated, the cost would be much lower. In lieu of this concern, the local government places all of the ironing workshops in a designated area of a local industrial park, where heating is centrally supplied. As a result, the starting capital for opening an ironing workshop in the designated zone is very low, only about 40,000 yuan (less than 5,000 US dollars).

When a cluster attracts more business, crime rates often go up. Security is like oxygen. Without oxygen, organisms cannot survive. Without a secure environment, it becomes hard for a cluster to attract traders and suppliers to do business. In many Chinese clusters, local governments hire private security guards to patrol the street using their own resources (Fleisher et al., 2010).

Sonobe and Otuska (2006) postulate that cluster development follows two phases. The first phase is quantity expansion and the second one is quality upgrade. Low product quality is pandemic in many clusters in developing countries. Due to lower entry barriers and easy information flow, it is easy for enterprises to imitate product designs and technologies from others in a cluster. Thereby, many enterprises do not have incentives to invest heavily on R&D and improve product quality. This may create a problem of "race to the bottom", wherein everyone competes for the lowest price, regardless of quality. It is very hard for any individual enterprises to produce high quality products in such an environment. It requires collective actions to break out of the trap and to shift the cluster development to the second phase – quality upgrade (Ruan and Zhang, 2010).

Because different clusters produce different products, the exact interventions can be quite different. For example, in Wenzhou footwear cluster, in response to a consumer boycott on the extreme low quality of its shoes in 1987, Wenzhou's government and local business worked out several indigenous ways to resolve the quality problem. A business association was created with a main purpose for quality control.[5] The association blacklisted enterprises producing fake and low-quality shoes, shaming them among its members. In addition, it worked in concert with the city's industrial and commerce administration to ban those on the blacklist from posting advertisements in Wenzhou. Since Wenzhou was one of the largest footwear clusters, traders came over to Wenzhou to place orders. If a firm's name could not be seen anywhere, it would lose its customers very soon. So the blacklisting and ban of advisement turned out to be an effective strategy to regulate firms' behavior.

In Zhili child garment cluster, the local government used different strategies to curb the production of low quality clothes. The local government set up a quality inspection center to randomly check product quality to filter out bad apples (Fleisher et al, 2010). In addition, the local government provided incentives, such as tax breaks, cheap credit, and access to land, in order to attract enterprises with sound brand names and high-quality products to the industrial park.

One may wonder why the local governments in China are so interested in facilitating cluster development. This may be related to China unique institutional structure, which is marked by a decentralized fiscal system and centralized political system (Zhang, 2006; Xu, 2011). Because the promotion of local officials is closely tied to economic growth indicators and local expenditure is largely determined by local revenues, local officials have a strong incentive to develop the local economy (Li and Zhou, 2005). Given their informational advantages, local governments are more likely to identify their binding constraints and figure out the best local solutions than the central government. In fact, many successful industrial policies on cluster development originate from the local level in China.[6] A research question arises: how can the interests of local government officials in other developing countries become aligned with local economic development?

4.1.6 Conclusions

Using China as an example, we show that the cluster-based production mode is a viable production structure and has several key advantages in easing financial and institutional constraints.

First, start-up costs are lower in clusters because each business can specialize in a narrow segment of production thanks to the fine division of labor in clusters. Thereby, clustering enables many farmers with entrepreneurial talents to move into industrial production.

Second, the extensive use of trade credit helps enterprises lessen the working capital constraints in daily operations.

Third, repeated transactions in clusters make reputation effects particularly important. The presence of multiple competitors in clusters producing similar goods deters dishonest behaviors. Therefore, it is possible to maintain the proper functioning of market transactions through private order in clusters, even if the formal legal institution is still weak.

Even though the cluster-based industrialization model has proven its viability in China and other developed countries, particularly during early stages of industrialization, its importance has not been fully recognized by policy-makers in large because many enterprises in clusters are very small and informal, completely flying off the radar of official statistics. Moreover, in many countries, local officials' incentives are not embedded in the process of local economic development. Since many binding constraints to cluster development are context specific, the solutions are often local and unorthodox, which are naturally harder for outsiders to figure out. Thereby, a one-size-fits-all type of industrial policy at the national level may not apply to a particular cluster, similar to Rodrik's argument against using one recipe for all countries (Rodrik, 2008). Even if it luckily works once, it is likely to fail next time. After all, the cluster-based model of industrial development calls for more fine-tuned industrial policies at the local level, which requires local governments to continuously experiment and readjust.

In the end, we would also like to draw a cautious note on the limitations of clusters. Clusters fit particular well to areas with high population density and low capital/labor ratio and with divisible technologies. As labor costs rise and capital becomes more abundant, the cluster-based production model may be replaced by the factory system as attested in the UK and the US in the past one hundred years. Accordingly, industrial policies must respond to these changing endowment structures and external environments (Lin, 2007). Even with proactive industrial policy, there is not guarantee that an industry will survive forever. As shown in history, some of the once prosperous clusters, like the gun cluster in Birmingham, have disappeared or been replaced by other industries (Allen, 1929).

Notes

1. "In Roaring China, Sweaters Are West of Socks City" by David Barboza, *New York Times*, December 24, 2004. Available from http://www.nytimes.com/2004/12/24/business/worldbusiness/24china.html?pagewanted=print&position=.
2. This section is largely from Ruan and Zhang (2009).
3. Even in the USA where the capital market is more developed, Delgado, Porter, and Stern (2010) find that clusters play a positive role in facilitating entrepreneurship.
4. See Sonobe, Hu, and Otsuka (2002) for the role of specialized market in the formation of Zhili children's garment cluster and Ruan and Zhang (2009) on marketplace development in Puyuan cashmere sweater cluster.
5. See Ruan and Zhang (2010) for details.
6. Thun (2004) warns that decentralization alone may not induce local governments to develop competitive local industries and increasing international competition can help reduce the local obstacles to change. In this regard, the central government has played an important role in introducing market competition, including but not limited to setting up special economic zones, opening China up to foreign direct investment, joining WTO, reforming the state-owned enterprises, and building national highways and high-speed railways.

References

Allen, George C. (1929) *The Industrial Development of Birmingham and the Black Country, 1860–1929* (London: G. Allen & Unwin Ltd).

Agrawal, Ajay and Cockburn, Iain M. (2003) "The Anchor Tenant Hypothesis: Exploring the Role of Large, Local, and R&D-intensive Firms in Regional Innovation Systems," *International Journal of International Organization*, vol. 21, pp. 1227–1253.

Ayele, Gezahegn, Moorman, Lisa, Wamisho, Kassu, and Zhang, Xiaobo (2011) "Infrastructure and Cluster Development: A Case Study of Handloom Weavers in Ethiopia," IFPRI Discussion Paper, No. 0980.

Chinitz, Benjamin (1961) "Contrasts in Agglomeration: New York and Pittsburgh," *American Economic Review*, vol. 51, no. 2, pp. 279–289.

Delgado, Mercedes, Porter, Michael E., and Stern, Scott (2010) "Clusters and Entrepreneurship," *Journal of Economic Geography*, vol. 10, no. 4, pp. 495–518.

Fleisher, Belton, Hu, Dinghuan, McGuire, William, and Zhang, Xiaobo (2010) "The Evolution of an Industrial Cluster in China," *China Economic Review*, vol. 21, no. 3, pp. 456–469.

Goldsmith, Raymond W. (1969) *Financial Structure and Development* (New Haven, CT: Yale University Press).

Huang, Zuhui, Zhang, Xiaobo, and Zhu, Yunwei (2008) "The Role of Clustering in Rural Industrialization: A Case Study of Wenzhou's Footwear Industry," *China Economic Review*, vol. 19, pp. 409–420.

Li, Hongbin and Zhou, Li-An (2005) "Political Turnover and Economic Performance: The Incentive Role of Personnel Control in China," *Journal of Public Economics*, vol. 89, nos 9–10, pp. 1743–1762.

Lin, Justin (2007) *Development and Transition: Idea, Strategy, and Viability*, Cambridge University Marshall Lecture.

Long, Cheryl and Zhang, Xiaobo (2011) "Cluster-Based Industrialization in China: Financing and Performance," *Journal of International Economics*, vol. 84, no. 1, pp. 112–123.

Long, Cheryl and Zhang, Xiaobo (2012) "Patterns of China's Industrialization: Concentration, Specialization, and Clustering," *China Economic Review*, vol. 23, no. 3, pp. 593–612.

Marshall, A. (1920) *Principles of Economics* (London: Macmillan).

North, Douglas C. (1990) *Institutions, Institutional Change, and Economic Performance* (New York: Cambridge University Press).

Oyelaran-Oyeyinka, B. and McCormick, D. (eds) (2007) *Industrial Clusters and Innovation Systems in Africa* (Tokyo: United Nations University Press).

Piore, Michael J. and Sabel, Charles F. (1984) *The Economic Industrial Divide: Possibility for Prosperity* (New York: Basic Books).

Porter, Michael E. (1990) *The Competitive Advantage of Nations* (New York: The Free Press).

Rajan, Raghuram G., and Zingales, Luigi (1998) "Financial Dependence and Growth," *American Economic Review*, 88 (June), pp. 559–587.

Rodrik, Dani (2008) *One Economics, Many Recipes: Globalization, Institutions, and Economic Growth* (Princeton, NJ: Princeton University Press).

Ruan, Jianqing and Zhang, Xiaobo (2009) "Finance and Cluster-Based Industrial Development in China," *Economic Development and Cultural Change*, vol. 58, pp. 143–164.

Ruan, Jianqing and Zhang, Xiaobo (2010). "'Made in China': Crisis Begets Quality Upgrade," IFPRI Discussion Paper No. 1025, International Food Policy Research Institute.

Saxenian, AnnaLee (1994) *Regional Advantage: Culture and Competition in Silicon Valley and Route 128* (Cambridge, MA: Harvard University Press).

Sonobe, Tetsushi, Hu, Dinghuan, and Otsuka, Keijiro (2002) "Process of Cluster Formation in China: A Case Study of a Garment Town," *Journal of Development Studies*, vol. 39, no. 1, pp. 118–139.

Sonobe, Tetsushi, and Otsuka, Keijiro (2006) *Cluster-Based Industrial Development: An East Asia Model* (New York: Palgrave Macmillan).

Stigler, George J. (1951) "The Division of Labor is Limited by the Extent of the Market," *Journal of Political Economy*, vol. 59, no, 3, pp. 185–193.

Thun, Eric (2004) "Keeping Up with the Jones': Decentralization, Policy Imitation, and Industrial Development in China," *World Development*, vol. 32, no. 8, pp. 1289–1308.

Xu, Chenggang (2011) "The Fundamental Institutions of China's Reforms and Development," *Journal of Economic Literature*, vol. 49, no. 4, 1076–1151.

Xu, Chenggang and Zhang, Xiaobo (2009) "The Evolution of Chinese Entrepreneurial Firms: Township-Village Enterprises Revisited," IFPRI discussion papers 854, International Food Policy Research Institute.

Zhang, Xiaobo (2006) "Fiscal Decentralization and Political Centralization in China: Implications for Growth and Inequality," *Journal of Comparative Economics*, vol. 34, no. 4, pp. 713–726.

Zhang, Xiaobo and Hu, Dinghuan (2011) "Overcoming Successive Bottlenecks: The Evolution of a Potato Cluster in China," IFPRI Discussion Paper 1112.

4.2

Capability Failure and Industrial Policy to Move beyond the Middle-Income Trap: From Trade-based to Technology-based Specialization*

Keun Lee
Seoul National University

4.2.1 Introduction

The disappointing economic performance of the past two decades under the Washington Consensus of the 1980s and 1990s and the impact of the 2008 global financial crisis have resulted in the revival of industrial policy as a keyword in development literature. New literature in the same vein includes the works of Cimoli, Dosi, and Stiglitz (2009), as well as those of Lin (2012), Lee and Mathews (2010), and Wade (2012). Industrial policy is a broad concept. According to Johnson (1982), it refers to policies that improve the structure of a domestic industry in order to enhance a country's international competitiveness. Variants of industrial policies existed in successful countries, such as the UK from the 14th to the 18th centuries, the USA and Germany in the 19th century, Japan in the late 19th century, and Korea and Taiwan in the late 20th century (Cimoli et al., 2009).

Empirical studies report conflicting results on the effectiveness of industrial policy. Although there is qualitative evidence indicating that industrial policy has been used in East Asian economies, which have grown rapidly as they changed their industrial structures (Johnson, 1982; Amsden, 1989; Wade, 1990), the impact of industrial policy has often been unverified quantitatively. According to Beason and Weinstein (1996), tariff protection, preferential tax rates, and subsidies did not affect the rate of capital accumulation or total

*An earlier version of this paper was presented at the Conference on New Thinking in Industrial Policy, held in the World Bank, Washington DC, May 22–23, 2012. The author thanks the participants, including J. Lin, J. Stiglitz, and A. Fiszbein, for comments and discussion.

factor productivity (TFP) in Japan from 1955 to 1980. Moreover, nominal tariff was negative and significant to the growth rate of labor productivity and TFP at the sectoral level in Korean industries from 1963 to 1983 (Lee, 1996). Nevertheless, several studies verify the positive contribution of industrial policy. Shin and Lee (2012), using the same period and sectoral data as Lee (2006), find that tariff protection, especially when combined with export market discipline, leads to the growth of export share and revealed comparative advantage (RCA). They also argue that the goal of industrial policy was not productivity at the early stage – as in the 1970s – but output or market share growth. Aghion, Dewatripont, Du, Harrison, and Legros (2011) also find that subsidies widely distributed among Chinese firms have had a positive impact on both TFP and the innovation of new products in the sectors with a high level of competition. Both of these recent studies identify competition or discipline as a common precondition for effective industrial policy.

One way to interpret this diverse outcome is that it might be difficult to verify the average positive impact of industrial policy because the effects tend to appear only in certain conditions, depending upon specific contexts (countries or sectors). Moreover, these studies indicate the significance of the criteria used in assessing the effectiveness of industrial policy. For example, productivity has become an important criterion only since the late 1980s, that is, after the Korean government shifted its policy tools from tariffs to research and development (R&D) subsidies as well as joint R&D; actually, enhanced innovation capabilities led to Korean firms' productivity catch-up with Japanese firms from 1985 to 2005 (Jung and Lee, 2010). Given that structural change in an economy is a long-term process, the idea of adopting different policy tools over time is consistent with the reasoning that industrial policy should deal with the various dimensions of capabilities of firms and industries in the latecomer countries. In other words, different tools are necessary depending on whether the target involves simple operational or production capabilities, investment capabilities, or technological capabilities at the advanced level.

The current paper suggests a capability-based view of industrial policies and recommends specific implementation strategies to build specific capabilities at various stages of economic development. For a developing country, it is critical to enhance its capability to produce and sell products in the international market so that the country may earn foreign currency that it can then use to pay for imports of investment goods. However, the challenging part of this process is increasing that capability. Thus, capability building is the focus of a World Bank study compiled by Chandra (2006). A World Bank (2005) assessment of the reform decade of the 1990s also states that growth entails more than the efficient use of resources, and that growth-oriented action may be needed, for example, in relation to technological catch-up or the encouragement of risk-taking accumulation of capabilities. According to studies on reform in Latin America carried out by ECLAC, macroeconomic stability is not a sufficient condition for long-term growth, which is more closely tied to the dynamics of the production structure (Ocampo, 2005). Lee and Mathews (2010) synthesize capability-based view as the Beijing–Seoul–Tokyo (BeST) consensus, which is commensurate with their firm-level study (Lee and Mathews, 2012) and country-level study of Korea (Lee, 2013b).

The capability-based view of development can be compared with the institution-focused view. The recent literature on economic development has argued on the relative importance of institutions, policies, and geography as determinants of growth. Although more works have been reported in favor of the first factor, that is, institutions (for example Acemoglu, Johnson, & Robinson 2001, 2002; Rodrik et al., 2004), there is also criticism against its relevance, and certain scholars propose that human capital is a more robust determinant (Glaeser et al., 2004). Although institutions are, undoubtedly, a fundamental factor in long-term economic growth, they also have to be formed over the long run by specific policies. Specific policy ideas often precede the legislation embodying the goals. Ocampo (2005) argues that a well-functioning broader institutional context is essential; however, it generally does not play a direct role in bringing about changes in the momentum of growth, and that the latter is more closely related to the dynamics of the production structure. In an econometric study using country panel analysis, Lee and Kim (2009) reveal that institutions and secondary education are significantly related to growth, but only in lower- and lower-middle income countries. According to their study, technological development and higher education are the significant growth factors for upper-middle- and high-income countries, because the levels of institutional development are similar in these countries. This implies that middle-income countries aiming to reach high-income status should start emphasizing their technological capabilities.

This line of thinking brings the issue of technological capabilities into the debate on the middle-income trap. This concept is defined as a situation wherein middle-income countries struggle to remain competitive as low-cost, high-volume production ultimately hinders their transition to high-income status (World Bank, 2010; Yusuf and Nabeshima, 2009). This condition is relevant considering that numerous developing countries have achieved growth for a certain period (usually less than a decade) but are unable to sustain such growth over a longer period (Jones and Olken, 2005; Hausmann et al., 2005). Rodrik (2006) also cites the greater importance of sustaining growth than initiating it. We find more instances in Latin American countries, such as Brazil and Argentina, where growth was more or less stalled during the 1980s and 1990s (Lee and Kim, 2009: Table 1; Paus, 2011). By contrast, several countries moved beyond middle-income status to join the rich-country club. Examples include Korea and Taiwan, whose per capita incomes increased threefold from the 1980s to the 1990s, from original levels similar to those of Latin American countries in the early 1980s. Although a significant volume of the literature on the poverty trap is relevant to low-income countries, there are few empirical studies on how to sustain growth beyond the middle-income level. Even the recent World Bank-sponsored growth commission report and a book by the leader of the commission (Spence, 2011) do not deal with the issue of sustaining growth in developing countries by targeting industries with comparative advantages. However, this issue is gaining increasing attention in a number of recent studies, such as those by Griffith (2011), Ohno (2010), Eichengreen et al. (2011), and Paus (2011).

One might ask why growth beyond the middle-income status is important, or is more important than spurring growth in low-income countries. One answer is that only when some middle-income countries move beyond the stage of producing and exporting low-cost, labor-intensive goods can low-income countries achieve growth and sustain it, thereby attenuating the adding-up problem (Lee, 2013a). The adding-up problem occurs when all the developing countries flood the market with the same goods that they produce well, resulting in a decrease in the relative prices of these goods and lower profits for the concerned sectors (Spence, 2011). From this perspective, it is crucial for China to move beyond its current specialization in low-cost, labor-intensive goods and shift toward manufacturing higher-end ones so that other latecomer countries can avoid the continuing competition with Chinese goods.

Thus, the current paper focuses on industrial policy for middle-income countries. Echoing the argument of Lee (2013a), we argue that the goal of industrial policy for middle-income countries is to promote technology-based specialization, as opposed to traditional trade-based specialization that may be more relevant to low-income countries. The new structural economics of Justin Lin also points out the need for dynamic comparative advantage, suggesting that the latecomers should target the industries with latent comparative advantage or mature industries from the countries that are slightly ahead of them. Although this is a sound practical guideline, a more theoretically grounded criterion is needed. As a more specific, differentiating criterion for targeting technology, this paper suggests a cycle time for technologies based on empirical evidence at the country, sector, and firm levels earlier proposed by Lee (2013a). The proposed guideline is also based on the fact that the successful catching-up countries, such as Korea and Taiwan, have specialized in short-cycle technology-based sectors. This strategy makes sense because in sectors with shorter technology cycle times, existing technologies become obsolete rapidly, and new technologies tend to emerge frequently (that is, more opportunities emerge). Thus, the latecomers do not have to master existing technologies dominated by the incumbent.

In section 4.2.2, the paper introduces the notion of capability failure, which is contrasted with the market and system failures that have also been used as a justification for state activism. We argue that the capability failure is more unique and serious in the context of developing countries, and that industrial policy should aim to cultivate the capabilities of the actors (private firms) in developing countries. Section 4.2.3 discusses the idea that the tools of industrial policy should be different and must change depending upon the stage of development, if not by country; it also presents the technology policy criteria for the middle-income countries, focusing on the cycle time of technologies. By presenting certain examples, section 4.2.4 elaborates on the process of raising the technological capabilities of the firms along the three stages of development and learning. The capability building of the latecomer firms is explained along the three stages of learning: from the license/FDI-based learning, to the learning from contract/joint R&D with an external agent as the teacher/leader, and to the learning from the public–private R&D consortium with the latecomer firm as the main actor. Section 4.2.5 concludes the paper.

4.2.2   Market failure, system failure, and capability failure

A classical argument for government activism, particularly industrial policy, has been made in the context of market failure. The new structural economics of Lin (2012) as well as the initiatives put forward by Cimoli, Dosi, and Stiglitz (2009) argue for the proactive role of the government. Governments are advised to promote infant industries as well as facilitate industrial upgrading and diversification, which are justified by identifying issues of information and coordination failure, as well as external conditions that can be regarded as instances of broadly defined market failure. Knowledge is rightly considered as the least mobile endowment of a country; thus, it is an optimal target area for industrial policy, which is defined as closing the knowledge gap (Greenwald and Stiglitz, 2013). The source of market failure is the fact that knowledge is a public good. Industrial policy is justified due to possible underinvestment in learning when there are flaws in the capital and risk markets, as well as market failure associated with imperfectly competitive industries and a spillover in learning. From this perspective, the actual amount of R&D is often less than the optimal amount that would prevail without market failure. Therefore, government subsidies to support R&D are suggested given the externality involved in the production of knowledge.

Another view that supports a proactive government is the system failure view based on neo-Schumpeterian economics, specifically the concept of the national innovation system of Nelson (1993) and Lundvall (1992). It calls for government activism with a different basis from that of the market failure view. One of its earliest proponents is Metcalfe (2005), whose work suggests the rationale for innovation policy in advanced economies. He argues that the process of innovation depends on the emergence and success of innovation systems connecting the various actors (components) engaged in the process. Then, the need for government activism arises, because effective interaction among the actors in the innovation systems does not exist naturally but has to be constructed, instituted for a purpose. In particular, some scholars (that is, Bergek et al., 2008; Dodgson et al., 2011) observe that system failure often exists where missing or weak connections (and synergies) among actors tend to lead the system to lower performance. Innovation systems consist of firms, universities, public research laboratories, and government and financial institutions. The problems arise due to cognitive distance (Nooteboom, 2009) among these actors and/or tacitness of knowledge, which results in cognition failure. In this situation, the main function of the government is not to promote individual innovation events but to set the framework conditions in which innovation systems can better self-organize across a range of economic activities.

There is a need to reassess the aforementioned views to see whether or not they can be considered as an effective rationale for the degrees and forms of government activism in developing countries, and applicable to their context. For instance, their common and hidden presumption is that the firms and other economic actors are already capable of production and innovation, and that the government must simply try to modify the extent of their activities or promote interaction among them. Let me dwell upon this point.

In the innovation system literature, the system is defined by the components in the boundaries and their interactions. The main focus is on the interaction among the actors, although the availability of knowledgeable or capable actors is also addressed.[1] However, the stark reality in developing countries is that the actors, especially the firms, have extremely weak levels of capability. This is a serious problem because, in the system failure view, the firms are regarded as the leaders in defining the system itself.

Typical market-failure-based justifications of R&D subsidy indicate the positive externality of R&D and its resulting undersupply. In the market failure view, the firms are assumed to be capable of conducting R&D, and their only problem lies in their inability to produce the optimal amount. The reasons for such situation are sought outside the firm, such as in the capital market or risk market, and these are the areas where the government's corrective action is suggested.

However, the reality in a number of developing countries is that private firms are unable to pursue and conduct in-house R&D, which they consider as an uncertain endeavor with uncertain returns. Thus, the problem is not less or more R&D but 'zero' R&D. Figure 4.2.1 illustrates the flat R&D-to-GDP ratio among the middle-income countries, which does not rise proportionally with per capita income. This is a serious condition because middle-income countries are the ones that should start paying more attention to innovation efforts. This information clearly suggests that this is the root of the middle-income trap. Actually, using country panel analysis, Lee and Kim (2009) verify that in transitioning from a middle- to high-income status, one of the constraints faced by countries is R&D effort or innovation capabilities. Thus, weak R&D effort is a critical matter that brings up the various capabilities of firms. In fact, the basic rationale for the market or system failure view is equally valid in the context of both advanced and developing countries. Therefore theory should be developed further to reflect the specificities of developing countries.

R&D expenditure
(% of GDP)

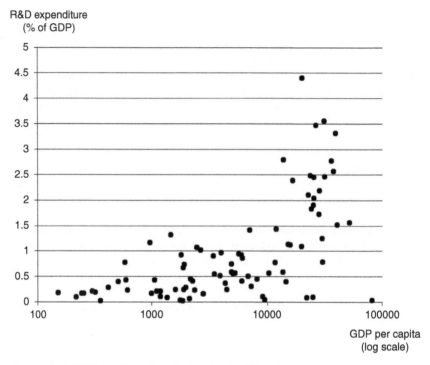

Figure 4.2.1   R&D-to-GDP ratio of countries in different income groups
Note: Drawn by the author using the data from the UNESCO (R&D figures) and World Bank (WDI).

In contrast to the typical argument for government activism based on market failure or system failure, this paper emphasizes "capability failure" as a justification for government activism, and suggests specific ways to raise the capabilities of firms in developing countries. In developing countries where firms have a low R&D capability, a safer way of doing business is to buy or borrow external technologies or production facilities, as well as to specialize in less technical methods or assembly manufacturing. To move beyond such states, effective forms of government activism had better include not the simple provision of R&D funds but various ways to cultivate R&D capability itself. An innovation survey on Thailand conducted by Chaminade et al. (2012) identifies one related problem, that is, the tendency of government policy to be limited only to tax incentives without implementing explicit measures to encourage Thai firms to take on greater risk in innovation. More effective and alternative forms of intervention may include the transfer of R&D outcomes performed by public research institutes and a public-private R&D consortium, which gained success in Korea and Taiwan.[2]

Such direct intervention is important because learning failure happens not only due to the fact that knowledge is a public good but also because there has been no opportunity for effective learning due to historically inherited conditions or policy failure. Seen from this angle, industrial policy is not about choosing winners but about choosing good students and matching them with good teachers or bringing them to good schools. Good schools may be in the form of licensing-based learning (of tacit knowledge) or public–private joint R&D projects, in which direct and cooperative learning take place. By contrast, banks that merely supply R&D money might not serve as good schools. Continuing with this analogy, the market failure view can be expressed as, "I will pay for your school so that you may take more classes," whereas the system failure may be expressed as, "Go to school and make more friends." However, both views pay insufficient attention to such factors as the initial aptitude of students, what is taught to them in schools, who the teachers are, and how they teach their students. In the capability view, these aspects are crucial to a successful industrial policy. Thus, the capability failure view essentially believes in the importance of raising the level of capabilities of the firms (students) and the various learning methods to be provided over the dynamic course of learning, not only in the elementary schools but also in the secondary and tertiary institutions. In sum, we need both tuition fees (R&D money) and good friends (linkages to other components in the system) in schools, but the critical factors are the student himself, a good curriculum, a knowledgeable teacher, and an effective teaching method. Table 4.2.1 summarizes these arguments.

Table 4.2.1   The three types of failure

	Market failure	**System failure**	**Capability failure**
Focus	Market institutions	Interaction among actors	Actors (firms)
Source	Knowledge as public good	Cognition failure from tacitness of knowledge	historically given; No learning opportunity
Example problem	Sub-optimal R&D	Lower R&D effects	No R&D
Solutions	R&D subsidies	Reducing cognitive distance	Access to knowledge and help in learning
School Analogy	Tuition support	Making more friends	Targeting student learning
Relevance	Developing and advanced countries	Developing and advanced countries	More unique to developing countries

Source: The author.

4.2.3   From industrial policy to technology policy: from low- to middle-income countries

4.2.3.1   The need for a dynamic shift of policy tools

Although economic development is a lengthy dynamic process that hinges on the specificities of the countries concerned, literature has not paid sufficient attention to the simple requirement of having corresponding policy tools for countries at different stages of development. An example is the recent debate on the relative importance of policies, institutions, and geography. Most of the studies on this subject search for one universal determinant of economic growth regardless of the stage of development. The opposite extreme is the argument presented by Rodrik and other scholars who emphasize the importance of identifying the binding constraints for each country (Rodrik, 2006; Hausmann et al., 2008).

An ideal compromise may come in the form of stage- or group-specific factors for economic growth that are neither universal nor country-specific. This last view is consistent with Lin's (2012) concept of new structural economics, which states that development policy should consider structural differences between developed and developing countries. One similar study is that of Lee and Kim (2009), which finds that technological development and higher education are more effective in generating growth for upper middle- and high-income countries, whereas secondary education and political institutions seem important for lower-income countries.

If we extend this logic to industrial policy, we realize that the tools of such policy should also depend on the stage of development, if not on the country itself. The traditional industrial policy tools come in the form of infant industry protection by tariffs or undervaluation of local currencies. However, if we consider industrial development as a long-term process that takes over 10 or 20 years, it is natural for the tools of policy to change over the course of economic growth. Such a dynamic view of industrial policy is warranted, because the capability level of the beneficiaries of such intervention would change over time as well.

Let us consider the example of industrial policy in Korea. Shin and Lee (2012) report that tariffs and other forms of protection led to export and output expansion through fixed investment during the early period (that is, the 1970s and 1980s), whereas Jung and Lee (2010) find that for a later period (that is, from the mid-1980s to 2005), R&D investment stimulated by tax exemptions led to productivity growth. These two studies find that for both periods, the disciplinary impact of export orientation is significant, because it pushed the rents associated with tariffs (earlier period) and with an oligopolistic market structure (late period) used for fixed (earlier period) and R&D investments (later period), respectively. This finding suggests that the form of government activism in Korea has evolved from traditional industrial policy (that is, trade policy) to technology policy (R&D policy).

Such a dynamic shift in policy tools is not simply imposed by the government but also reflects the available and/or desired level of firm capabilities that have been changing over time. Although Korea has grown fast with exports of labor-intensive and low-end goods, this growth strategy already reached its peaks by the mid-1980s. Around that time, Korea saw an increase in its own wage rate, which coincided with the emergence of lower-wage countries that competed against it in the world market. Given Korean firms' realization of the need to upgrade to higher-end or value-added goods, they began, for the first time, to establish in-house R&D centers, after which the tools for industrial policy switched toward tax exemption on R&D (Lee, 2013b; Lee and Kim, 2010). Another new and important form of state activism comes in the form of a policy to target directly the learning process of firms by involving them in the public–private R&D consortium. One prime example is the local import-substituting development of telephone switches (TDX) that occurred in the 1980s (Lee, Mani, and Mu, 2012).

The Korean example indicates a dynamic shift in the form of government activism from the traditional industrial policy (tariffs and undervaluation) in the early stage of development, to technology policy (R&D subsidies and P-P R&D consortium) in the later stages. This dynamic shift is required for a developing country to evolve from a low-income to a middle-income status, and eventually move on up to a higher-income status. In the mid-1980s, Korea reached the level of a middle-income country with per capita GDP of approximately US$1,673 in nominal terms and US$3,223 in 2000 dollar terms (Lee and Kim, 2009: Table 1). It can be argued that without such a shift, any country may be stuck in the so-called middle-income trap, in which it struggles to remain competitive as a site for low-cost, high-volume production (World Bank, 2010; Yusuf and Nabeshima, 2009). One cause of the middle-income trap is the adding-up problem that occurs when all the developing countries flood the market with the similar goods that they tend to produce well (Spence, 2011).

Then, the connection between the two problems of the middle-income trap and adding-up becomes clearer. In other words, only when more successful middle-income countries advance from selling low-end goods to producing and selling higher-value-added or high-end goods can there be room for less successful or low-income countries to continue selling low-end goods and gain profit from it (Lee, 2013a). From this perspective, it is extremely important for China to move beyond its current specialization in low-cost labor-intensive goods to higher-end goods. Such succession has happened in Asia, with the Korean and Taiwanese taking over the void left by the Japanese. Subsequently, as Korea and Taiwan moved further ahead, the next-tier countries occupied the positions they left.

Table 4.2.2 summarizes the preceding discussion. Different tools of industrial policy are suggested for lower- and middle-income countries. For the former, traditional tools such as tariffs, the undervaluation of currencies, and

Table 4.2.2   Dynamics of industrial policy from low- to middle-income and beyond the middle-income trap

Stages	Low or lower-middle income	Upper-middle income toward high income
Policy tools	Industrial policy: (tariffs, undervaluation of currency, entry control)	Technology policy (public-private R&D consortium, R&D subsidies, standardization policy)
Access to External/ Foreign knowledge	FDI, OEM/ Assembly work/ Licensing	Collaboration with public research labs and universities, Overseas R&D outposts, International M&As, contracted R&D (based on in-house R&D efforts)
Type of specialization	Trade specialization	Technology specialization
Criterion of Specialization	Labor or resource-intensive industries	Short cycle/emerging technologies
End goal	Competitive export industries	Indigenous knowledge creation and diffusion
Background theory	Product life cycle (inheriting)	Catch-up cycle (leapfrogging)

Source: The author.

entry control into sectors are suggested; for the latter, technology policy tools, such as R&D subsidies, public–private R&D cooperation and standard policies, are recommended. Corresponding to these tools, the channels of access to foreign or external knowledge from the perspective of local firms are listed herein (Lee, 2005). Lower-income groups learn from FDI, OEM/assembly arrangement and licensing, whereas middle-income groups benefit from collaboration with public research labs and universities, overseas R&D outposts, international mergers and acquisitions (M&As) and contracted R&D, all of which should be combined with in-house R&D efforts. Given these channels, the goal of lower-income groups must be to establish competitive export industries, whereas middle-income groups must focus on the consolidation of a local basis for knowledge creation and diffusion.

4.2.3.2   Cycle time of technologies as a criterion for technology targeting

A remaining concern is the nature and criterion of specialization, which is one of the classical issues in industrial policy. There is an established answer for the low-income groups: specialization based on initial endowments, such as labor and natural resources or comparative advantages associated with resource endowments (Lin, 2012). These industries usually produce low-value-added or low-end goods in the global division of labor, which essentially resembles trade-based specialization.

Now, an intriguing issue is identifying the criterion of specialization that can be applied to the group of middle-income countries that strive to upgrade their industrial structure from low to higher value added. Value added per worker or labor productivity might be a criterion, but it is too general and there are too many sectors with similar levels of labor productivity. Lin's structural economics points out the need for dynamic comparative advantage, suggesting that latecomers should target the industries with latent comparative advantage or mature industries from the countries slightly ahead of them. Nevertheless, though this is a good practical guideline, we still need a more theoretically grounded criterion, or a more specific, differentiating criterion for middle- or higher-income countries attempting to mobilize new tools of technology policy. For example, suppose that a country is ready to form a private–public R&D consortium to develop certain technologies or products. In this case, one thorny issue is identifying which technologies or products to target. Korea or Taiwan actually faced this problem in the mid-1980s. Let us say that two possible choices are pharmaceuticals or semiconductors. Both types of products have a higher value-added component than the apparel or calculators these countries produced and exported in the 1970s.

This question of specialization has also been raised in Greenwald and Stiglitz (2013) as the question of which country endowments determine its comparative advantage when a country is advised to follow its (current or latent) comparative advantages. Greenwald and Stiglitz (2013) also suggest that a society's learning capacity is influenced by its knowledge after discarding capital, skilled labor, and even institutions that tend to be mobile. This criterion makes sense because learning capacity eventually determines a country's long-term competitiveness. The next question, then, is which sectors would have a greater degree of learning capacity.

Allow me to suggest the cycle time of technology as a criterion for the specialization of middle-income countries. Conceptually, the length of cycle time of technologies refers to the speed by which technologies change or become obsolete over time, causing new technologies to emerge more often. In the literature (for example, Jaffe and Trajtenberg, 2002), the cycle time of technologies is measured by the mean citation lag, which is the time difference between the application year of the *citing* patents and that of the *cited* patents. A long cycle time indicates greater importance of old knowledge, hence the greater need for latecomers to study such knowledge. When knowledge in the field changes quickly (that is, essentially meaning of short cycle time), the disadvantages for the latecomer might not be significant. Thus, it is advantageous for qualified latecomers to target and specialize in these sectors.

Technologies based on short cycle time possess two key properties, namely, the sector has less reliance on existing technologies, and it have a greater opportunity for the continued emergence of new technologies. New opportunities indicate more growth prospects, and less reliance on existing technologies may lead to the faster localization of a knowledge creation mechanism. In this sense, these sectors would be those with higher learning capacities as emphasized by Greenwald and Stiglitz (2013). Additionally, this criterion satisfies the condition of viable profitability and competitiveness. This is because it indicates lower entry barriers and the possibility of higher profitability brought about by fewer collisions with advanced countries' technologies, less royalty payments, and even first- or fast-mover advantages or product differentiation. If we apply this criterion to the issue of choice over two sectors, semiconductors with shorter cycle time should be chosen rather than pharmaceuticals that correspond to longer cycle technologies. Although this is an *ex post* judgment, one can say that if Korea or Taiwan decided to target the pharmaceuticals sector in their industrial policy, either country would not have been as successful as it is now.

The validity of this argument and the criterion for specialization has been verified by extensive econometric analysis conducted by Lee (2013a) at the firm, sector, and country levels. The findings are as follows. First, at the firm-level comparative analysis of Korean and American firms, the former tend to specialize in technologies based on short cycle time, which are linked to higher profitability. At the sector level, the question was identification of the fields in which technological catch-up may or may not occur, as well as the factors that influence the speed of technological catch-up. It was found that this occurs in the fields with shorter cycle times, and that the advanced countries tend to have a higher share in long-cycle technology-based sectors. At the country level, it was found that the successful catching-up countries, such as Korea, Taiwan, Hong Kong and Singapore, used to have longer or similar cycle time technologies as the high- and other middle-income countries until the mid-1980s. However, the cycle times of their patent portfolios began to shorten significantly since then. Country panel analysis confirms that specialization in technologies with shorter cycle times is positively related to economic growth in the successful catching-up economies of Asia, whereas growth is associated with specialization in technologies with long cycle times in both high- and other middle-income countries (excluding the Asian four).

4.2.4   How to enhance the capabilities of firms in developing countries

This section focuses on the issue of how to move away from long-cycle to short-cycle technology-based sectors, or from the low value-added segment to the higher value-added segment in the same industries. Such a transition does not occur automatically even if a country is open to trade and FDI. Rather, it always involves deliberate learning and risk taking by companies and other public actors, combined with the exogenously open windows of opportunity. Short-cycle technology-based sectors matter because these are where new opportunities emerge more frequently and where business activities take place with lower entry barriers. The market mechanism serves not as a triggering factor but as a facilitating factor that stimulates risk-taking and rewards the successful actors.

For example, Taiwan's successful settling down with shorter-cycle technology-based sectors or higher value-added industry segments would have taken a longer time had there been no public–private R&D cooperation, the first successful example of which is the consortium to develop laptop computers (Mathews, 2002). However, we should note that there were several attempts and failures prior to this achievement. Such private–private joint effort does not guarantee immediate success, but is the only way out of the old specialization in longer-cycle technology-based sectors, and, hence, out of the middle-income trap. In Korean history, the first case of a successful public–private R&D consortium was the development of digital telephone switches. This marked the beginning of the country's emergence as a leader in telecommunication and IT devices, because that success was the source of learning and confidence that, in turn, led to further public–private cooperation in the production of memory chips, mobile phones, and digital TVs. With this series of public–private R&D collaborations to enter new industries, Korea gradually reduced its reliance on longer-cycle technology-based industries that produce such goods as apparel, textiles, processed sugar, radios, cookers, ovens, refrigerators, and other consumer products.

The following section describes the three-step process of entering and specializing in shorter-cycle technology-based sectors.[3]

4.2.4.1 Licensing/transfer/FDI-based learning to build initial absorptive capacity

Since the publication of the influential article by Cohen and Levinthal (1990), absorptive capacity has come to be recognized as one of the major binding constraints of economic development of the latecomers. Specifically in the case of Korea, scholars have emphasized the importance of absorptive capacity that has enabled companies to learn and assimilate the inflow of external knowledge (Evenson and Westphal, 1995; Pack, 1992; Kim and Dahlman, 1992). Efforts to build up such capacity should focus on not only enhancing the level of generic human capital but also providing learning opportunities for workers in private firms. The Korean experience verifies this point.

In the 1960s, when Korea began to modernize with export drives, its human capital base was poor: in 1965, enrolment rates in the primary, secondary, and tertiary schools were 29.6 percent, 10.9 percent and a mere 2.6 percent, respectively. Thus, the main emphasis was on increasing the general level of human capital, so that by the mid-1970s, there was considerable improvement compared with the previous decade. In 1975, primary school enrolment rose to 106.86 percent and those for secondary and tertiary schools were 56.35 percent and 6.9 percent, respectively (World Bank, 2005).

The other aspect of enhancing absorptive capacity was increasing the imports of technology embodied in equipment, combined with training to acquire the know-how and skills needed to operate the imported facilities. Korean firms, especially during the 1960s and 1970s, chose to acquire know-how (tacit knowledge) that could help them construct and operate manufacturing facilities with which they were initially unfamiliar (Chung and Lee, 2011). The typical know-how bundle consisted of technological contents in printed form as well as related training and services provided on site by expatriate engineers. Korean engineers were occasionally sent to the transferor's firm to learn the implementation process. According to Chung and Lee (2011), the technology inclusive of patent rights would come later, when Koreans already gained better capabilities to decipher the codified contents of the patents.

Chung and Lee (2011) show through firm-level data on know-how licensing that Korean firms actually went through a lengthy period of learning, assimilating, and adapting foreign technology in the 1970s before beginning to conduct in-house R&D in the mid-1980s. Specifically, foreign technology flowed into Korea in three forms: licensing contract of know-how, patented know-how, and licensing of patented technology. Chung and Lee (2011), based on the cases of the leading Korean firms, show the phases of foreign technology acquisition, leading to in-house R&D and own patent applications. In the case of LG Electronics, it was in 1969 (the year of its establishment) that it contracted for know-how licensing, followed by know-how plus patents, and then patent-only licensing. It first recorded its R&D expenditure in its financial statement for 1976, and filed for patent applications in 1978. This seems to be the typical sequence followed by Korean companies although there have been certain variations.

Another important means by which to enhance absorptive capacity is to set up public research institutes that can conduct R&D and problem-focused development, and then transfer the outcome to the private sector. For example, in the late 1960s, the Korean government recognized the need for advanced training for scientists and engineers in preparation for the development of indigenous technologies. In 1972, the government established a new graduate school of engineering and applied sciences, the Korea Advanced Institute of Science (KAIS), which was later renamed the Korea Advanced Institute of Science and Technology (KAIST). This academic institution has served as a vital scientific and technological institute that ensures, with adequate research funding, excellent education for the best minds of Korea.

Finally, establishing joint ventures with foreign partners or working in an OEM assembly arrangement with foreign firms is also an effective channel for learning basic operational skills and production technologies (Hobday, 2005). Attracting FDI is one of the best strategies to guarantee learning and access to knowledge. However, it may not be reliable for longer-term purposes, and there are certain conditions that must be met, including local controllership and local content requirements. Amsden and Chu (2003) state that technological catch-up requires the use of assets related to project execution, product engineering, and a form of R&D that straddles applied research and exploratory development. If such assets are to be accumulated at all, the responsible party tends to be a nationally owned organization. By its nature, FDI firms have no reason or incentive to develop their own development capabilities in host countries, because these reside in the mother companies abroad. Thus, ownership matters at least in R&D, and FDI might not be effective as a device with which to learn higher-tier capabilities (e.g., R&D). In their early days, many Korean chaebols had FDI or OEM relationships with foreign MNCs. According to Lee and He (2009), during its early days, Samsung Electronics was a joint venture with the Japanese firm, Sanyo, from which the Korean company – having no prior experience in the electronics industry – acquired know-how and technologies. Meanwhile, Hyundai Motors was an OEM assembler for the US-based Ford, although it soon broke up with the latter. Taiwan's path from OEM to OBM via ODM also involved a great deal of interaction with foreign firms in FDI.

4.2.4.2   Learning R&D capabilities in in-house R&D and as a co-R&D partner

Once a firm builds a certain level of absorptive capacity, it must establish and initiate its own in-house R&D center. Independent R&D efforts are required because foreign firms would become increasingly reluctant to grant technology licenses to the rising latecomer firms, especially when the latter attempt to enter the skill-intensive markets dominated by the advanced countries. Thus, investment in R&D is required not only for the further absorption of advanced technology, but also for the development of the latecomers' own technological capabilities. Developing in-house R&D capabilities is critical also because the initial success leads to an increase in local wage rates, resulting in losing competitiveness compared to other economies offering cheaper costs or wages (Lee and Mathews, 2012).

With the establishment of in-house R&D labs, the firms at this stage have to explore more diverse channels of learning and access to foreign knowledge. The new alternatives include co-development contracts with foreign R&D specialist firms and/or with public R&D institutes, gaining mastery of the existing literature, setting up overseas R&D outposts, and initiating international M&As. For example, it was also from the early 1990s that a small number of Korean firms began to establish overseas R&D posts, mainly to obtain easier and faster access to foreign technology that used to be difficult to acquire through licensing. These overseas posts also served as a window on recent trends in technological development (OECD, 1996).

Arranging access to foreign knowledge and trying new modes of learning is critical, because isolated in-house R&D efforts are often insufficient to build indigenous R&D capabilities. In this regard, allow me to elaborate on the two important modes of new learning at this stage: (1) co-development contracts with foreign/external R&D specialist agencies or firms, and (2) participation in a public–private R&D consortium. In both cases, the best targets for R&D are those industries or technologies that are relatively mature, but which the latecomer economies are importing or buying at monopoly prices from foreign companies. In this situation, import-substitution targeting involves taking the rents away from the foreign companies and giving them to the local companies. In this scheme, local efforts face fewer uncertainties or risks, because the targeted technologies are often mature ones that are not impossible to emulate through the concerted effort of the local R&D consortium. One reason that could hinder targeting is the uncertainty involved in making the right choices in industries or technologies. For example, no one can tell which industries or technologies will prosper in a particular country. This concern makes more sense in the context of developed countries, where firms at the forefront of technologies face greater uncertainties. In the context of the latecomers who are below the frontier, a ready justification for targeting industries exists.

A good example of the first mode (co-development) is the case of Hyundai Motors of Korea. The main business of the Hyundai group used to be construction, a long-cycle technology-based sector. Hyundai entered the shorter-cycle business of automobiles in the early 1970s as an assembly maker for Ford, the US car manufacturer. Such a story is common in developing countries. However, Hyundai Motors and Korea's current status as stronghold of the automobile business would not have been possible without the company's brave decision to cut its ties with Ford and to sell its own brand of automobiles equipped with its own engines. Hyundai then became a joint venture with the Japanese car maker, Mitsubishi, wherein the Japanese company provided engines and other key components, while Hyundai merely assembled them. In that partnership, Hyundai was a licensed producer but not an OEM producer, as it used its own brand in the local and export markets. However, when Hyundai wanted to develop its own engines, Mitsubishi (which held 20 percent of the equity) refused to teach the former how to design and produce these engines on its own. Most developing country businessmen would have given up at that point, but Hyundai's founding chairman, Chung Ju-yung, did not. He decided to spend an enormous amount of money on R&D, with efforts focused on engine development.[4] Fortunately, Hyundai was then able to gain access to the external knowledge of specialized R&D firms, such as Ricardo in England. The process was not easy; Ricardo did not just provide an engine design. It was basically a co-development of a completely new design by the two companies. In fact, the partners had to try more than 1,000 prototypes until they finally succeeded seven years after the project was launched in 1984 (Lee and Lim, 2001).

The second mode, participation in a public–private R&D consortium, can also be an effective school for private firms when their capability is low. Given their low R&D capabilities, the private firms cannot take the lead in the consortium, in which public research agencies play the key R&D roles and teach and transfer the outcomes to participating private firms. We can find many examples of this process from Korea, Taiwan, and other catching-up countries.

A noteworthy example would be the government-led R&D consortia in the telecommunication equipment industry, specifically the accompanying local development of telephone switches. This led to the successful localization of telephone switches in the 1980s and 1990s in several latecomer countries, including China, Korea, India, and Brazil (Lee, Mani, and Mu, 2012). Most of the developing countries used to have serious telephone service bottlenecks in the 1970s and 1980s; they had neither their own telecommunication manufacturing equipment industry nor their own R&D program. As a result, they used to import expensive equipment and related technologies, and local technicians merely installed foreign switching systems into the country's domestic telephone networks. With industrial and commercial bases developing rapidly – along with population growth – a number of countries decided to build their own manufacturing capabilities.

Starting with Brazil in the 1970s, followed by Korea and India in the mid-1980s, and finally by China toward the late 1980s, all of these countries crafted a state-led system of innovation in the telecommunication equipment industry, with a government research institute at the core. The research institute developed more or less "indigenous" digital telephone switches that were then licensed to public and private domestic enterprises. In these four countries, a common pattern in the indigenous development of digital switches was the tripartite R&D consortium among the government research institutes (GRIs) in charge of R&D functions, state-owned enterprises (SOEs) or the ministry in charge of financing and coordination, and private companies in charge of manufacturing at the initial or later stages. However, the subsequent waves of industry privatization and market liberalization in Brazil and India versus the consistent infant industry protection in Korea and China differentiated the trajectory of the industries in these four countries (Lee, Mani, and Mu, 2012). At one extreme, the indigenous manufacturers of China and Korea took over from the importers and MNCs. Their enhanced capabilities in wired telecommunication, which were accumulated over the preceding decades, led to the growth of indigenous capabilities in wireless telecommunication as well. At the other extreme, Brazil and India have increasingly become net importers of telecom equipment, and their industries are now dominated by affiliates of the MNCs.

As noted by 이것이 Lee and Mathews (2012), examples from Taiwan include the cases of calculator and laptop PC production. The calculator case is an example of the acquisition of more fundamental design capability or the basic design platform, which is made possible with the help of a government entity such as the Industrial Technology Research Institute (ITRI). Another example is the public-private R&D consortium to develop laptop PCs from 1990 to 1991 (Mathews, 2002). This consortium developed a common mechanical architecture for a prototype that could easily translate into a series of mass-produced standardized components. The consortium represented an industry watershed, and even after several failed attempts, it succeeded in establishing new "fast follower" industries in Taiwan.

4.2.4.3   Final stage of learning: leapfrogging into shorter-cycle sectors

The final stage is leapfrogging, in which the latecomers do not aim to imitate the existing products or plants, but explore ways to develop emerging products in short-cycle technologies. A Korean example is digital TV development, which can be regarded as the decisive and final watershed that enabled Korea to begin taking over Japan in the TV business. An example from China would be its recent move toward electric-engined cars and the use of solar power. In these areas, there are no products to imitate from the latecomers' point of view; instead, the advanced and latecomer countries enter the market at the same time. If the former latecomers succeed first, there would be a strong momentum for them to surpass the middle-income group and join the rich country club. In this leapfrogging endeavor, the public–private R&D consortium takes a more vital role given that the risk involved is huge and different. Furthermore, coordinated initiatives for exclusive standards and incentives for early adopters would be important in reducing the risk faced by the weak initial market.

Although both the second and third stages involve the public–private R&D consortium, there is a marked difference between the two. In the third stage, private firms take the lead over the public labs in conducting R&D jointly, whereas in the second stage, public research labs are mainly in charge of R&D, with the private actors doing the manufacturing. Thus, in the final stage of the R&D consortium, the role of public research arms is to monitor the trend of technologies as well as to provide information and knowledge about the choice of proper technology standards and the identification of suitable foreign partners in collaborative development. Examples of the foreign partner include Qualcomm for mobile phone development and Zenith for digital TV development. Furthermore, a foreign company usually has a different role. In the second stage, the foreign company is the direct teacher in the co-development contract; however, in the final stage, it becomes the supplier of source technology to be commercialized by the latecomer firms or their consortium. This has been case with Korea's entry into the mobile phone or digital TV market (Lee et al., 2005). In terms of relationships with foreign actors, the final stage features horizontal collaboration or alliance based on complementary assets. Some Korean firms (for example, Samsung) have reached this stage, and are now engaged with Intel, Sony, Toshiba, and Microsoft in diverse modes of alliances.

In light of the above, the success probability of leapfrogging may be higher when a new techno-economic paradigm or a new generation of technologies begins to emerge. Perez and Soete (1988) and Freeman and Soete (1997) observe that some latecomers may be able to leapfrog older versions of technology, bypass heavy investments in previous technology systems, and jump on new technologies to take over the market from the incumbent firms or countries. This leapfrogging strategy makes more sense at the time of a paradigm shift, because every country or firm is a beginner in using the new techno-economic paradigm, and the entry barriers tend to be low. Furthermore, the so-called winner's trap may operate in the sense that the incumbent tends to ignore new technologies and continue to use the existing dominant technologies until it exhausts its sunk investment in the existing facility. The concept of leapfrogging is consistent with the idea of technological discontinuity proposed by Anderson and Tushman (1990, 1986) that competence-destroying discontinuity may lead to the emergence of new entrants.

Korea's catch-up with Japan in the development of high-definition TVs (HDTVs) would not have been successful if Korean electronics companies, such as Samsung and LG, had not targeted the emerging digital technology-based products more aggressively than Japanese companies that opted to continue manufacturing the dominant analogue products.[5] In the late 1980s the Japanese firms developed, for the first time, analogue-based HDTV, and suggested that Korean companies follow new technologies and products by learning from them. Initially, the Korean companies considered going in that direction as they used to do in the 1970s and 1980s. Instead, they decided to try a leapfrogging strategy of developing an alternative and emerging technology, that is, producing digital technology-based HDTVs. These companies succeeded by forming the public–private R&D consortium, which marked the beginning of the Korean hegemony in the global display market previously dominated by Japan. Without such risk-taking and leapfrogging strategies, Korean catch-up with Japan would have taken much longer or might have never happened.

Leapfrogging is more likely to happen when there are more frequent changes in technologies or generation changes in products, and when there are certain technological sectors with such features. As argued, such features are closely linked with the length of the cycle time of technologies, as they indicate the speed with which technologies change or become obsolete over time, paving the way for the continued emergence of new technologies. We can reason that it is advantageous for qualified latecomers to target and specialize in such sectors. Although this is considered a risky venture, it would prove to be a logical one because the latecomers do not have to rely substantially on the existing technologies dominated by the incumbents;

moreover, there are always more growth opportunities associated with ever-emerging technologies.

Finally, we should note the importance of carefully handling the risks involved in opting to implement the leapfrogging strategy. As Lee et al. (2005) explain, one of the biggest risks is choosing the right technologies or standard in the *ex post* sense. In the competition for standard setting and market creation, the role of the government is to facilitate the adoption of specific standards, thereby influencing the formation of markets at the right time. In general, when the involved target is in the area of information or another emerging technology, the critical function of standard setting should be emphasized. Aiming to achieve isolated development without consideration for standards might lead to a failure of the entire project. In a standard setting, collaboration and partnership with rivals or suppliers of complementary products are essential. Another key factor is determining who creates and reaches the market first, given the fact that market size determines the success or failure of one standard in relation to another.

4.2.4.4   Summary of the process[6]

This section summarizes the entire process of moving from longer-cycle to shorter-cycle technology-based sectors.

Let us suppose an initial stage, in which the latecomer countries tend to specialize in longer-cycle technology-based sectors or in the low-end segment of the relatively short-cycle technology-based sectors. An example of longer-cycle technology-based sectors is textile products. An example of the low-end or low value-added segment of the shorter-cycle technology-based sectors is the OEM- or FDI-based assembly-type products in consumer electronics or automobiles. These arrangements are typical of low-income or several middle-income countries. Although the longer-term prospect of this model is somewhat uncertain, it tends to promote economic growth, which is sometimes accompanied by protectionist measures in the form of tariffs and undervaluation of local currencies.

At this stage, the goal of industrial policy is to prioritize job creation and output growth rather than technological learning. Thus, policy tools often include tariffs and undervaluation of currencies that are less sector-specific or more horizontal than vertical tools, such as targeting certain technologies in the form of specific R&D grants or projects. Other forms of horizontal intervention are needed in the areas of hard infrastructure (for example, transportation, energy, and communication), although these would not be classified as industrial policy in a narrow sense. If any degree of specialization is needed, the traditional criterion of comparative advantage along with resource endowments would suffice.

When a country reaches middle-income status, it would need greater sector-specific or vertical intervention because it must now identify its niche between low- and high-income countries, with limited options than before.

At this stage, industrial policy becomes less concerned with job creation but more focused on the creation of or entry into new industries to upgrade the overall industrial structure.

This paper suggests short-cycle technology-based sectors as a niche for latecomers. Although this criterion does not guarantee success in the deterministic sense, it is more likely to lead to success under certain conditions. In other words, one critical factor that must be considered is how to break into shorter-cycle technology-based products or into the higher value-added segment of the existing short-cycle technology-based sectors. This transition involves moving from the license-based production of consumer products to their own design (IPRs)-based production. Good targets for such an entry are those products that the latecomers were unable to manufacture but had to import at higher prices due to their economic significance. For example, for Nigeria and Cameroon, it as crude oil without refining it for higher value-added quality, the target should be to build an oil refinery in their respective countries. The task is not impossible given that the technology needed to build an oil refinery is old and mature and is, therefore, easily available at cost. Its nature is similar to Korea's decision to build its own steel industry in the early 1970s because it did not want to pay higher prices for steel products to be used by local steel-consuming industries, and instead wanted to promote products such as automobiles and ships. A recent example is China's move to target and develop high-speed trains as a latecomer. As a large nation, China needs such a transportation system, and it would incur substantial costs if it would continue to rely on foreign technology rather produce its own trains.

In terms of policy tools, this indigenous endeavor tends to involve R&D grants and collaboration with public or foreign partners, combined with infant industry protection in the form of sector-specific tariffs and credits or public procurement. By contrast, undervaluation of currencies would not be effective, because it is not discriminatory enough. In other words, it is now time to look for sectors in which to invest the rents earned through undervaluation in the preceding stage.

The final stage of leapfrogging involves public–private R&D efforts that target emerging, rather than existing, technologies. In this case, the role of the government and public labs is to share the risk involved in the choice of technologies and to promote the initial markets. Specifically, coordinated initiatives on exclusive standards and incentives for early adopters would be essential in reducing the risk faced by the weak initial market.

Throughout the stages of leapfrogging, it is necessary for the latecomers to gain access to a foreign knowledge base, without which their endeavors would be more difficult and are likely to fail. The latecomers can and should utilize diverse access channels, such as tacit knowledge held by specialized R&D firms or individual scientists or engineers in universities in the form of contracts, reverse brain drains, and/or overseas R&D outposts (Lee, 2005).

To imitate existing product designs or concepts, the latecomer firms may have to rely on the memory of those who are previously involved in the R&D projects of the forerunning companies. Of course, the latecomers also have to rely on explicit knowledge in the form of licensing, literature, or other forms of public knowledge. The idea that the dynamic process of learning capabilities requires matching with different teachers (learning sources) is also a key aspect of the capability-based view of industrial policy.

4.2.5   Summary and concluding remarks

This paper began with a theoretical distinction of market, system, and capability failure as a justification for industrial policy. Although these concepts have varying degrees of relevance in different contexts, this paper argues that capability failure is the most serious and unique problem in the context of developing countries compared with developed economies. This paper also identifies failure of capability, especially technological capability, as the source of the middle-income trap faced by many developing countries as they attempt to upgrade to higher value-added industries or segments. As a solution to this problem, this paper proposes technology-based specialization and elaborates on how to build the necessary capability.

In the literature, a low-income country is advised to follow trade-based specialization to exploit the comparative advantages associated with its natural resources. In this manner, such countries can command international competitiveness in certain industries, which are typically inherited from higher-income countries. This process is predicted by the product life-cycle theory (Vernon, 1966). Along this line, low-income countries may grow to reach middle-income status. However, the medium-term risk to the initial comparative advantage of industries operating in these countries is associated with wage rate increases in the labor-intensive industries that are dependent on low wages. By comparison, new and cheaper labor sites in next-tier countries are always at hand, ready to emerge and assume previously occupied by their predecessors in the global value chain. Thus, so-far successful latecomers may be falling into the middle-income trap associated with the so-called adding-up problem. Thus, a long-term challenge for low-income countries is to move to higher value-added activities in the same industries and/or gain entry to newly emerging industries.

For a developing country to go beyond the middle-income stage, this paper suggests the implementation of technological specialization in shorter-cycle or emerging technologies, or finding an upgraded niche in a new value segment in the current industries. The empirical analysis in the work of Lee (2013a) shows that the successful catching-up economies and their firms have specialized in short-cycle technologies, thereby promoting a higher degree of localization of knowledge diffusion and creation. This strategy has also allowed the successful catching-up countries to upgrade further based on their indigenous capabilities. This strategy makes sense due to the fact that in sectors with shorter technology cycle times, new technologies emerge frequently and existing ones become obsolete quickly. Thus, the latecomers do not have to master existing technologies dominated by the incumbent. In fact, advanced countries tend to be more active in sectors with longer cycle times. A complementary relationship also exists between specialization in short-cycle technologies and localization of the knowledge creation mechanism, because using short-cycle technologies means relying less on existing technologies dominated by incumbent advanced countries.

This paper suggests an implementation strategy to facilitate the transition from trade-based specialization to technology specialization. The goal is to acquire technological and design capabilities based on a combination of acquired external knowledge and in-house R&D efforts. Three stages are described herein. The first stage involves the assimilation of foreign technology (mostly operational skills and production technology) and know-how (through licensing, OEM or FDI arrangements) or technology transfer from public research agencies. In the second stage, the learning and access channels change to co-development contracts and public–private consortia once the latecomer firms establish their own in-house R&D labs as a physical basis for more indigenous learning. In this stage, the R&D target can be mature segments in the short-cycle technology sectors, which translate into fewer uncertainties in terms of feasibility and market potential. The varied experiences in the production of telephone switches in China, India, Brazil, and Korea comprise the prime example. The final stage of learning is the more ambitious strategy of leapfrogging to emerging technologies, with digital TV development in Korea or indigenous 3G wireless standard development in China as the examples. When technological specialization involves leapfrogging, two kinds of risk may be involved: whether or not the countries are making a right choice over technologies or standards, and whether or not there is an initial market for these technologies. Thus, gaining entry into new, emerging industries must involve government assistance in the form of technological policies that guide public-private R&D consortia and/or exclusive standard policy, procurement, and user subsidies for initial market provision.

One might ask whether or not it makes sense to say that every middle-income country should specialize in the same short-cycle technologies. This question is analogous to the question of the adding-up problem, which refers to the risks involved in the strategy of labor-intensive specialization in all low-income countries. However, specialization in short-cycle technologies does not entail a fixed list of technologies; instead, the sectors with short-cycle technologies imply the fields or sectors, in which new technologies always emerge to replace obsolete ones. The continuous emergence of new technologies suggests the availability of new opportunities for new entrants that are not confined to the old dominant technologies. This idea is contrary to the concept of the product life cycle, in which latecomers only inherit old or mature industries or segments from the incumbent economies. If industrial policy is akin to a concentrated commitment of resources into certain sectors to obtain returns and improve a sector's chances of success, then choosing long-cycle technologies would mean a reduced chance of success. This is because such technologies require more resources, thereby requiring more time to build a minimal level of competitiveness required for international competition.[7] For example, had Korea decided to enter the pharmaceuticals market in the 1980s, it would not have become successful not only in that industry itself, but also in terms of the growth of related industries and subsequent entries into newer ones.

Finally, we should point out the double-edged nature of short-cycle or frequently changing technologies, that is, they can serve either as windows of opportunity or as additional barriers to entry. Although Korea and Taiwan achieved successful catching-up in short-cycle sectors, other lower-tier countries, such as those in Latin America, did not experience success in those sectors (Lee, 2013a). This condition has to do with the notion of truncated learning (Lall, 2000), in which frequent technological changes interfere with the effectiveness of learning, and acquired knowledge becomes obsolete or useless with the advent of new technologies. This explains why the proposal in this paper involves a three-stage entry into shorter-cycle-based sectors, focused on the gradual development of capabilities. Entry into the next stage requires the successful accumulation of capabilities in the preceding stage. Although this is a narrow path rife with risks and requirements, it is the only available way toward high-income country status.

Notes

1. For instance, Metcalfe notes that systems are not only defined in terms of their components, and the availability of knowledgeable actors is a necessary but not a sufficient condition for the emergence of an innovation system.
2. For details, see Mathews (2002), Lee and Lim (2001), Lee et al. (2005), and OECD (1996).
3. For a fuller detail, see chapter 7 of Lee (2013a).
4. For details on the history of Hyundai Motors, see Lee and Lim (2001).
5. The case of digital TV production is further explained by Lee et al. (2005). A direct comparison of Samsung and Sony can be found in the work of Joo and Lee (2010).
6. This subsection is based on chapter 7 of Lee (2013a).
7. Certainly, if we are concerned only with domestic markets that are more or less closed to competition, the significance of a short or long cycle might not matter as much as it does with the present discussion.

References

Acemoglu, Daron, Johnson, Simon, and Robinson, James A. (2002) "Reversal of Fortune: Geography and Institutions in the Making of the Modern World Income Distribution," *Quarterly Journal of Economics*, vol. 117, pp. 1231–1294.

Acemoglu, Daron, Johnson, Simon, and Robinson, James A. (2001) "The Colonial Origins of Comparative Development: An Empirical Investigation," *American Economic Review*, vol. 91, pp. 1369–1401.

Aghion, Philippe, Dewatripont, Mathias, Du, Liqun, Harrison, Ann, and Legros, Patrick (2011) "Industrial Policy and Competition," CEPR Discussion Papers 8619, CEPR Discussion Papers.

Amsden, Alice (1989) *Asia's Next Giant: South Korea and Late Industrialization* (Oxford: Oxford University Press).

Amsden, Alice and Chu, W. (2003) *Beyond Late Development* (Cambridge, MA: MIT Press).

Anderson, Philip, and Tushman, Michael (1990) "Technological Discontinuities and Dominant Designs: A Cyclical Model of Technological Change," *Administrative Science Quarterly*, vol. 35, pp. 604–633.

Beason, Richard, and Weinstein, David E. (1996) "Growth, Economies of Scale, and Targeting in Japan (1955–1990)," *The Review of Economics and Statistics*, vol. 78, no. 2, pp. 286–295.

Bergek, Anna., Jacobsson, Staffan, Carlsson, Bo, Lindmark, Sven, and Rickne, Annika (2008) "Analyzing the Functional Dynamics of Technological Innovation Systems: A Scheme of Analysis," *Research Policy*, vol. 37, no. 3, pp. 407–429.

Chaminade, Cristina, Intarakumnerd, Patarapong, and Sapprasert, Koson (2012) "Measuring systemic problems in National Innovation Systems. An application to Thailand," *Research Policy*.

Chandra, V. (ed.) (2006) *Technology, Adaptation and Exports: How Some Countries Got it Right* (Washington, DC: World Bank).

Chung, Moon Young, and Lee, Keun (2011) "How Absorptive Capacity is Formed? Technology Licensing to Indigenous R&D and Innovation in Korea," Paper prepared for the Asia-Pacific Economic and Business History Conference 2011, held in Berkeley, California, USA.

Cimoli, Mario, Dosi, Giovanni, and Stiglitz, Joseph E. (eds) (2009) *Industrial Policy and Development* (New York: Oxford University Press).

Cohen, Wesley M., and Levinthal, Daniel A. (1990) "Absorptive Capacity: A New Perspective on Learning and Innovation," *Administrative Science Quarterly*, vol. 35, no. 1, pp. 128–152.

Dodgson, Mark, Hughes, Alan, Foster, John, and Metcalfe, J.S. (2011) "Systems Thinking, Market Failure, and the Development of Innovation Policy: The Case of Australia," *Research Policy*, vol. 40, no. 9, 1145–1156.

Eichengreen, B., Park, D., and Shin, K. (2011) "When Fast Growing Economies Slow Down," NBER Working Paper No. 16919 (Cambridge, MA: NBER).

Evenson, R. E., and Westphal, Larry (1995) "Technological Change and Technology Strategy," in Jere Behrman and T.N. Srinivasan (eds.), *Handbook of Development Economics*, vol. 3 (Amsterdam: North-Holland).

Freeman, C. and Soete, L. (1997) "Development and the Diffusion of Technology," in C. Freeman and L. Soete (eds), *The Economics of Industrial Innovation* (London: Pinter Publishers).

Glaeser, Edward, La Porta, Rafael, Lopez-de-Silanes, Florencio, and Shleifer, Andrei (2004) "Do Institutions Cause Growth?," *Journal of Economic Growth*, vol. 9, pp. 271–303.

Greenwald, Bruce, and Joseph Stiglitz. (2013) "Industrial Policy, Creation of a Learning Society and Economic Development," in J. Stiglitz and J. Lin, (eds), Industrial Policy Revolution (New York: Palgrav MacMillan).Griffith, B. (2011) "Middle Income Trap," in R. Nallari et al. (eds), *Frontiers in Development Policy* (Washington, DC: World Bank).

Hausmann, R., Pritchett, L., and Rodrik, D. (2005) "Growth Accelerations," *Journal of Economic Growth*, vol. 10, pp. 303–329.

Hausmann, R., Rodrik, D., and Velasco, A. (2008) "Growth Diagnostics," in N. Serra and J.E. Stiglitz (eds), *The Washington Consensus Reconsidered towards a New Global Governance.* (Oxford: Oxford University Press), pp. 324–355.

Hobday, M. (2005) "Firm-level Innovation Models: Perspectives on Research in Developed and Developing Countries," *Technology Analysis and Strategic Management*, vol. 17, no. 2, pp. 121–146.

Jaffe, Adam B. and Trajtenberg, M. (2002) *Patents, Citations, and Innovations: A Window on the Knowledge Economy* (Cambridge, MA: MIT Press).

Johnson, Chalmers (1982) *MITI and the Japanese Miracle: The Growth of Industrial Policy, 1925–1975* (Palo Alto, CA: Stanford University Press).

Jones, Benjamin F. and Olken, Benjamin A. (2005) "The Anatomy of Start-Stop Growth," NBER Working Papers 11528 (Cambridge, MA: National Bureau of Economic Research).

Joo, S.H. and Lee, K. (2010) "Samsung's Catch-up with Sony: An Analysis Using US Patent Data," *Journal of the Asia Pacific Economy*, vol. 15, no. 3, pp. 271–287.

Jung, Moosup and Lee, Keun (2010) "Sectoral Systems of Innovation and Productivity Catch-up: Determinants of the Productivity Gap between Korean and Japanese Firms," ,*Industrial and Corporate Change*, vol. 19, no. 4, pp. 1037–1069.

Kim, Linsu, and Dahlman, Carl J. (1992) "Technology Policy for Industrialization: An Integrative Framework and Korea's Experience," *Research Policy*, vol. 21, no. 5, pp. 437–452.

Lall, Sanjaya (2000) "The Technological Structure and Performance of Developing Country Manufactured Exports, 1985–1998," *Oxford Development Studies*, vol. 28, no. 3, pp. 337–369.

Lee, Jong-wha (1996) "Government Interventions and Productivity Growth," *Journal of Economic Growth*, vol. 1, pp. 391–414.

Lee, Keun (2013a) Schumpeterian Analysis of Economic Catch-up: Knowledge, Path- creation and the Middle Income Trap (Cambridge: Cambridge University Press).

Lee, Keun (2013b) "How Can Korea be a Role Model for Catch-up Development? A 'Capability-based View'," in Augustin K. Fosu (ed.), *Achieving Development Success: Strategies and Lessons from the Developing World* (Oxford: Oxford University Press (for WIDER)).

Lee, Keun (2006) "The Washington Consensus and East Asian Sequencing: Understanding Reform in East and South Asia," in J. Fanelli and G. McMahon (eds), *Understanding Market Reforms*, vol. 2 (Basingstoke: Palgrave Macmillan).

Lee, Keun (2005) "Making a Technological Catch-up: Barriers and Opportunities," *Asian Journal of Technology Innovation*, vol. 13, no. 2, pp. 97–131.

Lee, K. and He, X. (2009) "The Capability of the Samsung Group in Project Execution and Vertical Integration: Created in Korea, Replicated in China," *Asian Business and Management*, vol. 8, pp. 277–299.

Lee, K. and Kim, B.Y. (2009) "Both Institutions and Policies Matter but Differently at Different Income Groups of Countries: Determinants of Long Run Economic Growth Revisited," *World Development*, vol. 37, no. 3, pp. 533–549.

Lee, K. and Kim, Y.K. (2010) "IPR and Technological Catch-Up in Korea," in H. Odagiri, A. Goto, A. Sunami, and R. Nelson (eds), *Intellectual Property Rights, Development, and Catch Up: An International Comparative Study.* (Oxford: Oxford University Press).

Lee, K. and Lim, C. (2001) "Technological Regimes, Catching-up and Leapfrogging: Findings from the Korean Industries," *Research Policy,* vol. 30, pp. 459–483.

Lee, K., Lim, C., and Song, W. (2005) "Emerging Digital Technology as a Window of Opportunity and Technological Leapfrogging: Catch-up in Digital TV by the Korean Firms," *International Journal of Technology Management,* vol. 29, nos 1–2, pp. 40–63.

Lee, K., Mani, S., and Mu, Q. (2012) "Divergent Stories of Catchup in Telecom: China, India, Brazil, & Korea," in F. Malerba and R. Nelson (eds), *Economic Development as a Learning Process* (Cheltenham: Edward Elgar).

Lee, K. and Mathews, J. (2012) "Firms in Korea and Taiwan: Upgrading in the Same Industry and Entries into New Industries," in J. Cantwell and Ed Amann, *The Innovative Firms in the Emerging Market Economies* (Oxford: Oxford University Press).

Lee, K. and Mathews, J. (2010) "From the Washington Consensus to the BeST Consensus for World Development," *Asian-Pacific Economic Literature,* vol. 24, no. 1, pp. 86–103.

Lin, Justin Yifu (2012) *New Structural Economics: A Framework for Rethinking Development and Policy* (Washington, DC: World Bank).

Lundvall, B.Å. (1992) *National System of Innovation-Toward a Theory of Innovation and Interative Learning* (London: Pinter Publishers).

Mathews, John A. (2002) "The Origins and Dynamics of Taiwan's R&D Consortia," *Research Policy* 31, 633–651.

Metcalfe, J.S. (2005) "Systems Failure and the Case for Innovation Policy," in Patrick Llerena, Mireille Matt, and Arman Avadikyan (eds), *Innovation Policy in a Knowledge-based Economy: Theory And Practice* (Berlin: Springer).

Nelson, R. (1993) *National Innovation Systems: A Comparative Analysis* (New York: Oxford University Press).

Nooteboom, B. (2009) *A Cognitive Theory of the Firm. Learning, Governance and Dynamic Capabilities* (Northampton, MA: Edward Elgar).

Ocampo, J.A. (ed.) (2005) *Beyond Reforms: Structural Dynamics and Macroeconomic Stability* (Washington, DC: Stanford University Press for the UN Economic Commission for Latin America (ECLAC)).

OECD (1996) *Reviews of National Science and Technology Policy: Republic of Korea* (Paris: OECD).

Ohno, K. (2010) "Overcoming the Middle Income Trap," in L. Yueh (ed.), *Future of Asian Trade and Growth* (London: Routledge), pp. 199–221.

Pack, Howard (1992) "Technology Gaps between Industrial and Developing Countries: Are there Dividends for Latecomers?," Proceedings of the World Bank Annual Conference on Development Economics (Washington, DC: World Bank).

Paus, E. (2011) "Latin America's Middle Income Trap," *Americas Quarterly,* winter.

Perez, C. and Soete, L. (1988) "Catching-up in Technology: Entry Barriers and Windows of Opportunity," in Dosi et al. (ed.), *Technical Change and Economic Theory* (London: Pinter Publishers).

Rodrik, Dani (2006) "Goodbye Washington Consensus Hello Washington Confusion? A review of the World Bank's Economic Growth in the 1990s: Learning from a Decade of Reform," *Journal of Economic Literature,* vol. 44, no. 4, pp. 973–987.

Rodrik, Dani, Subramanian, Arvind, and Trebbi, Francesco (2004) "Institutions Rule: The Primacy of Institutions Over Geography and Integration in Economic Development," *Journal of Economic Growth,* vol. 9, pp. 131–165.

Shin, Hochul, and Lee, Keun (2012) Asymmetric Trade Protection Leading not to Productivity but to Export Share Change: The Korean Case from 1967 to 1993, Economics of Transition, Vol. 20, no. 4, pp. 745-785.

Spence, Michael (2011) *The Next Convergence: The Future of Economic Growth in a Multispeed World* (New York: FSG Books).

Tushman, Michael and Anderson, Philip (1986) "Technological Discontinuities and Organizational Environments," *Administrative Science Quarterly*, vol. 31, pp. 439–465.

Vernon, Raymond (1966) "International Investment and International Trade in the Product Cycle,". *The Quarterly Journal of Economics*, vol. 80, pp. 190–207.

Wade, Robert Hunter (2012) "Return of Industrial Policy?," *International Review of Applied Economics*, vol. 26, no. 2, pp. 223–239.

Wade, Robert Hunter (1990) *Governing the Market: Economic Theory and the Role of the Government in East Asian Industrialization.* (Princeton, NJ: Princeton University Press).

World Bank (2005) *Economic Growth in the 1990s: Learning from a Decade of Reform* (Washington, DC: World Bank).

World Bank (2010) "Exploring the Middle-Income-Trap," *World Bank East Asia Pacific Economic Update: Robust Recovery, Rising Risks*, vol. 2 (Washington, DC: World Bank).

Yusuf, S. and Nabeshima, K. (2009) "Can Malaysia Escape Middle Income Trap? A Strategy for Penang," Policy Research Working paper 4971 (Washington, DC: World Bank).

4.3
Comments on "Capability Failure and Industrial Policy to Move beyond the Middle-Income Trap: From Trade-based to Technology-based Specialization"

Ariel Fiszbein
World Bank

This paper looks at the question of economic development from the perspective of countries seeking to transition from middle to high income. The so-called middle-income country trap (that is, countries succeeding in growing to middle-income level but not being able to sustain that growth to become high income) provides the background and motivation to the paper.

The underlying premise is that, while the transition from low- to middle-income status can probably be understood in terms of a simple model of comparative advantage (whereby low-income countries need to concentrate on the production of labor-intensive goods and seek to exploit that advantage through export orientation and the adoption of simple technologies) the transition from middle- to high-income country status demands *technological innovation*. The core argument of the paper is that in defining the strategy for technological innovation (and the associated catch-up) middle-income countries will be better off by *specializing in dynamic industries* in which there exist more opportunities for fast (faster) changes in technologies –the so-called *short-cycle technologies*. In doing so, they increase their chances of leapfrogging in a way that would be more difficult if they were investing and competing in industries in which there are less opportunities for innovation.

Two aspects of this argument are worth noticing. First, specialization (as opposed to broad-based growth) is seen as essential (similarly that in the case of transitions from low- to middle-income status). Second, the hypothesis can be formulated in both deterministic and probabilistic ways. My reading of the paper is that the author has a deterministic perspective (that is, specialize in short-cycle technologies and you'll become rich, specialize in long-cycle technologies and you will face the middle-income trap). The same argument could also be seen as one of deciding under uncertainty (for example, specialization in industries with short-cycle technologies having higher expected returns but also being riskier).

The empirical "testing" of the hypothesis relies on two strategies. First, is the comparison of the level and type of innovation (understood as the acquisition, creation, diffusion and use of knowledge for productive purposes, and measured by patents) that different groups of countries experience. Secondly, through the comparison of the experience of East Asia (specifically South Korea and Taiwan) and Latin America (mostly through references to Argentina and Brazil).

While I found the general argument intriguing (and plausible, particularly under its probabilistic formulation), in my view the empirical strategy was not persuasive for two reasons.

First, while I understand the practical appeal of using patents as the key indicator, the paper did not succeed in convincing me that, by themselves, differences in the number, type and distribution of patents registered, adopted and used is a strong factor explaining differences in growth rates over long periods of time. Doing this would require, in my view, long-term series for a large number of countries (high and middle income at different points in time) which at least this paper does not seem to use. A more detailed explanation of the pros and cons of using patent data (including its reliability) and how the different indicators were constructed would have been useful as well.

Second, the comparisons between East Asia and Latin America also left me wanting. While the discussion on Korea and Taiwan (and the experience in sectors such as micro-chips, laptops, etc.) is useful and does suggest that at least those two countries succeeded in developing strong industries through the development of new technologies, the references to Argentina and Brazil and the interpretation of their experience during the 1980s and 1990s are rather limited. It is clearly true that during that period the Latin American countries lost terrain relative to East Asia. And, with the caveats on data expressed before, we can also accept the difference in the type of technologies they seem to have pursued. But attributing one to the other implies heroic assumptions, particularly considering the enormous differences in policies between these countries during that period (for example, unsustainable macroeconomic policies leading to the adoption of stabilization policies, debt crises, sharp fluctuations in trade and financial liberalization policies, and so on.).

The paper does not provide an explanation of the factors that enabled the adoption of "short cycle technologies" in some countries and not in others. It is not clear whether this was the result of "successful" business strategies by specific firms (the Hyundai story points in that direction) or the result of specific policies and institutions that enabled and/or promoted such strategies. Areas of particular interest in this regard involve basic education (does the fact that Latin American countries have, overall, dismal performance in international tests matter?), higher education (do Korea and Taiwan have more emphasis on STEM fields relative to Latin America), university–firm links, and so on. The role (or lack of) of public institutions in charge of technology promotion (which during that period, for example, in Argentina suffered a major dislocation) is also a matter of interest.

In summary, in my view the paper raises some important questions and fosters debate. However, I would hope to see more detailed econometric work and more careful comparative analysis of policies and institutions.

4.4

What's New in the New Industrial Policy in Latin America?

Robert Devlin
Johns Hopkins SAIS
Graciela Moguillansky
International consultant

4.4.1 Introduction

Latin America has long been a laggard in terms of economic catch-up, on repeated occasions over its history it has witnessed less developed countries leapfrogging it in economic growth and development (Coatsworth, 1998; Dominguez, 2008; Devlin and Moguillansky, 2011). The post-war period has been no exception, with countries in East Asia only being the most notable.

In the period from 1950 to 1980 Latin America was an aggressive practitioner of industrial policies (IP). During much of the period the practice was in line with the then mainstream thinking in development economics. Significant growth, industrialization and modernization took place (Ocampo, 2006), although not enough for catch-up in a generally expansive world economy. The IP approach, however, began to be seriously challenged in the 1970s when military governments in the Southern Cone shifted to policies favoring Chicago School monetarist thought, which had been much less influential in the development practice of the time. A profound Latin American debt crisis in the 1980s, coupled with the ascendance of Thatcher/Reagan arguments for the retrenchment of the state in economics and life, created a pendulum swing in the region to what has been called neoliberal economic policy. Major structural adjustments and reforms designed to bring the free market forward and push back the market governance of the State dominated the 1980s and 1990s.

In recent years, however, countries in Latin America have witnessed a renaissance in the deployment of systematic industrial policies. This paper will give an overview of the phenomenon, citing a number of cases which we think reflect the current state of affairs in the region. It will highlight why the new shift (albeit not of the pendulum type) has occurred, why it is in principle a positive development and why important dimensions of the current industrial policies in the region are different from thoseexperienced in the past and offer hope for greater success. It will also identify some bad habits that linger and which need to be addressed with urgency if the new trend is to be successfully consolidated.

Section 4.4.2 will outline why we think the application of intelligent and well-executed industrial policies are important for the catch-up of Latin American economies. Section 4.4.3 will address what is new in the new industrial policy in Latin America. Section 4.4.4 will review what is still "old" in the new industrial policy of the region. Section 4.4.5 will address some slightly "existential" issues that have us still thinking about more complete answers. Section 4.4.6 offer our conclusions.

4.4.2 Why industrial policy is necessary in Latin America

There is an extensive literature justifying the deployment of industrial policy via government interventions in the market. The most generally acknowledged reason is the existence of so-called market failures that, when pervasive enough, will significantly retard the efficient allocation of resources. These typically fall into categories involving the existence of dysfunctional monopoly power, Marshallian externalities/spillovers of different types and the undersupply of public goods. However, modern justifications go beyond the static equilibrium-inspired market failure argument. These additional considerations incorporate dynamic factors such as systemic failures related to the generation of learning opportunities, capacity building, experimentation, innovation as well as the incorporation of technical change for the diversification of productive activities and exports that are needed to climb up the world's hierarchy of production. This latter perspective moreover acknowledges that not all productive activities are the same in terms of their dynamic effects on agents; hence the role of industrial policy is to provide incentives to market stakeholders to explore the adoption of new processes and activities of a higher order, often in the face of obstacles that are not easily bridged by the autonomous forces of the market (Peres and Primi, 2009).

Latin America was a good student of the structural reforms of the Washington Consensus era (Lora, 2007). While this period has generated considerable debate about the effects of these reforms (Birdsall, de la Torre and Valencia, 2011), most would probably conclude that the era's positive legacy is the emergence of a consensus in the region that macroeconomic stability is essential for growth, the role of the private sector as a primary agent of investment and innovation, the importance of articulating with a globalizing world economy and the need to attend to the poor.[1] However, the growth experience in the 1980s and 1990s was disappointing. This, coupled with the emergence of big competitive challenges in trade arising from liberalization – especially new free trade areas with industrialized countries – and the better performance of countries less observant of the "market fundamentalism" that arose out of some of the more enthusiastic interpretations of the Washington Consensus, contributed to the gradual reemergence of the state as an active promoter of productive transformation. In effect, following Evans's (1995) terminology, Latin American governments have begun to advance from their mostly "custodian" role in markets – regulating at arms' length – to a more proactive stance aimed at being a "handmaiden" of private sector competitiveness and productive transformation.

The stylized facts of Latin America's economic profile would suggest that there is considerable space for industrial policies to promote structural change and endogenous drivers of the high and sustained rates of growth needed to converge with rich countries.

The Caribbean Basin countries gained comprehensive preferential market access to the United States beginning in 1984 with that country's launch of the Caribbean Basin Initiative (CBI) and its "augmented version" in 2000. In the mid-2000s the CBI was converted into a comprehensive free trade area for Central America and the Dominican Republic. Meanwhile, in 1994 Mexico entered into a comprehensive free trade area with the USA called the North American Free Trade Agreement (NAFTA). Both agreements gave rise to a strong growth in exports. The Economic Commission for Latin America and the Caribbean (ECLAC, 2008) showed that the preferential access also contributed to a very marked diversification of exports, generally considered to be a factor supportive of growth and development (Imbs and Wacziarg, 2003; Klinger and Lederman, 2006). The diversification additionally witnessed a sharp increase in the participation of low-, medium- and high-tech manufactured exports, which could provide important opportunities for learning and entrance into new "product spaces" that would be conducive to economic upgrading (Hausmann and Klinger, 2006). But the same ECLAC study also showed that these advantages were not being fully exploited: the expansion of value added in low-medium and hi-tech manufactures was markedly lower than the increase in the value of exports, reflecting the dominance of import–re-export assembly activities ("maquila") with the U.S. market. Moreover, in Central America the growth of many exports was in "undynamic" products that were losing shares in world trade.

The story for natural resource exporters in South America has also been uneven. The commodity boom of the 2000s drove a concentration on exports, especially in the Andean area and Chile. These latter countries, which have their manufactured exports based to a large degree of natural resources, exhibit low intensity in engineering even when compared to other natural resource-based exporters such as Australia and New Zealand. Moreover, their exports have been overly represented by relatively undynamic products in terms of their growth in shares of world trade (ECLAC 2008). And while in the 2000s Latin America's economic growth was the best in 40 years, its overreliance on high commodity prices to drive that growth is a source of vulnerability (Inter-American Development Bank, 2008; ECLAC, 2010). Moreover, that growth has been undistinguished when compared to other developing regions (Table 4.4.1).

Table 4.4.1 Growth rates in developing regions (average annual % growth)

	2000–2009	2010	2011	2012
East Asia and the Pacific	9.4	9.7	8.2	7.8
China	10.9	8.5	9.1	8.4
Europe and Central Asia	5.8	5.2	5.3	4.0
Turkey	4.9	9.0	8.2	2.9
Latin America and the Caribbean	3.8	6.0	4.2	3.6
Brazil	3.6	7.5	2.9	3.4
Colombia	4.5	4.3	5.6	4.4
Mexico	2.2	5.5	4.0	3.2
Argentina	5.4	9.2	7.5	3.4
Middle East and N. Africa	4.7	3.6	1.7	2.3
South Asia	7.3	9.1	6.6	5.8
India	7.9	8.7	6.5	6.5
Sub-Saharan Africa	5.1	4.8	4.9	5.3

Sources: World Bank (2012) and World Bank, *World Development Indicators 2011.*

Finally, the entire region underperforms in competiveness. The region's participation in world exports of manufactures has grown little and its participation in services has fallen (ECLAC 2011). Meanwhile, only Chile and Barbados are in the top 50 of the more than 140 countries in the World Economic Forum's Global Competitiveness Index; and even so they do not perform well in dynamic sub-indexes like education and innovation.[2] This situation is of concern since the region risks being squeezed by China moving up into higher tech areas where Latin America has excelled (for example, aeronautics, autos) and by low-wage countries emerging as new labor-intensive exporters (for example, in Africa and South Asia).

These outlined handicaps facing Latin America have been overcome by other countries that have actively deployed industrial policies. Countries such as Singapore, Taiwan and Ireland began their respective productive transformations with labor-intensive assembly operations for export, much like Central America and the Dominican Republic today, primarily geared to the creation of employment. However, with ambition, forward-looking strategies and proactive horizontal, as well as selective, public promotional policies, they diversified and upgraded into higher-value and more skill/knowledge-intensive local production for export to eventually become wealthy countries (Devlin and Moguillansky, 2011). Likewise, countries such as Finland, Sweden, and Malaysia moved beyond their original dependence on an abundance of natural resources to diversify into much higher value-added skill- and knowledge-based products and activities.[3] This did not happen through the "invisible hand" of the market, as public sector industrial policies of both a horizontal and a vertical nature (including government procurement) helped build the local capacities needed to make the transition. These countries, along with Australia and New Zealand, which through local innovation have built value-added around natural resource exploitation, attest to the arguments of Stijns (2001) and Lederman and Maloney (2007) that natural resources are not a curse. However, they are a blessing only as long as one has a strategy that provides an answer to "how" natural resources can be exploited in a way that progressively diversifies and upgrades the overall level of skills and economic activity in the country for catch-up. Unfettered market forces are unlikely to do this; indeed, they may drive a country deeper into its static comparative advantage.[4]

Industrial policies can address the low-productivity traps of SMEs, which typically are major employers in Latin America. Horizontal policies for SMEs often are not enough. SMEs are highly heterogeneous in their potential and specific in their needs; hence assistance programs must be designed with that heterogeneity in mind.

Industrial policies also can promote much-needed economic linkages from local firms that have become important international players, but have generated little spillover effects in the local economy. As an illustration, the conglomerates Arauco and CMPC are among the principal economic groups in Chile. In 2008 they entered into the top 30 forestry companies of the world, being higher ranked than some Canadian and Australian lead firms in that industry. But rising to become big and important world players hides a stark national reality: There is no real public policy to promote the spread effects of activity in the sector. While in Australia and Canada the industry leaders are integrated into a large export-oriented cluster involving small, medium-sized and large firms, in Chile the two conglomerates mentioned, along with a third, Massisa, dominate practically all segments of the market. The lack of a competition policy, as well as comprehensive public policy promotion of economic transformation, has impeded the upgrading and/or entrance of small and medium-sized firms into the sector.[5] Unlike in either Australia or Canada, the activities have not led to real "territorial" development of which the three firms are a contributing member. Rather, the firms oversee a strategy based on extensive exploitation and precarious employment situations in areas with the highest indices of poverty and where there is an absence of community involvement.

The privatizations of the Washington Consensus era contributed to the enlargement and diversification of the economic activities of local economic groups,[6] some of which have become multinational in their economic activities.[7] However, while these firms have scale, talent, and import the latest machinery and equipment, many have not been leaders in locally-based development (Tavares, 2005) or innovation and investment in R&D, which tends to be very low in almost all Latin American countries. Indeed, the whole area of promotion of innovation and R&D, as well as creating networks of collaboration among business, academia and government, is a prime area of action for industrial policies in Latin America. Meanwhile, although almost all Latin American countries have programs of FDI attraction, that is not the case regarding effective strategies to leverage FDI for economic upgrading and spread effects in the local economy (Mortimore, 2008). Ireland, Singapore, Malaysia, among others, have used industrial policies to do precisely this with their FDI attraction programs (Devlin and Moguillansky, 2011).

Another area ripe for industrial policies in Latin America is the preparation for climate change. Climate change brings not only threats, which should be anticipated and addressed by firms and society, but also opportunities in terms of new technologies and emerging comparative advantages. Latin America was very late in responding to the opportunities of the advances in ITC (ECLAC, 2008). The systemic dimensions and implications of climate change are unlikely to be addressed with alacrity by the autonomous forces of Latin American markets. Promotion of strategic thinking and research in this area, and coupling it with the commercial needs of defending and/or creating comparative advantage, is a natural area for industrial policy.

4.4.3   What's new in the new industrial policy in Latin America?

Industrial policy itself is nothing new to Latin America. In the early 19th century, reforms of the newly independent Latin American countries significantly reduced the Spanish colonial legacy of state intervention in the economies, but did not eliminate it. Nevertheless, the power of the normative laissez-faire economic framework of the second half of that century contributed to putting the State in a decidedly subsidiary role vis-à-vis private sector market initiatives. However, in the early 20th century state enterprises began to take on a higher profile in the economies of the region, including in directly productive activities. Then in the interwar period State interventions in the economy gained much more traction when private markets faltered due to the Great Depression and wars.[8]

While much of the state intervention in the interwar period was reactive – filling in where markets objectively failed – in the post-war era of 1950–1980 state expansion in the economy became proactive, leading Ocampo (2006) to label it the era of "state-led industrialization." In this period of "mixed capitalist economies" public sector indicative planning became the norm in the region and public sector promotion of industrialization was quite pervasive.[9] Planning exercises moreover received support from the World Bank and the US official sector as part of the Alliance for Progress.

The strategy at the time was largely "inward-looking" and more popularly identified with the moniker "import substitution industrialization," or ISI.[10] The period witnessed important advances in industrialization, institutional modernization and respectable average rates of economic growth. However, growth was volatile and was punctuated by episodes of fiscal and balance of payments crises (Ocampo, 2006). Moreover, political instability was reflected in cycles of authoritarianism and democracy. The imbalances of the ISI process had its counterpart in the accumulation of foreign debt, especially with international commercial banks, starting in the mid-1960s. Contagion in the international financial market in 1982, sparked by payment problems in Mexico, delivered a full-blown debt crisis to the region. The crisis of the 1980s and the consequent wrenching and asymmetric adjustments between debtors and creditors contributed to politically delegitimizing the state-led industrialization model of development (Devlin, 1989).

Latin America's economic policy and adjustments throughout the decade of the 1980s were supported by the conditional financing programs of the IMF, the World Bank, regional development banks and the linked debt rescheduling/refinancing by international commercial banks. The policy platform advocated by these institutions, and which was generally in line with the thinking of a new guard of economic policymakers that emerged in the region, was directed at macroeconomic stabilization, liberalizing the economy and dramatically reducing the footprint of government in the promotion of industrialization. The ethos of the time was expressed in the policy lines of action of the so-called Washington Consensus (Williamson, 1990).

The Consensus involved reforms in ten rather generic policy categories. Rodrik (2006) later added ten more of an institutional orientation which he thought reflected the expanded thinking of the Washington Consensus reforms promoted in the 1990s. The interpretation of "how" to give policy and institutional reforms a precise configuration was open to interpretations. The space for interpretation sometimes led to rather unnuanced "one size fits all" recommendations and applications of reforms (such as rapid privatizations at any price and relatively rapid and across-the-board liberalizations), some of which probably caused Williamson himself to stutter.

What united the advocates of the Washington Consensus was "more market, less government intervention," pushing the state back mostly to what we termed earlier a "custodian role" in the governance of markets. In the more extreme interpretations of this approach, government almost became an "inferior good" that perhaps had to be tolerated but certainly could be dramatically shrunk. A logical conclusion in this framework is that the best industrial policy is no industrial policy at all.

Be that as it may, during the 1980s and 1990s the idea of industrial policy was highly polemical and very out of step with mainstream thinking in academic circles, the policies of Washington-based institutions and the thinking of policymakers in Latin America. This is not to say that industrial policies disappeared altogether. Governments did introduce gentle incentives, largely of the horizontal type; for example, to promote exports or attract FDI. Even sector-specific incentives were sometimes introduced.

However, these were generally not a well-focused strategic application of incentives beyond faith in the benevolent forces of the market; they were often the result of the pressure of some interest group. Ad hoc interventions would accumulate over government cycles, creating a virtual "archeological park" of incentives.[11]

The late 1990s witnessed the onset of reform fatigue in Latin America. As mentioned earlier, despite being a good student of the Washington Consensus, economic growth was generally unremarkable – a sensation of "pain but no gain" emerged in the region. Moreover, ambitious unilateral, multilateral, regional, and bilateral trade liberalization created major challenges for the private sector, which was now supposed to be the engine of growth (Giordano and Devlin, 201; Tussie, 2011); indeed, new free trade areas with the USA and Europe – where the liberalization was very asymmetrically weighted by the Latin American economies – were an especially strong wake-up call for the private sectors. Parallel to this there was increasing criticism of the "one size fits all" and "fundamentalism" perceived in interpretations of the Washington Consensus (for example, Stiglitz, 2002; French-Davis, 2005; Rodrik 2006). There also emerged some major studies highlighting the role of industrial policies in the development of success cases of the post-war era (for example, Wade, 1990; Evans 1995; Devlin and Moguillansky, 2011) and new thinking about frameworks of modern industrial policy (e.g., Wade, 1990, Chang, 1994; Evans, 1995; Rodrik, 2004; Hausman and Klinger, 2006; Hausmann and Rodrik, 2006; Hausmann, 2008; Sabel, 2009; Reinert, 2009; Cimoli, Dosi, and Stiglitz, 2009; Lin and Monga, 2010; and Aghion et. al., 2012).

It is in this environment that more proactive state action expressed in strategically designed industrial policies began to reemerge in Latin America. There was a sense in many countries that good macroeconomics and market liberalization was not enough for structural transformation and accelerated growth for catch-up. However, the industrial policy being deployed in the region has a number of new dimensions that contrast with the "old" industrial policies pursued in the Post-war era prior to the crisis of the 1980s.

4.4.3.1 A significantly different context for deploying industrial policies

Context matters for the implementation of effective industrial policy. Today Latin America is the most democratic developing region in the world meaning that governments are more accountable than ever before for their decisions. A culture of macroeconomic stability has taken root regardless of ideology with a consequent reduction of vulnerability to internal and external shocks. Most countries see the private sector as the lead agent of productive transformation. The countries' economies are now relatively open, while export diversification and upgrading are now appreciated as handmaidens of productive transformation. FDI is generally welcome.

4.4.3.2   A main focus on international competitiveness

The old industrial policy in Latin America was designed to catapult countries rapidly into the higher echelons of industrialization. An iconic initiative in this regard was Brazil's Second National Development Plan 1975–79, which in the face of serious uncertainty in the world economy aimed to build self-sufficiency in strategic areas.[12] In this era of Latin American industrial policy there was something of a denial of comparative advantage, while competiveness was at best an afterthought given the high levels of industrial protection of that time – average nominal tariffs typically well exceeded 100 percent (Thorp, 1998).[13] Effective protection, of course, was much higher due to significant tariff escalation. In contrast, the new industrial policy in the region has been primarily motivated by a goal of enhancing the international competitiveness of existing industries, what Hausmann, Rodrik and Sabel (2008) call industrial policy "in the small." This reflects the pressures arising from more open economies in the age of globalization, competition from free trade partners and the specter of losing domestic and international market shares to Asia. Illustrations of this trend in developing strategic competitiveness strategies are found in Brazil, Chile, Colombia, the Dominican Republic, Ecuador, El Salvador, Mexico, Panama, Peru, and Uruguay (Table 4.4.2).

Table 4.4.2 also shows that some of the strategies combine with promotion of new activities, which would fall into the Hausmann, Rodrik and Sabel industrial policies "in the large." However, many of these more ambitious initiatives are "in the large '*light*'," that is, they are not grand bets distant from existing comparative advantages or learning capabilities. As an illustration, Table 4.4.3 lists the initiatives in Colombia for productive transformation that aim to build capacities leading to new world-class sectors/activities in that country. In Chile, the 2007 innovation strategy's push for new activities was focused on cluster development of eight carefully selected sectors, but most are based on activities close to country's abundant natural resources.[14]

Latin America's most ambitious industrial policy has been implemented in Brazil, which began in continuum with the Industrial, Technological and Trade Policy, or PITCE (2003–07), continued with the Productive Development Policy, or PDP (2008–10), and now is expressed in its closely related follow-up Plano Brazil Maior. While one of the objectives of the industrial policy in the PDP period has been the diversification of the productive structure, enhanced productivity and exports with special emphasis on innovation, in fact much of the effort appeared to have focused on consolidating competitiveness as well as the international investment expansion of existing national champions in resource-based industries (Programs to Consolidate Leadership in Figure 4.4.1).[15] Promoting national champions for market positioning, learning and upgrading, linkages to the

Table 4.4.2 Illustration of industrial policy strategies in selected countries

Country	Program	In the Small	In the Large
Brazil	PITCE (2003–07)	X	X
	Productive Development Policy (PDP)-2008–10	X	X
	Plano Brasil Maior 2011–14	X	X
Colombia	Vision Colombia 2019 and 2032	X	X
	National Competitiveness Policy	X	
	National Development Plan 2010–14 (PNP)	X	X
	Program to Promote World Class Sectors (included in PNP)	X	X
Chile	2007 and 2008 National Strategy for Innovation	X	X
	Competitiveness Agenda 2010–20*	X	X
Dominican Republic	National plan for Systemic Competitiveness	X	
	30 Year Development Strategy	X	
Ecuador	National Development Plan 2007–11	X	
El Salvador	National Development Plan 2010–14	X	
Mexico	Vision 2030	X	X
Panama	National Concertation	X	
Peru	National Competitiveness Plan 2003–10	X	
	National Competitiveness Agenda	X	
Uruguay	Industrial Development Strategy (2008)	X	X
	Sectoral Industrial Plans (2011)	X	X

Note: *Discontinued by the current government.
Source: The authors based on official data.

Table 4.4.3 Colombia: industrial policy in the large

Program to Promote World Class Sectors	PND New Sectors based on Innovation
Outsourcing of Business Services	ITC
Software	Health
Cosmetics	Biotech
Fashion and design	Electronics
Electric energy and transmission	Logistics
Auto parts and vehicles	Design
Chocolate Confection	Energy and Natural Resources
Health Tourism	Creative industries

Note: Titles in italics represent new major export sector under the program of World-Class Sectors.
Source: Ministry of Planning, National Development Plan 2010–2014.

domestic and international economies, and so on, is a legitimate goal of industrial policies. Whether the promotion of Brazilian national champions is serving as an eventual platform for new upgraded comparative advantages, and whether the already large firms needed BNDES financing to conquer the world market, are issues that merit more investigation (Almeida and Schneider, 2012).[16]

Apparently the new Plano Brazil Maior is now increasingly focusing on infrastructure, strengthening productive chains, promoting export diversification with more value added and innovation, oriented especially to SMEs, and more recently to defending domestic industry from the effects of merciless exchange rate appreciation and economic slowdown.[17] In spite of risks of overly defensive adjustments to confront potentially destabilizing external developments, some of the spirit of Brazil's reentry into comprehensive industrial policy expressed characteristics which have been associated with success in economic catch-up: concern for "what" one produces in the world hierarchy of production and ambition to build capacities to upgrade the level of economic activities.[18] The challenge will be to progressively translate that spirit into effective forward-looking programs.

As for Mexico, Vision 2030 and the National Plan focus mostly on horizontal[19] and specific sectoral initiatives to improve competitiveness; however, there also are robust industrial policies at the state level.[20] In Peru, the National Competitiveness Plan of the National Competitiveness Council started out with an enormous number of initiatives and goals, but few got off the ground due to difficulties in priority setting and financing (Devlin and Moguillansky 2011). The major achievement has been accomplishment of a "Doing Business Initiative." The government is currently focusing on developing a new two-year initiative focused on competitiveness. In Panama, the National Concertation has an ambitious social and economic agenda through 2025. One of its four pillars is competitiveness, although goals set out here are more aspirational and less precise than some of the social-related pillars.

In the context of the renewed interest in medium-to long-term strategic thinking and industrial policy, it also should be mentioned that a new dimension is the explicit focus on innovation. This led the launch of industrial policy in the aforementioned Chilean initiative and is an important complement in the strategies of Brazil,[21] Uruguay, Mexico and, more recently, Colombia. This too is a healthy development since innovation is now leading transformation strategies in many of the region's competitors in the developed and developing world (Devlin and Moguillansky, 2011).

In sum, the application of the new industrial policy is aimed primarily at achieving international competitiveness around existing comparative advantages, and where it strays into new activities the distance from the former is generally far from heroic. Moreover, although there are so-called vertical initiatives in many of the national strategies (especially Brazil),

PDP – Level 2: structuring programs (areas)

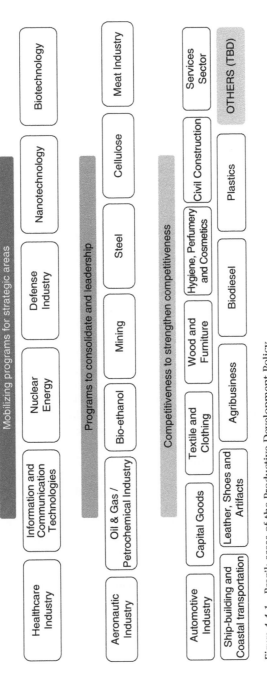

Figure 4.4.1 Brazil: areas of the Productive Development Policy
Source: Federal Government of Brazil.

horizontal, or relatively neutral interventions, seem to have a high profile in most of the schemes.[22] Ambition and intelligent strategic bets aimed at experimentation, learning, and upgrading for catch-up are hallmarks of successful countries (Devlin and Moguillansky, 2011). However, the conservative and gradual approach exhibited in Latin America seems appropriate given the past tendencies of "overreach" and capability limits of a public sector that is now just beginning to reemerge as a proactive player in productive transformation. One must learn to walk before running.

4.4.3.3   Financing

Another new feature of the new industrial policy is financing. The formal national plans of the old industrial policy were often unfinanced in whole or in part and hence their words often did not translate into deeds. The new industrial policy displays more financial commitment in a significant number of countries, perhaps also reflecting more efficient fiscal management. Brazil's industrial policy has the active participation of the Ministry of Finance and the robust support of the BNDES, the largest public lender in Latin America. Through a number of instruments the BNDES has financed exports adversely affected by exchange rate appreciations, credits for small and medium-sized enterprises to raise their competitiveness, innovation and the international expansion of national champions.[23] Chile's program had a special Innovation Fund financed from copper mining royalties. Panama's National Concertation plan, with many precise goals up through 2025, receives earmarked commitments from receipts of the newly, expanded Panama Canal. Meanwhile, Colombia's National Competitiveness Policy is annually fully budgeted as an integral part of the National Development Plan. The National Planning Department is also studying multi-annual budgeting for competitiveness initiatives that require long term investments. Moreover, this could be facilitated by a new regime of royalties on petroleum and mining. As for the World Class Sectors Initiative, it had been without financing (Moguillansky, 2012).

In El Salvador, the government transparently indicates (and itemizes by the goals in its National Development Plan) that about 35 percent of the financing is secure with the rest explicitly under negotiation with donors. In Uruguay, the country's industrial sector plans do not have *ex ante* financing, but rather they must be solicited once there is tripartite agreement; sources are a national training agency, multilateral agencies, bank loans or special funds under the administration of a ministry.

Meanwhile, Peru and the Dominican Republic have relied exclusively on multilateral agencies and donors, which has some disadvantages. There is the conditionality of the lender or donor's agenda; one is forced into the external agencies' financial cycle and the time-consuming procedures for approval and disbursement; and coverage often falls short of the complete spectrum of activities needed to integrally enhance competitiveness and upgrade economies. Finally, heavy reliance on external funding can dilute ownership of the initiative and commitment within the government itself.

Notwithstanding the mentioned advances, there are other weaknesses exhibited in Latin America. Budgets for executing agencies can be weighted more to operational expenses than promotional programs leading to too few resources being spread over too many programs. This problem was observed in Chile in the area of innovation and competitiveness, leading to the recommendation that resources be concentrated in the most promising initiatives (Agosin, Larraín and Grau, 2009). Excessively complex procedures and slow bureaucratic responses to applications submitted to support programs discourage private sector participation. Another common problem is that initiatives which are medium- or long-term in nature, such as research and innovation, are prisoners of the uncertainties of short-term budget cycles; this uncertainty can affect the credibility of the program for potential clients. Establishing special earmarked funds such as one finds in some European countries – and what Chile did for innovation and which may emerge in Colombia – could be an approach to consider.[24]

4.4.3.4 Public–Private Alliances

In the old industrial policy in Latin America, strategies and programs were very much state-led in a relatively "top-down" spirit. In Evans's (1995) framework the state at that time in many ways acted as a kind of "demiurge." This was due to distrust of private sector capacities, coupled in many cases with sharply diverging ideological stances on economic development and politics. The picture has changed quite dramatically in the age of the new industrial policy.

One of the new dimensions of thinking about industrial policy is the recognition that it is not possible for governments to formulate effective industrial policy on their own; that is, the bureaucratic model of development that was associated with many of the post-war success cases is no longer viable. Today the world is different place for countries aiming to catch-up. Globalization has retaken its path of hyperexpansion after shedding the effects of the Great Depression and war. Liberalization of national and international markets has been pervasive and privatizations have pushed back direct state participation in productive activities. The private sector is now considered by most to be the engine of growth. Technological change and world competition is of increasing intensity. Globalization is creating centripetal forces of world integration. Manufacturing, and even services, are increasingly articulated by global production chains, world networks and domestic or regional clusters. Innovation is still taking place in vertical settings, but increasingly new knowledge and its diffusion is network-based with a growing international character (Sabel, 2009). Policy space for State action is circumscribed by WTO rules which have many gray areas that must be identified and navigated. New, still not fully defined challenges and opportunities are on the horizon due to climate change. Hence with all this, while probably always a truism, today more than ever, as Radosevic (2009) observes, "all views are partial" in assessing market developments.

Consequently the new industrial policy disassociates itself from the notion of the government "picking winners." Rather governments should work with the private sector in search of opportunities and related obstacles to experimentation, learning and upgrading economic activities. In this context industrial policy becomes an "outcome" of a "social process" of exploration and problem- solving carried out by relevant players in the private sector and government (Rodrik, 2004). Moreover, this collaboration must be close, but accomplished without capture of the state by special interests, or what Evans (1995) called the government's achievement of "embedded autonomy."

Ultimately governments are, as Hausmann and Rodrik (2006) point out, "doomed to choose" among different policy options for supporting private sector articulation with market opportunities. Thus the idea is that working together in a socially constructive way that recognizes mutual interdependence, an alliance of government and business can contribute to the development of more intelligent strategies and more effective public programs to enable market-based productive transformations than if each addresses challenges individually (and possibly in a context of mutual distrust). In other words, the whole can become more than the sum of its parts in a joint governance of the market.[25]

Other social actors may potentially contribute valuable insights and information depending on the issue(s) in question. And/or they may have veto power over policies and hence must be brought in under the tent. Labor unions have valuable contextual information in the workplace and issues such as wage and work rules that condition the action of firms and their productivity. Moreover they can politically veto public policies favorable to the business environment. Academia has technical expertise and can verify/ reject/ add information provided by stakeholders. And certain organized social groups have de facto vetoes over the allocation of public resources, so they too may be bought into the tent to enhance public understanding of strategies, policies and programs.[26] Moreover, democratic principles are increasingly ruling developing countries in the era of globalization, creating demands for more civil participation and transparency in policy processes and more public accountability for the policies pursued. Latin America is no exception.

It is also very important to add that public–private alliances for productive transformation are not only about building new capacities in the private sector. Government must be able to be a credible technical partner of the private sector if the latter is to actually commit time and resources to serious collaboration.

Alliances can operate at different levels: national, department, region, or even a municipality. They can also operate with a view to the economy-as-whole for an overall national strategy, to a sector, across sectors and themes. Ideally the different levels should "talk" to each other, as illustrated in Figure 4.4.2. In terms of organization of alliances, the dominant structure in any country can be formal forums or councils, ad hoc task-specific committees, informal networks of tacit information or some combination of these (Devlin and Moguilansky, 2011).

Since the second half of the 1990s Latin America has seen the emergence of public–private alliances geared towards giving strategic direction to industrial policies and overseeing their implementation. Table 4.4.4 illustrates a number of them. Some of the alliances "fly" higher over the policy terrain than others.

Certain alliances are meant to provide advice to the executive on the overall direction of the economic policy and to have a strong political dimension as well given their intention to draw stakeholders together into a common

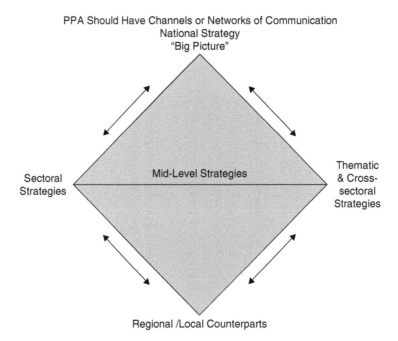

Figure 4.4.2   Public–private alliances talk to each other
Source: Devlin (2012).

Table 4.4.4 Selected public–private alliances in Latin America

Field/country	Alliance	Type of Alliance	Structure
Brazil			
National	Economic and Social Development Council (CDES) Advisory body to the president on state reform and on medium/long-term issues	Formal, structured	Representatives of workers, businesses, social movements and the government organized in thematic groups. More than 100 council members chosen by the President
Sectoral	National Industrial Development Council (CNDI) Supervises industrial development polices	Formal, structured	23 ministries, 14 representatives of industry and the President of the BNDES
Sectoral	Sectoral and state-level councils and forums for public–private alliance dialogue on the implementation of the PDP	Formal *ad hoc* but in the process of being structured	Sectoral and thematic business associations and representatives of sectoral and thematic public agencies
Chile			
Sectoral	Productive Development Forum – Council for productive development (1994–99)	Formal, structured	Tripartite partnership: Government-unions-business 24 council members chaired by the Minister of Economy
National	Various alliance forums set up at different times on different issues	Formal *ad hoc*	
	National Innovation Council for Competitiveness Defines the innovation strategy and advises the presidency on innovation policies	Formal, structured	A president, 5 ministers, and 11 representatives of business, science, and academia. The alliance operates on different levels: at the executive and grassroots levels, among the leaders of the clusters and through participation in the Regional Productive Development Agencies (ARDP)

Colombia			
National	National Planning Council Consensus building on the National Development Plan	Formal, structured	Composed of representatives of the various civil society groups
National	National Competitiveness Commission Implementation of the strategy for productivity and competitiveness	Formal, structured	Chaired by the President with the participation of businesses, academia and unions, public agencies, private organizations, and regional competitiveness commissions
Dominican Republic			
National	National Competitiveness Council	Formal Structured	President, Ministry of Economy, Planning and Desarrollo, 8 representatives from ministries or sectoral associations and 8 private sector individuals.
El Salvador			
National	Economic and Social Council	Formal, structured	24 business associations, 24 representatives of social groups, 5 government representatives
Ecuador			
National	The National Council of Production with its Consultative Council	Formal, Structured	The National Council is made up of government and the Consultative Councils has as members. Business Associations that comment on government plans.
Sectoral	Sectoral Councils	Formal, Structured	14 tripartite councils to identify and overcome productive constraints and negotiate wage pacts.

(continued)

Table 4.4.4 Continued

Field/country	Alliance	Type of Alliance	Structure
Mexico			
National	Consultations by the Presidency	Formal *ad hoc*	Private sector participation through consultations and negotiations with business associations, unions, other members of civil society.
Panama			
National	National Concertation for Development Preparation of national development strategy	Formal, structured	Council with 58 representatives of business, unions, the Church, social sectors, indigenous groups, political parties and the government at the central and local levels
Peru			
National	National Accord	Formal Structured	More than 40 members made up of political parties, business, labor, farmers, univerisites, churches, regional representatives, government ministers and chaired by the President of the Council of Ministers
National	National Competitiveness Council	Formal Structured	President of the Council of Ministers, ministers of state, representatives of business, labor and INDECOPI (NGO that oversees competition issues)
Uruguay			
National	Sectorial Tripartite Councils	Formal Structured	Sectoral ministries, sectoral business associations, labor of the sector and sometimes a representative of the innovation agency ANNI.

Source: Authors based on official data.

national endeavor which gives legitimacy to industrial policies. This would be the case of the formally structured Economic and Social Development Council (CDES) of Brazil, the National Accord in Peru, the National Planning Council in Colombia, the Economic and Social Council of El Salvador, the Consultative Council of Business in Ecuador and the ad hoc consultations by the Mexican Presidency to construct Vision 2030. All but the mentioned Ecuadorean council have very broad civil society representation. The National Concertation of Panama – involving broad civil society participation – is particularly interesting; it generated a real national pact on objectives, goals and strategic directions for the economy up through 2025, with commitments of financing from the Panama Canal revenue. Moreover, the National Concertation pressured and got a Fiscal Responsibility Law passed that requires every new government to present a plan on how it will spend Canal revenues in light of the national agreement on development priorities.

Other alliances are not without political dimensions, but are set up to fly closer over the policy terrain. Brazil's CNDI, consisting of 23 ministries, 14 representatives of business and the president of the BNDES, had its origins in the PITCE and continued in the era of the PDP for the officially stated purpose of defining and assisting in the coordination of the strategies. The alliance for the PDP also extended to public–private sectoral and state councils.

Colombia has a tradition going back to the mid-1990s of public–private collaboration in the design of economic initiatives. Collaboration suffered from discontinuities between governments, but there has been greater continuity since 2006. The National Competitiveness Commission, with government, business, academic, union and regional representation, has guided the strategy and policy underpinning the National System of Competitiveness. The government, business, and labor representation on Peru's National Competitiveness Council was formed with a similar function in mind, as is the government–business National Competiveness Council of the Dominican Republic. Meanwhile Chile's National Innovation Council is a government–business–academic forum that was overseeing the country's innovation strategy during the Bachelet government.

The existence of these public–private alliances in Latin America is a positive development. Public–private policy alliance councils, even in the most advanced industrialized countries, are always a work in progress, involving trial and error, given that they are a complex human endeavor promoting the interaction of multiple actors with different interests in a democratic setting (Devlin, 2012). The structure and governance of alliance councils are by their natures *sui generis*, as they must accommodate the idiosyncratic nature of each society and the objectives set out; that is, there are no formulas. Nevertheless, observation of experiences in countries with a longer history of public–private alliances suggests some serious governance problems in Latin America councils that need to be addressed. While space will not allow a comprehensive itemization of problems that can be observed in the region's councils, an illustration would be:[27]

- The formation of national-level public–private alliances signal a priority initiative. That is why political authorities of the highest level in the central government are normally on them.[28] However, some of the councils in Latin America are not yet embedded in the national political culture; that is, they can be more councils of government than councils of state, which means that their political relevance and credibility for the participating members and the country often ebbs and flows according to the personal interest of the nation's Executive. The National Accord of Peru was launched by the Toledo government where it was active in recommending initiatives for socio-economic development, but fell into disuse in the subsequent government with signs of renewal in 2012 in another government. Likewise, the National Concertation of Panama was initially kept at arms' length at the beginning of two successive governments and later embraced by the Executives due to the political commitment and persistence of its broad civil membership, strong legal footing and eventual realization by the Executive of its political utility for the government. In Chile, the National Innovation Council for Competiveness appears not to have had broad political support as attempts to give it legal status failed in Congress, eroding its legitimacy and making its sustainability vulnerable to changes in government (Devlin and Moguillansky, 2011).
- The civil representativeness of the Council can be in question, which erodes its credibility. This was a problem in Brazil's CNDES ("friends of Lula") and the Dominican Republic's CNC (Moguillansky, 2012). The Secretariat of the Concertation National of Panama is currently reviewing its representatives with the aim of strengthening their representativeness.
- Participation of multinationals with important operations in the country seems to be largely absent. This could be lost opportunities to encourage more linkages with domestic firms and gain an international "antenna" for strategic thinking.[29]
- A large number of representatives in the Council's plenary ensures wide circulation of information, but it trades off with the ability to do real dialogue, problem-solving and consensus building. The more than one hundred members of Brazil's CNDES may present challenges in this regard.[30]
- Lack of engagement by the minister of finance can dilute the council's link to the national budget. The ministers of finance in Brazil and Colombia are active in those countries' councils, which is an asset. Brazil has the added heft of the active participation of the BNDES.[31]
- The Councils (including their technical commissions) can be relatively inactive, which erodes credibility and the interest of participation by high-level civil representation. Brazil's CNDI apparently had not been meeting (although the Plano Brasil Maior apparently is trying to revive

it).[32] Peru's National Accord has had extended periods of inactivity (with a recent attempt of the current government to revive it). The CNC of the Dominican Republic has been inactive, although its executive arm has been very effective serving as a liaison between government and business (Moguillansky, 2012).

- Major players are not discouraged by the government in their efforts to bypass the council for the tradition of intensive bilateral lobbying. This bypass of course is inevitable if the council does not meet regularly, or is not a credible interlocutor with the government. In Colombia the Executive apparently discourages private conversations with members of the National Competitiveness Commission (Moguillansky, 2012).
- The councils' governance structure and method of dialogue do not serve to overcome distrust, or indifference, between government and business. This has been a problem in Chile. The National Competiveness Council of Peru also appears to have been ineffective in creating sustained real engagement between government and business. In Uruguay the ministries' attention to, and priority for, the tripartite sectoral councils is quite variable.
- Generally, the councils do not have well-financed independent and neutral technical secretariats that can facilitate problem-solving deliberations in the national interest and monitoring of the degree to which recommendations or agreements are really translated into policy and a budget. This raises the risk of capture of the government by private interests, or the capture of civil society representatives by the government. The Concertation National of Panama has a financed Secretariat that provides these services and the additional support of UNDP. Peru's resuscitated National Accord recently secured financing for a small secretariat in charge of administrative and technical support.
- Transparency in the councils' governance is not always the best.
- The communication between the National Councils discussing the "big picture," which advise the Executive, and the National Competitiveness Councils, is either sparse or non-existent. This lack of articulation can "balkanize" dialogue and erode the credibility and/or political legitimacy of either or both councils, thereby reducing their effectiveness as advisory or technical tools.[33]
- National council members, or their counterparts in the regions (whether associations or individuals), can lack the capacities to effectively participate. The regional shortcomings have been a problem in Colombia and Chile. Financing, technical assistance and capacity building can be a remedy for this problem.[34]

4.4.3.5 Coordination and monitoring

Coordination. The effective coordination and monitoring of industrial (or for that matter any) policies are critical for their effective implementation.

Coordination is always a major challenge for any government. Moreover, as seen in Figure 4.4.3, the complexity of coordinated management rises sharply the more ministries/executing agencies must leave their "silos" to address cross-sectoral, regional or interregional policy initiatives.

Coordination and monitoring within government was another major weakness of the old industrial policy. It continues to be a weak point today in many governments. However, a number of countries have made serious efforts to break the status quo with new ambitious schemes that attempt to improve coordination. Several illustrations are presented here.

In Brazil, Figure 4.4.4 outlines the coordination that was set up for the PDP strategy.[35] One virtue is that it was a first attempt to break out of the disconnected "silos" that traditionally plagued program implementation and replace it with a more whole-of-government approach. As can be seen, the Ministry of Development, Industry and Trade was the general coordinator of the programs in the PDP. It also was a member of a managing council in which the Casa Civil of the Presidency is represented, the organ that linked the PDP to other initiatives such as the one in science and technology (this link apparently was quite effective).[36]

The day-to-day Executive Office importantly had the presence of the major financial arms of government, facilitating their full engagement with the PDP. Meanwhile, assignments were given for the execution of the

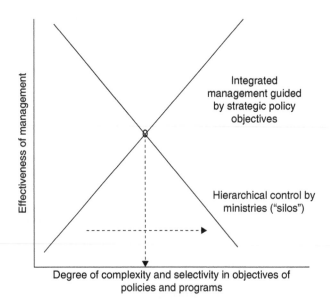

Figure 4.4.3   Coordination of management of industrial policies
Source: Marshall (2009).

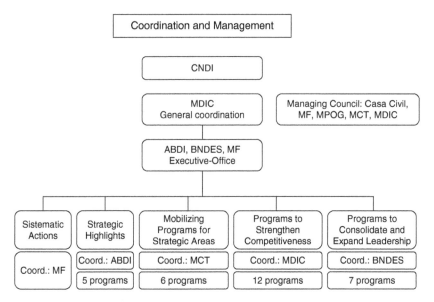

Figure 4.4.4 Coordination of the Productive Development Policy (PDP)
MF= Ministry of Finance, MPOG=Ministry of Planning, MCT= Ministry of Science and Technology
MDIC=Ministry of Development, Industry and Trade, BNDES= National Development Bank,
ABDI=Agency for Industrial Development, CNDI= National Industrial Development Council.
Source: Government of Brazil.

specific areas of the PDP. The Plan Brasil Maior includes more activities
in the areas of technology, services and trade. Adjustments involve direct
integration of the Ministry of Science, Technology and Innovation and the
Ministry of Management and the Budget.[37] If results are an indicator of the
effectiveness of the coordination of the PDP (it is too early to evaluate Plano
Brasil Maior), they suggests that it has been quite respectable. *Ex- ante* performance targets were met in 2008, while a number of shortfalls were registered in subsequent years. However, after 2008 the world economy entered
into turmoil and hence results probably were affected by shifts of attention
to shorter term economic management issues.

In Colombia, it is the High Council of the Presidency and the Department
of Planning that lead the coordination of the execution of the strategy, with
the latter assuming an ever greater role. The Department of Planning has a
history of competence and internally mirrors the ministerial portfolios. It
coordinates the mixed public–private technical committees (the workhorses
under the National Competitiveness Council) that enter into the details
of policies and their execution. However, in coordination of the transversal initiatives of the National Competiveness Policy there have been some
vacuums in sectors and regions. Meanwhile, coordination between the

Competitiveness Strategy and World Class Sectors Strategy (coordinated by the Ministry of Commerce, Industry and Tourism) reflects a lack of whole-of-government priorities and weak communication. With a view to addressing some of these problems the 2010–14 National Plan aims to have all branches of public agencies supporting enterprise development put under the umbrella of the Regional Competitiveness Councils instead of dispersed ministries. While in theory this could improve coordination, the scheme will have to address capacity building of the weaker regional councils and more transparency in their criteria for the selection of representatives and the use of funding (Moguillansky, 2012).

In the Dominican Republic, notwithstanding the dormant nature of the National Competiveness Council, the Executive Office of the Council has acted as an effective, proactive de facto coordinator between government agencies and businesses, with a view to enterprise and cluster development under the National Plan for Competitiveness for which it also was a catalyst.[38] Meanwhile, in Uruguay, the central government formed a Cabinet-level Productive Committee, led by the Ministry of Industry, that meets every 15 days to coordinate the implementation of industrial policies by the sectoral ministries. However, within the Cabinet Committee there is not always consensus, which makes the task of executing agencies more difficult.

Ecuador undertook a wholesale diagnosis and reform of its central government to strengthen the coordination of the public sector's delivery of the objectives in the country's national plan (Apaza, 2011). To eliminate identified duplication and overlap, the competencies of ministries and their decentralized agencies have been clarified. Coordination of industrial policy is the responsibility of the Coordinating Ministry of Production, Employment and Competitiveness, which participates in the National Council of Production. There is, however, an institutional weakness in the implementation capacity of the ministries and agencies subordinated to the coordinating minister.

Coordination has traditionally been a problem in Chile. Perhaps reflecting weaknesses in the National Innovation Council for Competitiveness, it continued to be a problem even in this new institutional arrangement. However, the government agencies began to take matters into their own hands. For example, ProChile, located in the Ministry of Foreign Affairs, and CORFO, which supported industrial promotion and innovation, traditionally worked in silos. During the government of President Bachelet, given that the innovation strategy was designed to innovate for export, the heads of the two agencies took the initiative to join forces in a common program (Devlin and Moguillansky, 2011).

Monitoring. As for monitoring implementation, there are some advances that can be identified. An innovative formal system is in place in Brazil. In Colombia, the Private Sector Competitiveness Council – made up of signature Colombian firms and selected hosted multinationals[39] – has effectively assumed this responsibility. In Panama it is the Secretariat of the National Concertation that monitors; a review of implementation of commitments by the government is currently underway. Meanwhile, Mexico has detailed annual reports of the progress in implementing the goals set out in its national plan.

4.4.4 What's old about the new regionalism?

We have observed some illustrations of advances in the application of industrial policies in Latin America. However, there also are some lingering bad habits that are more than just exceptions to the norm in the region. Since these weaknesses have been around for a long time, and hence are not new, we can be more brief.

4.4.4.1 Continuity between governments

Strategies have to be continuously monitored, adjusted, refined, and abandoned when they clearly are not working. However, Latin American public policy has traditionally suffered from what Machinea (2005) has termed a "refounding syndrome": each new government negates the policy and programs of the previous government and introduces a new program without evaluating what of its predecessor worked and what did not. In the area of macroeconomics this tradition may have ended as successive governments in the region seem now to share a common bond of preoccupation about the primacy of macroeconomic balances regardless of political party or ideology. Drawing on our illustrations, progress has also been seen industrial policy too. The switch from the Lula to Rousseff governments brought a new plan, but it built on the former PDP. Meanwhile, in Colombia, the switch from the Uribe to Santos governments witnessed new initiatives, but these too built on the earlier effort. Relative continuity has been maintained in Uruguay as well. This perhaps has been aided by the fact that the Presidents came from the same party.[40]

In Panama, as mentioned, the current government initially did not show interest in the National Concertation that emerged during the previous government. However, that changed, perhaps because the National Concertation has strong political roots and it named a new Secretary General respected by the Executive of the country. In the case of Chile, the current government suspended the national innovation strategy for competitiveness developed over the life of the two previous governments of the now opposition "Concertación." This could be a setback for industrial policy in that country. The planning of the innovation initiative had respectable domestic and international support and the pieces were put in place for implementation. A major dismantling of the programs along with related technical personnel and the dedicated forums behind the strategy would erase the new capabilities that the country was gaining in managing a sorely needed innovation strategy. Its fate may have been sealed by the fact that the initiative appears to have been more of an "initiative of government than of state" (a sufficient national consensus was not built around it). Moreover, the country faced the inertia of "path dependency" in terms of both a long contemporary "custodial-like" public management of industrial development and a legacy of relatively marked ideological differences between the two coalitions of political parties about the role of government in the economy.[41]

4.4.4.2 Government capabilities

The Missing Merit-based Professional and Technically Capable Civil Service. Most Latin American countries have civil service laws on the books. But few have implemented and updated them (Grindle, 2010). Beyond central banks and ministries of foreign affairs, most countries in the region still have ad hoc personnel arrangements that do not come close to the criteria of a professional and technocratic civil service (see Table 4.4.5 and Figures 4.4.5 and 4.4.6). Lack of systems geared to merit-based recruitment of the "best and the brightest" for career streams, coupled with poor pay and esteem for public service, means that low- and mid-level posts often have staff of middling technical caliber which makes needed professional delegation difficult. Meanwhile, more senior management positions are filled by political appointments or consultants with special income arrangements

Table 4.4.5 A definition of a professional civil service

"Civil service systems are those in which the preponderance of non-elected public sector jobs are filled through a process of credentialing based on education, examination or some other test of merit; in which a career ladder exists and is accessed through regularized demonstration of credentials of education, examination, tenure in office or other form of assessing merit; in which tenure is secure barring malfeasance in office; and in which movement in and out (through retirement, for example) is regulated and compensated. In such a system, the official performs duties for the state or the service, not for the patron or party. The rules of the game in the system are formal and objectified through rules and procedures."

Source: Grindle (2010).

Table 4.4.6 Singapore minister on the salaries for civil servants

"It is necessary to avoid a gap between the wages of public and private sectors in order to recruit qualified personnel who will remain in the public sector; otherwise, Singapore would lose a key advantage over other countries: the existence of a public administration that is honest, competent and effective."

Source: *Straits Times*, 3 March 2007.

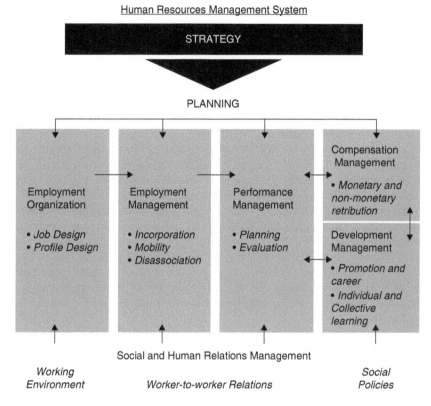

Human Resources Management System

Figure 4.4.5 Characteristics of professional civil service personnel management.
Source: Longo (2004)

and are subject to high turnover between governments, thereby eroding institutional memories.[42] This situation is also an environment fertile for corruption of different types. Ministries and executing agencies charged with industrial policies are often the ones most plagued by this problem.

This general characteristic of a lack of a well-motivated, stable, technically competent, and accountable civil service at all the corresponding levels of government – and especially at those levels charged with productive transformation – is the Achilles' heel of industrial policy in Latin America. Indeed, no countries have successfully caught up with rich countries without a competent professional and technocratic civil service. Moreover, if the new industrial policy requires public–private alliances, the weak condition of the civil service structure will discourage businesses and other civil society leaders to ally themselves with government, unless they can see it as a channel for special favors.

Hence, in our view the building and strengthening of a competent professional civil service in Latin America has the urgency of a state emergency and should be an endogenously driven priority component of industrial policies.

There are two related issues that also are legacies of the past.

Structure of Ministries and Executing Agencies. Many ministries are still structured as they were in the bygone era of ISI and need to have their internal structure and processes evaluated and updated to the realities of globalization and the new industrial policies. Moreover, executing agencies of ministries – the workhorse of industrial policies – are typically an integrated part of the ministerial bureaucracy. Consideration could be given to making these agencies statutory bodies under the ministries with public–private boards of directors. This would provide for the delegation of authority and the flexibility in personnel and program management that are needed to face the fast-moving challenges of globalization and international competitiveness.

Tax Pressure. An effective government needs revenue to finance a professional civil service and incentive programs for productive transformation. In Latin America the countries with the most need for structural change exhibit central governments applying the lowest tax pressure, typically in the low teens.

4.4.4.3   Evaluation of impacts

"Does it work? Let's try it and if it does work, fine, let's continue it. If it doesn't work, toss it out, try another one": the ex-Prime Minister of Singapore commenting on the government's support programs for productive transformation (Mydans and Arnold, 2007).

One of the dictums of the new industrial policies is knowing when to quit; learning how to "pick losers" and eliminate/phase them out.[43] Evaluation of the impact and effectiveness of the program vis-à-vis the objectives set out is a critical component of modern industrial policy. Rigorous assessment based on appropriate methodologies and empirical data gathering can be challenging and bear significant cost. But it has to be done and countries like Finland have led the way (Devlin and Moguillansky, 2011).[44]

There are many advantages of rigorous evaluation. Most obviously, it helps to evaluate value for the money spent on the program, identifying needed adjustments or the wisdom of termination. Just as importantly, it can justify to taxpayers the public outlay of resources for the program – and highlight its contribution to growth and an eventual fiscal return. Or evaluation can provide ammunition to terminate in the face of lobbying by beneficiaries of the incentive. In Latin America the systematic evaluation of the impacts of IP programs vis-à-vis objectives set out is a new frontier that must be conquered.[45]

4.4.4.4 Weak regional/local counterparts

This was a problem in the old regionalism too, but in today's environment, where production and intellectual networks are increasingly important for competitiveness and learning, the low capacity of actors not on center stage nationally is a handicap for effective industrial policies.

4.4.4.5 Corruption

When talking about the new industrial policies in Latin America, the issue of corruption always rears its head. We have not attempted to explore this important issue, but one thing is for sure: warnings of corruption in Latin America existed in the era of the old industrial policy and in the era of the Washington Consensus too. Moreover, even countries that have successfully applied industrial policies for catch-up have not been a community of saints (Khan, 2006). So while corruption is for many reasons an important issue for governance, it should not detract from the arguments for doing effective industrial policies.

4.4.5 Addendum: two slightly existential issues

One issue that requires more research and exploration is Ricardo Hausmann's (2008) "high bandwidth" dilemma, which is now gaining more attention in light of growing interest in public–private collaboration. Hausmann has been one of the innovators in the thinking about the new industrial policy. In terms of his high bandwidth argument, it points out that the market is complex. Hence, just as decentralized decision-making, as found in the "invisible hand" of Adam Smith's free market, is more efficient than central planning, decentralized self-organizing bodies in society are the best interlocutors for government in its search of information for the provision of public goods to service industrial policy. Thus Hausmann proposes that an "open architecture" of public–private collaboration is better than forums that are organized by governments around predetermined groups.

He and others, pointing to the US experience, toy with the idea that lobbying – while recognizing warts that make it suboptimal – could be a second-best decentralized approach to elicit information from the private sector for the provision of public goods. This seems to lead to a conclusion that Latin America should explore strengthening institutionally based lobbying to support its industrial policies. If we are interpreting this correctly, we find the idea unpalatable. Many think that the drivers of the USA's competitive success are waning as its congress and executive branch are bogged down in discrete initiatives, but not an overall strategic policy approach to improved competitiveness.[46] Moreover, it is common to hear that the malaise of the U.S. economy is due to the fact that the country's congress has been literally bought out by special interests. In any event, lobbying seems to be an odd channel for formulation of public interest-based industrial policy given its lack of transparency, information asymmetries, the leverage of money and a significant number of less than engaged voters.[47]

On these grounds – notwithstanding lobbying which will always go on – we think that there is a strong argument for well-governed public–private forums whether of the aforementioned formal structured or ad hoc types. They provide for transparency, formal or tacit rules of the game, contestable dialogues/problem-solving and can provide mechanisms for technical support which can balance capacities of the players, among other things. The argument for "open architecture" in terms of who participates makes sense particularly for mid-level strategies (Figure 4.4.2) that often require coordination of cross-sectoral interests (for example, innovation) and/or where these interests have a degree of practice in self-organization/cooperation.[48] Nevertheless, governments will have to be more proactive in organizing representation for umbrella forums setting out national public interest-related priorities and providing cohesion for medium- to long-term development strategies that guide and legitimize industrial policies at the different levels of Figure 4.4.2;[49] and for forums aiming to develop sectors or activities that do not yet exist, or where self-organizing stakeholders are not naturally acting in the public interest.

Finally, in terms of the bandwidth argument, true, economies are complex. However, in the more backward Latin American countries that are lagging in structural transformation the complexity at the sectoral level should not be an overwhelming puzzle to significantly unravel and hence get started with applying industrial policies. It would require the set up of well-governed, problem-solving public–private collaboration and progressive capacity building of the civil service. In many of these economies the obstacles to adding value to "maquila" and natural resources are often quite basic and identifiable (even with rough and ready methodologies), especially if there is technical assistance. So the real dilemma may be a different one: (i) how to achieve the creation and institutional strengthening of professional and technically- capable public bureaucracies; and (ii) the formation of well-governed mechanisms of public–private collaboration and problem solving that are rooted in political culture and have the serious engagement of the Executive in the spirit of "embedded autonomy."

The second, slightly existential issue is public–private collaboration and the engagement of the big business groups that operate in Latin American countries. Schneider (2012) has some relevant observations in this regard. They are very important: for example, in Chile the 20 largest firms account for half of GDP. Their upside is that they hire the best talent, and being diversified, family controlled and hierarchical they are agile in the allocation of resources and can take a medium- to long-term perspective. But they have serious downsides in that they often exercise oligopolistic power; they leverage political power bilaterally and personally; they grow through acquisition and invest little in R&D. We would also add that their allegiance and linkages to the domestic market are often underexploited.

A common reaction is that if government attempts to engage these powerful groups it will be captured. We think there is no alternative but to address the potential of this national resource. Determined political leadership, coupled with engagement of these business groups in national public–private alliances to support industrial policies that benefit their competitive self-interest to move up the world's productive hierarchy, would seem to be a way to exploit the upside characteristics of their operations.[50] Schneider suggests that industrial policies be targeted specifically to the firm, which makes sense given the personality-based nature of management. However, this will require that public sector find ways for engagement to be practiced with the "embedded autonomy" that is needed to protect the public interest.

4.4.6 Conclusions

After a hiatus during the era of the Washington Consensus, the proactive State and strategic industrial policy initiatives aiming to promote productive transformation and accelerated growth "are back" in Latin America. However, in important ways the industrial policies of today have new characteristics compared to the old industrial policies of 1950–80 – which generated advances but had serious and costly vulnerabilities too.

The region has consolidated a culture of macroeconomic stability and engagement with a globalizing world economy. Policy is now formed in a democratic setting. However, the structural weaknesses exhibited in the economies of the region even after two decades of reform, coupled with the challenges of globalization and an unexceptional growth performances compared to other developing regions, have created demands for more active State support of productive transformation. The types of structural weaknesses exhibited in Latin America are exactly the ones that industrial policy is best able to address. Moreover, mostly all countries that have achieved sustained economic catch-up have been practitioners of industrial policies.

What's new in the new industrial policies compared to the old? While we have not been able to do a "10 digit" survey of the nature of industrial policies in all the countries of the region, looking at a selected number of different types of countries suggests the following stylized facts:

- Industrial policies are being aimed at much more open economies now led by the private sector which faces international competition in traded goods and services. Moreover, the industrial policies are mostly geared to improving existing international competitiveness, while the promotion of new activities is more limited and generally does not attempt heroic leaps forward that totally ignore comparative advantage or realistic possibilities for building new upgraded knowledge and capacities. Thus the deployment of the new industrial policies generally reflects the prudence of attempting to "walk before running" in terms of industrial promotion.

- One observes the gradual emergence of innovation as a priority in industrial policies—an area where Latin America has seriously lagged. This means that the region is following the lead of successful catch-up developing countries which began to place strategic emphasis on innovation in the 1990s.
- Fiscal management is better and strategies/plans have closer links to budgets; hence, words in national plans/strategies are more likely to translate into deeds.
- There is a much heighted preoccupation about mechanisms for coordinating government action and monitoring outputs of planned industrial policies.
- Public–private policy alliance councils have emerged in many countries to guide governments in the direction, content and implementation of industrial polices. This is important since modern industrial policy recognizes that for market economies in an era of globalization all views are now, more than ever, very partial. Hence, industrial policy cannot be designed "top-down." Rather it is really a question of finding an effective social process and corresponding institutional arrangement of public–private collaboration that problem solves and elicits information for the effective provision of public goods supporting private sector experimentation, learning and upgrading without capture of the State by special interests.

While these advances are encouraging and major, one also sees serious limitations, some of which are hangovers from the past. These must be addressed if industrial policies are to be done right and progressively raise their ambition.

- Public–private policy alliance councils are a welcome new development in the region. However, they still must be viewed as a work in progress. All the councils exhibit flaws in their structure and the tangible and intangible dimensions of governance. These limit their effectiveness as a social process for the search of information and consensus to support the deployment of strategies and support programs for productive transformation.
- Sometimes there is less than enthusiastic private sector participation in public–private alliances along with a preference for bilateral lobbying. This may sometimes be attributed to the above-mentioned flaws in the governance of the alliances, which sometimes include less than sincere participation of the leaders of government.

- While there are signs of improvement, the continuity of programs over the political cycles can still be breached by the old "refounding syndrome" in the region, whereby a new government unilaterally aborts the program of a predecessor without serious evaluation of what worked and what did not.
- An Achilles' heel of industrial policies in Latin America is the lack of a merit-based and technically capable professional civil service in most countries of the region. No country with a capitalist economy has managed to achieve economic catch-up without a competent public bureaucracy to partner with the private sector. Hence this weakness in Latin America should be treated as a "national emergency" that makes the building, or strengthening, of a professional technocratic civil service an endogenous priority component of industrial policies. Only with a stronger civil service (*cum* political leadership) will the region be able to raise the ambition of IP to accelerate scaling up for the diversification and upgrading of economic activities that will allow it to eventually reach the higher echelons of the world's productive hierarchy.
- Competent states need finance and hence adequate tax pressure, something which many countries in the region still lack. Moreover, the structure and processes in ministries and their executing agencies – often not much different that the era of import substitution industrialization – need to be reformed to respond better to the private sectors' challenges of a globalized world economy.
- While the countries are advancing in their ambition for coordination and monitoring, they have not yet entered into the vital terrain of evaluation of the impact of specific industrial policy support programs vis-à-vis their intended objectives. This is a vital gap in efficient industrial policy because one of the tenants of modern industrial policy is to know how to identify losers and abandon them. In addition, evaluation supports another tenant: close public collaboration with the private sector without capture of the State by special interests. It is also necessary to justify the cost of government interventions to the taxpayer.
- Regional counterparts of national public–private alliances are often weak in finance, technical capacities and interest, compounding communication bottlenecks in the network of alliances in the nation.

We also observe that the exploration of a decentralized "open architecture" for public–private alliances can make sense for certain mid-level strategies under the right conditions. However, proposals that lobbying should be a major vehicle to achieve this is unpalatable due to, *inter alia*, the lack of transparency, the leverage of money, asymmetric capacities of players and the risks of weak mediation of private interest by the public interest. We also agree with some analysts that argue that industrial policy must give special focalized and customized attention to exploiting the upside of large domestic business groups for development and upgrading of the domestic economies at large.

In sum, industrial policies have returned to Latin America and their character is quite different from the much maligned (not totally fairly) policies of the ISI era. But the secret of successful industrial policies still depends on doing it right. Advances in this regard are significant, but there is considerable room yet for improvement.

Notes

1. This concern about poverty would be part of Rodrik's (2006) "augmented" Washington Consensus.
2. The OECD Program for International Student Assessment (PISA) scores for Latin American participants reveals poor student performances. Available online at www.oecd.org/edu/pisa/2009.
3. Yla-Anttila and Palmberg (2007); Blomstrom and Kokko (2003) and Mamood (2000).
4. This seems to be a problem in oil-rich Norway.
5. Interview with a high-level official in the Ministry of Agriculture. Also see "Colegio de Ingenieros Forestales (n.d.).
6. For example see Paredes and Sanchez(1994); Gechunoff and Canovas (1994); Fernandez(2000); Alarco and del Hierro (2010).
7. See Santiso (2008) and *AméricaEconomía* (2010).
8. See, for example, Solari and Franco (1978), Pinto (1973), Ortega (1989), Ocampo (1984), Devlin (1994) and Gonzalez (2012).
9. See Table 6.1 in Devlin and Moguillansky (2011), which presents the national plans of the era.
10. Ocampo's (2006) moniker is more technically correct.
11. Baruj, Kosakoff and Porta (2006)
12. The Plan gave birth to some notable successes in ethanol based on sugar cane and the development of deep sea oil drilling by Petrobras. Previous plans gave rise to other Brazilian champions of today such as its agroindustry and Embraer.
13. Exports were seen as more of a balance of payments financing tool than a vehicle for learning, innovation and growth.
14. The current government, which entered power in 2010, suspended the strategy launched by the opposition. The National Innovation Council for Competitiveness announced a review of the strategy of innovation in April 2011: http://www.cnic.cl/.
15. The focus on competitiveness of areas of existing comparative advantage gained a higher profile in the PDP after public criticism of the PITCE, which aimed principally at four high technology sectors: biotechnology, ITC, semiconductors and pharmaceuticals.
16. Zebral (2011) argues that the PDP was aimed at bolstering the traditional "clientelist" network of big Brazilian firms.
17. See Gobierno Federal de Brasil (2011)
18. A paradigmatic case is Korea which rejected advice "to do what it does best and trade for the rest". The strategy was to continuously build new capacities in order to climb up the world's hierarchy of production. (Prestowitz, 2012).

19. A special emphasis has been placed on the competitiveness of SMEs.
20. See Palacios (2008) for an example of industrial policy initiatives in Jalisco.
21. While innovation is part of recent Brazilian strategies, the fact is that the country has a long history of innovation in agro-business, energy and natural resources, aeronautics, etc. Brazil is the only country in Latin America that has consistently stood out for its expenditure on R&D (recently 1.1 percent of GDP).
22. For instance, in Chile 90 percent of the resource allocation was envisioned for "neutral" support of innovation (Consejo de Innovación de Chile, 2008). In Colombia, the National Competitiveness Policy has focused on transversal initiatives across sectors involving five strategic pillars and 15 plans of action. Meanwhile, Brazil's Central Bank President has recently indicated that his country will strengthen the horizontal modes of industrial policies (Wheatley and Rathbone, 2012).
23. Some have expressed concern for inadequate allocation of resources to SMEs, which perhaps is being remedied in Plano Brasil Maior.
24. A management rule of thumb for innovation is that the closer the supported activity is to the market, the more there should be full pay or co-pay by the beneficiary, while the more distant it is to the market the more likely a grant is appropriate (Devlin and Moguillansky, 2011).
25. Some strains of thought doubt business and government can work together without capture. The origins of this go back to Adam Smith (1965) as cited in Herzberg and Wright (2006): "People of the same trade seldom meet together, even for merriment and diversion, but the conversation ends in a conspiracy against the public, or on some contrivance to raise prices...But though the law cannot hinder people of the same trade from sometimes assembling together, it ought to do nothing to facilitate such assemblies, much less to render them necessary." Some modern day schools of economic thought have tended to be skeptical of private–public economic policy alliances because of distaste for its corporatist overtones and belief in the logic that self-interest leads attempts at collective action to degenerate into concessions for special interests (for example, Buchanan and Tullock, 1962). However, there is ample evidence that private-public alliances can be an effective tool for industrial policies and reforms more generally (Herzberg, 2004 and Griffins and Zammuto, 2005).
26. In Ireland the national public-private alliance council was critical in developing a social consensus on the allocation of a large sum of public monies to support innovation rather than on more popular social issues that had gained the attention of the public (Devlin and Moguillansky, 2011).
27. Also see Devlin and Moguillansky (2011) and Devlin (2012).
28. The presence of an engaged and committed high level authority like a president, vice president or prime minister has various advantages. It signals political commitment. It attracts the participation of high level representatives of the private sector. The high level authority can also pressure ministries to convert words into deeds, including budget allocations. Since Presidents are usually busy people it is important to have a powerful ministry in charge of follow-up (Devlin, 2012). In Peru the CNC has had leadership from a powerful minister, but not always the engagement of the Executive. This may partly explain why priorities set out in the CNC were not very effectively sorted out and translated into action.
29. Countries that have caught up by initially relying on FDI have incorporated multinational representation on their councils, directly, or through participating business associations (Devlin and Moguillansky, 2011). Colombia's Private Sector Competitiveness Council, which participates actively in that country's strategy, has representation of multinationals hosted by the country.

30. Surveys show that the participants' satisfaction with the CNDES was only moderate and some of the major players lost interest (Zebral, 2011).
31. The Competiveness Council in Peru is now housed in the Ministry of Finance, but as mentioned earlier, financing is largely provided by donors and multilateral agencies
32. This may explain why many business interests initially did not feel well informed about the PDP (Devlin and Moguillansky, 2011). The tripartite sectoral councils did involve significant private–public interaction.
33. This became a major problem in the Irish Alliance which perhaps contributed to the country's crisis (Devlin and Moguilansky, 2011).
34. Spain, in order to have effective private sector interlocutors for the government, helped finance the strengthening of business associations (Devlin and Moguillansky, 2011).
35. Interestingly, the cascading of responsibilities is somewhat similar to how Singapore managed its most recent flagship development strategy (Devlin and Moguillansky, 2011).
36. Personal rapport also matters in this issue and that apparently existed between the teams of the BNDES and the Ministry of Science, Technology and Innovation.
37. Also linked to the coordination network are public-private councils that oversee implementation of the sectoral and systemic actions, respectively, of the Plan.
38. The role of the Executive Office of the CNC seems to mirror the story of Czech Invest, where a dynamic director and staff absorbed a de facto role in coordinating investment attraction and local enterprise development. (Devlin and Moguillansky, 2011).
39. Also participating in associate status are representatives of several universities and business associations.
40. As Ocampo (2012) points out, while having essentially the same objectives, prior to the mid-2000 successive presidents abandoned competitiveness programs of their predecessors.
41. A very similar situation explains the demise of the Growth and Innovation Board of New Zealand (Devlin and Moguillansky, 2011).
42. The Commonwealth tradition is interesting. In this type of civil service a high ranking civil service manager (for example, a secretary general) is just under the minister and his/her position is not affected by changes in governments/ ministers, which provides institutional memory to management.
43. This is something the Asian Tigers did even in the "old" days.
44. Finland has shown that well designed and implemented subsidies for innovation actually generate a positive fiscal return for the government (Devlin and Moguillansky, 2011). Brazil has broad macro-like target indicators, but no program-specific impact evaluations which are a critical tool for evaluating effectiveness (Almeida and Ross Schneider, 2012).
45. Apaza (2011) reports that Ecuador's planning ministry is in the process of developing a methodology for evaluations of impact.
46. For example, Porter (2008).
47. Articles in the *Washington Post* of May 13 on lobbying in the oil and gas as well as beef industries are helpful reminders.
48. Finland's Research and Innovation Council has recently decided that it membership in the future will be less based on social representation and more based on expertise (Devlin, 2012).

49. One of the shortcomings in Australia is that its innovation strategy may be too decentralized and lacks an overarching coherence (Cutler, 2012).
50. These firms could be motivated by the fact of "doing more of the same" in a competitive world can a losing strategy.

References

Aghion, P., M. Dewatripont, L.Du, Harrison, A. and Legros, F. (2012), "Industrial Policy and Competition".

Agosin, Manuel, Larraín, Christian and Grau, Nicolas (2009), "Industrial Policy in Chile", Documento de Trabajo No. 294, Department of Economics, University of Chile, Santiago, Chile.

Alarco, German and del Hierro, Patricia (2010)" Crecimiento y concentración de los principales grupos empresariales en México", *Revista de la CEPAL* No. 101, August.

Almeida, Mansueto and Schneider, Ben Ross (2012), "Globalization, Democratization and the Challenges of Industrial Policy in Brazil," Korean Development Institute, July.

AméricaEconomía (2010), "Ranking Multilatinas 2010."

Apaza, Carmen (2011) "Estudio comparativo sobre proceso de reforma de estructuras públicas en países seleccionados," Departamento para la Gestión Pública Efectiva, Organization of American States, Washington, DC.

Baruj, Gustavo, Kosacoff, Bernardo and Ramos, Adrián (2006), "Políticas nacionales y la profundización del Mercosur: el impacto de políticas de competitividad," Project Paper 74 (Santiago, Chile: Economic Commission for Latin America and the Caribbean).

Bizberg, Ilan (2008) "Alianzas public-privadas, estrategias para el desarrollo exportador y la innovación: el caso de México," Economic Commission for latin America and the Caribbean, Mexico City (June).

Birdsall, Nancy, de la Torre, Agusto, and Valencia Caicedo, Felipe (2011) "The Washington Consensus: Assessing a 'Damaged Brand'," in José Antonio Ocampo and Jaime Ros (eds), *The Oxford Handbook of Latin American Economics* (Oxford: Oxford University Press).

Blomstrom, Magnus and Kokko, Ari (2003) " From Natural Resources to High-Tech Production: The Evolution of Industrial Competitiveness in Sweden and Finland, No. 3804 CEPR Discussion Paper.

Chang, Ha-Joon (1994) *The Political Economy of Industrial Policy* (New York: St. Martin's Press).

Cimoli, Mario, Dosi, Giovanni, and Stiglitz, Joseph (eds) (2009) *The Political Economy of Capital Accumulation: The Past and Future Policies for Industrial Development* (Oxford: Oxford University Press).

Colegio de Ingenieros Forestales (n.d.) "Propuesta para la Formulación de Una Política Forestal Nacional," Santiago de Chile.

Consejo de Innovación de Chile (2008) *Hacia una estrategia de innovación para la competitividad*, vol. 2 (Santiago, Chile: Consejo de Innovación de Chile).

Coatsworth, John (1998) "Economic and Institutional Trajectories in Nineteenth Century Latin America," in J. Coatsworth and A. Taylor(eds.), *Latin America and the World Economy Since 1800* (Cambridge, MA: David Rockefeller Center for Latin American Studies, Harvard University).

Cutler, Terry (2012) "The Challenge of Industrial Policy: A Sectoral Perspective from Australia" (North Melbourne, Australia: Cutler and Company).

Devlin, Robert (1989) *Debt and Crisis in Latin America: The Supply Side of the Story* (Princeton, NJ: Princeton University Press).

Devlin, Robert (1994) "La Crisis de la Empresa Pública, Las Privatizaciones y a Equidad Social », Serie Reformas de Política Pública No. 26, Economic Commission for Latin America and the Caribbean, Santiago.

Devlin, Robert (2012) "National Public–Private Strategic Policy Alliance Councils: Their Governance Matters," forthcoming Working Paper (Washington, DC: Inter-American Development Bank).

Devlin, Robert and Moguillansky, Graciela (2011) *Breeding Latin American Tigers: Operational principles for Rehabilitating Industrial Policies* (Washington, DC: World Bank Publishers).

Dominguez, Jorge (2008) "Explaining Latin America's Lagging Development in the Second Half of the Twentieth Century: Growth Strategies, Inequality, and Economic Crisis," in Francis Fukuyuma (ed.), *Falling Behind* (New York: Oxford University Press).

ECLAC (2008) *Structural Change and Productivity Growth 20 Years Later: Old Problems, New Opportunities* (Santiago, Chile: ECLAC).

ECLAC (2010), "Latin America and the Caribbean in the World Economy 2009–2010", Santiago, Chile.

ECLAC (2011) *Latin America and the Caribbean in the World Economy 2010–2011* (Santiago, Chile: ECLAC).

Evans, Peter (1995) *Embedded Autonomy. States and Industrial Transformation* (Princeton, NJ: Princeton University Press).

Fernandez Jilberto, Alex (2000) "América Latina: el debate sobre los nuevos grupos económicos y conglomerados industriales después de la reestructuración neoliberal," *European Review of Latin American and the Caribbean Studies*, no. 69, October.

French-Davis, Ricardo (2005) *Reformas para América Latina después del fundamentalismo neoliberal* (Buenos Aires: Siglo XXI).

Giordano, Paolo and Devlin, Robert (2012) "Regional Integration," In José Antonio Ocampo and Jaime Ros (eds), *The Oxford Handbook of Latin American Economics* (Oxford: Oxford University Press).

Gobierno Federal de Brasil (2011) "Plano Brasil Maior 2011–2014. Innovar para competir. Competir para crecer".

Gonzalez, Francisco (2012) *Creative Destruction? Economic Crisis and Democracy in Latin America* (Baltimore: Johns Hopkins University Press).

Griffins, Andrew and Raymond Zammuto (2005) "Institutional Governance Systems and Variations in National Comparative Advantage," *The Academy of Management Review*, vol. 30, no. 4 (October).

Grindle. Merilee (2010) "Constructing, Deconstructing, Reconstructing Career Civil Service Systems in Latin America," CID Working Paper 204 (Cambridge, MA: Center for International Development, Harvard University).

Guerchunoff, Pablo and Cánovas, Guillermo (1994) "Las privatizaciones en Argentina: impacto micro y macroeconómicos," Serie de Reformas en Política Pública No. 21 (Santiago de Chile: CEPAL).

Hausmann, Ricardo (2008) "The Other Hand: High Bandwidth Development Policy," Research Working Paper 08-060, Kennedy School, Harvard University, Cambridge MA.

Hausmann, Ricardo and Klinger, Bailey (2006), "Structural Transformation and Patterns of Comparative Advantage in the Product Space", Faculty Research Working Paper RWP06-041, Kennedy School of Government, Harvard University, Cambridge MA (September).

Hausmann, Ricardo and Dani Rodrik (2006) "Doomed to Choose: Industrial Policy as a Predicament," Kennedy School of Government, Harvard University, Cambridge MA, (September).

Hausmann, Ricardo, Dani Rodrik and Charles Sabel (2008) "Reconfiguring Industrial Policy: A Framework with an Application to South Africa," CID Working Paper 168, Center for International Development, Harvard University, Cambridge MA, May.

Herzberg, Benjamin (2004) "Investment Climate Reform: Going the Last Mile," Policy Research Working Paper 2290 (Washington, DC: World Bank).

Herzberg, Benjamin and Wright, Andrew (2005) "Competitiveness Partnerships: Building and Maintaining Public–Private Dialogue to Improve the Investment Climate", World Bank, Multilateral Investment Guarantee Agency.

Herzberg, Benjamin and Wright, Andrew (2006) *The PPD Handbook* (Washington, DC: World Bank).

Imbs, Jean and Wacziarg, Romain (2003) "Stages of Diversification," *American Economic Review*, vol. 93, no. 1.

Inter-American Development Bank (2008) *All That Glitters Is Not Gold* (Washington, DC: World Bank).

Khan, Mushtak Husain (2006) "Governance and Anti-Corruption Reforms in Developing Countries: Polices, Evidence and the Ways Forward," Secretariat of the G-24 of Developing Countries, Washington, DC.

Klinger, Bailey and Lederman, Daniel (2006), "Diversification, Innovation and Imitation Inside the Global Technological Frontier," Policy Research Working Paper 3872 (Washington, DC: World Bank).

Lederman, Daniel and William Maloney (eds) (2007) *Natural Resources: Neither Curse or Destiny* (Palo Alto, CA: Stanford University Press).

Lin, Justin Yifu and Monga, Célestin (2010), "Growth Identification and Facilitation: The Role of the State in the Dynamics of Structural Change," Policy Working Paper 5313 (Washington, DC: World Bank).

Longo, Francisco (2004), "La calidad de los sistemas de servicio civil en América Latina y el Caribe: una metodologia de evaluación", Revista del CLAD Reforma y Democracia, No. 28, February.

Lora, Eduardo (2007) "State of Reform in Latin America: A Silent Revolution," in Eduardo Lora (ed.), *The State of State Reform in Latin America* (Palo Alto, CA: Stanford University Press).

Machinea, José Luis (2005) "Competitividad y bienestar :balanceando el corto y largo plazo," in *Las visions de país importan. Lecciones de experiencias* (Washington, DC: International Institute for Democracy and Electoral Assistance/World Bank/ Economic Commission for Latin America and the Caribbean).

Mahmood, Amir (2000) "Export Specialization and Competitiveness of Malaysian Manufacturing: Trends, Challenges and Prospects," Department of Economics, University of New Castle, Australia, October.

Marshall, Jorge (2009) "La reforma del estado: visión y proceso," Expansiva, Instituto de Políticas Públicas, Santiago, Chile.

Moguillansky, Graciela (2011) "Comisiones y Consejos Nacionales de Competitividad: Aunando los intereses público-privado en Colombia y República Dominicana," Notas Técnicas #IDB-TN-374, Sector KLN (Washington, DC: Inter-American Development Bank).

Mortimore, Michael (2008) "Can Latin America Learn from Developing Asia's Focused FDI Policies?" (Santiago, Chile: ECLAC).

Mydans, Seth and Arnold, Wayne (2007), "Creator of Modern Singapore is Ever Alert to Perils," *New York Times*, September 2.

Organization of American States (n/d) *Country Guide on Transparency Rules in the Americas*. Available online at www.oas.org/es/sap//dgpe/guia.

Ocampo, José Antonio (2012) "Boom Times a Threat to Diversification," in "Investing in Colombia," *Financial Times*, May 8.

Ocampo, José Antonio (2006) "Latin America and the World Economy in the Long Twentieth Century," in K.S. Kumo (ed.), *The Long Twentieth Century, the Great Divergence: Hegemony, Uneven Development and Global Inequality* (New Delhi: Oxford University Press).

Ocampo, José Antonio (1984) "The Colombian Economy in the 1930s," in Rosemary Thorp (ed.), *Latin America in the 1930s: The Role of the Periphery in the World Crisis* (New York: St Martin's Press).

Ortega, Luis et. al. (1989) *CORFO: 50 años de realizaciones, 1939–1989* (Santiago: Department of History, University of Chile, Santiago).

Palacios, Juan José (2008) "Alianzas publico-privadas y escalamiento industrial. El caso del complejo de alta technologia en Jalisco," Studies and Perspectives Series 98, Economic Commission for Latin America and the Caribbean, Mexico City (May).

Paredes, Ricardo and Sanchez, José Miguel (1994) "Organización industrial y Grupos Económicos: el Caso de Chile," Economics Department, University of Chile.

Peres, Wilson and Primi, Annalisa (2009) "Theory and Practice of Industrial Policy. Evidence from the Latin American Experience," ECLAC, Productive Development Department, Santiago, Chile.

Pinto, Aníbal (1973) *Chile, un caso de desarrollo frustrado* (Santiago: Editorial Universitaria).

Porter, Michael (2008) "Why America Needs an Economic Strategy," *Business Week*, October 30.

Prestowitz, Clyde (2012) "Whatever Japan Can Do, Korea Can Do It Better," June 11, Busbybrown@gmail.com.

Radosevic, Slavo (2009) "Polices for Promoting Technological Catch Up: Towards Post-Washington Consensus Approach," *International Journal of Institutions and Economics*, vol. 1, no. 1.

Reinert, Erik (2009) "Emulation vs. Comparative Advantage: Competing and Complementary Principles in the History of Economic Policy," in Mario Cimoli, Giovanni Dosi and Joseph Stiglitz (eds), *The Political Economy of Capital Accumulation: The Past and Future Policies for Industrial Development* (Oxford: Oxford University Press).

Rodrik, Dani (2004) "Industrial Policy for the Twenty-First Century," Kennedy School of Government, Harvard University, Cambridge, MA (September).

Rodrik, Dani (2006) "Goodbye Washington Consensus, Hello Washington Confusion? A Review of the World Bank's Economic Growth in the 1990s: Learning from a Decade of Reform," *Journal of Economic Literature*, vol. XLIV, December.

Sabel, Charles (2009) "What Industrial Policy is Becoming: Taiwan, Ireland and Finland as Guides to the Future of Industrial Policy," Colombia Law School, New York.

Sachs, Jeffrey (2011) *The Price of Civilization* (New York: Random House).

Schneider, Ben Ross (2012) "Business–Government relations in Latin America: Institutions, Business Groups and Electoral Systems", Department of Political Science, Massachusetts Institute of Technology, Cambridge, MA.

Smith, Adam (1965) *Wealth of Nations* (New York: Modern Library).

Solari, Aldo and Rolando Franco (1978) "La inserción de las empresas públicas en el aparato estatal uruguayo," ST/CEPAL/CONF.65/L.5 (Santiago, Chile: Economic Commission for Latin America and the Caribbean).

Santiso, Javier (2008) "La emergencia de las multilatinas," *Revista de la CEPAL*, no. 95, August.

Stiglitz, Joseph (2002) "Freedom to Choose," in Joseph Stiglitz, *Globalization and its Discontents* (New York: Norton).

Stijns, Jean Philippe (2001) "Natural Resource Abundance and Economic Growth Revisted," University of California at Berkeley, March.

Tavares, Marcia (2005) «Las multilatinas, tendencias y política pública¨ Boletín Informativo TECHINT 320. Available online at http://es.scribd.com/doc/28666981/Tavares-Marcia-Las-Multi-Latin-As-Tendencias-y-Politica-Publica.

Thorp, Rosemary (1998) *Progress, Poverty and Exclusion: An Economic History of Latin America in the 20th Century* (Baltimore: Johns Hopkins University Press).

Tussie, Diana (2011) "Latin America in the World Trading System" in José Antonio Ocampo and Jaime Ros (eds), *The Oxford Handbook of Latin American Economics* (Oxford: Oxford University Press).

Wade, Robert (1990) *Governing the Market: Economic Theory and the Roel of Government in East Asian Industrialization* (Princeton, NJ: Princeton University Press).

Wheatley, Jonathan and Rathbone, John Paul (2012) "Brazil Bank Chief Upbeat on Economy," *Financial Times*, July 27.

Williamson, John (1990) *The Progress of Policy Reform in Latin America* (Washington D.C.: Institute for International Economics).

World Bank (2012) *Global Economic Prospects* (Washington, DC: World Bank).

Yla-Anttila, Pekka and Pamberg, Cristopher (2007) "Economic and Industrial Policy Transformation in Finland," *Journal of Industry, Competition and Trade*, vol. 7, nos 3–4.

Zebral, Silverio (2011) "Alianzas public–privadas efectivas para el desarrollo: los caos de CDES y del CNDI en el 'capitalismo de enlace brasileño'," Seminario GOES, OEA, CEPAL, Seminario alianzas public–privadas para una nueva visión del desarrollo, January 10, San Salvador, El Salvador.

4.5

Comments on "What's New in the New Industrial Policy in Latin America?" by Robert Devlin and Graciela Moguillansky

Carlos Alvarez V.
Deputy Director, OECD Development Centre

4.5.1 Introduction

In their recent publication, *Breeding Latin American Tigers: Operational Principles for Rehabilitating Industrial Policies* (2011), Robert Devlin and Graciela Moguillansky managed to transcend the old and endless discussion about the desirability of implementing industrial policies, and focused instead on characterizing *how* a group of countries successfully implemented industrial policies and were able to close or substantially narrow the development gap with more advanced economies. The authors make a major contribution since they analyze the complexities of consensus building, institutional development and policy implementation, thereby identifying lessons that are extremely valuable for industrial policy practitioners.

Now, armed with this analytical framework the authors focus on the recent experience of industrial policies in Latin America, providing a fairly accurate description of recent developments in this field. They provide evidence that an increasing number of countries in the region are recognizing the need to implement policies to promote competitiveness and long-term growth, although not yet calling them "industrial policies." And they are advancing in their implementation.

The authors welcome these developments and I also celebrate this revival, especially if it is bringing new approaches that fit with changes in the world scenario. However, based on my reading of the article and my own experience, I cannot avoid the impression that that in many countries these efforts are made in a half-hearted way. But the challenges that Latin America is facing are significant and more decisive action is needed.

4.5.2 Why industrial policy in Latin America?

I agree with the reasons given by the authors in their call for a more active industrial policy in Latin America. While an important segment of the region has shown a high dynamism during the first decade of the century, like many other developing countries, and without denying the important played by sensible macroeconomic management, it is quite clear that an important part of this phenomenon is explained by exogenous factors, particularly the emergence of China in world trade and the commodity boom that this has generated. But simultaneously, and probably as a part of the same phenomenon, export diversification has tended to fall,[1] and productivity growth has not departed from its weak historical performance (IDB, 2010).

Under these circumstances the reinvigoration of industrial policies as a crucial component of the development policy mix is imperative. We are talking about policies that facilitate transformation of the economies towards higher levels of productivity by removing the obstacles that block structural change, combining horizontal with sector-specific selective measures.

Having said that, however, the task is by no means simple.

4.5.3 What is new? A new scenario

The current scenario is very different from that of the 1960s and 1970s when industrial policy was actively deployed in the region.

The current scenario offers new opportunities for catching up. The globalization process has resulted in the expansion of goods and services markets for developing countries; at present. multinational enterprises invest in developing countries not only looking for access to natural resources or attractive domestic markets, but also in a search for favorable locations to produce and export, and even carry out research and development; the unbundling of global value chains reduces the entry barriers to export certain productive activities; and the emergence of a dynamic global services market offers employment opportunities to people of varying skills.

Simultaneously, new threats emerge. Trade liberalization increases the levels of vulnerability of domestic enterprises and the establishment of provisions for the protection of intellectual property in bilateral free trade agreements and global trade regulations, increases substantially the cost of the technological learning processes, especially in smaller countries.

The entry of China into global trade is a powerful singular phenomenon that has had and will have a strong impact on Latin America at different levels. Chinese companies, with their cost advantages, have been a strong competitor to Latin American companies, having managed in many cases to displace them from both local and international markets. On the other hand, China has been a source of massive demand for raw materials, especially from South America, creating a price boom with a positive impact on growth in the subregion. In this context, the course of China's economy in the coming years is an essential variable to consider in the design of industrial policies in Latin American countries.

The combination of these phenomena has intensified the process of the declining share of the manufacturing sector in Latin American economies and the increase in the production of commodities. In many countries the drastic and rapid process of trade liberalization and the entry of China to the global market destroyed whole branches or industrial sectors. Thus, the possibility of building on capacities developed in the import substitution period no longer exists. More recently, the commodity prices boom has exacerbated the interest of local talent to look for business around these exporting sectors in search of a portion of the revenue windfall.

And, on the other hand, the policy space in the field of industrial policy has also changed. It should be noted that industrial policymakers currently lack the traditional policy instruments of selective protection or export promotion that countries like Korea, Chinese Taipei and even China, used in their expansion processes. Intellectual policy regulations also constrain the use of technology policy instruments used in the past.

4.5.4   Industrial policies for a new scenario

This is not a scenario in which weak industrial policies can succeed. *Breeding Latin American Tigers...* establishes that successful industrial policies should be based on medium- and long-term strategies, built on the basis of a solid public–private alliance and implemented by strong and well-aligned public institutions. Yet satisfying these requirements is by no means a straightforward matter, especially in a region where the Washington Consensus doctrine was applied with the highest strength producing a significant weakening of institutional capabilities in this field.

However, a process of reconstruction seems to be underway. Several countries have crafted development strategies which focus on international competitiveness, on the basis of the work of public–private arrangements and establishing formal allocation of resources for their implementation. Many countries have also established coordination mechanisms to facilitate a coherent implementation. But while progress has been made in matters of strategy building it is not so clear that improvement has reached the stage of implementation, what can be inferred from the concerns raised by the authors about the weak implementation capabilities and lack of continuity of policies.

Similar concerns emerge from a more detailed observation of the specific implementation of the policies, the volume of resources effectively committed and the breadth of the adopted measures.

First of all, in general *industrial policy initiatives don't enjoy adequate budgets*: There are no reliable figures on the total public expenditure allocated to different components of industrial policies in Latin America, but the total public expenditure in R&D acts a reasonable proxy. The average participation of R&D financed by the government in GNP in the year 2008 in a sample of Latin American countries was 0.18 percent, compared with the same indicator in OECD which was 0.67 percent in the same year. The only country in Latin America whose effort in this field get closer to the OECD average is Brazil with 0.58 percent.[2] Those countries that have successfully caught up made significant resource commitments, and this does not seem be the case in Latin America at present.

Second, *essential factors for economic transformation, such as long term-finance or skilled personnel, are not readily accessible.* Horizontal programs designed to solve these shortages have not been particularly effective. In the case of the access to credit, even accepting that financial services have expanded in Latin America in recent years, it has taken the form of trade (short-term) credit, forcing firms to resort to this kind of credit to finance long-term investments that enhance productivity, which is not efficient and expose firms to the possibility to interrupt their investment plans (IDB, 2010). So far, development banks have played a limited role in compensating for this weakness. Something similar occurs in the field of training, where relatively weak training and vocational education schemes are not being able of satisfying skills demand by industry. This situation is more critical in the field of research personnel.

Third, there is a *hesitant movement toward sector- or cluster-based programs*: the revival of industrial policies in the region has typically started with the establishment of horizontal and demand-driven instruments. That operates on the base of reasonable principles (contestability, pertinence, transparency, and so on). But usually the result is a dispersed set of initiatives that do not have a significant impact. The constraints to growth faced by companies in high-potential sectors, are usually specific to the sector or cluster to which they belong, and typically require of a simultaneous resolution. That's why a sectoral or cluster-based approach is needed. Many countries in the region have implemented cluster-inspired initiatives, but on a very small scale, and without the capacity to organize around them robust interventions. There are some examples of sectoral programs at national level, but mostly organized around one dimension, such as innovation, and not dealing with constraints in other fields.

Fourth, the *scarce use of high-powered instruments*. If protection instruments are unavailable it is necessary to deploy other instruments with a real capacity to modify behaviors in the direction signaled by national strategies. Most of them are at present used extensively in OECD countries, but not in many Latin American countries. That is the case of

- Pre-competitive and mission-oriented research: finance of research oriented to solve national economic or societal challenges, including the introduction of new products to the export portfolio of the country. This kind of research has been critical for the introduction of salmon farming in Chile or the development of the bio-ethanol industry in Brazil, but its use is not widespread in the region.

- Sectoral innovation programs: medium- and long-term programs that promote the implementation of constellations of R+D+i initiatives aimed at strengthening the competitiveness of strategic clusters or sectors. They are critical to building innovative capacities to compete in more demanding markets.
- Selective investment attraction: This permits a rapid entry to sectors where the country has latent competitive advantages and where important opportunities of technical and managerial learning exist. It maximizes its impact when it is coherently integrated in broader strategies. It has been used only in some countries like Costa Rica, Uruguay and Chile.
- Innovation-oriented public procurement which lowers barriers to the market introduction and diffusion of innovations, in areas with high learning externalities or social impact.

There is space for diversifying and strengthening industrial policy set of instruments. The experimentation of some countries in the use of more innovative approaches is a source of knowledge that can be harnessed by their peers through policy dialogue exercises.

4.5.5   Conclusions

Latin American countries are in the process of rebuilding their industrial policies, with a special emphasis on crafting medium- and long-term strategies, guaranteeing the participation of the private sector in the design and implementation of them and making an important effort of public sector internal coordination in its execution. These positive efforts at the level of design should be translated into robust programs, endowed with adequate budgets and materialized with effective instruments by strong institutions, which seems not yet be the case in many countries.

Latin America needs to move decisively toward a next stage in industrial policy, channeling a part of the rents produced from the export boom in national resources to more ambitious initiatives that facilitate the transit toward a more diversified and productive industrial structure.

The strengthening of the industrial policy framework should consider the combination of horizontal policies aimed as guaranteeing the access of critical inputs for production upgrading with sectoral or cluster-based initiatives materialized through the use of high-powered instruments.

If recent advances consolidate as long-term trends, the social and political legitimacy of industrial policy will be restored, permitting a continuous process of capacities upgrading toward more productive industrial structures and higher welfare for the citizens of Latin American countries. Robert Devlin and Graciela Moguillansky provide very valuable insights to governments that have decided to persevere in this direction.

Notes

1. The Herfindahl–Hirschmann Index on export concentration by product increased during the last decade in Argentina, Brazil, Chile, Colombia and, to a lesser extent, Mexico.
2. The figures for some countries that have followed active catch-up policies are: Korea (0.85 percent), Finland (0.81 percent), and the Czech Republic (0.58 percent).

References

Devlin, Robert and Moguillansky, Graciela, (2011) *Breeding Latin American Tigers: Operational Principles for Rehabilitating Industrial Policies* (Washongton, DC: World Bank).

Pages, Carmen (ed.) (2010) *The Age of Productivity: Transforming Economies from the Bottom Up* (Basingstoke: Palgrave Macmillan).

Part V
Country Case Studies of Successful and Unsuccessful Industrial Policies

5.1

The Return of Industrial Policy in Brazil

David Kupfer, João Carlos Ferraz and Felipe Silveira Marques
BNDES

5.1.1 An account of the past experience in industrial policy

Up to the 1970s, Brazil implemented an industrial policy aimed at substituting imports that was consensually acknowledged for being active and strong.[1] Such activeness was the result of the broadness and depth with which the Brazilian state was willing to intervene in markets, taking on a leading allocating role in the economy. The strength of the industrial policy at that time stemmed from the meeting of three essential conditions to boost it: (i) co-existence with a favorable macroeconomic environment; (ii) intensive use of classic instruments (tariff barriers, financial and fiscal incentives for prioritized sectors in two National Development Plans); and (iii) use of state-owned companies (some existing since the 1950s, some created in the 1970s).

This active and strong industrial policy was undeniably successful in industrializing the country, but resulted in hits and misses. The policy was successful in structuring new sectors, such as petrochemicals and pulp & paper, but was unable to boost-up pre-existing sectors, such as textiles and automotives. For sectors with greater technological intensity, and thus more dependent on the capacity to innovate, both positive and negative results have been achieved, having been highly successful in the aeronautics industry, but not so much in the computer industry.

After the 1980s, the industrial policy was progressively relaxed and eventually abandoned, due primarily to the macroeconomic difficulties stemming from very high levels of internal and external debt, coupled with the ideological obstacles that marred the 1990s in Brazil. In the middle of this decade, once the hyperinflation issues were finally subdued, the macro environment, the stabilization of prices based on fiscal contraction and overvalued exchange rates, as well as privatization left little room to engage in a new industrial policy.

In the 2000s, industrial policy made a comeback in Brazil, and with growing importance. Three policies have been put into practice since then: the Industrial, Technological and Foreign Trade Policy (PITCE), from 2004 to 2007; the Productive Development Policy (PDP), from 2008 to 2010, and the Brasil Maior Plan (PBM), launched in 2011 and still underway. Nevertheless, the macroeconomic and institutional framework conditions must evolve further towards explicit actions to promote industrial development.

This article argues that the lack of these elements and the difficulties in the excessive but much-needed attention to the short-term management of the economy have hindered the design and implementation of industrial policy which, by definition, is a long-term endeavor. It is as if the conditions for activism have been re-established, but some essential prerequisites for a strong industrial policy have not. Nevertheless since 2011, short-term and long-term actions are converging, opening the path for interesting developments in the years to come.

The remainder of this paper analyzes three recent industrial policies enacted during the 2000s, and discusses their connections with the macro environment. With this analysis, the idea is to outline key challenges for Brazilian industrial development for the next few years.

5.1.2   Three recent experiences

Since the return of industrial policy to Brazil in 2004, and under a new government with an ideology that was more favorable to this type of action, there were three specific policies:

- The Industrial, Technological and Foreign Trade Policy (PITCE, 2004–2007), which aimed at strengthening the institutional framework by creating agencies and modernizing legislation to make innovation-inducing instruments more effective, focusing on, above all, technology-intensive sectors.
- The Productive Development Policy (PDP, 2008–2010), which focused on investment and innovation, but ended up having an anti-cyclical role that proved crucial in the federal government's efforts to combat the effect of the 2008 international financial crisis.
- The *Brasil Maior* Plan (PBM, 2011–14), whose main priority is to aggregate value through innovation, but which has tended more and more toward defending the internal market and recovering the systemic conditions for competitiveness, which is evident in the efforts that are more and more focused on reducing the elements that make up the "Custo Brasil" (costs related to doing business in Brazil).

These experiences, despite some similarities, offer distinct importance. On the timeline of Brazilian industrial policies, there is a clear concern to maintain continuity, but lined with flexibility. Innovation and competitiveness, for example, are clear priorities in each case. However, it is equally visible that the focus and the organization in each case were altered to tackle the different economic challenges that each of these policies had to face. The PITCE was conceived to tackle sectors with large and growing trade deficits (capital goods, semiconductors, software, as well as pharmaceuticals and medication). The PDP, in its turn, was conceived within a context of international growth and an abundance of foreign currency stemming from improvements in the terms of trade. The aim of the policy was to leverage investments and innovation to sustain growth, and the number of sectors benefited rose. The context of the PBM, in its turn, has been marked by the international crisis and fierce international competition including the expansion of imports, while emphasis is being given to innovation and to aggregating local value.

The following sections detail the guidelines of the three policies and establish a connection with the macro environment at the time they were elaborated.

5.1.3   PITCE: the return of the phoenix

The PITCE is a milestone marking the return of industrial policy in Brazil.[2] This happened, however, in a hostile macroeconomic environment, in terms of severe restrictions on external accounts. The sharp devaluation of the Brazilian real against the dollar due to uncertainties in the electoral campaign in 2002[3] put pressure on the balance of payments and the country's sovereign risk, already weakened by a deterioration of the balance of payments that had generated a currency crisis at the end of the previous decade. Then the PITCE arose deeply framed by the context of external vulnerability which, again, restricted the development of Brazil.

The policy, launched in November 2004, sought to face this situation by modernizing the industrial structure and make the country's balance of payment more robust. The focus was on technology-intensive industries, such as capital goods, semi-conductors, software and pharmaceuticals, which could provide gains in productivity and windows of opportunity to develop robust scientific and technological systems in areas, such as energy, health and agriculture.

The goal of the PITCE was to induce a change in the technological level of Brazilian industry, aiming at more innovation and differentiation of products. The expectation was that developing the country's technology sectors would favor an upgrade in exports, fostering gains in more sophisticated segments in the international market.

Efforts were focused on three different dimensions. The first was related to horizontal actions, mainly: innovation and technological development; exports; industrial modernization and improvements in the institutional environment. The second, referred to as "Strategic Options," was concentrated on the policy's vertical focus: semiconductors; software; capital goods, and pharmaceuticals. Last of all, the third focus was on the so-called Future Opportunities, favoring biotechnology, nanotechnology and biomass/ renewable energy.

Considering the measures as a whole, one of the most relevant outcomes was the improvement of incentive mechanisms for innovation, with the Innovation Law, A law expanding fiscal incentives for innovative activities, the Bio-security Law and the Biotechnology Development Policy. The Trademark and Patents Registration Office (INPI) was restructured to speed up the processing of intellectual property rights, and new sectorial programs for financing were created at the Brazilian Development Bank (BNDES), such as Profarma (pharmaceuticals). Also, the science and technology sectorial funds, which had been created a decade before, but which were then shortened as part of the effort to reduce public spending, were allowed to operate with full budget thus providing sufficient resources for R&D in priority areas.

Another substantial contribution from the PITCE were the important institutional advances to foster the comeback of industrial policy in Brazil. These include the creation of the National Industrial Development Council (CNDI), a three-pronged political structure involving government, the business sector and workers functioning as an advisory board, and the Brazilian Industrial Development Agency (ABDI), which is responsible for providing technical support for the policy. The two institutions are focused on filling institutional gaps that the dismantling of the industrial policy, which had been taken to the hilt some years earlier, had left as the main negative legacy.

As of 2004, the swift and intense improvements in the terms of trade, linked primarily to the effects of China's growth in markets to which Brazil was exporting commodities, quickly generated robust figures in the trade balance, due to basic products, rather than the sophisticated goods that had been proposed in the PITCE. The high profitability of these activities attracted foreign investments which, coupled with the strong inflow of short-term capital owing to the gains in arbitration stemming from the glaring difference between domestic and foreign interest rates, put the exchange rate on a strong evaluation track.

This gave rise to a rupture in the economic scenario in which the PITCE was based four years earlier. PITCE lasted until mid-2008 when, amidst a new economic and political framework, it was succeeded by the Productive Development Policy (PDP).

5.1.4   PDP: sailing in favorable winds and stormy weather

The PDP was conceived under an international context of strong growth and a national context of abundant reserves due to significant improvements in the terms of external trade. This new framework resulted in some trends which the policy sought to work with, of which three structural changes stand apart.

The first transformation marks the return to the importance of the domestic sources of economic dynamism, especially gross fixed capital formation (GFCF), as a strategic engine for expressive and sustained growth, which can be summarized in the idea that a virtuous cycle of inclusive growth had been established in the country.

This change was brought about by many causes. The most important came in the form of a reaction to the effects of income policies adopted by the Brazilian government, among which another virtuous cycle stands out: the restructuring of the labor market. Having started with programs of income transfer and then continued with a intensification of the policy of real increases in the minimum wage, which had been practiced since the mid-1990s, a formidable formalization of jobs took place. This formalization was accompanied by a significant increase in consumer´s credit, especially to low income families. These combined factors were fostering the most significant of all the changes underway throughout these years: a strong cycle of investments was established in the country the likes not seen since the end of the 1970s.

The PDP sought to foster investment and innovation to maintain growth. With this goal in mind, the policy, launched in May 2008, established four challenges:

(i)   expand the supply capacity of the Brazilian economy in sustainable and competitive bases to avoid bottlenecks and inflationary pressure;
(ii) increase the innovation capacity of Brazilian companies to expand competitiveness in the domestic market and strengthen their foreign insertion;
(iii) maintain the robustness of the balance of payments, staying on the path to expand and diversify exports and create favorable conditions to attract direct foreign investments; and
(iv) improve access to markets for micro and small companies (MSEs), generating positive competition and distribution effects – in conjunction with initiatives aimed at developing business systems a of larger scale and with compatible governance through better international practices.

With reference to these challenges, four macro-targets were set for the PDP:

(i)   an increase in the participation of the gross fixed capital formation (GFCF) in the GDP from 17.4 percent in 2007 to 21 percent in 2010;
(ii) an increase in the participation of corporate spending in R&D in the GDP from 0.49 percent in 2005 to 0.65 percent in 2010;
(iii) an increase in the participation of Brazilian exports in worldwide exports from 1.16 percent in 2007 to 1.25 percent in 2010; and
(iv) an increase of 10 percent in the number of exporting Micro and Small Enterprises (MSEs) by 2010 (11,792 in 2006).

To reach these goals, when the PDP was launched, initiatives and all-encompassing programs were announced. On the one hand, initiatives were outlined and aimed at favoring measures that directly affected the aggregate performance of the economy, especially fiscal measures, finance to investment and innovation, and legal certainty.

At the same time, 34 programs were structured, with implementation slated for the 2008–10 period, aimed at boosting the short-, medium- and long-term competitiveness of the Brazilian economy. The task of carrying out each one of these programs, which requires permanent and systematic dialog with the private sector, was given to Executive Committees comprising representatives from several governmental entities, with the plan to integrate and bring together efforts of the programs with the policies underway. These programs were divided into sectorial and systemic actions. The structure of the policy is explained in Figure 5.1.1.

Related to industrial structure, the PDP was organized into three groups:

(i)   Mobilizing Programs in Strategic Areas, chaired by the Ministry of Science and Technology (MCTI), whose focus was to overcome the scientific-technological challenges for innovation;

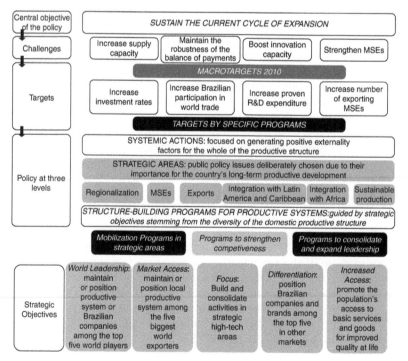

Figure 5.1.1   Structure for the Productive Development Policy
Source: Brasil (2008, p. 29).

(ii) Programs to Strengthen Competitiveness, chaired by the Ministry of Development, Industry and Foreign Trade (MDIC), whose focus was to increase domestic competitiveness and expand production links;

(iii) Programs to Consolidate and Expand Leadership, chaired by BNDES, which brought together sectors with international projection and competitive capacity, focusing on innovation and the internationalization of companies.

The sectors that are part of these three groups are outlined in Figure 5.1.2.

The PDP contributed to sustaining the growth of the Brazilian economy until the onset of the international financial crisis. The crisis, nevertheless, affected the achievement of the four macro-targets.

Throughout this adverse time, the policy was focused on resisting and overcoming the international crisis, strengthening the structure of Brazilian industry within a more competitive environment. However, these actions occurred concurrently with emerging and undesirable microeconomic transformations. Compared to industrialized nations and, principally, to emerging Asian countries, the more visible signs of industrial weakening was to be found in the slow evolution of productivity and increasing imports. The result was a sharp increase in imports of manufactured goods, and, as a consequence, the hollowing out of several industrial value chains

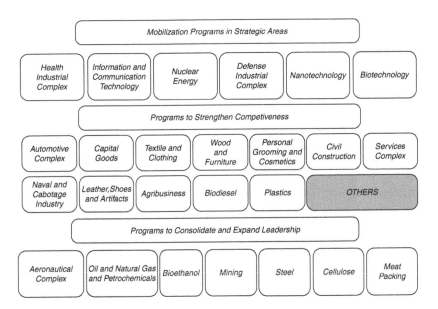

Figure 5.1.2 Sectoral dimension of the PDP
Source: Brasil (2008: 30).

installed in Brazil. Inverting this undesirable situation became a challenge to be addressed by Brasil Maior Plan (PBM). In 2011, at the end of the Luiz Inácio Lula da Silva eight years' administration (two mandates) and the rise of President Dilma Roussef, the PDP was replaced with the PBM.

5.1.5   PBM: facing a hostile environment, attention to costs and value added

The Brasil Maior Plan (PBM), launched in August 2011, was aimed at providing answers to challenges arising from slow growth in the international environment. In the internal plan, the Brazilian economy had shown signs of having overcome the most daunting part of the international crisis, which was proven by the 7.5 percent growth in GDP in 2010. Due to the economy's performance, everything suggested that the permanent objective objective of the different versions of Brazilian industrial policies in the 2000s – add value through innovation – could finally be placed at the helm. Within this context, four guiding priorities were defined.

The first guiding principle is to build and strengthen critical competencies. The aim is to enable Brazilian companies to strengthen operations in sectors in which technological innovation plays a fundamental role. There are two main targets in this area. First, large-scale Brazilian companies that already hold strategic positions in national and worldwide markets. Second, small and medium technology-based firms, associated, or not, with foreign firms, in market niches characterized by design and knowledge-intensive product lines.

The second guideline is to enhance productivity and technology upgrade along value chains. This is aimed at facing the hollowing-out process. This replacement of national products with imports is concentrated in: (i) labor-intensive industrial activities, such as textile production, footwear and toys; (ii) inputs, parts, and components in engineering-intensive businesses, such as the case of several segments in the capital goods sector and auto-parts.

The third guideline is to expand the domestic and foreign markets for Brazilian companies. This guideline seeks to invert the specialization in primary products. Over the past few decades, international insertion of the Brazilian economy has passively reflected the logic of the country's static comparative advantages. This translated into progress concentrated in primary products and industrial inputs based on natural resources, such as meat production, pulp and paper, mining, steel and agribusiness. Building dynamic and comparative advantages require broad and concerted efforts in terms of industrial policy.

The fourth and final guideline is to ensure socially inclusive and environmentally sustainable growth. There are enormous opportunities, especially in the energy sectors. The country's large reserves of renewable and non-renewable resources open much room for Brazil to step in as a reliable

energy provider for the world. In a similar vein, the rich biodiversity constitute a huge opportunity for industrial development.

Based on these guidelines, ten strategic objectives were outlined with
respective goals for the 2011–14 period,[4] as seen in Figure 5.1.3.

As with the PDP, the organization of the PBM has not only a structural
dimension, but also a systemic range. For the PBM, some 19 sectorial committees and nine systemic coordination teams were created, as shown in
Figure 5.1.4.

The Sectorial Committees were organized into five groups. This organization aims to reflect the different technical and economic characteristics of
several sectors that make up the Brazilian industrial sector.

Group I, which includes Mechanics, Electro-electronics and Health Industries,
contains sectors with a higher capacity to transform the production structure
due to their ability to disseminate innovation throughout the economy: suppliers for Oil & Gas industries; Health; Automotive; Aeronautics and Defense;
Capital Goods and ICT/Electronics.

Group II includes Scale-Intensive Industries, as activities that are at the
top of the country's export list: Chemical-Petrochemical; Bio-ethanol and
Renewable Energies; Toiletry, Perfumery and Cosmetics; Mining; Metallurgy;
and Pulp and Paper.

Group III includes Labor-Intensive Industries, which concentrate most
small and medium-sized companies in the country.

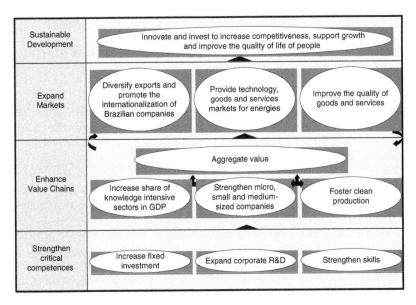

Figure 5.1.3 Strategic map for the Brasil Maior Plan (PBM)
Source: Brasil (2011: 18).

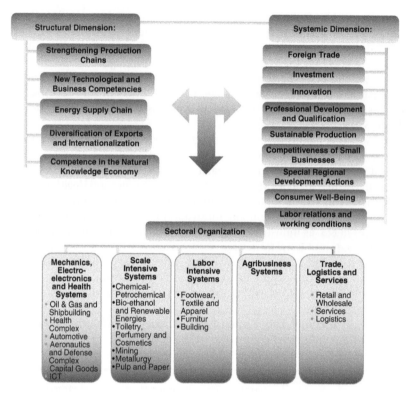

Figure 5.1.4   Sectoral dimensions and organization of the Brasil Maior Plan (PBM)
Source: Brasil (2011: 8).

Group IV, Agribusiness Systems, includes an important part of Brazilian exports that now has been boosted by the science push in biological science and the demand pull brought about by the new geopolitics driven by the problems in food safety and biofuels.

Group V, focused on Wholesale and Retail Trade, Logistics and Business Services, is a pioneering initiative in Brazilian industrial policy to explicitly include services, reflecting the growing importance of these sectors to generate qualified jobs and income.

Conceived to foster a sweeping restructuring of Brazilian industry, the PBM had to face a challenging national and international economic context. The slackening of Brazilian economy exposed an important deterioration in the competitiveness of national industry. Fierce international competition, sweeping protectionist initiatives in several countries and, above all, the loss of exchange rate competitiveness due to the overvaluation of the Brazilian Real at the beginning of 2011, placed a check on Brazilian industry's capacity to react.

Faced with these new constraints, one remarkable novelty in the PBM is the concern with defending the internal market. With this aim, the PBM has put into practice a broad number of short-term measures to reduce costs: interest rates reduction for capital goods acquisition, tax cuts on the payroll, investment and exports, and reduction in the energy bill. Associated with these short-term actions, the government reinforced the emphasis it has been putting on long-term investment plans in infrastructure (urban mobility, highways, railways, harbors and airports, energy). Most of these policies consider the importance of developing a local supply industry. The goal is to guarantee profitability in industrial operations and to encourage positive return on capital investments, which has shown a significant drop in the second half of 2011 and the first half of 2012.

PBM also acted upon sectors on two fronts. Firstly, the legal framework to enhance preference for national products and services in government purchases was updated and policy action were made more expedient. Second, special sectorial regimes were reinforced or revised with the aim of providing incentives for those firms willing to: invest in innovation; introduce energy and consumer efficient products and foster a local supply industry, all under WTO regulations.[5] In short, against incentives, explicit counterpart efforts are demanded to those firms willing to participate in sectoral program. If successful, initiatives with such references may become a model to be followed up and expanded to other economic activities.

5.1.6 Brazilian industrial development: the main challenges

The recent experience in industrial policy in Brazil has shown that, despite efforts to set quantitative targets, mobilize relevant instruments and establish interaction between public and private sectors,[6] a series of issues remain unanswered.

First, improvements in the external sector throughout the 2000s led to the accumulation of abundant international reserves. This suggested that the industrial policy could break away from the need for short-term competitiveness, required by the pressure to equilibrate the balance of payments, and move towards building a competence-based economy. Nevertheless, the volatility of the international scenario after the 2007–08 crisis gave rise to uncertainties which compromised these goals.

Particularly challenging for Brazil is the result of China's growing aggressiveness in international trade. The nature of China's dual role in the world economy – demanding commodities and offering low-cost manufactured goods implies the reorganization of international trade and capital flows. The increasing relevance of China has placed Brazil on the backfoot, evident in the fact that Chinese industrial structure is becoming increasingly competitive rather than complementary to Brazilian production. Changes in Brazilian trade dynamics, moving its focus from Europe and the USA to China, has, at least temporarily, given rise to a trend that goes against local aggregation of value.

The second challenge lies in the institutional dimension. How to combine the traditional catching-up efforts with the new redistributive objectives of the new development model is a question with as yet no clear answer. And with a political consensus concerning the future of Brazil's industry still to be consolidated, it may be difficult to mobilize the necessary resources and competences required to put in place projects and initiatives required to upgrade Brazilian productive structure.

The third is the capacity of the policy to adapt to a changing external environment. Short-term and long-term actions must converge toward a sustained development path that find resonance with interests of the business sector.

Efforts to try to face these questions are essential in a country whose macroeconomic environment has shown continuous improvements, with increasing social inclusion. Competitiveness, nevertheless, remain a challenge to be tackled.

5.1.7   Final reflections

The success of an industrial policy depends on some crucial prerequisites. One is the relevance of an explicit vision about the future and a clear strategy to build it, which will provide its essence. Another is its convergence with the macroeconomic policy, which will provide its vital signs of life. A third is the consistency of the institutional model, which will provide the capacity to improve and adapt in light of the varying economic situations that will materialize.

The 2000s were characterized by the return to industrial policy in Brazil, with growing importance and three policies in practice since then (the PITCE, 2004–07, the PDP, 2008–10, and the PBM, 2011–14).

The PITCE and the PDP represented moves ahead in relation to the first prerequisite, that is, the relevance of strategy. Above all, they represented the final resolution of the debate about the existence of, and even the need for, industrial policy, which explained the (lack of) industrial policy throughout the 1990s.

The PBM advanced towards the second prerequisite, that is, the convergence between macroeconomic management and industrial policy. Improvements in the macro environment with the recent fall in interest rates to levels that are more compatible with those in effect in the international financial system pave the way to build more long-term efforts aimed at Brazilian industrial development, with no excessive focus on short-term oscillations.

In fact, throughout these almost ten years of the return of industrial policy in Brazil, the front seat was many times taken up by the necessary management of undesired effects derived from economic uncertainties brought about, mostly by the boom of commodity prices and the international financial crisis.

The time has come to advance into the third prerequisite: the strengthening of institutions. Effective industrial policies require effective institutional coordination at all levels: among public agencies; among private entities; and between public and private sectors. Efforts along these lines should be at the forefront of the agenda of all relevant actors.

Notes

1. For a historical account of Brazilian industrial policy, see Suzigan and Villela (1997).
2. Coutinho, Ferraz, Nassif and Oliva (2012) analyze the return of Brazilian industrial policy in the 2000s.
3. The exchange rate in 2000 went from R$/US$ 2,5 in May to around R$/US$ 3,8 in October.
4. The goals are available in Brasil (2011: 19s).
5. Worthy of mention is the Automotive Regime that provides the opportunity for federal tax reductions if firms engage in R&D and engineering investments; internal supplier's development and energy and environmental efficiency improvements.
6. Ferraz, Kupfer and Marques (2012), using the Brazilian experience, discuss factors of success in implementing industrial policies, while Perez and Primi (2009) do the same using the Latin-American experience.

References

Brasil (2008) *Productive Development Policy: Innovation and Investment for Sustainable Growth* (Brasília: MDIC).

Brasil (2011) *Brasil Maior: Innovate to Compete. Compete to Grow* (Brasília: MDIC).

Coutinho, L., Ferraz, J.C., Nassif, A., and Oliva, R. (2012) "Industrial Policy and Economic Transformation," in Javier Santiso and Jeff Dayton-Johnson (eds), *The Oxford Handbook of Latin American Political Economy* (Oxford: Oxford University Press).

Ferraz, J.C., Kupfer, D., and Marques, F. (2013) "Industrial Policy and Development: Lessons from Brazil," in Richard Kozul-Wright and Jose Manuel Salazar-Xirinachs (eds), *Growth, Productive Transformation and Employment: New Perspectives on the Industrial Policy Debate* (UNCTAD/ILO). forthcoming.

Peres, W. and Primi, A. (2009) "Theory and Practice of Industrial Policy. Evidence from the Latin American Experience," *Serie Desarrollo Productivo* no. 187 (Santiago de Chile: CEPAL).

Suzigan, W. and Villela, A. (1997) *Industrial Policy in Brazil* (Campinas: Unicamp).

5.2

Comments on "New Thinking on Industrial Policy: Country Case Studies of Successful and Unsuccessful Industrial Policies – The Return of Industrial Policy in Brazil"

Volker Treichel
World Bank

Industrial policy and development: Lessons from Brazil

I am grateful for the opportunity to comment on this paper discussing industrial policy and Brazil's economic development. Over the past ten years, Brazil has made remarkable progress in achieving macroeconomic stability and high growth, while at the same time markedly reducing poverty. Indeed, over the period 2004–10 growth more than doubled to over 4.2 percent (from about 1.9 percent during the period 1996–2003), while inflation fell sharply from a peak of 15 percent in 2003 to an average of 3 to 5 percent during 2004–10. Most remarkably, poverty declined from 35 percent in 2000 to 22 percent in 2009. The paper draws appropriate attention to the role that industrial policy has played in fostering growth and to the need for sound principles of implementation to effect the expected results.

Brazil's industrial policy, as implemented in the plan "Brasil Maior," uses instruments such as tax incentives, access to concessional financing, and providing infrastructure, education, and research and development (R&D) to promote growth in a large number of sectors that have been grouped into five broad categories. One of the most important institutions in charge of industrial policy in Brazil is the national development bank, the BNDES. With assets and disbursements in excess of those of the World Bank, BNDES plays a crucial role in Brazil's economic development and has earned a return on earnings significantly above that of other development banks.

My main comment on the paper is that, while it provides information on the strategic goals and the design of Brazil's industrial policy, it does not sufficiently address the question on the type of interventions that have been implemented by the BNDES and other agents of industrial policy in Brazil and the extent to which Brazil's industrial policy has been effective in reaching its objectives. In addition, the paper argues that Brazil's stance of macroeconomic policy over the last decade has not been appropriate. Yet, it is precisely the tight monetary and fiscal policies implemented since the crisis in 2000/2001 that have succeeded in overcoming a legacy of macroeconomic instability and creating an environment more conducive to investment by the private sector. This macroeconomic stability was certainly a prerequisite for the effectiveness of industrial policy interventions.

More information on the effectiveness of industrial policy is important: Brazil, like other countries in Latin America, has shown high growth yet remains trapped in middle-income status, as shown in Figure 5.2.1.

This phenomenon is even more surprising, given that Brazil's labor productivity has been rising rapidly since 2002, as shown in Figure 5.2.2.

An indication of the root cause of Brazil's failure to break out of the middle-income trap is the failure of Brazil to achieve greater sophistication in products, as measured by the EXPY indicator developed by Hausmann. EXPY is a measure of the export sophistication of the product basket for each country. Technically speaking, it is the sum of the country's export share of each product weighted by the PRODY measurement for that product. The PRODY index is the sum of weighted per capita GDPs of all nations for each product, with the weight being the country's export share

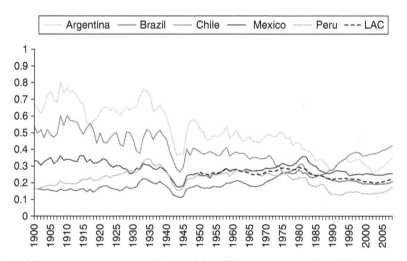

Figure 5.2.1 Ratio of Selected LAC Countries' GDP per capita to US GDP per capita (1990 International Geary-Khamis dollars)
Source: Maddison (2010).

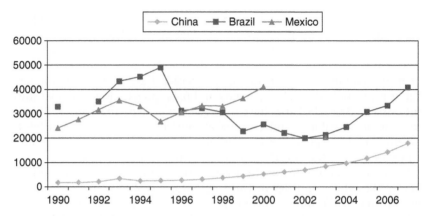

Figure 5.2.2 Labor productivity in manufacturing (value added per employee, US$)
Source: UNIDO (2011).

for the product divided by the aggregate of all nations' export share for the product. With the notable exception of Costa Rica, the sophistication of whose exports greatly benefited from the investment by INTEL, most Latin American countries have not managed to increase their EXPYs over the past decade, in fact the EXPY of Brazil seems to have declined somewhat. Figure 5.2.3 powerfully illustrates what appears to be Brazil's key problem in exiting the middle-income trap, namely the lack of industrial upgrading.

This absence of industrial upgrading in Brazil and Latin America more generally is particularly problematic in view of the rise of China. Since 1979, China has had an average annual growth of nearly 10 percent and an average annual trade growth of over 16 percent. China's emergence as a dominant player in the world economy creates significant opportunities and challenges for other regions in the world, including Latin America. China's dynamic growth has already contributed to a global resource boom which has been crucial in supporting Latin America's strong growth performance in the recent decade. China has also become an important source of FDI. Yet, China's rising competitiveness in light manufacturing products – a major export good for the region – has crowded out the manufacturing sector in a number of countries, in particular in Mexico.

Against this background, Brazil, and Latin America more generally, will have to undertake more sustained efforts at becoming competitive in industries with higher value added. In all successful countries, industrial policy has played a crucial role in facilitating structural transformation. In designing and implementing industrial policy, it will be important to undertake sector-specific coordination, given that the contents of coordination often differ by sector. Focusing on specific sectors is also important given that

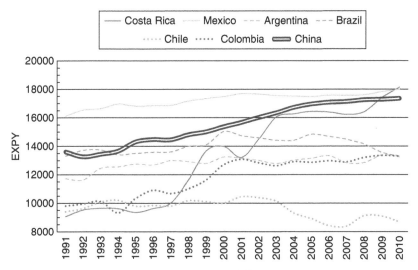

Figure 5.2.3 EXPY Trends for Latin America and China
Source: World Bank calculations based on Comtrade.

the government's resources and capacities are limited and need to be used strategically.

Picking winners in this fashion has been a controversial subject. In the past, picking winners has often had disastrous results with public resources being wasted through inefficient public enterprises and development banks. Yet the main issue with this old form of structuralism was not the use of industrial policy per se, but the choice of the target sectors as they were not in line with the country's comparative advantage. Hence, the strategy adopted was actually a comparative-advantage-defying strategy, leading to nonviable firms in competitive markets whose survival depended on generous government policy support both for their initial investment and their continuous operation. These policies led to rent-seeking, corruption and political capture and contributed to macroeconomic instability and poor growth performance in the region, thus laying the ground for economic crises in many countries in the late 1990s.

The adoption of market-oriented policies under the Washington Consensus since the late 1980s and early 1990s aimed to address these shortcomings and marked a broad shift away from the interventionist and inward-looking policies followed in the past. The Washington Consensus policies focused on government failures, notably macroeconomic instability and constraints to free development of the private sector, and assumed structural changes could happen spontaneously. The shift in policy direction of Latin American countries was promoted by the international community – which sought to help the region overcome a history of default and possibly embark on a high-growth path of the type seen in East Asia – also through the substantial debt reduction through the Brady Plan in the late 1980s.

Yet the Washington Consensus advised the government to eliminate all distortions immediately, subsequently leading to the collapse of old priority sectors. At the same time, the Washington Consensus was strongly opposed that governments play a proactive role in facilitating firms' entry into sectors that were consistent with the country's comparative advantage.

Yet experience from dynamically growing countries in East Asia and elsewhere indicates that the government continuously provided transitional support to non-viable firms in the old priority sectors and removed distortions only when firms in those sectors became viable or the sectors became very small. The governments in these countries also facilitated private firms' entry to sectors that were consistent with the country's comparative advantage.

What lessons can we learn from these countries' successful experience?

- It is important for a government to select sectors for industrial policy interventions that are in line with the country's latent comparative advantage. For this purpose, it should identify tradable goods and services that have been growing dynamically for about 20 years in fast-growing countries with similar endowment structures that have a per capita GDP about 100 percent higher than that of the middle-income country. In many cases, given that wages tend to rise in the growth process, a fast-growing country that has produced certain goods and services for about 20 years may begin to lose its comparative advantage in those sectors, leaving space for countries with lower wages to enter and compete in those industries. Additional screening criteria such as availability of raw materials, size of the domestic market, and availability of skills provides additional relevant information to confirm the choice of target sectors.
- Second, among the identified industries, the government may give priority to those in which some domestic private firms have already entered spontaneously. The government may then try to identify: (i) the obstacles that are preventing these firms from upgrading the quality of their products; or (ii) the barriers that limit entry to those industries by other private firms. This could be done through the combination of various methods such as value chain analysis or the Growth Diagnostic Framework suggested by Hausmann, Rodrik, and Velasco (2008). The government can then implement policies to remove those binding constraints and use randomized controlled experiments to test the effects of releasing those constraints so as to ensure the effectiveness of scaling up those policies at the national level.
- Third, some of the identified industries may be completely new to domestic firms. In such cases, the government could adopt specific measures to

encourage firms in the higher-income countries identified in the first step to invest in these industries. Firms in these higher-income countries will have incentives to relocate their production to the lower-income country so as to take advantage of the lower labor costs. The government may also set up incubation programs to catalyze the entry of domestic private firms into these industries.

- Fourth, in addition to the industries identified on the list of opportunities for tradable goods and services in step one, developing country governments should pay close attention to successful innovations by domestic private enterprises and provide support to scale up those industries. Due to rapid technological changes, many new opportunities may arise – opportunities that would not have existed a decade or two ago, as those industries did not exist in the rapidly growing comparator countries.
- Fifth, in developing countries with poor infrastructure and unfriendly business environments, the government can invest in industrial parks or export processing zones and make the necessary improvements to attract domestic private firms and/or foreign firms that may be willing to invest in the targeted industries. Improvements in infrastructure and the business environment can reduce transaction costs and facilitate industrial development. However, because of budget and capacity constraints, most governments will not be able to make the desirable improvements for the whole economy in a reasonable timeframe. Focusing on improving the infrastructure and business environment in an industrial park or an export processing zone is, therefore, a more manageable alternative. Industrial parks and export processing zones also have the benefits of encouraging industrial clustering. The industrial parks would need to be tailored to the specific requirements of the targeted industry, however.
- Sixth, the government may also provide limited incentives, such as tax holidays or preferential access to credits and/or foreign exchanges, to domestic pioneer firms or foreign investors that work within the list of industries identified in step one in order to compensate for the non-rival, public knowledge created by their investments. Incentives should not, and need not, be in the form of monopoly rents, high tariffs, or other distortions as the firms in the targeted industries should be viable in open, competitive market.

Taking into account Latin America's relative comparative advantage in factor costs, especially in wages – Colombia's wages are broadly in line with those in China which is competitive in labor-intensive manufacturing – the role of government will be to help reduce transaction costs, in particular for transportation and logistics. This can be accomplished also by encouraging clustering of companies in the same sectors. China's experience shows that clusters have been most effective.

For middle-income countries, a key element and question at the outset is: (i) which high value-added industries that exist in advanced countries are missing in their industrial structure, and (ii) among their existing industries which are still *within* the global technological frontier (even if more advanced than similar sectors in low-income countries) and (iii) which are already *on* the global technological frontier. Most middle-income countries have economic structures that include all three types of industries. Even high-income countries possess those three types of industries, but often most of their existing industries are already at the global technological frontier. A preliminary step should be to separate existing domestic industries into categories, and adjust the sequential GIF steps accordingly.

For industries that are already *on* the global technological frontier, if the country intends to stay in those industries, firms in the industries need to create continuously new processes, new products, and new technologies – thus advancing the frontier. Governments can facilitate such industrial upgrading by providing support for R&D – with a view to creating the required innovative activities – as well as by acquiring the necessary cutting-edge technology and equipment. For a country to upgrade or diversify to new industries that locate *within* the global technological frontier, the six steps in the GIF framework are useful for selecting the industries and identifying the required government interventions.

This type of industrial policy supports firms in the targeted sectors that are viable because they are in line with the country's latent comparative advantage. Government interventions to support industrial upgrading and diversification based on this framework will be consistent with the goal of competition policy. This is because the government's incentives for investments are used to compensate first movers for the externalities they create, rather than address the firms' viability problem. A limited tax holiday or discrete subsidy would be sufficient. The government's interventions focus mainly on areas that overcome the coordination failures to facilitate the competitiveness of the targeted industries.

To summarize: to achieve dynamic growth, Brazil should develop industries according to its comparative advantage, which is determined by the country's endowment structure, and tap into the potential advantages of backwardness in industrial upgrading. In order to be competitive in the new world economic order and exit from the middle-income trap, Latin America needs to upgrade its industrial structure continuously. At this juncture, Latin America's product mix lacks diversification, has not improved in terms of sophistication and has not been adaptable to changes in demand in key export markets. Latin America has lost competitiveness and is now at risk of deindustrialization which could exacerbate its exposure to fluctuations of the world economy and the business cycle in main export markets in advanced and emerging markets.

Industrial upgrading and diversification would be essential to avoid further deindustrialization arising from the competitive pressures of the rise of

China, broaden the base for economic growth and create the basis for further sustained reduction in unemployment and poverty and improvements in income inequality. Brazil's comparative advantage lies in sectors that are intensive in natural resources, scientific knowledge, and unskilled labor. To facilitate upgrading to these sectors, Brazil should make a concerted effort to improve education, R&D, and physical infrastructure. With a view to maximizing the effectiveness of these interventions, it will be important for the region to pick winners, that is, sectors that correspond to the latent comparative advantage of the economies, and calibrate supporting policies in close collaboration with the private sector through public–private sector alliances. Different from the experience under the old structuralism, industrial policy measures inspired by New Structural Economics will be consistent with the principles of free and fair competition, as the sectors are in line with a country's latent comparative advantage and therefore sustainable.

5.3

The *Chaebol* and Industrial Policy in Korea*

Wonhyuk Lim
Korea Development Institute (KDI)

5.3.1 Introduction

Many in the developing world have interpreted the global financial crisis as the death knell for the Washington Consensus, and are taking a close look at more proactive policy alternatives that depart from the standard package of liberalization, privatization, and stabilization and focus on developing local capabilities to add value and manage risks (Winters et al., 2010). Industrial policy, in particular, has once again become a hot topic (Cimoli, Dosi, and Stiglitz, 2009; Ohno, 2009).

Korea occupies a special place in this policy debate. One of the poorest countries in the world at the beginning of the 1960s, Korea joined the ranks of industrial democracies within a single generation, becoming a member of the Organization for Economic Co-operation and Development (OECD) in 1996. Even among successful economies characterized by sustained high growth, Korea stands out with its impressive industrial upgrading and indigenous private sector development covering such advanced industries as electronics, motor vehicles, shipbuilding, steel, and chemicals. Developing countries are showing a great deal of interest in how Korea managed to combine market mechanism and extra-market arrangements to generate rapid, resilient, and shared growth.

In general, development may be conceptualized as the result of synergies between enhanced human capital and new knowledge, involving complementary investments in physical and social capital. Three externalities are central to the development challenge: coordination externalities in the organization of economic activities through markets and hierarchies; innovation externalities in the production and utilization of knowledge; and institutional externalities influenced by the quality of governance and institutions (Lim, 2011).

---

* This is a slightly revised and expanded version of the author's paper of the same title in *Asian Economic Policy Review* 7(1), June 2012.

Three solutions to coordination and innovation externalities suggest themselves: government, business groups, and financial institutions. The standard "big push" line of argument calls for the state's coordinating role in promoting the concurrent development of upstream and downstream industries when these industries depend on each other to be viable (Rosenstein-Rodan, 1943; Murphy et al., 1989). Government can also address innovation externalities by providing support for the production, utilization, and dissemination of knowledge. Business groups are another solution. By definition, a business group is a corporate structure that consists of legally independent firms, operating in multiple industries and bound together by formal and informal ties (Khanna and Yafeh, 2007). It can be a rational and efficient corporate form under the constraints of imperfect markets for goods and services (Okazaki, 1999). Moreover, when the constituent firms of a business group are operating in related industries, they can internalize the returns from innovation to a greater extent than would otherwise be the case. Financial institutions, such as banks and venture capital firms, are a third solution, as they can intermediate between people with ideas and people with money. The quality of institutions and governance influences the effectiveness of these extra-market arrangements in addressing coordination and innovation externalities.

As far as coordination is concerned, standard logic suggests that while the benefits of extra-market arrangements may dominate the costs in the early stages of development, their relative merits are likely to decline as market transactions become increasingly viable. The dynamic is somewhat different for innovation. As a country approaches the technological frontier, the role of government as a risk partner to support R&D may remain important, because of large externalities in basic research, especially in such fields as defense and health. However, the need to rely on government research institutes to perform applied R&D will be reduced as the capacity of the private sector is improved and intellectual property protection is strengthened. Thus, even in the realm of innovation, the value of using extra-market arrangements is likely to decline.

However, transition from extra-market arrangements is not preordained because institutional substitutes for missing markets can become entrenched. By no means are they passive rule-takers, and the problem of "institutional overhang" can complicate transition dynamics.

This is arguably a greater problem in Korea than elsewhere because of the extent to which its development relied on extra-market arrangements. In the Korean economic system, the government and family-controlled business groups, known as the *chaebol*, played a dominant role. By contrast, financial institutions played a relatively minor independent role because, for the most part, they were under the control of either the government or the *chaebol*. The government and the private sector made joint efforts to address coordination and innovation externalities while minimizing negative government externalities such as corruption. They developed "a big-push partnership" in which the government shared the investment risks of the private sector and provided support largely based on performance in competitive global markets, systematically filling the missing links in the domestic value chain and moving up the quality ladder. The reinforcement of successful experiments through the feedback mechanism of performance-based rewards led to dramatic changes over time (Lim, 2011).

This paper is organized as follows. Section 5.3.2 presents a conceptual overview of business groups and industrial policy from theoretical perspectives. Section 5.3.3 looks at the evolution of the *chaebol* and industrial policy in Korea: transition to export-oriented industrialization in the 1960s, heavy and chemical industry (HCI) drive in the 1970s, and information technology (IT) industry promotion in the 1980s and 1990s. Section 5.3.4 then highlights a shift from industrial policy to competition and corporate governance policy. This shift has been part of a more fundamental transition from a developmental state to a democratic market economy in Korea. Section 5.3.5 concludes.

5.3.2   Business groups and industrial policy in theoretical perspectives

The Korean word *chaebol*, or its Japanese equivalent *zaibatsu*, consists of two Chinese characters: While *chae* (*zai*) means wealth or finance, *bol* (*batsu*) means lineage, faction, or clique. Thus, *chaebol* literally means "a wealth clique." In Japan, by the end of World War II, *zaibatsu* had come to mean "a business group in which one parent company (holding company) owned by a family or an extended family controlled subsidiaries operating in various industries with large subsidiaries occupying oligopolistic positions in the respective industries."[1] This definition reflects the usual concerns about firm size and market dominance associated with big business, a primary concern of antitrust and competition policy. However, the definition also encompasses three structural elements: the business structure of high diversification; the governance structure of family control; and the organizational structure of holding companies (multi-subsidiaries rather than multi-divisions). To a large extent, these elements also characterize family-controlled business groups around the world.

As Table 5.3.1 shows, there are essentially three different theoretical avenues for exploring the nature of business groups, which may be family-controlled, state-controlled, or widely-held but with controlling mechanisms to bind constituent firms together. The first approach is an efficiency model that focuses on the firm's make-or-buy decisions, using the concept of transaction costs, especially within the context of underdeveloped or imperfect markets for inputs and services. The second explanation for business groups is a principal–agent model that focuses on the conflict of

Table 5.3.1 Theoretical approaches to business groups

Theoretical approach	Central concepts	Analytical focus
Efficiency model	– Transaction costs – Risk diversification	Market development and extent of the firm (monolith)
Principal–agent model	– Agency problem – Entrenchment problem	Conflict of interest among stakeholders
Political economy model	– Rent-seeking – Developmental state	Business–government relations

interest among stakeholders. The third explanation is a political economy model that tends to emphasize the role of the government–business alliance in the evolution of business groups, incorporating such concepts as the developmental state and rent-seeking.[2]

Industrial policy is broadly defined as a nation's effort to influence sectoral development and, hence, the nation's industry portfolio. Using such instruments as tax and financial subsidies, trade protection, and public–private consultation, industrial policy can target either emerging industries (infant industries) or declining industries—or anything in-between. Targeting can be either sector-specific (vertical) or non-discriminatory (horizontal). The case for state intervention is weaker for those industries with a clear revealed comparative advantage and few externalities, as the private sector can presumably realize profit opportunities in these industries with relative ease.

As Table 5.3.2 shows, scholars have a wide range of views on identifying and promoting promising sectors. Because of the characterization of traditional industrial policy as incompetent and corrupt governments "picking winners" in a top-down manner without a concrete plan for implementation and phase-out, "new" industrial policy has tended to emphasize "winners picking themselves" through experimentation and positive reinforcement (Rodrik, 2007). Lin and Monga (2010) go beyond "self-discovery" and advocate international benchmarking based on the latecomer's advantage. In particular, based on the notion of comparative advantage, they suggest that developing countries focus on "tradable goods and services that have been produced about 20 years in dynamically growing countries with similar endowment structures and a per capita income [measured in purchasing power parity] that is about 100% more than their own." However, more is likely to be needed if developing countries are to move beyond the middle-income trap, when catch-up economies may have to take considerable strategic risks to jump into *non-mature* industries to compete with advanced economies.

This is not an easy task. In fact, countries tend to move through the product space by developing goods close to those they currently produce, and can reach the core from the periphery "only by traversing empirically

Table 5.3.2   Literature on industrial policy

Schools	Insights on sector identification and promotion
Developmental state (Johnson, 1982; Amsden, 1989; Wade, 1990)	Government picks winners (in consultation with business).
Rent-seeking (Krueger, 1974)	Government can't and shouldn't pick winners. (Self-fulfilling incompetence and corruption?)
Self-discovery (Rodrik, 2007)	Winners pick themselves, with help from search and problem-solving networks.
New structural economics (Lin and Monga, 2010)	Latecomers can pick winners in mature industries by benchmarking early movers (based on comparative advantage).
Product space (Hidalgo et al., 2007)	Winners are readily identifiable, but how do we go from the periphery to the core?
Strategic risk-taking	Winners are readily identifiable through international benchmarking and experimentation, but the key is to take strategic risks, weighing the challenges of skill accumulation, scale economies, and complementary investments against the possibility of capacity underutilization and financial distress.

infrequent distances," which may explain why poor countries fail to converge with the income levels of rich countries (Hidalgo et al., 2007: 482).

Existing empirical research on industrial policy sheds little light on these issues. Ideally, to evaluate the impact of industrial policy on industrial upgrading, we should focus on the subset of industrial policy whose objective is to promote industrial upgrading, rather than maintaining social cohesion or propping up declining industries. We should look at the full set of industrial policy instruments, not just readily quantifiable subsidies, and compare the productivity or domestic value added of a targeted sector before (without) the introduction of industrial policy with that after (with) the introduction of industrial policy over a sufficiently long time horizon so as not to miss the full impact of industrial policy on industries with a long gestation period. Unfortunately, existing empirical studies on industrial policy miss out on these points. For instance, in their study on Japanese industrial policy, Beason and Weinstein (1996) include mining—not an "emerging" industry by any stretch of imagination in the Japanese context. The Japanese government imposed minimal tariffs on mineral imports to make inputs available at international prices but compensated for this with generous financial and tax subsidies for the declining domestic mining sector; one should not be surprised that sectoral targeting did little to improve the comparative productivity of the Japanese mining sector in a cross-sectional exercise. Also, the lack of correlation between high-performance sectors and industry policy instruments is not really a serious problem in a cross-sectional setting, if these industries have a strong revealed comparative advantage and can thrive without much support from the state. What we need to look at is the impact of industrial policy on potentially promising industries with a weak revealed comparative advantage when compared with the counterfactual. As for the empirical analysis of Korea's industrial policy reported in Lee (1996), the selected time horizon (namely, 1962–83) is a problem because the heavy and chemical industries, promoted during the 1970s, suffered underutilization until the early 1980s. It was after the 1986–88 boom that the general assessment of the heavy and chemical industry drive began to change. Survey papers, such as Pack and Saggi (2006), which cite the results of these empirical studies to draw unfavorable conclusions about industrial policy, are equally problematic.

In fact, history and product space theory suggest that promising sectors are often identifiable through international benchmarking and experimentation, but the real challenge is how to address coordination and innovation externalities to make the transition from the periphery to the core. As Figure 5.3.1 shows, developing countries typically start their industrialization in the assembly and production segment of the value chain, in such labor-intensive industries as garments. Most countries fail to move to higher value-added segments along the value chain (for example, product design) or to shift up to higher value-added sectors (for example, machinery and equipment) for two reasons. They neglect to address coordination and innovation externalities in education, R&D, and infrastructure development

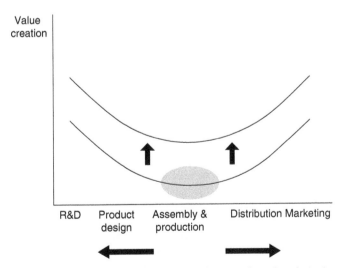

Figure 5.3.1 Double smile: moving along and shifting up the value chain (reproduced from Ohno, 2009, p.16)

Source: Economic Planning Unit of the Prime Minister's Department, Malaysia (edited).

and/or rush to promote sophisticated industries without the requisite scale economies and skill accumulation. International benchmarking and close public–private consultation is key to solving information and incentive problems in this stage.

If a country makes huge investments to promote "core" industries but fails to achieve international competitiveness, the resulting capacity underutilization and financial distress may bankrupt its economy. In addition, even if technological challenges could be overcome at the individual country level, the world would be awash in overcapacity if too many countries build optimal-scale plants for the global market. This "fallacy of composition" effect further increases the risks of industrial policy. Accordingly, a country must carefully weigh the challenges of skill accumulation, scale economies, and complementary investments against the possibility of capacity underutilization and financial distress before embarking on ambitious industrial policy.

5.3.3   Korea's experience with industrial policy

Korea's experience with industrial policy offers an illustrative case. In the early 1960s Korea embarked on export-oriented industrialization, correcting its previous bias against exports and using its latent comparative advantage to develop labor-intensive manufacturing industries. While continuing to pursue export-oriented industrialization for its resource allocation, scale economies, and dynamic learning effects, Korea did not just wait for its income and skill levels to rise before developing its potential comparative advantage in more sophisticated industries. Instead, the government and the private sector systematically studied what had to be done to fill the missing links in the domestic value chain and move up the quality ladder, and made concerted efforts to aim for international competitiveness from the outset. Korea sought to indigenize intermediate inputs imported from foreign upstream industries, through technology acquisition, human resource development, and the construction of optimal-scale plants aimed for the global market (Lim, 2011). The corporate histories of Samsung, Hyundai, LG, and SK, among others, suggest that they were willing to pursue vertical integration or related diversification even on their own, but usually worked in conjunction with government policy when they ventured into unrelated industries (Lim, 2003).

Although the degree of sector targeting changed dramatically from the 1960s to the 1970s and then the 1980s onward, Korea maintained an outward-oriented, bottom-up, integrated approach to industrial policy, relying on close publicprivate consultation and international benchmarking. In the 1970s, Korea targeted heavy and chemical industries based on national security as well as industrial upgrading considerations. In the 1980s, Korea began to promote IT industries and pay greater attention to small and medium-sized enterprises (SMEs), especially after Korea's democratization in 1987. As the capacity of the private sector increased and sectoral targeting became a more difficult proposition, Korea shifted to a more sector-neutral approach. The Industry Development Law of 1986, in particular, marked a watershed as it scrapped previous sector-specific promotion laws and provided support for industry rationalization and R&D regardless of sectors.

5.3.3.1 Transition to export-oriented industrialization

A student revolution in 1960 that overthrew the previous corrupt government and a military coup in 1961 that placed economic modernization at the top of its agenda changed Korea's political economy and helped to establish a strong yet responsive and responsible "developmental state." Under popular pressure, whoever came to power could not advocate a return to "the good, old days," and had to present a development strategy for the nation. The new, democratically elected Chang Myun government prepared a five-year economic development plan as well as a blueprint to establish a superministry in charge of planning, budget, and coordination. The Chang government also established national meritocratic examinations for recruiting civil servants. Park Chung Hee, who seized power through the 1961 coup, built on these institutional innovations and relentlessly pursued economic modernization, which he believed was the best antidote for the communist threat on the divided Korean peninsula. The Park government also took over the task of dealing with "illicit wealth accumulators," or business leaders who were accused of having grown rich through corruption in the 1950s, and demanded and received their equity shares in commercial banks in lieu of fines for tax evasion and other illegal practices. This drastic measure enabled the government to exert direct control over commercial banks (Lim, 2011).

Having nationalized commercial banks, the Park government tried to mobilize domestic savings to promote basic industries through a currency reform in 1962. However, this effort was botched because the Korean government had not consulted with the United States, which at the time was providing more than half of Korea's budget through aid. Upset by the lack of prior consultation, the United States used its aid leverage to roll back the currency reform and force the military government to uphold its pledge to restore the electoral regime by 1963. Although the military government had little choice but to acquiesce, the lessons were not lost on the policymakers (Kim, 2011). Reassessing the import-substituting industrialization strategy that they had initially favored, they began to search for radically different options that would save them from ever being trapped in such a vulnerable position again (Mason et al., 1980: 196–7). Seeking to tap into foreign capital while limiting the influence of foreign governments or multinationals, the government primarily relied on foreign loans, reduced aid dependence, and restricted FDI, the combination of which would allow Korea to take advantage of the domestic–international interest rate differential and be the residual claimant on its investments – if it successfully invested the capital. The relatively minor role of FDI meant that Korea had to acquire technologies through licensing, reverse engineering, and indigenous development – all of which required progressive local capacity accumulation. At the most fundamental level, Korea's export-oriented industrialization was a strategy to secure political as well as economic independence (Lim, 2011). Lacking democratic or pro-independence credentials, Park Chung Hee also felt that the best way for him to prevail in elections was to deliver improving living standards.

Although Park and his followers had initially condemned some of Korea's business leaders as "illicit wealth accumulators," they apparently concluded that combining state monitoring with private entrepreneurship would be the most effective means of carrying out the economic development plans. The government's partners were not yet large business groups but family-owned firms, typically involved in the production of light manufactures.[3] Their owner-managers had autonomy in decision making, but they were subject to high-level monitoring by government, because government controlled the formal banking sector and offered repayment guarantees to foreign financial institutions that extended loans to Korean companies. Through direct monitoring and performance-based support, the government tried to contain the potential costs of state-backed debt financing.

Korea introduced a number of measures to facilitate export-oriented industrialization. The short-term export credit system had been streamlined as early as 1961, with the automatic approval of loans to those with an export letter of credit (L/C), which allowed businesses to have access to trade financing without having to put up collateral. To provide institutional support in the area of foreign marketing and technology imports, the government established the Korea Trade Promotion Corporation (KOTRA) in 1962. The government also gave exporters various tax deductions, wastage allowances, tariff exemptions, and concessional credits (Cho and Kim, 1997: 36–7). The role of Korea's export subsidies should not be exaggerated, however. The average effective rate of subsidy on total exports in the second half of the 1960s was basically offset by the degree of currency overvaluation (Frank, Kim, and Westphal, 1975). More importantly, these subsidies took the form of performance-based rewards in a competitive setting rather than handouts with no strings attached.

After Korea achieved the annual exports of $100 million in 1964, the Minister of Commerce and Industry asked Park Chung Hee to chair monthly export promotion meetings. Attended by high-ranking government officials and business representatives, these meetings provided a forum to monitor progress and devise institutional innovations and solutions to emerging problems. At each monthly meeting, the Minister of Commerce and Industry gave a progress report on export performance by region and product relative to the targets set out in the annual comprehensive plan for export promotion. The Minister of Foreign Affairs gave a briefing on overseas market conditions. Government officials and business representatives then tried to identify emerging bottlenecks and constraints that impeded export performance and devise solutions to these problems. Subsequent meetings monitored progress. Export insurance was one of many institutional innovations that were introduced as a result of recommendations from monthly export promotion meetings (Shin, 1994). In short, these meetings between the government and the private sector provided opportunities to secure sustained attention from top leadership, monitor progress on a long-term vision, and detect and mitigate constraints as they emerged.

In addition, the Export Promotion Special Account Fund was established within the Korea International Trade Association (KITA) in 1969 as a public–private initiative to secure non-government funding for export promotion activities. It provided support for collective activities such as the dispatch of delegations to international trade fairs, improvement of design and packaging, and establishment of quality certification facilities. A small levy was imposed on imports to provide the funding (Kim, 2011).

Three points are worth emphasizing in regard to Korea's export promotion efforts. First, while the government drafted an annual plan for export promotion by product and by region, it was a reference against which progress could be measured at public–private consultation meetings, not a command-and-control instrument imposed on individual firms. Second, export incentives took the form of readily scalable rewards based on performance in a competitive setting (for example, L/C-based export financing) rather than rewards contingent on the accomplishment of preannounced targets. In other words, the exporter did not have to deliver or even commit to a certain firm-level target for export incentives to kick in; rather, the exporter received export incentives proportional to the exported amount, in the form of tax, duty, and interest rate reductions. Exports are affected by exporters' efforts and external conditions, two of the factors that the government does not want to get into the business of evaluating under information asymmetry. Third, and most importantly, Korea adopted an integrated approach to export promotion with comprehensive and inter-related measures, policies, and institutions. In fact, for Korea, export promotion – for which the nation had to change its mindset and measure itself against global benchmarks—served as the engine of growth and the organizing principle under which industrial upgrading, infrastructure development, and human resource development could be pursued. Because Korea took such an integrated approach, it would be inappropriate to analyze Korea's export promotion policy in isolation as a collection of tax and financial incentives to increase exports. Even under today's WTO rules, public–private consultations, performance-based rewards, and integrated policy approaches remain valid and effective instruments.

5.3.3.2   Heavy and chemical industry drive

If Korea's transition to export-oriented industrialization in the early 1960s had mostly to do with discovering its latent comparative advantage in labor-intensive manufacturing, Korea's subsequent development had more to do with upgrading its comparative advantage with a view toward increasing the domestic content of its exports. A new urgency for industrial upgrading was added in the early 1970s when the United States announced that it would reduce its troops in Asia in the wake of the Vietnam War. The policymakers felt that Korea must develop heavy and chemical industries if it was to have the ability to manufacture its own weapons and defend itself. Instead of setting up armories or factories for specific weapons, they established dual-use industrial complexes, with a target production ratio of 70 percent civilian and 30 percent military in peacetime (O, 2009; Kim, 2011).

Politically, in October 1972, Park Chung Hee declared a state of national emergency and adopted a new *Yushin* (revitalizing reform) constitution that gave dictatorial powers to the president, eliminated term limits, and abolished direct presidential elections. Under the new constitution, the president had the power to appoint one-third of the members of the National Assembly. Through a series of emergency decrees, Park subsequently banned discussions on the constitution. While tolerating little political dissent, Park relentlessly pursued two policy initiatives: New Village Movement (Saemaul Undong) to narrow the urban–rural gap (Park, 1998) and HCI drive to promote industrial upgrading and national security.

The HCI drive was formally launched in January 1973 with the objective of firmly establishing "a self-reliant economy" and achieving $10 billion in exports and $1,000 in per capita income by 1981. The master plan for the HCI drive envisaged that heavy and chemical industries would account for more than 50 percent of manufacturing value-added and contribute $5.63 billion to exports while light manufacturing and primary industries would add $3.67 billion and $0.70 billion, respectively, in 1981 (Table 5.3.3). Six were selected as leading industries: (1) iron and steel, (2) non-ferrous metals, (3) shipbuilding, (4) machinery, (5) electronics, and (6) chemicals (Table 5.3.4). Machinery in particular was regarded as a critical industry not only for its high value-added and extensive linkages with other industries, but also for its contribution to

Table 5.3.3   Targets for the HCI drive

	1972	1976	1981
GNP per capita	$302	$488	$983
HCI Share in Manufacturing Value-Added	35.2%	41.8%	51.0%
HCI Share in Manufacturing Exports	27.0%	44.0%	60.5%

Source: HCI Promotion Planning Board, cited in Kim (1988).

Table 5.3.4   Investment requirement estimates for the HCI drive (unit: million U.S. dollars)

	Foreign Capital	Domestic Capital	Total	Percent Share
Iron and Steel	1,502	674	2,176	22.7
Non-Ferrous Metals	222	123	345	3.6
Machinery	1,049	1,137	2,186	22.8
Shipbuilding	416	352	768	8.0
Electronics	593	599	1,192	12.4
Chemicals	1,523	662	2,158	22.8
Sub-Total	5,305	3,547	8,852	92.3
(Percent Share)	(59.9)	(40.1)	(100.0)	
Others	468	273	741	7.7
Total	5,773	3,820	9,593	100.0
(Percent Share)	(60.2)	(39.8)	(100.0)	

Source: HCI Promotion Planning Board, cited in Kim (1988).

defense industries. For a reference, Korean officials noted that when Japan reached $10 billion in exports in 1967, the machinery industry accounted for 43 percent of industrial production (Kim, 1988).

In December 1973, the government established the National Investment Fund (NIF) to finance long-term investment in heavy and chemical industries, estimated to be around $9.6 billion. The NIF interest rate was set at 9.0 percent, whereas the prevailing three-year interest rate on bank loans was 15.5 percent. Government-controlled banks also supported the HCI drive by providing policy-oriented loans on favorable terms. This was a dramatic departure from the second half of the 1960s.

To promote heavy and chemical industries, the government essentially had to secure scale economies, make massive complementary investments, and develop technical manpower with the requisite skills. Instead of relying on the market mechanism, Korea sought to address coordination and innovation externalities through integrated, forward-looking plans, even as it tried to aim for international competitiveness from the outset under the slogan of "the exportization of all industries."

In promoting upstream industries in the 1970s, Korea had to make a strategic choice. It could play safe and develop heavy and chemical industries for the small domestic market and risk inefficiency resulting from suboptimal scales and entrenched protectionism. Alternatively, it could promote these industries for the global market and risk capacity underutilization and financial distress. Korea chose the latter option because, despite considerable risks, it promised a dynamically efficient growth trajectory if Korea managed to develop technological prowess before the financial burden became overwhelming. To minimize time and exploit scale economies in establishing capital-intensive industries, the government decided to rely on a select group of state-owned enterprises and *chaebol* with successful track records such as Hyundai. The government felt that scale economies called for regulated monopoly or oligopoly in these industries until demand became large enough to support effective competition (O, 2009).

Before the term was in wide use, "a cluster approach" was evident in the HCI drive. To provide infrastructure such as water, electricity, and transportation and to secure backward and forward linkages, the government enacted the Industrial Complex Development Promotion Law in December 1973 and set up a machinery complex in Changwon, a petrochemical complex in Yeocheon, and an electronics complex in Gumi. National universities located near these industrial complexes were called upon to specialize in related engineering fields.

Last but not least, Korea greatly expanded technical and vocational training, strengthened science and engineering education, and set up government labs to conduct R&D, under the slogan of "the scientification of all people." According to the government's manpower development plan, demand for technicians, who graduated from technical high school and obtained at least three years of job experience, was projected to increase from 340,000 in 1969, to 980,000 in 1975, and to 1,700,000 in 1981. To supply high-quality technicians, the government established a number of technical high schools and provided incentives such as employment guarantees. Their curriculum emphasized practical training, and students were supposed to acquire technical certificates before graduation.

In the area of R&D, the government had already established the Korea Institute of Science and Technology (KIST) in 1966 and the Korea Advanced Institute for Science and Technology (KAIST) in 1971. In addition, it passed the Technology Development Promotion Law in 1972, providing tax and other incentives to encourage private sector R&D. It also established five industry-specific government research institutes (GRIs) in shipbuilding, electronics, machinery, metal, and chemical industries according to the Specialized Research Institute Promotion Law of December 1973. Through these efforts, the government sought to address innovation externalities critical to sustained growth.

Korea had a strong *and* increasing revealed comparative advantage in light industries when it made its strategic decision to promote heavy and chemical industries in 1973. After benchmarking advanced industrial nations with natural endowments similar to Korea's, such as Japan, Korea recognized that it had a potential comparative advantage in machinery and equipment industries and began to remove obstacles to achieving this objective, such as lack of technicians and engineers with the requisite skills in sophisticated industries (Lim, 2011).

The Korean government had to call off the HCI drive when serious macroeconomic imbalances and political problems forced it to adopt a comprehensive stabilization program in April 1979 (Stern et al., 1995). Although capacity underutilization was a major problem at the end of the 1970s, the HCI drive helped to build the foundation of many of Korea's leading industries such as steel, shipbuilding, machinery, electronics, and petrochemicals. It greatly strengthened backward and forward linkages among these industries, as well as related industries such as automobiles, to increase the local content of exports. It also enabled Korea to develop its own defense industry. Last but not least, the HCI drive set the stage for Korea's transition to an innovation-driven economy by expanding technical and engineering education and establishing a nucleus of R&D labs.

In the 1960s and 1970s, the public sector played a dominant role in R&D, mainly through newly established government labs. However, as Korean firms came to realize that they should go beyond imitation and assimilation and do their own innovation to succeed in global markets, they drastically increased their R&D spending. Gross R&D expenditure increased from less than 0.5 percent of GDP in the early 1970s to more than 3.5 percent of GDP in 2010. Over the same period, the private-sector share of the R&D spending increased from 20 percent to 75 percent. The number of researchers also increased from 6,000 to 220,000. As of 2010, there are more than 20,000 industrial labs in Korea.

5.3.3.3 IT industry promotion

Although international benchmarking and public-private consultation can play an important role in the identification of promising industries, they usually do not produce a decisive verdict and reasonable people can agree to disagree on the prospects of targeted industries. Such was the case with the IT industry in Korea's policy discussions at the end of the 1970s. While policymakers agreed that IT was an important sector with large spillovers, they were divided on Korea's prospects in this technologically advanced and fast-moving field. At the time, companies like LG were producing relatively simple IT products such as radio and TV sets, telecom services were poor, and the innovative capacity that was beginning to be developed in conjunction with the HCI drive was still low when compared with advanced industrial nations. The Economic Planning Board (EPB), for one, was unconvinced that Korea could become a major player in this knowledge-intensive and capital-intensive sector, and was opposed to making significant budget allocations to promote it. The Ministry of Commerce and Industry (MCI), on the other hand, was preoccupied with heavy and chemical industries and related industries such as automobiles. Although the Ministry of Post and Communication (MPC) could claim jurisdiction over at least some IT services, it did not have the stature within the government to lead industrial policy. In the end, Kim Jae Ik, Senior Presidential Secretary for Economic Affairs, restructured the Office of the Presidential Secretary for Science and Technology at the Blue House, and recruited those who believed that Korea had a realistic chance in the IT industry to lead promotion efforts in the 1980s, over the reservation of other policymakers (Oh and Larson, 2011).

The mode of government intervention in promoting the IT industry depended primarily on the relative capacity of the private sector. For TV sets and telephones, deregulation was the key policy instrument because multiple private-sector firms were ready to step in. Until 1980, to discourage "conspicuous consumption," only black-and-white TV broadcasting was allowed, even though Korean manufacturers were already exporting color TV sets abroad. Also, consumers had to purchase telephones through the MPC. To promote the IT industry, the government lifted the ban on color TV broadcasting and allowed consumers to purchase telephones on their own.

For more sophisticated IT products and services, however, the government played a more proactive role. The Blue House separated the communication business from the MPC and corporatized it as Korea Telecommunications Authority (today's KT) to make it more flexible and business-oriented. As much as 3 percent of its revenue was utilized for R&D and infrastructure improvement. Oh Myung, Presidential Secretary for Science and Technology, subsequently left the Blue House and took up the position of the Vice Minister of the Post and Communication to spearhead the effort. The government, working in collaboration with research institutes and private-sector companies, made extensive investments to develop TDX (digital electronic switching system for telephones), semiconductors, and computers. In the case of semiconductors, companies like Samsung and LG requested the government to lead R&D efforts because they lacked the resources to develop sophisticated products on their own, even though they knew that they had to move upstream if they were to survive in consumer electronics. The government also installed the National Backbone Information System as a way of creating procurement demand for IT products and services while computerizing essential information on personal identity and property. These programs helped to build the foundation of Korea's IT industry. Subsequently, in 1994, the Ministry of Post and Communication was expanded to the Ministry of Information and Communication, and worked with the private sector to develop mobile phones and to carry out a number of informatization projects.

Korea's industrial policy in the IT sector systematically reinforced weak segments of the domestic value chain through public–private consultation, under the objective to secure international competitiveness from the outset. Much like during the HCI drive, Korea set its sight on the global market instead of targeting only the domestic market. The government and the private sector proactively searched for solutions to the weak links in the value chain that runs from securing demand, developing human resources, strengthening R&D, producing parts and components, assembling the parts, to marketing and branding. In the process, the government played a critical role in addressing coordination and innovation externalities, by creating demand through its procurement projects and investing in R&D and education. Last but not least, the government tried to make merit-based appointments and abide by the principle of performance-based rewards so as to minimize the downside of government intervention.

5.3.4 Shift from industrial policy to competition and corporate governance policy

In the early stages of development, Korea had established "a big-push partnership," through which the government shared the investment risks of private-sector firms. This government protection against bankruptcy encouraged firms to undertake aggressive investment as they discounted downside risks. In order to maintain economic stability, the government thus found itself forced to intervene in the investment decisions of private-sector firms and place caps on the overall level of investment. In addition to the logic of the optimum efficiency scale required for international competitiveness, the government thus had another reason to limit entry into major industrial sectors such as automobiles. Consequently, although the fundamental solution to the problem of monopolization and collusion would have been to promote competition by scrapping entry barriers, the government was reluctant to take such action, for it would entail the overhaul of the government-managed economic system. The government had to make do with regulating the behavior of dominant firms.

On the last day of 1980, the Monopoly Regulation and Fair Trade Act (MRFTA) was enacted. The MRFTA was passed by the "Emergency Committee for National Security," the organization Chun Doo Hwan's new military regime set up after it declared martial law, disbanded the National Assembly and banned all political activities. The enactment of the MRFTA was primarily a response to the serious difficulties the Korean economy faced in 1980. The ambitious HCI drive and excessive intervention in the 1970s had driven the economy to the verge of a debt crisis. Extensive and prolonged price controls severely hampered the market mechanism and created substantial distortions. This experience prompted a reappraisal of the way the economy was run. The Chun government adopted macroeconomic stabilization measures to fight inflation. It also began to liberalize the economy, abolishing direct price controls and opening trade and investment.

Another significant factor in the legislation, however, was Chun's cynical attempt to gain popular support after having seized power through a military coup and a bloody suppression of the pro-democracy movement. In the wake of the HCI drive, there was a growing concern about the dominance of the *chaebol,* which had benefited enormously from favorable policy-oriented loans in the 1970s. For instance, the share of the top ten *chaebol* in GDP had more than doubled from 5.1 percent in 1973 to 10.9 percent in 1978. Chun presented the MRFTA as a symbol of political commitment to ensuring fairness as well as improving economic efficiency and promoting consumer welfare, incorporating such sociopolitical goals as protecting small producers from feudal business practices.

To prevent excessive concentration of economic power, the Fair Trade Commission began designating the largest business groups by asset size in 1987 and imposed various restrictions on intra-group, inter-firm transactions such as cross-holding of shares. As Table 5.3.5 shows, the ownership share of the founder families had drastically fallen over time by 1987. As is well known from the corporate governance literature, when ownership and control are separated, it is important to devise an incentive and monitoring scheme to ensure that the managers work in the interests of the owners rather than their own. As the gap between ownership and control widened in *chaebol*-affiliated firms, the lack of such incentive and monitoring schemes created increasingly serious problems. The desirability and effectiveness of the state-led monitoring and incentive system was greatly reduced, but few financial institutions or institutional investors were allowed to step in to serve these functions. The MRFTA was only an imperfect substitute.

Although the MRFTA signaled a shift away from industrial policy, institutional legacies did not disappear overnight. For instance, although Article 7 of the MRFTA prohibited mergers that would substantially restrain competition in any line of business, it provided for statutory exemptions for anti-competitive mergers if the Fair Trade Commission found it necessary to rationalize an industry or strengthen international competitiveness. With respect to collusion, the MRFTA required parties to a restrictive agreement to register it with the Fair Trade Commission for prior approval. Unlike in countries with a long tradition for antitrust, where collusion is held to be illegal per se except for a few special cases such as cooperative R&D, the MRFTA thus adopted something of a "government management" approach.

More importantly, although there was a shift in focus from industrial policy to competition and corporate governance policy, the resulting liberalization was asymmetric in that even as various entry restrictions and investment controls were lifted, institutional reforms and credible market signals (such as large-scale corporate failures) designed to replace weakening government control were not introduced. The *chaebol* expanded their influence in the non-bank financial sector and took advantage of the government's implicit guarantees to make aggressive investments. Moreover, although Korea's democratization in 1987 ushered in a new era of free and competitive elections, it took several years before Korea's civil society became strong enough to effect changes in campaign financing rules and introduce other anti-corruption measures designed to enhance transparency and accountability. Confident that they were too big and influential to fail, the *chaebol* discounted downside risks and aggressively expanded their businesses through debt financing. The average debt–equity ratio of the top 30 *chaebol* reached an astounding 519 percent in 1997. The explosive

Table 5.3.5 In-group ownership share of the top *chaebol* (%)

	1983	1987	1989	1990	1991	1992	1993	1994	1995	1996	1997	1998	1999	2000
Top 30	**57.2**	**56.2**	**46.2**	**45.4**	**46.9**	**46.1**	**43.4**	**42.7**	**43.3**	**44.1**	**43.0**	**44.5**	**49.6**	**43.4**
Family	17.2	15.8	14.7	13.7	13.9	12.6	10.3	9.7	10.5	10.3	8.5	7.9	5.4	4.5
Subsidiaries	40.0	40.4	31.5	31.7	33.0	33.5	33.1	33.0	32.8	33.8	34.5	36.6	45.1	38.9
Top 5	**n.a**	**60.3**	**49.4**	**49.6**	**51.6**	**51.9**	**49.0**	**47.5**	**n.a**	**n.a**	**45.2**	**46.6**	**53.5**	**n.a**
Family	n.a	15.6	13.7	13.3	13.2	13.3	11.8	12.5	n.a	n.a	8.6	n.a	n.a	n.a
Subsidiaries	n.a	44.7	35.7	36.3	38.4	38.6	37.2	35.0	n.a	n.a	36.6	n.a	n.a	n.a
Hyundai	81.4	79.9	n.a	60.2	67.8	65.7	57.8	61.3	60.4	61.4	56.2	53.7	n.a	n.a
Samsung	59.5	56.5	n.a	51.4	53.2	58.3	52.9	48.9	49.3	49.0	46.7	44.6	n.a	n.a
Daewoo	70.6	56.2	n.a	49.1	50.4	48.8	46.9	42.4	41.4	41.7	38.3	41.0	n.a	n.a
LG	30.2	41.5	n.a	35.2	38.3	39.7	38.8	37.7	39.7	39.9	40.1	41.9	n.a	n.a

Source: Korea Fair Trade Commission.

Note: The in-group ownership share for a *chaebol* is calculated by obtaining the weighted average of the combined ownership share of the founder's extended family and subsidiaries for all subsidiaries.

combination of weakening government control and remaining expectations for implicit government guarantees set the stage for Korea's economic crisis of 1997 (Lim, Haggard, and Kim, 2003).

In the aftermath of the crisis, Korea cleaned up massive nonperforming loans and adopted institutional reforms to reduce moral hazard, improve corporate governance, promote competition, and strengthen the social safety net. As a result of the crisis, during which 16 large business groups failed, firms reassessed default risks in making their investment decisions and increasingly focused on building core competence instead of aggressively expanding their businesses regardless of profitability.

Also, the problems that had initially plagued the application of the MRFTA were subsequently addressed through amendments and other changes in the direction of restricting government discretion in the wake of the 1997 crisis. The February 1999 amendment changed the provision on mergers and scrapped industrial policy considerations such as industrial rationalization and international competitiveness. This change was in line with the increasing competition advocacy role of the Fair Trade Commission. In fact, the Omnibus Cartel Repeal Act enacted in January 1999 removed legal exemptions for 20 cartels under 18 statutes. In the same year, the legal standard for anti-competitive practices was changed from "substantial restraint of competition" to "unreasonable restraint of competition," which means that it is no longer possible to defend a restrictive agreement on the grounds that it has an insignificant actual effect. Clearly in contrast to the approach taken by the government in the 1970s, these developments show that Korea has come a long way from the development dictatorship period. There has been a marked shift in emphasis from industrial policy to competition policy, increasingly relying on market mechanism rather than "the rule of government officials."

5.3.5   Conclusion

Korea's big push was much more successful than comparable programs implemented by most other developing countries. The student revolution of 1960 and the military coup of 1961 helped to establish a strong yet responsive and responsible "developmental state" in Korea. The subsequent adoption of meritocratic measures and incentives to contain rent-seeking and reinforce successful experiments was critical to the effectiveness of Korea's "big push" program. The government formulated indicative plans at the national level but delegated much of their implementation to business groups, which in turn tried to coordinate productive activities at the group level in addition to engaging in market transactions. Based on close public–private consultations and performance-based rewards, this two-tier approach to coordination helped to address information and incentive problems. Korea also promoted international trade as an essential component of its big push program. Not only did trade enable Korea to reduce the coordination problem and take advantage of scale economies, but it also provided learning opportunities and market tests for government policy and corporate strategy. Although the transition from an authoritarian developmental state to a democratic market economy was fraught with risks, as evidenced by increased room for rent-seeking immediately after the democratization of 1987 and the outbreak of the economic crisis in 1997, Korea's civil society successfully pushed for political and economic reforms to improve transparency and accountability.

As for industrial policy, although the degree of sectoral targeting changed dramatically from the 1960s to the 1970s and then the 1980s onward, Korea maintained an outward-oriented, bottom-up, and integrated approach, relying on close public-private consultation and international benchmarking. While continuing to pursue export-oriented industrialization for its resource allocation, scale economies, and dynamic learning effects, the government and the *chaebol* systematically studied what had to be done to fill the missing links in the domestic value chain and move up the quality ladder, through technology acquisition, human resource development, and construction of optimal-scale plants aimed for the global market. The government tried to make merit-based appointments and abide by the principle of performance-based rewards so as to minimize the downside of government intervention. As the capacity of the private sector increased and sectoral targeting became a more difficult proposition, Korea shifted to a more sector-neutral approach, which provided support for industry rationalization and R&D regardless of sectors. This was in line with a larger shift from industrial policy to competition and corporate governance policy, starting with the enactment of the Monopoly Regulation and Fair Trade Act in 1980.

Now that Korea has "caught up," Korea is trying to deal with the long shadow cast by the "big push" partnership between the *chaebol* and government. Suitably exposed to competition, the *chaebol* are among the most technologically and commercially advanced players, but their dominance of the Korean economy also has a downside. The *chaebol* may unduly concentrate and entrench economic and political power, and use this power to extract rents and influence policymaking in ways that favor the large-firm sector at the expense of the economy as a whole.

History provides three examples of how policymakers have dealt with this problem. Latin American countries simply allowed business groups to continue to expand, choosing to live with concentrated economic and political power. In Sweden, in contrast, the Social Democrats and family-controlled business groups reached a grand bargain through which the government imposed strict regulations and high income taxes on the groups but also provided subsidies and protection from takeover threats. Finally, the United States in the 1930s and the United Kingdom in the 1960s pursued a proactive anti-pyramiding strategy, using inter-corporate dividend taxes, strict takeover rules, and other measures to make pyramiding less attractive.

Rather than blindly adopting one or another foreign model, the best solution for Korea is for the government to strengthen investor protections and make it easier for shareholders to seek private remedies against "tunneling" and breaches of fiduciary duty, while enhancing intellectual property protection, strengthening competition, and expanding access to finance to promote the kind of entrepreneurship and entry that are vital to innovation but threaten to be stifled by the presence of very large business groups.

Notes

1. See Yasuoka (1976: 14). The translation of the cited definition into English is from Morikawa (1992: 250).
2. See Lim, Haggard, and Kim (2003) for a more detailed discussion of the three theoretical approaches and examples from Korean business groups. See Morck (2005) for a comparative perspective on business groups around the world.
3. Of the twenty-two largest business groups in Korea in 2000, only seven trace their origins to before 1945. The most prominent among these – Hyundai, Samsung, and LG – were little more than small, family-based enterprises until the 1940s. Eleven were founded during the American occupation (1945–48) and the Syngman Rhee government (1948–60). Four groups founded in the 1960s, including Lotte and Daewoo, expanded rapidly enough to be counted among the largest business groups in 2000. At the end of the 1960s, only Samsung and LG had made the list of the top ten business groups in Korea (Lim, 2003: 37–40).

References

Amsden, A.H. (1989) *Asia's Next Giant: South Korea and Late Industrialization* (New York: Oxford University Press).

Beason, R. and Weinstein, D.E. (1996) "Growth, Economies of Scale, and Targeting in Japan (1955–1990)," *Review of Economics and Statistics*, vol. 78, no. 2, pp. 286–295.

Cho, Y.J. and Kim, J.K. (1997) *Credit Policies and the Industrialization of Korea* (Seoul: Korea Development Institute).

Cimoli, M., Dosi, G., and Stiglitz, J.E. (2009) *Industrial Policy and Development: The Political Economy of Capabilities Accumulation* (Oxford: Oxford University Press).

Frank, C.R., Kim, K.S., and Westphal, L.E. (1975) *Foreign Trade Regimes and Economic Development: South Korea* (New York: National Bureau of Economic Research).

Hidalgo, C.A., Klinger, B., Barbasi, A.-L., and Hausmann R. (2007) "The Product Space Conditions the Development of Nations," *Science*, July 27, vol. 317, pp. 482–487.

Johnson, C. (1982) *The MITI and the Japanese Miracle: The Growth of Industrial Policy, 1925–1975* (Stanford, CA: Stanford University Press).

Kim, C.Y. (2011) *From Despair to Hope: Economic Policymaking in Korea, 1945–1979* (Seoul: Korea Development Institute).

Kim, K.M. (1988) *Korea's Industrial Development and Heavy and Chemical Industry Promotion Policy* (Seoul: Jigu Munhwasa) [in Korean].

Khanna, T. and Yafeh, Y. (2007) "Business Groups in Emerging Markets: Paragons or Parasites?," *Journal of Economic Literature*, vol. 45, no. 2, pp. 331–372.

Krueger, A.O. (1974) "The Political Economy of the Rent-Seeking Society," *American Economic Review*, vol. 64, no. 3, pp. 291–303.

Lee, J.W. (1996) "Government Interventions and Productivity Growth," *Journal of Economic Growth*, vol. 1, no. 3, pp. 391–414.

Lim, W. (2003) "The Emergence of the Chaebol and the Origin of the Chaebol Problem," in S. Haggard, W. Lim, E. Kim (eds), *Economic Crisis and Corporate Restructuring in Korea: Reforming the Chaebol* (Cambridge: Cambridge University Press), pp. 35–52.

Lim, W. (2011) "Joint Discovery and Upgrading of Comparative Advantage: Lessons from Korea's Development Experience," in S. Fardoust, Y. Kim, and C. Sepulveda (eds), *Postcrisis Growth and Development: A Development Agenda for the G-20* (Washington, DC: The World Bank), pp. 173–226.

Lim, W., Haggard, S., and Kim, E. (2003) "Introduction: The Political Economy of Corporate Restructuring," in S. Haggard, W. Lim and E. Kim (eds), *Economic Crisis and Corporate Restructuring in Korea: Reforming the Chaebol* (Cambridge: Cambridge University Press), pp. 1–31.

Lin, J.Y. and Monga, C. (2010) "Growth Identification and Facilitation: The Role of the State in the Dynamics of Structural Change," Policy Research Working Paper 5313 (Washington, DC: The World Bank).

Mason, E.S., Kim, M.J., Perkins, D.H., Kim, K.S., and Cole, D.C. (1980) *The Economic and Social Modernization of the Republic of Korea* (Cambridge, MA: Harvard University Press).

Morck, R. (ed.) (2005) *A History of Corporate Governance Around the World: Family Business Groups to Professional Managers* (Chicago: University of Chicago Press).

Murphy, K., Shleifer, A., and Vishny, R. (1989) "Industrialization and the Big Push," *Journal of Political Economy* 97(5): 1003–1026.

O, W.C. (2009) *The Korea Story: President Park Jung-hee's Leadership and the Korean Industrial Revolution* (Seoul: Wisdom Tree).

Oh, M. and Larson, J.F. (2011). *Digital Development in Korea: Building an Information Society* (London: Routledge).

Ohno, K. (2009) *The Middle Income Trap: Implications for Industrialization Strategies in East Asia and Africa* (Tokyo: GRIPS Development Forum).

Okazaki, T. (1999) "Corporate Governance," in T. Okazaki and M. Okuno-Fujiwara (eds), *The Japanese Economic System and Its Historical Origins* (New York: Oxford University Press), pp. 97–144.

Pack, H. and Saggi, K. (2006) "Is There a Case for Industrial Policy? A Critical Study." *World Bank Research Observer*, vol. 21, no. 2, pp. 267–297.

Park, J.H. (1998) *The Saemaul (New Village) Movement* (Seoul: Korea Rural Economic Institute).

Rodrik, D. (2007) *One Economics Many Recipes: Globalization, Institutions, and Economic Growth* (Princeton and Oxford: Princeton University Press).

Rosenstein-Rodan, P. (1943) "Problems of Industrialization of Eastern and South-Eastern Europe," *Economic Journal*, vol. 53 (June–September), pp. 202–211.

Shin, G. (1994) *Choices and Challenges for the Korean Economy on the Road to an Advanced Industrial Nation* (Seoul: Wooshinsa) [in Korean].

Stern, J.J., Kim, J.H., Perkins, D.H., and Yoo J.H. (1995) *Industrialization and the State: The Korean Heavy and Chemical Industry Drive* (Cambridge, MA: Harvard Institute for International Development).

Wade, R. (1990) *Governing the Market: Economic Theory and the Role of Government in East Asian Industrialization* (Princeton, NJ: Princeton University Press).

Winters, L.A., Lim, W., Hanmer, L. and Augustin, S. (2010) "Economic Growth in Low Income Countries: How the G20 Can Help to Raise and Sustain It," Working Paper 2010–01 (Seoul: Korea Development Institute).

World Bank (1993) *The East Asian Miracle: Economic Growth and Public Policy* (New York: Oxford University Press).

5.4
Comment on "The *Chaebol* and Industrial Policy in Korea" by Wohnyuk Lim

Shahid Yusuf
GWU, School of Business, Washington DC

There can be no denying Korea's remarkable industrial prowess sustained almost without interruption from the mid-1960s onwards. It is the stuff of legend and the subject of countless articles and book-length publications. Other developing countries, many of which were on a par with Korea in the 1960s and now lag far behind, have sought to learn from Korea's experience and to adapt the policies it followed – thus far with limited success. But the interest has not waned and in recent years it has risen to a new pitch as a number of middle-income countries find that their industrial momentum is faltering and conventional market-based incentives are proving less effective in the post-financial crisis environment.

In casting around for policies that could lead to a new round of industrialization and raise growth rates, policymakers are showing a renewed interest in the approach taken by Korea during the mid-1960s through the early 1980s, the period of "big push" industrialization which set the stage for later development. This approximately twenty-year stretch has been intensively studied and Wonhyuk Lim's paper traverses familiar ground. What the paper attempts is to summarize the key elements of Korea's industrial policy (IP) and to highlight the role of the large conglomerates, or *chaebol*, that are a conspicuous feature of the corporate landscape. Lim claims that "three externalities are central to the challenge of development" (p. 1). These are externalities linked with coordination, innovation and institutions and harnessing these for the purposes of development depends upon actions taken by governments, business groups and financial entities – presumably acting in concert although the paper does not underline this point here. Instead each is presented as an independent "solution" with governments playing the leading role in earlier stages when market imperfections abound, with businesses and financial institutions taking over at later stages. While Lim maintains that the *chaebol* had a major role, they are missing in action through much of the paper. Lim takes an inconclusive one-page stab at "exploring the nature of business groups" before turning to a discussion of government-led industrial and export promotion policies. He lists (in Table 5.3.2) some of the writing on IP without attempting to review the literature and his listing misses the recent attempts by Philippe Aghion and Karl Aiginger to bring IP more into the mainstream. Lim notes tellingly that the studies of IP shed little light on how governments can effectively "pick winners" and shift the focus of industrial activity from the fringes of the *product space* nearer to the *core*, and how, by mobilizing the full range of policy instruments, the state can induce IP to deliver superior results. There are plenty of papers on the topic, but the empirical basis of the claims made for or against IP is alarmingly slender. Addressing coordination and innovation externalities remains an art and there is potential for costly mistakes, something that many countries pursuing IP have painfully discovered. Lim urges governments to "carefully weigh the challenges" although how they should do so is left to the reader's imagination.

Section 5.3.3 is the core of the paper. It is an elliptical retelling of the Korean IP story with occasional references to the *chaebol*. According to Lim, the Korean government and business divined Korea's "latent comparative advantage" through careful study and "filled in the missing links in the domestic value chain." What this supposedly systematic study involved, the evidence of a paper trail and techniques employed that could be imitated by others, are passed over. This relatively successful period relied on "IP lite" with little by way of explicit targeting of industries with reference to externalities generated. Industrialization during the 1960s appears to have been guided largely by market forces with the then infant *chaebol* responsible for investment decisions albeit influenced by government export promotion policies (widely imitated by other countries with much less success).

IP entered a new phase in the 1970s and it is the vertical IP pursued during this decade that has attracted a vast amount of attention and is viewed by believers as contributing to Korea's later transition from a middle-income to a high-income economy. The creation of a Heavy and Chemical industry (HCI) starting in the early 1970s was clearly a top-down process pursued for political and defense reasons by President Park Chung Hee (with government agencies falling into line even though bureaucratic convictions were uncertain at best) and buttressed by the Yushin Constitution that gave the president "dictatorial powers." Lim claims that the HCI "had more to do with upgrading [Korea's] comparative advantage with a view toward increasing the domestic content of its exports" but this is belied by later statements and other writing on this phase of development that underscore President Park's belief in the transformative capacity of steel and engineering industries and by his desire to strengthen military capabilities in the face of uncertainties in respect of U.S. intentions regarding the defense of East Asia. The HCI drive was resisted by the *chaebol* and opposed by foreign bilateral and multilateral agencies which were unable to perceive Korea's latent or potential comparative advantage in these industries and in fact emphasized its "strong and increasing comparative advantage in light manufacturing." That Korean business and foreign observers were essentially correct in their assessment was brought home when "the ambitious HCI drive and excessive intervention in the 1970s [drove] the economy to the verge of a debt crisis" and several of the *chaebol* were bankrupted and had to be taken over by healthier conglomerates. Not only did the HCI drive saddle Korea with a vast industrial complex built at great cost with the help of subsidized financing channeled through state-controlled banks with the costs being borne by Korean households and taxpayers; it also strengthened the *chaebol* and increased their dominance as noted by Lim. This market power constrained domestic market competition and greatly increased the political influence of the *chaebol* – a source of concern for Korean governments ever since. It also encouraged borrowing practices that enormously increased the indebtedness of the *chaebol* and were in large part responsible for the severity of the crisis that gripped the Korean economy in 1997–98.

From the perspective of the early 21st century, President Park's decision to launch and persist with the HCI drive appears to have been advantageous in the long term. But it was an exceedingly perilous one that could easily have proven a colossal failure and ruinous for the Korean economy. It was a decision based mostly on personal convictions, on "gut feeling" and on a desire to replicate Japan's success. The economic justification of the IP pursued in the 1970s with reference to "latent" and "potential" comparative advantage is unconvincing. There is no evidence that a systematic effort was made to identify, forecast, and measure externalities, and single out the potentially most promising "infant" activities within broad "chemicals," "engineering," and "metallurgical" subsectors or to tailor infrastructure whether hard or soft for the purposes of these selected activities. Certainly little thought was given to the consequences of *chaebol*-led industrialization or to the impact on financial development of government control over banks and the use of directed credit to promote selected activities. By the early 1980s, the Korean authorities had recognized the shortcomings (and costs, "sectoral targeting changed dramatically") of vertical IP and shifted their focus to a market-based "competition and corporate governance policy."

Lim does not devote much space to the role of the *chaebol* in developing Korea's electronics industry, which is an interesting story and brings out both their independent role and their readiness to take bold initiatives. In this case, the government was a follower rather than the leader. The government had more of a hand in ICT development from the early 1990s onwards, jointly with the *chaebol* and a comparison of public–private interaction for the purposes of industrial development of the 1970s with the 1990s would have been insightful. The two pages Lim devotes to the IT sector only whet the appetite; the actual story is more complex. Incidentally, Kim Jae Ik died tragically in 1983 and his involvement with the electronics (not the ICT) sector had to do with helping introduce the production of electronic switches by the telecommunications industry early in the 1980s. Lim could have spelled out his and Oh Myung's contribution to ICT development from the early 1990s onwards.

Lim concludes by referring to the "responsive and responsible developmental state" established by the military coup in 1961. This scarcely chimes jives with his own recognition that the Korean state was "authoritarian" and that the Yushin Constitution rode roughshod over civil liberties. IP pressed home by authoritarian regimes in the 1970s and with diminishing conviction through the 1980s was highly risky and difficult to justify with reference to economic criteria or the outcomes of the HCI drive up to that point. Worse it entrenched the *chaebol*. And in Lim's words, "Korea is [still] trying to deal with the long shadow cast by the big-push partnership between the *chaebol* and the government."

As a long time Korea watcher, I am puzzled by the continuing fascination with the early Korean experience with vertical IP when more recent industrial development, innovation capability, and competitiveness is so much more compelling and relevant. Lim struggles to inject some freshness into the story and to respond to the renewed interest in IP by emphasizing the *chaebol* angle but in his paper, the *chaebol* remain a shadowy presence and the utility of IP then or in a form that would suit the purposes of countries today that are struggling to industrialize or reindustrialize, does not come through.

Index

Printed and bound in Great Britain by
CPI Group (UK) Ltd, Croydon, CR0 4YY